IVORY TOWERS
and SACRED FOUNTS

The Artist as Hero in Fiction
from Goethe to Joyce

IVORY TOWERS
and SACRED FOUNTS

The Artist as Hero in Fiction
from Goethe to Joyce

By Maurice Beebe

Professor of English

PURDUE UNIVERSITY

NEW YORK UNIVERSITY PRESS 1964

Publication of
this work was aided by a partial
subvention from THE FORD FOUNDATION,
to whom the publishers make grateful
acknowledgment.

PREFACE

ALTHOUGH the portrait-of-the-artist novel is a widely recognized genre of fiction, the study that follows is the first broadly extended discussion of the artist as hero. I have attempted to combine literary history with criticism by tracing the development of the artist-novel from the late eighteenth to the early twentieth century and by considering in detail some of the more important works within the tradition. Knowledge of that tradition seems to me essential to an understanding of individual portraits of the artist, which include some of the most important novels of the past century and a half, but the main justification for such a study is to be found in the special nature of artist-novels. These are stories which tell how they came to be written; most are self-portraits of their creators. To discover what they have in common is to learn something about the nature of the artist in general. Therefore, *Ivory Towers and Sacred Founts* is intended to be not only a critical history of a literary genre, but a study of the artistic temperament, the creative process, and the relationship of the artist to society.

It should be understood that I am using the term "artist" to mean anyone capable of creating works of art, whether literary, musical, or visual. In fact, actual production is not a requirement for the artist-hero, for some of the characters I discuss are only potential artists, and a few are not identified as artists at all, though they are obviously surrogates for their authors. There is some evidence outside the artist-novel that suggests basic differences among types of artists: the painter, for example, is likely to be more gregarious than the poet, and the ability to observe life clearly is obviously less important for the musician than for the painter or the writer. If we keep in mind the fact that though the hero of an artist-novel may be a sculptor or a composer, as a self-portrait of his creator he is always a writer, it is apparent that "the artist" established in fiction is always a literary man. And if the novelist sometimes seems to be a different breed of person from the poet or the dramatist (try to

v

imagine a lyric poem by Henry James!), then we must make a further qualification: the archetypal artist found in portrait-of-the-artist fiction is a more valid representation of the novelist type than of any other kind of writer. Nonetheless, there are ways in which artists, regardless of the art they practice, differ from nonartists, and in depicting these ways the novelist is a valid spokesman for all creative men.

Ivory Towers and Sacred Founts is divided into two main parts—the first tracing the major traditions of the genre, the second discussing at some length the work of four major novelists. My Introduction describes the three main themes of the artist-novel: the concept of the artist as a divided self, the equation of art with experience, and the conflicting ideal of detachment. In the three chapters of Part One these themes are taken up separately. The first chapter shows how the archetype of the artist became established in the writings of Goethe and Rousseau, the principal founders of the artist-novel, and in the "personal" or "confessional" novel that flourished on the Continent from 1785 to 1869. The second chapter discusses artist-novels of the nineteenth and early twentieth centuries that follow the Sacred Fount tradition—the assumption that the artist must "live" in order to create. I find the origins of this tradition in the Romantics, then consider its application in the English apprentice novel, a form first popular during the early Victorian period and again from about 1880 to 1920. The third chapter traces the development of the opposing view of art as religion—the Ivory Tower tradition as manifested in the representative figure of Poe's Roderick Usher, in French writers of the second half of the nineteenth century, and in the Aesthetic Movement in England during the same period. Part Two considers in detail the work of four writers—Balzac, James, Proust, and Joyce—who seem to me to achieve in different ways an effective balance between the Ivory Tower and the Sacred Fount. A concluding chapter suggests some of the implications of the pattern that has emerged in the preceding chapters.

Although artist-novels have appeared in great quantity since the 1920's, I have felt justified in stopping with Joyce, for he is, I think, the writer who brought the artist-novel tradition to a climax by achieving the most impressive synthesis of its basic themes. Portraits of the artist after Joyce seem to follow the tradition already established without changing it in any important way. But aside from that, I found a surplus of riches even within the restricted area I chose. I have singled out for individual discussion a number of novels and stories; these have been selected for their representative value in illustrating what I take to be the major themes of the artist-novel. Other important portraits of the artist could have been used as well, but they would only have offered additional support for a thesis that I hope is sufficiently demonstrated.

Like most works of literary scholarship, the present study owes much to the assistance and collaboration of other people. *Ivory Towers* was first conceived as the subject of a doctoral dissertation, and though the finished book bears little resemblance to the dissertation (Cornell University, 1952), my primary debt is still to the four professors who offered encouragement and constructive criticism at the time when they were needed most. It is a pleasure, therefore, to acknowldge my gratitude to Francis E. Mineka, David Daiches, Harold W. Thompson, and Baxter Hathaway. During the past decade I have drawn upon the intelligence of many friends and colleagues. At the risk of overlooking others, I should like to express my gratitude to Sophus Keith Winther, Frederick J. Hoffman, the late Richard Chase, J. Mitchell Morse, Oscar Cargill, Anthony Tommasi, Robert and Marlene Johnson, Barriss Mills, Darrel Abel, William T. Stafford, and Mark Rowan. Certain portions of this work first appeared in *PMLA, South Atlantic Quarterly, The Personalist, James Joyce Miscellany, Criticism, Bucknell Review,* and *Texas Studies in Literature and Language.* To the editors of these publications I am grateful not only for permission to reprint, but also for corrections and improvements that have been incorporated in the finished book. I am indebted to the Purdue Research Foundation for giving me three summer research grants that provided an opportunity to retreat, if only temporarily, into the Ivory Tower. But I am equally grateful to those unspecified persons—especially that one person—who prevented me from staying there.

CONTENTS

IVORY TOWERS
and SACRED FOUNTS

*The Artist as Hero in Fiction
from Goethe to Joyce*

Introduction

NO sooner has Denis Stone, the young poet in Aldous Huxley's *Crome Yellow,* confessed that he is writing a novel than he is chagrined to hear a new acquaintance describe the plot of the story:

"Little Percy, the hero, was never good at games, but he was always clever. He passes through the usual public school and the usual university and comes to London, where he lives among the artists. He is bowed down with melancholy thought; he carries the whole weight of the universe upon his shoulders. He writes a novel of dazzling brilliance; he dabbles delicately in Amour and disappears, at the end of the book, into the Luminous Future."

Denis blushed scarlet. Mr. Scogan had described the plan of his novel with an accuracy that was appalling. He made an effort to laugh. "You're entirely wrong," he said. "My novel is not in the least like that." It was a heroic lie. Luckily, he reflected, only two chapters were written. He would tear them up that evening when he unpacked.

Mr. Scogan paid no attention to his denial, but went on: "Why will you young men continue to write about things that are so entirely uninteresting as the mentality of adolescents and artists? . . . As for the artist, he is preoccupied with problems that are so utterly unlike those of the ordinary adult man—problems of pure aesthetics which don't so much as present themselves to people like myself—that a description of his mental processes is as boring to the ordinary reader as a piece of pure mathematics. A

3

serious book about artists regarded as artists is unreadable; and a
book about artists regarded as lovers, husbands, dipsomaniacs,
heroes, and the like is really not worth writing again." [1]

Mr. Scogan is not clairvoyant; he is simply well read. The story
of Percy could be that of several hundred sensitive young heroes of
novels, for by 1921, when *Crome Yellow* was published, both the
artist and the adolescent had become hackneyed subjects of fiction.
The tradition of artist fiction, which had developed steadily for more
than a century, reached a crest in the first two decades of the twentieth century. William York Tindall has gone so far as to say that
"from 1903 onwards, almost every first novel by a serious novelist
was a novel of adolescence." [2] Mr. Scogan is justified in linking
stories of adolescents with stories of artists, because the story of a
sensitive young man is usually that of a potential artist; when the
novel is autobiographical, as most are, it is the story of the artist who
wrote the book.

Less justified is Mr. Scogan's blanket dismissal of a form of fiction
which includes some of the most distinguished novels of the past
century: *Pierre, Lost Illusions, Sentimental Education, The Way of
All Flesh, Sons and Lovers, The Tragic Muse, Jean-Christophe,
Remembrance of Things Past, The Counterfeiters, Doctor Faustus,*
and *A Portrait of the Artist as a Young Man.*[3] If it be objected
that Mr. Scogan is speaking as the "ordinary adult man" and that
few of these novels have attained popular success, the list could
easily be expanded to include such nineteenth-century classics as
Wilhelm Meister, David Copperfield, Pendennis, and *The Ordeal
of Richard Feverel;* or such twentieth-century best-sellers as *Of
Human Bondage, Martin Eden, Maurice Guest, The Song of the
Lark, The Constant Nymph, Lust for Life, Sparkenbroke, Sinister
Street, The Fountainhead, The Horse's Mouth, The Alexandrian
Quartet,* and *Look Homeward, Angel.*

Fictional portraits of the artist are valuable in at least two ways.
First, a portrait of the artist helps us to understand the novelist
who wrote it. The novel can be seen in much the same manner as
the writer's letters, diaries, notebooks, prefaces, or memoirs—though,
of course, the careful critic will not make a one-to-one equation between a work of art and an autobiography. Nonetheless, the very
fact that the artist-novel is a product of the imagination, in which

1. (New York: Harper, 1922), pp. 30-32.
2. *Forces in Modern British Literature, 1885–1946* (New York: Knopf, 1947), p. 176.
3. Dates of initial publication of the many works of fiction referred to throughout this study are provided in the index.

the experience it uses is distorted and transcended, makes it often more revealing than primary documents, for writers frequently tell more about their true selves and convictions under the guise of fiction than they will confess publicly. The second main value of the portrait-of-the-artist novel is to be found in its cumulative impact. A comparative study of many portraits of the artist enables us better to understand the artist in general. Ideas that may seem eccentric or special in an individual portrait of the artist take on added significance when the same ideas are expressed again and again by other novelists. Thus a knowledge of the whole tradition helps to illuminate each work within that tradition.[4]

Artists have always prided themselves on their individuality, but the most surprising fact about portrait-of-the-artist novels is their similarity. From the beginnings of the genre in the late eighteenth century to the present time, the artist-hero is an easily recognized type. The person blessed (or cursed?) with "artistic temperament" is always sensitive, usually introverted and self-centered, often passive, and sometimes so capable of abstracting himself mentally from the world around him that he appears absentminded or "possessed." Granted most or all of these traits, he has an excellent chance of becoming an artist if he also has talent and the ability to apply himself. In many artist-novels, however, the story concludes with the hero not yet an accomplished artist. Except in temperament, Stephen

4. Aside from a few essays and specialized studies, little has been written on the general topic of the artist in literature. However, I have found the following useful in varying degrees: R. P. Blackmur, "The Artist as Hero," in his *The Lion and the Honeycomb: Essays in Solicitude and Critique* (New York: Harcourt, Brace, 1955), pp. 43–50; Theodore Robert Bowie, *The Painter in French Fiction: A Critical Essay*, University of North Carolina Studies in the Romance Languages (Chapel Hill, 1950); Van Wyck Brooks, "The Hero as Artist," in his *Sketches in Criticism* (New York: E. P. Dutton, 1932), pp. 93–99; Ralph Stokes Collins, *The Artist in Modern German Drama* (Baltimore: Johns Hopkins University Press, 1940); Gerald Jay Goldberg, "The Search for the Artist in Some Recent British Fiction," *South Atlantic Quarterly*, LXII (Summer 1963), 387–401; Philip Gilbert Hamerton, "Artists in Fiction," in his *Thoughts about Art* (Boston: Roberts Brothers, 1880), pp. 101–124; George C. Schoolfield, *The Figure of the Musician in German Literature*, University of North Carolina Studies in the Germanic Languages (Chapel Hill, 1956); Maurice Z. Shroder, *Icarus: The Image of the Artist in French Romanticism* (Cambridge: Harvard University Press, 1961); D. J. Smith, "Music in the Victorian Novel," *Kenyon Review*, XXV (Summer 1963), 517–532; and James M. Wells, "The Artist in the English Novel, 1850–1919," *Philological Studies* [West Virginia University], IV (September, 1943), 77–80. Proceedings of a panel discussion on the artist-hero novel held at the MLA Conference on English Fiction in Transition, December, 1961, are available in *English Fiction in Transition*, IV (third issue, 1961), 11–36, and V (first issue, 1962), 27–34.

Dedalus, in Joyce's *A Portrait of the Artist as a Young Man*, is still more young man than artist at the novel's conclusion, and when we reach the end of Proust's *A la Recherche du Temps Perdee*, we find that Marcel is at last ready to write the book we have just read. In both instances, as in many others, the hero attains this state only after he has sloughed off the domestic, social, and religious demands imposed upon him by his environment. Narrative development in the typical artist-novel requires that the hero test and reject the claims of love and life, of God, home, and country, until nothing is left but his true self and his consecration as artist. Quest for self is the dominant theme of the artist-novel, and because the self is almost always in conflict with society, a closely related theme is the opposition of art to life. The artist-as-hero is usually therefore the artist-as-exile.

Although the artist-hero claims individuality in that he is different from the majority of men, his quest for his true self usually ends in the discovery that he is very much like other artists, that in fact he embodies the archetype of the artist. Joyce's novel is not a portrait of *an* artist, but a portrait of *the* artist, and the distinction is important. In artist-novels the same themes appear so frequently that they assume the dimension of myths that may express universal truths, and just as we can distinguish between *an* artist and *the* artist, we can best understand individual portraits of the artist if we establish first the nature of the genre by finding an overall pattern in the works as a group. That pattern can be found, I think, in three interlocking themes: the Divided Self, the Ivory Tower, and the Sacred Fount. Each must be considered individually before we can see how they function together to form an archetype of the artist-novel.

I

MUCH literary scholarship is based on the assumption that the more we know about the life and background of a man, the better we can understand him as an artist and the more capable we are of interpreting his works. But an underlying assumption in the artist-novel is that creative man is a divided being, man *and* artist, a historical personage who merely serves as the medium through which the creative spirit manifests itself. The man is a human being of normal appetites and desires, for whom life is essentially the process of dying. The artist is a free, detached spirit which looks down on the man from a distance and is concerned not so much with the consumption of life as with the transcendence of life through creative effort. The man must spend himself, but the artist-spirit saves itself by becoming one with its works and thus escaping the bonds of time.

The theme of the Divided Self has a psychological basis in the nature of the introverted person. Thoreau, for example, writes:

> With thinking we may be beside ourselves in a sane sense. By a conscious effort of the mind we can stand aloof from actions and their consequences; and all things, good and bad, go by us like a torrent. We are not wholly involved in Nature. I may be either the driftwood in the stream, or Indra in the sky looking down on it. I *may* be affected by a theatrical exhibition; on the other hand, I *may not* be affected by an actual event which appears to concern me much more. I only know myself as a human entity; the scene, so to speak, of thoughts and affections; and am sensible of a certain doubleness by which I can stand as remote from myself as from another. However intense my experience, I am conscious of the presence and criticism of a part of me, which, as it were, is not a part of me, but spectator, sharing no experience, but taking note of it; and that is no more I than it is you. When the play, it may be the tragedy, of life is over, the spectator goes his way. It was a kind of fiction, a work of the imagination only.[5]

Alphonse Daudet recorded "that other self" which observed himself weeping beside his father's deathbed,[6] and Yeats, in *Per Amica Silentia Lunae*, built a theory of art around the second, inner self of the artist.

> I call to the mysterious one who yet
> Shall walk the wet sands by the water's edge
> And look most like me, being indeed my double,
> And prove of all imaginable things
> The most unlike, being my anti-self,
> And, standing by these characters, disclose
> All that I seek.[7]

The artist's double, most theorists agree, comes from the artist's subconsciousness, yet seems to look down dispassionately on the artist himself. Coleridge must have had something like this in mind when he wrote, "The eye hath a two-fold power. It is, verily, a

5. *The Variorum Walden*, ed. Walter Harding (New York: Twayne, 1962), p. 122.
6. Cited by Daniel Schneider, *The Psychoanalyst and the Artist* (New York: Farrar, Straus and Co., 1950), pp. 104–105.
7. (London, Macmillan, 1918), p. 7.

window through which you not only look out of the house, but can look into it too." [8]

If the artist-hero is usually an introvert, it is perhaps because the artist-novel, especially when it is autobiographical, is by its very nature an act of introspection. At any rate, many of the artists of fiction share an ability to step outside the self and to recognize a difference between the artist and the man. Disraeli's Contarini Fleming reflects on "the separation of the mere individual from the universal poet." [9] Arnold Bennett's frustrated artist, Edwin Clayhanger, discovers an "impartial observer" in himself.[10] Dreiser's Eugene Witla "was troubled with a dual point of view—a condition based upon a peculiar power of analysis—self analysis in particular, which was constantly permitting him to tear himself up by the roots in order to see how he was getting along." [11] The hero of St. John Ervine's *Changing Winds* "had a strange sense of fear that was inexplicable to him. He seemed to be outside himself, outside his own fear, looking on at it and wondering what had caused it." [12] The ability to become detached from the self is shared by artist-heroes as different from each other in other respects as Michael Fane, the hero of Compton Mackenzie's *Sinister Street,* and Edouard of Gide's *The Counterfeiters.* The former confesses, "Sometimes I feel as if there wasn't any me at all, and I'm surprised to see a letter come addressed to me." [13] Edouard writes: "It seems to me sometimes that I do not really exist, but that I merely imagine I exist. The thing that I have the greatest difficulty in believing in is my own reality. I am constantly getting outside myself, and as I watch myself act I cannot understand how a person who acts is the same as the person who is watching him act, and who wonders in astonishment and doubt how he can be actor and watcher at the same moment!" [14] So common are split selves in artists that Aldous Huxley was able to satirize the concept in his short story, "The Farcical History of Richard Greenow": from midnight to early morning the body of the sophisticated Greenow is occupied by the sentimental anti-self, "Pearl Bellairs," whose gushing best-sellers support, embarrass, and ultimately destroy the man through whom she acts.[15] Huxley's

8. George Whalley, *Poetic Process* (London: Routledge and Kegan Paul, 1953), p. 75.
9. Benjamin Disraeli, *Contarini Fleming: A Psychological Romance* (New York: Knopf, 1926), p. 255.
10. *Clayhanger* (New York, 1910), p. 568.
11. *The "Genius"* (New York: John Lane, 1915), p. 359.
12. (New York: The Macmillan Company, 1917), p. 482.
13. (London: Martin Secker, 1923), pp. 248–249.
14. *The Counterfeiters, with Journal of "The Counterfeiters,"* trans. Dorothy Bussy and Justin O'Brien (New York: Knopf, 1951), pp. 64–65.
15. From *Limbo* (1920). Reprinted in Cyril Connolly, ed., *Great English Short Novels* (New York: Dial Press, 1953), pp. 477–533.

story, like Henry James's "The Private Life," applies the *doppelgänger* theme common in fiction to the situation of the artist, but it may well be that there would be fewer stories about doubles if writers were not so peculiarly aware of a division in themselves.

Another psychological basis for the theme of the Divided Self may be found in the nature of the creative process. Any writer knows that there is a moment when calculation stops and the author seems to be carried along by a force beyond himself. Today we are likely to be scornful of "inspiration," and it may well be that the something that takes over in the creative process is not a divine afflatus descending upon the artist but a subconscious force arising from within. Whatever it is, thousands of artists have testified to the experience of inspiration, and there may be something after all in William Faulkner's insistence that "the writer's got to be demon-driven" [16] or Joseph Conrad's reluctance to revise one of his works because "all my work is produced unconsciously (so to speak) and I cannot meddle to any purpose with what is within myself.—I am sure you understand what I mean—it isn't in me to improve what has got itself written." [17] But the "I" here is not Conrad. It is Captain Korzeniowski, a humble seaman, who on another occasion said, "You know I take no credit to myself for what I do—and so I may judge my own performance. There is no mistake about this. . . . It [*Nostromo*] is a very genuine Conrad." [18] Critics of fiction often confuse the "I" of the storyteller with the person who wrote the work, but as early as 1877, Edward Dowden, discussing George Eliot, another novelist who, like Conrad, wrote under a pseudonym, noted that the personality which dominates her novel is "one who, if not the real George Eliot, is that second self who writes her books, and lives and speaks through them." This "second self," he continued, is "more substantial than any mere human personality" and has "fewer reserves"; while "behind it, lurks well pleased the veritable historical self secure from impertinent observation and criticism." [19]

Literary scholars may scoff at the separation of the person from the creator, but the psychologist Jung finds in this division the basis for his theory of the artist:

16. Frederick L. Gwynn and Joseph L. Blotner, eds., *Faulkner in the University: Class Conferences at the University of Virginia, 1957–1958* (Charlottesville: University of Virginia Press, 1959), p. 19.

17. Jocelyn Baines, *Joseph Conrad: A Critical Biography* (New York: McGraw-Hill, 1960), p. 160.

18. Baines, p. 287.

19. Quoted by Kathleen Tillotson, *The Tale and the Teller* (London: Rupert Hart-Davis, 1959), p. 22. An excellent discussion of the "second self" as it affects point of view is to be found in Wayne C. Booth, *The Rhetoric of Fiction* (Chicago: University of Chicago Press, 1961), pp. 67–77.

Every creative person is a duality or a synthesis of contradictory attitudes. On the one side he is a human being with a personal life, while on the other side he is an impersonal, creative process. Since as a human being he may be either sound or morbid, we must look at his psychic make-up to find the determinants of his personality. But we can only understand him in his capacity of artist by looking at his artistic achievement. We should make a sad mistake if we tried to explain the mode of life of an English gentleman, a Prussian officer, or a cardinal in terms of personal factors. The gentleman, the officer and the cleric function as such in an impersonal role, and their psychic make-up is qualified by a peculiar objectivity. We must grant that the artist does not function in an official capacity—the very opposite is nearer the truth. He nevertheless resembles the types I have named in one respect, for the specifically artistic disposition involves an overweight of collective psychic life as against the personal. Art is a kind of innate drive that seizes a human being and makes him its instrument. The artist is not a person endowed with a free will who seeks his own ends, but one who allows art to realize its purposes through him. As a human being he may have moods and a will and personal aims, but as an artist he is "man" in a higher sense —he is "collective man"—one who carries and shapes the unconscious, psychic life of mankind.[20]

Here, perhaps, is Stephen Dedalus' "uncreated conscience of my race." Willa Cather comes even closer to Jung's theory of the artist in her *The Song of the Lark*. Thea Kronborg becomes aware of a second, observing self when as a young girl she is seriously ill: "She did not realize that she was suffering pain. When she was conscious at all, she seemed to be separated from her body; to be perched on top of the piano, or on the hanging lamp, watching the doctor sew her up." [21] When she reaches maturity and achieves prominence as a singer, she realizes that this other self is her artistic personality. Why do people care for her?

It was something that had to do with her that made them care, but it was not she. It was something they believed in, but it was not she. Perhaps each of them concealed another person in himself, just as she did. Why was it that they seemed to feel and to hunt for a second person in her and not in each other? . . .

20. C. G. Jung, *Modern Man in Search of a Soul*, trans. W. S. Dell and Cary F. Barnes (London: Kegan Paul, Trench, Trubner and Company, 1945), pp. 194–195.
21. *The Novels and Stories of Willa Cather*, Library Edition (Boston: Houghton Mifflin, 1937), II, 11.

What if one's second self could somehow speak to all these second selves? . . . How deep they lay, these second persons, and how little one knew about them, except to guard them fiercely. It was to music, more than to anything else, that these hidden things in people responded.[22]

The time-and-eternity theme which appears frequently in artist-novels is, I think, closely related to the myth of the Divided Self. To escape death and become immortal, the artist-self would somehow remove himself from the bonds of the chronological time which drives him relentlessly from cradle to grave. Opposed to chronological time is subjective time, which cannot be clocked: minutes are sometimes hours, hours can be minutes. Subjective time is universal. But, for most of us, such time is as fleeting, as transitory as the seconds the clock ticks off. What the artist tries to do is to capture lost time and imprison it in the form of his art-work. The man must die, but the artist in him can achieve immortality in his works. This is a common theme in literature from Keats's Grecian Urn to Yeats's Byzantium. For instance, Gerald Lovel, the poet-hero of J. Westland Marston's unwieldy novel in verse, *Gerald*, finds his motivation as a poet in his desire to transcend time through art:

> A Statue's silence—is the Sculptor's voice.
> The Painter's immortality resides
> In his own forms, and objects. . . .

Even the objective, imitative work of art is, in this sense, capable of being immortal. But when the work of art is subjective, when it reflects the consciousness of its creator, the artist feels that he can achieve a personal self-extension through eternity:

> And thus the Sons
> Of Genius have prerogative to stand
> Exempt from Time's decree; Immutable
> In change! [23]

Joseph Frank, in his essay, "Spatial Form in Modern Literature," has shown that the attempt to capture time in the spatial form of the art-work is characteristic of many modern artists.[24] To explain the simultaneous appearance of this trend in a number of writers working independently of one another, Frank relies, in part, upon the theories of Wilhelm Worringer. In *Abstraktion und Einfühlung*,

22. *The Novels and Stories of Willa Cather*, II, 273.
23. *Gerald, A Dramatic Poem; and Other Poems* (London: C. Mitchell, 1842), pp. 8–9.
24. *Sewanee Review*, LIII (1945), 221–240, 433–456, 643–653.

Worringer demonstrated that historical fluctuations between naturalistic and nonnaturalistic art may be understood only if one substitutes what Alois Riegl called *Kunstwollen*, or will-to-form, for the
will-to-imitate which had been considered responsible for the creative
impulse. Naturalism is the prevailing style in cultures which have
attained harmonious balance with their environment; abstract styles
are produced when man is not in harmony with the universe, when
the artist, distrustful of the outside world, directs the will-to-form
to the subjective world. Because the modern era is of the second
type and because one characteristic of nonnaturalistic art is the attempt to remove all traces of time value, much modern art has
utilized spatial form. By emphasizing "climates of feeling," the Wor-
ringer-Frank theory overlooks the fact that the psychology of the
individual artist is also important in determining the art-form.

Acknowledging his debt to Riegl and Worringer, Otto Rank has
extended the theory of *Kunstwollen* to include the "urge to eternali-
zation" which he considers basic to the creative impulse: The artist
would escape time through the medium of his immortal art. The
kind of artistic personality, as well as the cultural environment,
determines the art-form:

> What the artist needs for true creative art . . . is life in one form
> or another; and the two artist-types differ essentially in the source
> from which they take this life that is so essential to production.
> The Classical type, who is possibly poorer within, but nearer to
> life, and himself more vital, takes it from without: that is, he
> creates immortal work from mortal life without necessarily having
> first transformed it into personal experience as is the case with
> the Romantic. For, to the Romantic, experience of his own ap-
> pears to be an essential preliminary to productivity, although he
> does not use this experience for the enrichment of his own per-
> sonality, but to economize the personal experience, the burden of
> which he would fain escape. Thus the one artist-type constantly
> makes use of other life than his own—in fact, nature—for the pur-
> pose of creating, while the other can create only by perpetually
> sacrificing his own life. From the spiritual point of view the work
> of the Classicist, more or less naturalistic, artist is essentially *par-
> tial*, and the work of the Romantic, produced from within, *total*.
> The totality-type spends itself perpetually in creative work with-
> out absorbing very much of life, while the partial type has con-
> tinually to absorb life so that he may throw it off again in his
> work.[25]

25. *Art and Artist: Creative Urge and*   1932, pp. 48–49.
    Personality (New   York: Knopf,

Although Rank does not specifically relate his classification of artist types to the question of spatial form, it is the Romantic, denying the chronology that common sense tells us exists in the world, who finds totality in the fusion of space and time within the individual consciousness. As Rank implies, it is the Romantic or totality-type of artist who is most likely to be alienated from the mundane world outside his ego. And it is this type of artist with whom I am dealing. Here again, though, we are faced with the paradox that what the artist is as artist is not necessarily what he is as man. In fictional portraits of the artist the artist-self is usually of the "totality-type," but this self may be in conflict with another self that yearns for experience and is of the partial type. The knowledge that "one must die to life in order to be utterly a creator" does not stop Thomas Mann's Tonio Kröger from envying and loving "the blond and blue-eyed, the fair and living, the happy, lovely, and commonplace." [26] In fact, Mann implies that if Tonio is superior to his Bohemian friends, it is largely because he embodies the perfect balance of artist and bourgeois.

II

IF we grant the divided nature of the artist, we can readily see why he is pulled in contrary directions. The man seeks personal fulfillment in experience, while the artist-self desires freedom from the demands of life. One result is that conflicting traditions of art have existed side by side for more than a century. What I call the Sacred Fount tradition tends to equate art with experience and assumes that the true artist is one who lives not less, but more fully and intensely than others. Within this tradition art is essentially the re-creation of experience. The Ivory Tower tradition, on the other hand, exalts art above life and insists that the artist can make use of life only if he stands aloof—"The artist, like the God of the creation, remains within or behind or beyond or above his handiwork, invisible, refined out of existence, indifferent, paring his fingernails." [27]

Crucial in this statement by Joyce is the comparison of the artist with God, for the Ivory Tower tradition equates art with religion rather than experience. The frequency with which the authors of artist-novels describe the creation of art as "divine," the sanctuary of the artist as "holy," or the nature of the artist as "godlike" or

26. "Tonio Kröger" in *Stories of Three Decades*, trans. H. T. Lowe-Porter (New York: Knopf, 1951), pp. 100, 132.

27. *A Portrait of the Artist as a Young Man* (New York: Modern Library, 1928), p. 252.

"priestly" is a heritage from the classic analogy of creator with Creator.[28] Until the nineteenth century, the analogy between God and artist could be assimilated into orthodox religious faith: the artist is *like* God; he is a kind of secondary god whose power comes from God. The artist imitates God, and the world-in-itself which is the work of art is like God's world in that it is ordered and unified by a just and benevolent power. Poetic justice reflects divine justice. With the gradual collapse of religious values during the nineteenth century, however, an important change appears in the artist-as-God concept. When the artist loses his belief in God and can see in the universe no evidence of a divine plan, but only chaos and disorder, then he no longer considers himself a secondary god, but a successor to God. The old God, as in Joyce's description, is an "indifferent" one who pares his fingernails and leaves the world to its own direction. But because the modern artist retains control over his creation, he feels justified in claiming that a "well-made" work of art is superior to the real world.

God looks down on the world. It is for this reason perhaps that when the artist assumes the role of God, he visualizes his place as one from which he can look down on his fellowmen, secure in his superiority and closer to the heavens than the earth. Scholars have attempted to find the first recorded use of the Ivory Tower as a metaphor for the artist's ideal retreat, but who originated the phrase during the early nineteenth century matters little.[29] That it was familiar by mid-century is shown by Gerard de Nerval's use of the term: "The only refuge left to us was the poet's ivory tower, which we climbed, ever higher, to isolate ourselves from the mob. Led by our masters to those high places we breathed at last the pure air of solitude, we drank oblivion in the legendary cup, and we got drunk on poetry and love." [30] If ivory implies the purity of the absolute, the tower implies height and open vistas. Traditionally, artists have preferred garrets to cellars. In one of its many forms, the Ivory Tower is that lofty perch from which Hawthorne, in "Sights from a Steeple," visualized himself a "spiritualized Paul Pry, hovering invisible round man and woman, witnessing their deeds, searching

28. The best discussions of the artist-God analogy are to be found in Meyer C. Abrams, *The Mirror and the Lamp: Romantic Theory and the Critical Tradition* (New York: Oxford University Press, 1953); Milton C. Nahm, *The Artist as Creator: An Essay of Human Freedom* (Baltimore: Johns Hopkins University Press, 1956); and Dorothy L. Sayers,

The Mind of the Maker (New York: Harcourt, Brace, 1941).
29. See, for example, Robert Finch, "Ivory Tower," *University of Toronto Quarterly*, XXV (October, 1955), 23–37.
30. *Sylvie* [1853] in *Selected Writings of Gerard de Nerval*, ed. Geoffrey Wagner (New York: Grove Press, 1957), p. 50.

into their hearts, borrowing brightness from their felicity and shade from their sorrow, and retaining no emotion peculiar to himself." [31] It is the Invisible Lodge of Jean Paul Richter, the Palace of Art of Tennyson, the Great Good Place of Henry James. It is the House of Usher, Axel's castle, Faust's alchemic chambers, and Joyce's Martello Tower. But whatever it may be called, the Ivory Tower is always the artist's private retreat.

In fact, the concept of the Ivory Tower is so familiar that it requires little elaboration. Just as Huxley satirized the theme of the Divided Self in his "Farcical History of Richard Greenow," Albert Camus could be sure that readers would recognize the target of his mock-serious story, "The Artist at Work." In this story Gilbert Jonas, a painter who believes only in his "star," is forced to work in a crowded apartment with his wife and children, where he is subjected to continual interruptions from his family, friends, and patrons. Fortunately the apartment has unusually high ceilings, and Jonas is able to build himself a loft high above the turmoil. As time passes, Jonas finds it increasingly disagreeable to leave his sanctuary. He begins to sleep there, and his meals and supplies are handed up to him by his wife, Louise, and his best friend, Rateau. His muse escapes him even there, and he sits in darkness patiently waiting for the return of the star that has abandoned him temporarily. The voices below become more and more distant, until finally

He put out the lamp and, in the darkness that suddenly returned, right there! wasn't that his star shining? It was the star, he recognized it with his heart full of gratitude, and he was still watching it when he fell, without a sound.

"It's nothing," the doctor they had called declared a little later. "He is working too much. In a week he will be on his feet again." "You are sure he will get well?" asked Louise with distorted face. "He will get well." In the other room Rateau was looking at the canvas, completely blank, in the center of which Jonas had merely written in very small letters a word that could be made out, but without any certainty as to whether it should be read *solitary* or *solidary*.[32]

Like other artist-thinkers of the past few decades, Camus reacted against the concept of the Ivory Tower. "The Artist at Work" sug-

31. "Sights from a Steeple," in his *Complete Works*, Riverside Edition (Boston: Houghton Mifflin, 1883), I, 280.

32. *Exile and the Kingdom*, trans. Justin O'Brien (New York: Knopf, 1958), pp. 157–158.

gests that when the artist denies his own humanity and rejects the
need for social engagement, he loses the ability to produce. For
Camus, the artist must leave his Ivory Tower to tap the Sacred
Fount of life.

III

THE Sacred Fount tradition is rooted in the concept of art as
experience. Prior to Freud and the twentieth-century view that the
artist is one who compensates through his work for his inability to
participate actively in society or to lead a satisfying passional life, it
was generally assumed that the artist differs from other men by the
intensity of his emotions and that he therefore lives more rather
than less fully than other men. For Wordsworth a poet is a man
"endowed with more lively sensibility, more enthusiasm and tenderness . . . a man pleased with his own passions and volitions, and
who rejoices more than other men in the spirit of life which is in
him." [33] And George Edward Woodberry summed up the conventional nineteenth-century attitude when he wrote: "The sign of the
poet . . . is that by passion he enters into life more than other
men. That is his gift—the power to live. The lives of poets are but
little known; but from the fragments of their lives that come down
to us, the characteristic legend is that they have been singularly
creatures of passion." [34]

To assume that the artist is by nature a man of feeling and passion
is to assume a close relation between art and experience. In fact, one
implication of the Sacred Fount myth is that life and art are inter-
changeable. Life can be converted directly to art, but to do so is to
destroy life. Similarly, art and the artist may be destroyed by life.
In Henry James's *The Sacred Fount*, the artist-narrator theorizes
that in any marriage or love affair one party becomes more vigorous,
youthful, intelligent as the other is drained of these qualities. Ironically, the narrator himself indulges in a love affair with the life
around him, turning human relationships into an elaborate, ingenious, artistic structure, but is himself left depleted when the life
he has tried to control and manipulate proves stronger than he. In
one of Balzac's parables of the artist, *La Peau de chagrin*, the fatal
skin shrinks in direct ratio to the intensity with which the artist
lives so that he can actually see the decreasing measure of his days.
Much the same idea is behind the many variations of the "magic
portrait" stories, such as Poe's "Oval Portrait," Hawthorne's "Pro-

33. Cited in Abrams, p. 102.   *The Way of the Makers* (New
34. Cited in Marguerite Wilkinson,   York: Macmillan, 1925), pp. 13–14.

phetic Pictures," or Oscar Wilde's *Picture of Dorian Gray*. In such stories the assumption is made that life can literally be transferred from flesh to canvas: as the portrait takes on life, the model's life seems to wane away, or, in Wilde's reversal of the myth, the portrait ages while the model remains as he was painted. The inference of the Sacred Fount myth is that life and art are so closely related that one can exhaust or destroy the other. Because there is only so much life to be lived, that which is turned into art is made unavailable for living: the more kite-string in the air, the less in the hand, and one cannot have it in both places at once. Hence the continual struggle between life and art.

To assume that creativity must be expended *either* in life *or* in art often leads to a confusion between sex and art. The religious of all times have defended chastity as a means of preserving creative energy. Thoreau writes in *Walden*: "The generative energy, which, when we are loose, dissipates and makes us unclean, when we are continent invigorates and inspires us. Chastity is the flowering of man; and what are called Genius, Heroism, Holiness, and the like, are but various fruits which succeed it." [35] And a century later the novelist-hero of Alberto Moravia's *Conjugal Love* feels that he can not complete his book unless he abstains from sexual relations with his wife. To assume that there is only one kind of creative energy leads to the view that the artist must spend himself, sacrifice his physical being, in artistic creation. In an extreme form this idea is expressed allegorically in "The Artist's Secret," one of Olive Schreiner's *Dreams*.

> There was an artist once, and he painted a picture. Other artists had colors richer and rarer, and painted more notable pictures. He painted his with one color, there was a wonderful red glow on it; and people went up and down, saying, "We like the picture, we like the glow."
>
> The other artists came and said, "Where does he get his color from?" They asked him; and he smiled and said, "I cannot tell you"; and worked on with his head bent low. And one went to the far East and bought costly pigments, and made a rare color and painted, but after a time the picture faded. Another read in the old books, and made a color rich and rare, but when he had put it on the picture it was dead.
>
> But the artist painted on. Always the work got redder and redder, and the artist grew whiter and whiter. At last one day they found him dead before his picture, and they took him up to

35. *The Variorum Walden*, p. 184.

bury him. The other men looked about in all the pots and crucibles, but they found nothing they had not.

And when they undressed him to put his grave-clothes on him, they found above his left breast the mark of a wound—it was an old, old wound, that must have been there all his life, for the edges were old and hardened; but Death, who seals all things, had drawn the edges together, and closed it up.

And it came to pass that after a while the artist was forgotten —but the work lived.[36]

The necessity to preserve creative force is one justification for the Ivory Tower. However, most of the writers in that tradition think of the artist as a being distinct from ordinary men and thus not subject in the same degree to the carnal appetites; he finds the source of his art in observation or introspection. For such artists the problem of the single creative force is less crucial than for those who find the source of art in experience. When the idea of the single force combines with the idea of art as experience, a conflict naturally arises. The artist *must* tap the Sacred Fount, but in doing so runs the risk of dissipating creative energy in the mere process of living and therefore proving incapable of transforming experience into art.

In the portrait-of-the-artist novel the Sacred Fount theme is most often expressed in terms of the artist's relationship to women. In many artist-novels—James's *Roderick Hudson*, Flaubert's *Sentimental Education* and Gissing's *New Grub Street*, to name but three—the artist is destroyed as artist because of his submission to love. In other novels, the artist feels that he cannot function without love. Hardy's *The Well-Beloved*, Wyndham Lewis's *Tarr*, Dreiser's *The "Genius"* and Norris's *Vandover and the Brute* are examples of novels in which the artist-hero must have romantic fulfillment to produce artistically. Although he may be destroyed by the search for such fulfillment, he must go to Woman in order to create—just as a man can father children only through women—and his artistic power is dependent on the Sacred Fount.

There are, of course, many variations of these three basic themes in the artist-novel, and there are many other themes as well. But the situation of the typical artist-hero is essentially what I have outlined here: the Divided Self of the artist-man wavering between the Ivory Tower and the Sacred Fount, between the "holy" or esthetic demands of his mission as artist and his natural desire as a human being to participate in the life around him.

36. *So Here Then Are Dreams* (East   1901), p. 55.
 Aurora, New York: Roycroft Press,

1. The Traditions

CHAPTER ONE

THE DIVIDED SELF

The Artist As Archetype

I *Beginnings*

ONE of the first alienated artists in prose fiction is the poet
Imlac in Samuel Johnson's *Rasselas*.[1] Imlac is the son of a man
"honest, frugal, and diligent, but of mean sentiments and narrow
comprehension." Through books and school, Imlac learns "the pleasure of intelligence . . . the pride of invention," indifference to
worldly riches, and a contempt for his tutors because they do not
seem "wiser or better than common men." His father starts him in
business with ten thousand pieces of gold and encourages him to
travel in search of ways to multiply his fortune. Instead, Imlac seeks
culture and a more intellectual society than his homeland can provide. After varied experiences, he decides that the life of the poet
is the noblest open to man, for the poet, he says, must content himself "with the slow progress of his name, contemn the applause of
his own time, and commit his claims to the justice of posterity. He
must write as the interpreter of nature, and the legislator of mankind, and consider himself as presiding over the thoughts and manners of future generations; as a being superior to time and place."
When Imlac finally returns to his homeland, he learns that his
father is dead, that he has been disinherited, and that those who
were once his friends are now contemptuous of his foreign manners.
"Wearied at last with solicitation and repulses," he tells the prince
of Abyssinia, "I resolved to hide myself for ever from the world and

1. *The History of Rasselas, Prince of*   beck Hill (Oxford University Press,
   Abyssinia [1759], ed. George Birk-   1887), pp. 54–71.

21

depend no longer on the opinion or caprice of others. I waited for the time when the gate of the *happy valley* would open, that I might bid farewell to hope and fear: the day came; my performance was distinguished with favour; and I resigned myself with joy to perpetual confinement."

Here are certain familiar features of the artist-hero tradition: dissatisfaction with the domestic environment, estrangement from a philistine father, a conviction that art is a vocation superior to time and place, the discovery that you can't go home again, and withdrawal to a Happy Valley (or Ivory Tower or Great Good Place). It is a story which we would not expect to find in a book by Doctor Johnson, for, despite his importance in helping to establish the independence of the man of letters and in awakening public interest in the nature of poets, he was himself too socially orientated, too fond of humanity to serve as a prototype of the alienated artist. Although scholars say that there is something of Johnson in Imlac, there is still a touch of irony in his portrayal of the poet. Imlac, after all, finds a role in society when he eventually escapes from the Happy Valley to serve as a mentor to the Prince of Abyssinia.

There could be no hint of satire in the story of Imlac if Johnson had not had a target for his satire; and though Imlac would seem to be an anarchronism—his early life, like his theory of the poet's vocation as "the interpreter of nature, and the legislator of mankind," is more Shelleyan than Johnsonian—there were alienated artists long before Johnson's time. Another story in *Rasselas* helps to point up this fact. Immediately before Johnson tells the story of Imlac, he recounts with amusement the successful attempt of a certain "artist" to build a flying machine in order that he might become a "pendent spectator" of the life beneath him. Just as the tale of Imlac seems to anticipate Shelley, the tale of the unnamed "artist" anticipates Joyce. Both writers use Daedalus as a prototype of the artist and thus remind us that the concept of the artist-as-exile is no discovery of the nineteenth and twentieth centuries. Plato presumably would not have banished the poet from his Republic if by his time the poet had not already established himself as an antisocial type inimical to accepted authority. The alienated artist is but a special kind of alienated man, and for the ultimate prototypes we should have to go back as far as Cain, Lucifer, or Prometheus.

Why, then the comparatively late emergence of the artist as a hero of prose fiction? One answer is to be found in his changing social status. Imlac had to seek refuge in the Happy Valley because there was no audience for the art he wanted to produce. As long as he had pieces of gold, he could scorn the philistines and write for posterity. When his money was gone, he had either to abandon his high ideals of the poet's vocation or find a patron. Not until the eighteenth century did the idea of art as a self-sufficient profession take hold in the public esteem. Until there was a large enough audience for books, music, and paintings, the artist was, of necessity, dependent upon either the Church or those few people with enough leisure, intelligence, and money to afford the luxury of art. When the public finally replaced the patron, the artist found it easy to set himself up as a superior person. But as long as his existence as artist depended upon the favor of the fashionable few, his position was subordinated to that of his audience: he was an entertainer, a servant, a court poet or fool.

The social history of art, which has been traced in detail by other writers,[2] may be summarized as a progression from decorative to didactic to self-expressive functions. Although the artist in earlier times was subordinated to aristocratic patrons or to the Church, the fact that he had been associated with the upper classes probably helped to give him a hold over the middle-class audience of later centuries. Art, it seemed, was related to the "better things in life," and the artist found himself the teacher of these things. When his lessons were rejected, when the middle class sought to reduce him to the status of an entertainer laboring for its amusement and benefit, the position of the artist was by then strong enough to permit him the freedom of proclaiming *non serviam*. Henceforth he would be content simply to express himself.

The rapid increase in public literacy during the eighteenth and early nineteenth centuries undoubtedly had an additional effect upon the rise of the artist-hero. As the ability to read became more widespread, more people became interested in the character of the storyteller; and each portrait of the artist helped to create an audience for another. At the same time, however, the increase in the

2. Studies which I have found especially useful include A. S. Collins, *The Profession of Letters: A Study of the Relation of Author to Patron, Publisher, and Public* (London: Routledge, 1928); Albert Guerard, *Literature and Society* (Boston: Lothrop, Lee and Shepard, 1935); Arnold Hauser, *Social History of Art* (2 vols.; New York: Knopf, 1951); Horace M. Kallen, *Art and Freedom* (2 vols.; New York: Duell, Sloan and Pearce, 1942); Leo Lowenthal, *Literature and the Image of Man: Sociological Studies of the European Drama and Novel, 1600–1900* (Boston: Beacon Press, 1957); Morse Peckham, *Beyond the Tragic Vision: The Quest for Identity in the Nineteenth Century* (New York: George Braziller, 1962); Levin L. Schücking, *The Sociology of Literary Taste*, trans. E. W. Dickes (London: Kegan Paul, Trench, Trubner and Co., 1944); and Raymond Williams, *Culture and Society, 1780–1950* (New York: Columbia University Press, 1958).

reading public encouraged the separation of the artist from the populace. As the nineteenth century advanced, there came to be two kinds of art—one for the masses, the other for "the happy few." It became necessary to distinguish between the hack and the man of letters, between "commercial" and "pure" art. As popular art became more available, serious art became more exclusive and thus helped further to exalt the position of the true artist.

No type of literature becomes popular unless it says something that the general reader finds related to his own interests or desires. Levin Schücking, commenting on the belated appearance of the artist as hero, says:

> It is particularly instructive to see how late the artist is in appearing in literature as an attractive figure. The hero in the romances of earlier centuries is a knight, a prince, a cavalier, an officer; sometimes in the eighteenth century a clergyman. . . .
>
> A hundred years later all this was changed. Interest centered, for the first time, in the artist. In Goethe's *Wilhelm Meister*, the hero, characteristically, is something of an artist, and . . . Thackeray, in *The Newcomes*, . . . also makes his hero an artist. The two novels had many successors, in which the newly revealed predilection of the dominant class is reflected. For the middle class, though originally it had established its dominance on the ideas of common sense and naturalness, had fallen victim to all sorts of affectation, had become aristocratized and narrowed by a thousand conventions. Half conscious of this inner discordance, it nurtured a secret affection for the untrammeled existence, as it saw it, of the artist. He was the embodiment of the human freedom for which it longed but which it scarcely dared to approve openly, still less to practise. He was almost a higher type of being.[3]

To credit the middle class with the vogue of the artist in literature is at first disconcerting. It is less so, however, if we recall that the early nineteenth century was a period of social upheaval and dislocation. "In the years following the Napoleonic wars," Raymond Williams has noted, "one did not have to be an artist to feel that society was indifferent or hostile to individual desires." [4] No doubt many readers saw something of themselves in the romantic outsiders of fiction. We may recall also that the Victorians liked sentimentality in their literature and sentimentality flourishes best when the average man considers himself a person of delicate sensibilities in sym-

3. Schücking, pp. 19–20.
4. "The Idea of Culture," *Essays in* *Criticism*, III (July, 1953), 259.

pathy with the victim of a cruel fate or an unfeeling society. Henry Murger's Bohemia, inhabited by convention-free artists and their mistresses, became popular because to many nonartists Bohemia seemed a form of Utopia.

But though the middle class may have admired the artist secretly and looked up to him, Thackeray's *The Newcomes*, which appeared from 1853 to 1855, shows that in England at least gentlemen continued to look down on him. Clive Newcome's decision to become a painter instead of attending Oxford, joining the army or the Church, or choosing a gentlemanly profession, shocks his relatives and friends. Typical is his uncle's attitude: "I ain't proud; I have not married an earl's daughter . . . but a painter! hang it, a painter's no trade at all—I don't fancy seeing one of our family sticking up pictures for sale." [5] Oddly enough, it is the commercial aspect of painting as profession which offends the gentleman banker. Clive's cousin, Ethel, writes to Colonel Newcome: "You will order Clive not to sell his pictures, won't you? I know it is not wrong, but your son might look higher than to be an artist. . . . An artist, an organist, a pianist, all these are very good people; but, you know, not de notre monde." [6] A gentleman could—indeed, should—compose poetry or music, paint pictures, or act in amateur theatricals, but he ceased to be a gentleman when he accepted payment for his esthetic activities. We are reminded of Byron's reluctance to accept money for his poems, and it is significant that Pope and Johnson, who are credited with establishing the financial independence of the man of letters during the eighteenth century, were offspring of lower-class parents. Whereas Clive Newcome had to fight against society in order to become a painter, his friend and protegé, J. J. Ridley, son of domestic servants, met little opposition. Philip Gilbert Hamerton, in what is perhaps the first essay on the subject of "Artists in Fiction," has commented on the distinction: "Gentlemen are the born officers in the social army, and they do not like to have their epaulettes torn off. But men in the ranks may do menial work of the world, because their position is so humble already that it cannot well suffer by any act not absolutely criminal. So the butler's boy may paint pictures as he might have brushed boots, and nobody considers it a degradation, except his parents, who probably had higher views for their son, and would have liked to see him in livery." [7]

5. *The Works of William Makepeace Thackeray,* Cornhill Edition (New York: Scribner's, 1923), V, 313–314.

6. *Works,* V, 457.

7. In *Thoughts about Art* (Boston: Roberts Brothers, 1880), pp. 101–124.

The painter lagged behind the poet and the composer in attaining social standing. Whereas the Romantic poets exalted their calling in poetry, the painters had to wait for John Ruskin before achieving recognition as superior members of society. Then, too, the painter's art is more obviously mechanical than that of the poet or the composer: because the painter or sculptor works with his hands, his profession seemed to early nineteenth-century society to be more menial, more analogous to that of a mere craftsman, than did poetry and music, which could claim a greater apparent reliance on inspiration and divine grace than upon manual skill. This explains, perhaps, why Ethel Newcome grouped "an artist, an organist, a pianist" in a single category and failed to recognize the distinction between creator and interpreter. Most of the authors of artist-novels would rank the composer higher than the musical performer, the dramatist higher than the actor, the original painter higher than the engraver or copyist. But such a distinction could not be made until the ideas of artistic originality, of creative genius, of art-as-expression rather than art-as-imitation, had gained currency. New theories of the creative process did much to improve the status of the artist.

The words *artist* and *artisan* are of course closely related.[8] Today we are likely to reserve the first term for the practitioner of the fine arts; the latter, for one skilled in mechanical art. In earlier times no such distinction was made. The classic idea of the artist was that of a craftsman with a talent as much manual as spiritual—hence Daedalus the "artist." But the eighteenth century saw a gradual change in the concept of art—and with it, the concept of the artist. Mimetic theories of art as the imitation of physical reality gave place to theories of art as the revelation of a superior reality, a fusing of the spirit in things with the soul of the observer-creator. The Romantic artist, Meyer Abrams has shown, thinks of himself not as a mirror reflecting reality, but as a lamp projecting outward upon reality.[9] As long as art was considered chiefly a matter of imitation, the artist seemed less important than his subject. When he claimed a special faculty—the imagination—which permitted him to perceive deeper truths than those known to the less visionary, he made *the one who sees* more important than *what is seen*. Eventually, as the new theories became dominant, the artist came to be considered not only a craftsman, but also a philosopher, a prophet, a legislator of mankind and, as we have seen, even a god.

8. See Maurice Z. Shroder, *Icarus: The Image of the Artist in French Romanticism* (Cambridge: Harvard University Press, 1961), pp. 2–11.

9. *The Mirror and the Lamp: Romantic Theory and the Critical Tradition* (New York: Oxford University Press, 1953), *passim*.

Whether as recipient of a divine inspiration which fuses through him as agent—a theory which goes a long way toward explaining the passive nature of the typical artist-hero—or as a god in a God-less universe forced to control, manipulate, or create new worlds through a careful, voluntary process, the artist came to be seen as a superior being. Only through such changes in basic artistic theory was the artist enabled to find an exalted position from which he could look *down* on society and to which readers could look *up* in search of truth and guidance. It is this which made the artist a hero in an age which saw what Mario Praz has called the "eclipse of the hero." [10]

But Praz is referring to the early Victorian period, when the first important portraits of the artist appeared in England. On the Continent, however, the artist was an established type long before 1850, and British writers could find in works by Goethe, Rousseau, and others adequate models for their artist-heroes. The rise of the artist-hero depends on the changes in the social status of art which I have summarized here all too briefly, but in any consideration of literary sources the chainlike influence of author upon author is surely as important as the general social and philosophical background.

II   *Goethe*

GOETHE deserves the major credit for initiating the vogue of the artist as hero, not merely because he pioneered the use of artists as central characters in fictional and dramatic works of considerable influence on his contemporaries and followers, but more importantly because a dominant theme of his work, from the early fragment "Prometheus" to the synthesis of the completed *Faust*, is the conflict between art and life. In dealing with this basic theme of the artist-novel, Goethe gave his followers an important lesson in methods of solving the main technical problem of the genre: how to present in dramatic, external terms a conflict which is within the artist-hero.

Because he achieved a personal balance between the self and the world, Goethe may be said to have earned his reputation as a universal genius. While he recognized the claim of the Ivory Tower upon the artist, he knew too the appeal of the Sacred Fount; and few writers have so clearly done justice to both sides of the age-old clashes between self and society, spirit and matter, art and life. In this way, Goethe as author gives the portrait-of-the-artist novel from its be-

10. *Eclipse of the Hero in Victorian*   (New York and London: Oxford *Fiction,* trans. Angus Davidson University Press, 1956).

ginning an example of balanced synthesis for those who followed him. Yet his most important portraits of the artist are studies of would-be artists who failed to become Goethes.

The early artist-heroes of Goethe find the conflict between art and society unsolvable. Prometheus, for instance, is not satisfied to be only the spiritual creator of mankind; he yearns also for experience and the fullness of life. Tasso, in Goethe's drama of 1788—a work frequently cited in later portraits of the artist—is described as one whose

> . . . eye scarce lingers on this earthly scene:
> To nature's harmony his ear is tuned.
>
> . . . .
>
> Though seeming to approach us, he remains
> Remote as ever; and perchance his eye,
> Resting on us, sees spirits in our place.

However, this description is countered with another:

> Thou hast with taste and truth portrayed the bard,
> Who hovers in the shadowy realm of dreams.
> And yet reality, it seems to me,
> Hath also power to lure him and enchain.[11]

One of the reasons why *Torquato Tasso* is, as Karl Viëtor says, "the first great work to deal with the problem of art and life, artist and society, a problem which has since played such a large role in the literature of Europe" [12] is the fact that the conflict is left unresolved. Young Tasso would shun the motley crowd and "hold free converse with himself in solitude," [13] but he wants also to love and to act. Flushed with pride at the completion of his great poem, he is immediately plunged into despair when he observes the respect shown to Antonio, a man of action.

> So strangely have his nature and his words
> Affected me, that more than ever now
> A want of inward harmony I feel,
> And a distracting conflict with myself.[14]

Jealous, he picks a quarrel with Antonio and drives himself into a self-imposed exile. Thus his talent as poet is not enough: the imprac-

11. *Torquato Tasso*, trans. Anna Swanwick. In *The Dramatic Works of Goethe* (New York: John D. Williams, 1882), pp. 91–92.
12. *Goethe the Poet* (Cambridge: Harvard University Press, 1949), p. 73.
13. *Torquato Tasso*, p. 194.
14. *Torquato Tasso*, p. 111.

tical visionary wants also to be consulted in affairs of state and to be loved as a man as well as respected as a poet.

Although Goethe may be said to have included within himself both a Tasso and an Antonio, he chose usually to separate the inner and outer aspects of his personality. Many of his works contain dramatic opposites, "doubles," who stand for the poles of action and thought. Until the final version of *Faust*, Goethe's ideal, synthesizing genius appears only by inference, the positive counterpart of what he chooses to present negatively. Hence, *The Sorrows of Young Werther* and *Wilhelm Meister's Apprenticeship*, which between them established the portrait-of-the-artist genre, are complementary studies in failure: Werther fails because he cannot accept the external world; Wilhelm gives up all pretensions to art when he becomes dominated by that world.

Werther, however, is usually interpreted not as the story of a young man incapable of accepting external reality, but as the story of a painter whose zest for life, represented by his desire to possess a woman married to another, is so strong that he kills himself in frustration. The reputation of Goethe's little novel has suffered from the fact that the general reader seems to be incapable of distinguishing between the author of a novel and its hero, especially when the story is told in the first person. Hence, *Werther* is still read and discussed as if it were a defense of illicit love and a championing of suicide written by Werther himself. The irony and detachment in Goethe's "editing" of Werther's letters is revealed only by close reading.

Yet we cannot deny that there is much of the young Goethe in Werther. The character is fully realized only because Goethe's own experience permitted him to describe Werther from within. We know from his autobiography that before writing *Werther* Goethe himself experienced an unhappy love affair and that he considered suicide.

Amongst a considerable collection of weapons I had a costly and well-polished dagger. I always put this by my bed, and before I extinguished the light I tried if I could succeed in forcing the sharp point a couple of inches into my heart. But since I could never succeed in this, I at last laughed myself out of it, flung away all hypochondriacal silliness and decided to live. But to be able to do this with cheerfulness I had to bring to execution a poetic task, in which all that I had felt, thought, and fancied on this weighty point should be put into words. I gathered together for this purpose the elements which had been moving about

around me for a couple of years; I brought to mind the things
which had most oppressed and vexed me, but nothing would take
shape; I wanted an incident, a story, in which all could be embodied.[15]

Finding that he could not plunge the dagger into his heart, he wrote
Werther as a means of killing a previous self. It is apparent that he
could not have cured himself in this way if he had not attained sufficient detachment from that earlier self to laugh at his own folly.
There are two Goethes in *Werther*—the Goethe of the past in the
character of Werther, and the Goethe of the present in the editor
and interpreter of Werther's letters.

It is significant too that though Goethe had the subjective material for his novel he could not write it until he found an incident
around which he could focus his still chaotic feelings. That incident
he found in the news of his friend Jerusalem's suicide because of
an attachment to a married woman. "At this moment," Goethe says,
"the plan of 'Werther' was found, the whole shot together from all
sides and became a solid mass, like water in a vessel which is on the
point of freezing is transformed into solid ice by the slightest agitation." [16] What happened apparently is that through the agency of
Jerusalem he was enabled to see himself outside himself. Until he
achieved detachment, he could not control his feelings or order them
into a unified work of art. "The *what* lies in us," Goethe declared,
"the *how* seldom depends on us." [17] His autobiography—which, incidentally, reveals so much self-detachment that the "I" of the book
may as well be in the third person—reveals clearly Goethe's need
for external stimuli. The variety of his art may be attributed to his
restless experimentation with new forms; if he read sonnets, he felt
compelled to master the sonnet form. And even the state of mind
which led him into his Werther period was not, he admits, original with himself, but in part his response to the melancholy reflec-
tiveness of the English literature he had been reading.

Werther kills himself for the very reasons which prevented
Goethe from committing suicide. Goethe found his cure outside
himself, in his acceptance of externality and the acknowledgement
of a necessary balance between external forces and the personal ego.
Werther lacks such balance. All satisfaction in life, Goethe says in
explanation of *Werther,* depends upon the regular return of outward
things—day and night, summer and winter—but if one is unrecep-

15. *Goethe's Autobiography: Poetry*   p. 516.
and Truth from My Own Life, 16. *Goethe's Autobiography,* p. 516.
trans. R. O. Moon (Washington, 17. *Goethe's Autobiography,* p. 420.
D. C.: Public Affairs Press, 1949),

tive to these outward things, he wearies of life and yearns for annihilation. "Nothing," he says, "gives rise to this weariness more than
the return of love." [18] The Lotte of the novel, we recall, was preceded by a Lenore, and after Werther's effort to play a part in the
world ends in failure, he can only return to Lotte and plunge deeper
into despair. Goethe says also, "The separation of the sensual from
the moral, which in the complicated, cultivated world severs the feelings of love and desire, gives rise here to an exaggeration which cannot produce what is good." [19] At no time does Werther have a conscious desire to possess Lotte carnally—"She is sacred to me. All lust
ceases in her presence." [20]—and we may speculate that it is fortunate
for him that she is unavailable. The only kind of love of which he
appears capable is platonic love, whereas Lotte is described as "heart
and soul, her whole body *one* harmony." [21]

Werther's changing attitude toward nature is perhaps the key to
his tragedy. He complains in one of his first letters that he cannot
paint because he is absorbed in nature: "I am so happy, so absorbed
in the sensation of a tranquil existence, that my art is suffering. I
could not draw a line at this moment, and yet I have never been
more of a painter than I am now." [22] If "Nature alone forms the
great artist," [23] it is the unnaturalness of his love for Lotte which
causes him to lose sight of his artistic mission. He proclaims after
meeting her, "Sun, moon and stars can journey calmly on their
round, I know not whether it is night or day and the whole world
about me has ceased to have any existence." [24] As he builds his
imaginative vision of an ideal Lotte, his powers of perception
weaken, and soon he is angry with nature: "It is the consuming
force latent in universal Nature that has formed nothing that has
not destroyed its neighbour and itself which saps my soul. And so
I reel along in anguish, surrounded by earth and sky and all the
weaving forces of Nature. I see nothing but a monster, eternally
devouring, eternally chewing the cud." [25] From temporary absorption in nature, he reverts to absorption in self. In neither condition is he capable of practicing his art.

The story of Werther's love for Lotte is interrupted by the letters

18. *Goethe's Autobiography*, p. 510.
19. *Goethe's Autobiography*, p. 510.
20. *The Sorrows of Young Werther*,
trans. William Rose, in *The Permanent Goethe*, ed. Thomas Mann
(New York: Dial Press, 1948), p.
387.
21. *The Sorrows of Young Werther*,
p. 374.

22. *The Sorrows of Young Werther*,
p. 363.
23. *The Sorrows of Young Werther*,
p. 368.
24. *The Sorrows of Young Werther*,
p. 378.
25. *The Sorrows of Young Werther*,
p. 399.

written during the time of his ill-fated attempt to establish himself in civic life. These letters are important not only because Werther's failure forces him to return to Lotte and thus back upon himself, but also because his failure is as important a motivation for his suicide as is his love for Lotte. Significantly, it is hurt pride which causes Werther to resign as secretary to the ambassador. The editor steps in to state this explicitly:

> He could not forget the rebuff at the embassy. He rarely mentioned it, but one could feel imperceptibly that he considered his honour irretrievably outraged, and that the episode had inspired him with a dislike for a profession or political activity. He therefore resigned himself totally to the odd emotional and mental idiosyncrasies with which we are acquainted from his letters, and to a bottomless passion which was bound to cause the eventual extinction of all his vital energies. The eternal monotony of a melancholy attachment to the charming and beloved being whose peace of mind he was upsetting, the tempestuous wearing down of his vitality, without hope or purpose, drove him at last to the dreadful act.[26]

Goethe describes Werther as an "unbalanced young man." He is unbalanced in the direction of self-absorption. Even his end, though sometimes interpreted as a noble act of self-sacrifice, is calculated for effect. Goethe's detachment from his hero comes out subtly in the conclusion. To the end Werther thinks only of himself: he pleads that his body be protected in some secluded and picturesque spot, in a symbolic gesture borrows Albert's pistols to make away with himself, and chooses Christmas Eve for the event, thus spoiling the holiday of Lotte and her children.

The Sorrows of Werther is important in the development of the portrait-of-the-artist novel for the wrong reasons. Although Werther fails as an artist, Goethe's supposed exaltation of his sensitive, rapturous hero helped to establish these qualities as essential to the popular conception of the artist. We note, for example, that the first Werther poem in English literature appears in Sir Herbert Croft's Love and Madness, which also contains the first extended account of the life of Thomas Chatterton. Croft's sensation novel, which first appeared in 1780 and went through seven editions in seven years, undoubtedly helped to establish the stereotype of the artist as a sensitive Werther or Chatterton destroyed by an unfeeling world.[27] And

26. The Sorrows of Young Werther, p. 431.
27. Stuart Pratt Atkins, The Testa-ment of Werther in Poetry and Drama (Cambridge: Harvard University Press, 1949), 17–20.

though *Werther* presents the story of a young artist destroyed by motivations other than frustration in love, it became a model for many stories of artists defeated by passion more carnal than Werther's. Hazlitt's *Liber Amoris,* James's *Roderick Hudson,* and Frank Norris's *Vandover and the Brute* are among the many novels which look back to *Werther* as a common source.

Although *Werther* did much to establish the popular conception of the artistic type, it was less important in the founding of the portrait-of-the-artist novel than *Wilhelm Meister*—a novel in which the hero turns out to be no artist at all. Wilhelm writes poetry, adapts *Hamlet* for the German stage, and fancies himself an actor, but he discovers eventually that none of these activities in itself represents his true vocation. In matters of art he is at best a dilettante and amateur. Throughout much of the narrative his main purpose is the cultivation of his own personality; in the remainder he prepares himself for the cultivation of others. Yet Goethe in *Wilhelm Meister* helped to establish the nature of the true artist by showing what he is not.

The puppet theater which Wilhelm acquires as a child sets the pattern of his later life. A sensitive, passive child, he develops an interest in the arts partly because such a predilection appears to be an inheritance from his art-collecting grandfather, partly because he is repelled by the materialistic and narrowly utilitarian life of his family and neighbors. One of his first poems, "The Muse of Tragedy," represents Trade as a "nervous old housekeeper . . . always diligent, always restless, quarrelsome and thrifty, mean and troublesome." [28] The puppet theater not only establishes his interest in the theater, but also, one may say, stimulates his desire to play providence. His later transition from art to society seems less abrupt if we remember that the most social of the arts is the one most appealing to him. When his love for Mariana is thwarted by misunderstanding, he burns his early poems and abandons his plan to become an actor because he reasons that a true genius would not be vulnerable to such a disappointment. If shortly thereafter he does join a theatrical troupe, it is more by accident than deliberation, though he tries to justify his move by the desire to "awaken among the populace good and noble feelings." [29]

At this stage of his career, however, he is not ready to help others because, like Werther, he is absorbed in self. He is not even a very good actor, for he lacks the ability to project in a variety of roles. Unlike Serlo, who "always saw the outer peculiarities of men and

28. *Wilhelm Meister: Apprenticeship*   1947), I, 29.
and Travels, trans. R. O. Moon   29. *Wilhelm Meister,* I, 91.
(London: G. T. Foulis and Co.,

gathered them into his collection of mimicry," [30] Wilhelm "was able to speak and tell of feelings and thoughts, of many experiences of the heart and mind, but not of outward objects, to which he . . . had not paid the smallest attention." [31] His only role is himself, and if his only acting success is the part of Hamlet, this is because he interprets the character as himself—"a beautiful, pure, noble, highly moral nature without the sensuous strength which makes the hero." [32] When Serlo's gifted sister Aurelia says to Wilhelm, "nothing comes to you from without; I have not readily seen anyone who knows so little of the people with whom he lives and so fundamentally misunderstands them as you do," he replies, "From my youth I have been wont to direct the eyes of my spirit more inwards than outwards, and so it is very natural that I should have got to know mankind up to a certain point without understanding in the least or having any conception of men." [33]

The inwardness of Wilhelm's temperament is brought out by contrast with his more outward-directed opposites. In his notes Goethe labelled Wilhelm "aesthetico-moral dream" as distinguished from Lothario as "heroically active dream." [34] But Lothario is only one of Wilhelm's doubles. During the early part of the novel the other side of the picture is represented by his friend and eventual brother-in-law Werner, whose eloquent eulogy of Trade, compared with Wilhelm's attack upon it, provides evidence of Goethe's own balanced attitude. During his theatrical period, Wilhelm's opposites are Serlo, the true actor, and Laertes, the "unqualified will" of the notes, who abandons the stage for a more aggressive career as a businessman. When Wilhelm leaves the theater to carry Aurelia's dying message to Lothario, he finds the latter living in a castle in which, significantly, "all outward symmetry, every architectural appearance seemed to have been sacrificed to the requirements of internal convenience." [35] With the change of setting, Wilhelm's character becomes more outward-directed, and Lothario's utilitarian castle is the headquarters for that strange fellowship in which Wilhelm enrolls. But perhaps the most significant contrast is that between Wilhelm and Jarno. When they first meet, both young men seem aloof and withdrawn from society, but whereas Wilhelm's aloofness is the result of his introversion, Jarno's is the product of his desire to be a detached observer capable of knowing the world as it is. After he, like Wilhelm, has been taught the values of social participation by the Abbé, he sums up his experience:

30. *Wilhelm Meister*, I, 234.
31. *Wilhelm Meister*, I, 229.
32. *Wilhelm Meister*, I, 211–212.

33. *Wilhelm Meister*, I, 221–222.
34. Viëtor, *Goethe the Poet*, p. 125.
35. *Wilhelm Meister*, I, 361.

From my youth up I had looked at what is clear and wished in all things nothing but what is clear. I had no other interest but to know the world as it was, and infected with this inclination the remainder of my best companions, and in consequence our whole culture had almost taken a false direction; for we began to see only the faults of others and their limitation, and to regard ourselves as splendid people. The Abbé came to our assistance and taught us that we ought not to observe people without taking an interest in their culture, and that one can really only be in a position to observe through action in a state of activity and to watch ourselves.[36]

The key point of this passage on the ethics of observation—that we can know ourselves only by comparison and that fair comparison can be made only through mutual participation—comes close to being the main idea of *Wilhelm Meister*. Significantly, at the end of the novel the differences between Wilhelm and his doubles tend to disappear.

A technical device closely related in purpose to the use of the double and also influential on later novelists is Goethe's use of dreams and prevision. Much of what happens in *Wilhelm Meister* is the external expression of what has been internally envisioned. Wilhelm asks himself: "May it not be . . . that in youth as in sleep images of future destiny hover around us and become forebodingly visible to our unobstructed eye? Are not the seeds of what is to befall us already scattered by the hand of destiny? Should not a foretaste of the fruits which we hope some time to gather be possible for us?" [37] The questions are answered affirmatively when Wilhelm has symbolic dreams and fleeting intimations of what is to occur to him and his friends. Such foreshadowing permits Goethe to overcome through the suggestion of inevitability what would otherwise seem excessive coincidence in the unravelling of the mysteries at the conclusion of the novel.

A third thematic-technical device is the repeated motif of seeing one's self outside one's self. When Mignon steals into Wilhelm's room to share his bed, she finds herself anticipated by a rival: the shock to Mignon is attributed in part to her seeing her own half-known desire acted out by another. A parallel incident is that of the deception played upon the countess. Wilhelm is persuaded to trick her by impersonating her husband, but when the count returns unexpectedly to find Wilhelm in his place, he is made so distraught by the experience of seeing what he thinks is himself that he under-

36. *Wilhelm Meister*, I, 470.   37. *Wilhelm Meister*, I, 125.

goes a religious conversion and changes his way of life. After Wilhelm reads his own life story as prepared by the mysterious fellowship, he too becomes capable of standing detached from himself: "For the first time he saw his figure outside himself—not as in a mirror a second self, but as in a portrait a different self." [38] All three of these devices—dramatic opposites or doubles, prevision, and the repetition of the self-seeing motif—involve an interplay between what is inward and what is outward; hence, the theme of the novel, the interdependence of self and soceity, is a basic part of the novel's structure.

For Wilhelm, as for the count, the experience of seeing himself outside himself enables him to achieve freedom from his enslavement to ego. It is this which qualifies him for membership in the fellowship. Soon thereafter he asks the Abbé if Felix is really his child—information which previously he had tried to avoid. The answer is affirmative; Wilhelm embraces the child, accepting him and, with him, his responsibility to society. "Your years of apprenticeship are over," says the Abbé. From this moment the emphasis changes from character to action. With the conventionalizing of the story— through the crowding of the stage with new characters, the unravelling of the mysteries by apparent coincidences, and the melodrama of the old harper's story—what promised to be the first portrait-of-the-artist novel becomes a typical eighteenth-century romance. Yet it is easy to exaggerate the difference between the first three quarters of the novel and its conclusion, between the earlier and the later Wilhelms. When he accepts his responsibility to society, he does not abandon what was true in his previous position to become a Werner, Lothario, or Jarno; rather, he assimilates the positive aspects of their characters and achieves a balance between himself and the world. He awakens from his "aesthetico-moral dream" and begins to apply for the benefit of society his innate aptitude for beauty and goodness.

One of the best known sections of *Wilhelm Meister* is the discussion of the differences between the novel and the drama. "The hero of the novel must be suffering," we are told; "at least he must not be in a high degree active." [39] Even after his transition, Wilhelm continues to be a passive hero; things still happen *to* him. The decisions he makes on his own—the offer of marriage to Theresa, for example—prove to be wrong, and even his proper union with the beautiful "Amazon" Natalia, who complements his character, is brought about by the drunken Frederike. *Wilhelm Meister*, regard-

38. *Wilhelm Meister*, I, 432.   39. *Wilhelm Meister*, I, 265.

less of its conclusion, helped with *Werther* to establish the type of
the passive, sensitive hero and thus offered a prototype for the
Stephen Dedaluses and Marcels of later fiction. The character of
Wilhelm is the more convincing because Goethe, like Joyce in
Ulysses, associates his hero with the earlier prototype, Hamlet.

Another aspect of *Wilhelm Meister* which was important in the
development of the artist-novel is the idea of self-development as a
necessary preliminary to the improvement of society. Goethe insists
all capacity is inborn, but that it must be cultivated.[40] The individual
must find a happy balance between thought and action because
"thought enlarges, but disables; action enlivens, but narrows." [41]
It is better for a youth to go astray on a path of his own than "to
wander aright on a path which is foreign" to him.[42] Such ideas
helped the artist not only to justify the cultivation of his own character without particular regard for the values of his less sensitive
society, but to claim the right of leadership. The Romantic notion
of the artist as the "unacknowledged legislator," the proper leader,
of mankind owes much to *Wilhelm Meister*.

A third major influence upon the portrait-of-the-artist novel is
found in Goethe's concept of the artistic vocation, for we may say
that if Wilhelm is not a true artist, it is partly because Goethe held
an uncompromisingly exalted notion of what the true artist ought
to be. Wilhelm burns his poems "because a poem is either first-rate,
or ought not to exist; because everyone, who has no talent for producing the best should restrain himself from art and earnestly beware of every temptation leading to it." [43] Because Wilhelm knows
that he is vulnerable to experience and he is eager to be liked, he
lacks confidence in his artistic talents. The true poet, he argues, is
indifferent to the minor frustrations and disappointments of life:
"Destiny has placed the poet, like a god above all this. He sees the
whirl of the passions, families and kingdoms exciting themselves
aimlessly; he sees the insoluble riddles of misunderstandings, for
which often only a word of one syllable is lacking to explain, cause
unspeakably ruinous disorders. He feels the sorrow and the joy of
every human lot. . . . And so the poet is at once teacher, prophet,
friend of gods and of men." [44]

In his autobiography Goethe wrote: "True poetry proclaims itself thus, that, like a gospel of this world, it understands how to
free us from the earthly burdens which oppress us by means of
inward serenity and outward enjoyment. Like an air-balloon, it

40. *Wilhelm Meister*, I, 63.   43. *Wilhelm Meister*, I, 70.
41. *Wilhelm Meister*, I, 471.   44. *Wilhelm Meister*, I, 71.
42. *Wilhelm Meister*, I, 446.

raises us with the ballast, which clings to us into higher regions, and lets the confused labyrinths of the earth lie unravelled before us as in a bird's-eye view." [45] Such statements make it clear that for Goethe the best art, though not intentionally didactic, has a social function in the amelioration of passion and spiritual despair. To objectify subjective experience is to bring it under control for both artist and audience. Writing of his early drama *Götz von Berlichingen*, Goethe said, "I pursued again the traditional poetic confession, so that by this self-tormenting penance I should become worthy of an inward absolution." [46] It is in this sense that his works are "fragments of a great confession."

If the poet must be detached in order to see and control the whole —"one can only create anything of importance when one is isolated"—[47] he must also "grasp the fullness of the external world, where alone he can find nourishment for his growth and at the same time a standard for it." [48] True art is the product of the interplay between the internal and external forces which find unity in the oneness of the form-giving genius. For Goethe, therefore, the true artist stands midway between the Ivory Tower and the Sacred Fount.

III   *Rousseau*

IN establishing the archetype of the artist, it is more difficult to assess the importance of Jean-Jacques Rousseau, for, compared with the balanced and emotionally stable Goethe, Rousseau seems erratic and contradictory. The Rousseau of legend is a sentimentalist who introduced the concept of the Noble Savage, urged a return to nature, and exalted sensibility and passion over reason and restraint. Yet there were times when Rousseau considered sensibility the cause of his misfortunes, and though he may have exalted the Noble Savage and urged a return to primitivism, he also argued for the perfectibility of society through reason and religion. The real Rousseau was a rebel from society who loved mankind, an individualist who believed that true freedom depends upon conformity. Yet the Rousseau of legend is real too, in the historical sense, for it was that Rousseau who most influenced his contemporaries and followers and, perhaps more than any other individual, served as the prototype of a new kind of man.

If we had to deal only with the Rousseau of legend, his significance in the rise of the artist as hero would seem paradoxical. On

45. *Goethe's Autobiography*, p. 512.   47. *Goethe's Autobiography*, p. 566.
46. *Goethe's Autobiography*, p. 459.   48. *Goethe's Autobiography*, p. 351.

the one hand, his assumed exaltation of sensibility helped to make the artist seem superior to the mass of men, for the artist could lay claim to feelings at once more delicate and more intense than those of his less imaginative followers. However, if Rousseau was arguing for a return to primitive nature, his message was anti-esthetic, for art is the controlling of nature and flourishes best in a highly civilized society. Fortunately, we now see that Rousseau was not championing a return to nature. He made room for art in his ideal society, and behind his theories of life lay not the nihilism of the romantic rebel but an awareness of the sanctity of life not unlike that of many later artist-visionaries.

For Rousseau, we must remember, was an artist. His influence as thinker has been so pervasive that we are likely to overlook the fact that he was more artist than philosopher. True, his musical compositions, operas, and dramas are today forgotten, and justly so. His one novel, *Julie ou La Nouvelle Héloïse,* is of historical importance but virtually unreadable. Putting these artistic failures to one side and his philosophical works to the other, we should still, however, have the autobiographical writings. The *Confessions* and *Reveries of a Solitary* live on because they are the products of a deeply artistic temperament and a poetic skill better adapted to self-analysis and mystical reverie than to the abstract philosophizing with which Rousseau's name is more often associated.

For all his ability at self-analysis, Rousseau could never satisfactorily explain the forces which made him an artist. In his *Dictionary of Music* he tried to define *genius:* "Ask not, young artist, what is genius! If you have it you will feel it yourself; if you have it not, you will never comprehend it. The genius of the musician includes the whole world in his art. . . . The emotions which he expresses he finds in the depths of his heart. . . . His soul bears a sense of life that never deserts him and that he communicates to hearts formed for understanding it." [49] Rousseau, however, never stopped asking the question. Among his minor works are several portraits of the artist: *Narcisse,* an early drama, deals with a young man who falls in love with his own portrait; in *Pygmalion* (which Goethe particularly admired) an artist falls in love with his own work; the opera-ballet, *Les Muses Galantes,* is concerned with the amours of poets. But most often the question, What is genius?, framed itself in terms of the question, What am I? It is to this desire for self-understanding that we owe the *Confessions,* the first fully developed self-portrait of the artist in modern literature.

49. Matthew Josephson, *Jean-Jacques Rousseau* (New York: Harcourt, Brace and Co., 1931), p. 206.

Rousseau admitted that he set himself up as a professional musician because of a desire to emulate a young man named Venture who had dazzled the ladies of Annecy: "I was so fired by this idea that without thinking that I had neither his charm nor his talents I took it into my head to play the little Venture at Lausanne, to teach music, of which I was ignorant, and to say that I came from Paris, where I had never been." [50] In doing this, Rousseau was scarcely true to his own nature, which explains perhaps why his first music and writings, the art of a consciously motivated dilettante, are of little interest today. It was not until 1749, when he was thirty-seven, that he became a real artist, and then almost unconsciously. The moment of transformation he described in a letter to M. de Malesherbes:

I was on my way to see Diderot, then a prisoner at Vincennes. I had a copy of the *Mercure de France* in my pocket and I took to leafing through it along the way. My eyes lit on the question of the Academy of Dijon which occasioned my first piece of writing. If anything was ever like a sudden inspiration it was the impulse that surged up in me as I read that. Suddenly I felt my mind dazzled by a thousand lights; crowds of lively ideas presented themselves at once, with a force and confusion that threw me into an inexpressible trouble; I felt my head seized with a vertigo like that of intoxication. A violent possession oppressed me, made me gasp for breath, and being unable any longer to breathe as I walked, I let myself drop under one of the trees of the wayside, and there I spent half an hour in such a state of agitation that when I got up I perceived the whole front of my vest moistened with my own tears which I had shed unawares. Oh, Sir, if ever I could have written even a quarter of what I saw and felt under that tree, with what clarity should I have revealed all the contradictions of the social system, with what force would I have exposed all the abuses of our institutions, in what simple terms would I have demonstrated that man is naturally good, and that it is through these institutions alone that men become. All I have been able to retain of those crowds of great truths that illuminated me in a quarter of an hour under that tree has been scattered quite feebly in my three principal writings. . . . That is how, when I least thought of it, I became an author almost in spite of myself.[51]

50. *The Confessions of Jean-Jacques Rousseau,* trans. J. M. Cohen (Penquin Books, 1953), p. 144.
51. Charles William Hendel, *Citizen* *of Geneva: Selections from the Letters of Jean-Jacques Rousseau* (New York: Oxford University Press, 1937), pp. 208–209.

Apparently this moment of consecration—a parallel to many such moments in artist-novels—brought to the surface something which had lain concealed in Rousseau's subconscious. What is surprising is that it did not reveal itself earlier, for that the seeds of true artistic impulse were in Rousseau's basic temperament is seen clearly in the *Confessions*.

Rousseau begins his autobiography disarmingly:

> I have resolved on an enterprise which has no precedent, and which, once complete, will have no imitator. My purpose is to display to my kind a portrait in every way true to nature, and the man I shall portray will be myself.
>
> Simply myself. I know my own heart and understand my fellow man. But I am made unlike any one I have ever met; I will even venture to say that I am like no one in the whole world. I may be no better, but at least I am different. Whether Nature did well or ill in breaking the mould in which she formed me, is a question which can only be resolved after the reading of my book.[52]

Perhaps because the *Confessions* became a model for subsequent artists, Rousseau's claim to uniqueness seems extravagant to the modern reader. Every individual is, of course, different in some ways from all others, but the type to which Rousseau belongs has become a stereotype. The "I" of the *Confessions* or *Reveries of a Solitary*, like the autobiographical hero, Saint-Preux, of *Julie*, is a man strikingly familiar to those acquainted with the heroes of James, Proust, Joyce, Mann, Gide, and others.

In fact, we find in Rousseau virtually all of the traits traditionally associated with the "artistic temperament." Among these qualities is sensitivity. Far from exalting this gift, as he is assumed to have done or as later writers do, Rousseau seemed to feel that sensitivity led only to nervous imbalance and eventual misery: a "sensitive heart" was "the cause of all the misfortunes in my life." [53] The sensitive person is likely to be either jubilant or depressed, impetuous and timid, quick to take umbrage. Saint-Preux writes to Julie:

> Ah, Eloisa! too much sensibility, too much tenderness, proves the bitterest curse instead of the choicest blessing: vexation and disappointment are its certain consequences. The temperature of the air, the change of the seasons, the brilliancy of the sun, and thickness of the fogs, are so many springs to the unhappy possessor, and he becomes the wanton sport of their arbitration; his

52. *Confessions*, p. 17.   53. *Confessions*, p. 19.

thoughts, his satisfaction, his happiness, depend on the blowing
of the winds, and the different points of east and west can sadden,
or enliven his expectations: swayed as he is by prejudices, and
distracted by passions, the sentiments of his heart find continual
opposition from the axioms of his head. Should he perchance
square his conduct to the undeviable rule of right, and set up
truth for his standard, instead of profit and convenience, he is
sure to fall a martyr to the maxims of his integrity; the world will
join in the cry and hunt him down as a common enemy. But sup-
posing this not the case, honesty and uprightness, though ex-
empted from prosecution, are neither of them the channels of
honour, nor the road to riches; poverty and want are their inseparable attendants, and man, by adhering to the one, necessarily
attaches himself to the inheritance of the other; and by this means
he becomes his own tormentor. He will search for supreme happiness, without taking into the account the infirmities of his nature.
Thus his affections and his reason will be engaged in a perpetual
warfare, and unbounded ideas and desires must pave the way for
endless disappointments.[54]

The sense of a split between head and heart appears also in many
passages of the *Confessions*. For example, Rousseau describes his
temperament in terms of "a heart at once proud and affectionate,
and a character at once effeminate and inflexible, which by always
wavering between weakness and courage, between self-indulgence
and virtue, has throughout my life set me in conflict with myself,
to such effect that abstinence and enjoyment, pleasure and prudence
have alike eluded me." [55] He writes elsewhere: "I have a passionate
temperament, and lively and headstrong emotions. Yet my thoughts
arise slowly and confusedly, and are never ready till too late. It is
as if my heart and my brain did not belong to the same person." [56]
To discover a means of escape from this conflict, to attain peace and
harmony through self-understanding and self-acceptance, is one of
the motives of the *Confessions*.

His sensitivity, he tells us, was an inheritance from his parents,
but fostered and intensified by his precocious early reading:

In a short time I acquired . . . not only an extreme facility in
reading and expressing myself, but a singular insight for my age
into the passions. I had no idea of the facts, but I was already
familiar with every feeling. I had grasped nothing; I had sensed

54. Anonymous   translation   from
Eloisa; or, A Series of Original Let-
ters (London: T. Becket, 1776), I,

86–87.
55. *Confessions*, p. 23.
56. *Confessions*, pp. 112–113.

everything. These confused emotions which I experienced one after another, did not warp my reasoning powers in any way, for as yet I had none. But they shaped them after a special pattern, giving me the strangest and most romantic notions about human life, which neither experience nor reflection has ever succeeded in curing me of.[57]

It was not long before young Rousseau began making up his own stories, building dream castles as it were:

> My restless imagination took a hand which saved me from myself and calmed my growing sensuality. What it did was to nourish itself on situations that had interested me in my reading, recalling them, varying them, combining them, and giving me so great a part in them, that I became one of the characters I imagined, and saw myself always in the pleasantest situations of my own choosing. So, in the end, the fictions I succeeded in building up made me forget my real condition, which so dissatisfied me. My love for imaginary objects and my facility in lending myself to them ended by disillusioning me with everything around me, and determined that love of solitude which I have retained ever since that time.[58]

Imaginative reverie as a means of retreat from unpleasantness became habitual with Rousseau. It explains the appearance of *Julie* —he professed embarrassment at the way in which that story shaped itself within his consciousness almost in direct opposition to his will —and eventually he came to see in reverie the best means of attaining the harmony which he could find in neither himself nor society.

We would expect a person with this introspective tendency to be passive in his actions. Rousseau also illustrates this characteristic of the totality-type. The celebrated trance which made him an author was, of course, a passive experience; and he confessed that he could never create deliberately: "I did not foresee that I should have ideas. They arrive when they please, not when it suits me. Either they do not come at all, or they come in a swarm, overwhelming me with their strength and their numbers." [59] It is significant that when he decided to study philosophy he tried to be completely receptive to each author he read, vowing to adopt the ideas of each without mingling them with his own. In this way he was to build up a storehouse of ideas upon which he could later base his own system of thought. This passivity extended even to Rousseau's sexual life.

57. *Confessions*, p. 20.   59. *Confessions*, p. 158.
58. *Confessions*, p. 48.

He expected women to be the aggressors, and he was quite ready "to fall on my knees before a masterful mistress, to obey her commands, to have to beg for her forgiveness." [60]

The totality-type is likely to be absorbed in one thing at a time, indifferent to all distractions. "Except for the one object in my mind," Rousseau wrote, "the universe for me is non-existent." [61] Each time he takes up a new interest it becomes "a passion, and soon I can see nothing else in the world but the amusement that occupies me." [62] One reason for his disillusionment with society was his feeling that polite usage demanded a restraint foreign to his nature: "I have never been capable of moderation in my relationships, or of simply fulfilling the duties of society. It has always been all or nothing with me." [63]

Considering these basic characteristics of temperament, it is not surprising that Rousseau found himself at odds with society. What may well surprise us today, though, is that his preference for solitude seems actually to have offended his contemporaries. There was for Diderot ("only the wicked man is alone"), Voltaire, Grimm, and his other acquaintances something indecent about this man who refused to accept the rewards of his fame and who continued to live modestly as a music copyist even after the success of his books had secured him entrance into the best salons and earned him financial independence. So intent was Rousseau upon maintaining his personal freedom that he even refused a government pension. After the success of his opera, *Le Devin du Village*, he was invited to an audience with Louis XV, who was said to be willing to grant a pension to its author. Rousseau seems never to have regretted his refusal to meet the king, for if he lost a pension, he was free also of "the dependence it would have imposed." [64] It was this stubborn insistence that he be left alone which set Rousseau apart from his contemporaries. He would have approved William Faulkner's refusal to dine at the White House because a hundred miles is a long way to go "just to eat."

Temperament alone, however, does not fully explain Rousseau's withdrawal from society. There were also physical and ideological as well as psychological motives involved. For one thing—and his critics make much of it—Rousseau suffered from an embarrassing malady, a congestion of the ureter, which forced him to urinate frequently. Such an ailment undoubtedly contributed to his sense of awkwardness in society. But there can be little doubt also that it

60. *Confessions*, p. 28.
61. *Confessions*, p. 44.
62. *Confessions*, p. 174.

63. *Confessions*, p. 483.
64. *Confessions*, p. 354.

served Rousseau as a convenient "wound," giving him an excuse to avoid activities in which he was not eager to participate. That Rousseau made little effort to secure proper medical attention causes one to suspect that he was less distressed by the malady than a more gregarious person would have been. For the man who prefers his own company, there are certain advantages in sickness.

To a considerable degree, Rousseau's rejection of society was a rejection of the expedient values of his time. He came to believe eventually that participation in society is innately evil. In one of his letters he defended his solitude thus: "The state in which I have placed myself is the only one where man can be good and happy, since it is the most independent of all, and the only one where he never finds himself under the necessity of harming others for his own advantage." [65] And in *The Reveries of a Solitary*: "If I had remained free, obscure, isolated, as I was made to be, I should have done nothing but good, because I have not the germ of any harmful passion in my heart; if I were invisible and powerful as God, I should have been beneficent and good like Him." [66] Because true merit is disinterested, the good man avoids involvement with others. One of Rousseau's spiritual descendants is Natty Bumppo, who refused to return to the settlements because "never again shall I be seen running wilfully into the danger of immoralities." [67]

But the underlying cause of Rousseau's alienation was his mystic tendency. His habit of imaginative reverie, I have shown, appears to have begun as a compensatory escape from reality: the world of his daydreams was that ideal society of his philosophy, a world in which man could live in harmony within himself and with his environment. The sense of the whole, the escape from an awareness of dissociation, appears to have been the ultimate goal of Rousseau's reveries. Such a religious purpose made him impatient with the obligations of a temporal and transitory existence: "I have never been able to compel myself to keep good time. I enjoyed my lessons while I was giving them, but I did not like being obliged to go to them, nor being tied to time. In all matters constraint and compulsion are unbearable to me; they would make me dislike even pleasure. It is said that among the Mohammedans a man goes through the streets at dawn to command all husbands to do their duty by their wives. At that hour I should be a bad Turk." [68] And Ernst Cassirer tells us that "it was one of the happiest moments of his life

65. Hendel, p. 210.
66. Translated by John Gould Fletcher (London: Routledge, 1927), p. 129.
67. James Fenimore Cooper, *The Prairie: A Tale* (New York: Rinehart Editions, 1950), p. 433.
68. *Confessions*, pp. 183–184.

when, renouncing all plans for the future in order to live from day to day, he got rid of his watch. 'Thank heavens!' he exclaimed in a transport of joy, 'I shall no longer need to know what time it is!' " [69]

Rousseau found that he could escape time best by losing himself in contemplation. During his later years, when he was writing *Reveries of a Solitary,* he found comfort even in his sensitivity: "The more a contemplator has a sensitive soul, the more he yields himself to ecstasies which excite in him this harmony. A profound and pleasing reverie then fills his senses, and he loses himself with a delicious intoxication in the immensity of the beautiful system with which he feels himself identified. Then all particular objects escape him; he does not see and does not feel anything but everything." [70] And how different this is from normal, temporal existence:

> All is in a continuous flux upon earth. Nothing keeps a constant and fixed form, and our affections which attach themselves to exterior things pass away and change necessarily like them. Always in advance or behind us, they recall the past, which is no more, or presage the future, which often is not to be; there is nothing solid there to which the heart can attach itself. Therefore one has scarcely here below anything but passing pleasures; for the happiness which lasts, I doubt if it is known. Scarcely is there, in most living delights, a moment where the heart can truly say to us: I wish that this moment should last forever. And how can one call that happiness which is a fugitive state which leaves our heart unquiet and empty, which makes us regret something beforehand or desire something after?
>
> But there is a state where the soul finds a position sufficiently solid to repose thereon, and to gather together all its being, without having need for recalling the past, nor to climb on into the future; where time counts for nothing, where the present lasts forever, without marking its duration in any way, and without any trace of succession, without any other sentiment of privation, neither of enjoyment, of pleasure nor pain, of desire nor of fear, than this alone of our existence, and which this feeling alone can fill entirely: so long as this state lasts, he who finds it may be called happy, not with an imperfect happiness, poor and relative, such as that which one finds in the pleasures of life, but with a sufficing happiness, perfect and full, which does not leave in the soul any void which it feels the need of filling. . . .

69. *The Question of Jean-Jacques Rousseau,* trans. and ed. Peter Gay (New York: Columbia University Press, 1954), pp. 41–42.
70. *Reveries of a Solitary,* p. 138.

What is the nature of one's enjoyment in such a situation? Nothing external to oneself, nothing except oneself and one's own existence; so long as this state lasts, one suffices to oneself, like God.[71]

As John Gould Fletcher has remarked, Rousseau was like the holy men of old in that he tried to live a "life of dissociated consciousness." It was his misfortune to live at a time when "the type of the holy man . . . was no longer permitted to exist." [72]

For Rousseau after all failed in his purpose. It was only at isolated moments in his life that he was able to find in his reveries a sense of harmonious oneness. The story of Rousseau would have a happier ending if we could assume with some of his biographers that he achieved in his last years a conquest of his inner conflict through what psychologists call "subsidence"—"a final, pure detachment of self from the world, by one who sinks wholly into an inner life." [73] But *The Reveries of a Solitary* tell us otherwise. There are passages in which he claims complete detachment from the world's opinion, but the very fact that he makes the statements indicates that he remained on the defensive. Thus the *Reveries* begin:

> Here am I, then, alone upon the earth, having no brother, or neighbour, or friend, or society but myself. The most sociable and loving of human beings has been proscribed by unanimous agreement. They have sought in the refinements of their hatred whatever torment could be most cruel to my sensitive soul, and they have violently broken all the links which attached me to them. I would fain have loved men in despite of themselves; they have not been able to conceal themselves from my affection, except by ceasing to be men. They are, then, strangers, unknown, nothing finally for me, because they have wished it.[74]

For all the passages which suggest an inner harmony through calm meditation there are others which are bald attacks upon his enemies or attempts at self-justification. The genuinely detached man, as Henry James remarked of Flaubert, does not thrown stones at society. Thus there is a defensiveness about Rousseau's continual harping on the joys of solitude which implies a need for self-justification and for communication with others. In this, as in other aspects, Rousseau is the prototype of those who follow him—those tormented sensitives who even while proclaiming their distaste for society and

71. *Reveries of a Solitary*, pp. 112–114.
72. "Introduction," *Reveries of a Sol-*   itary, p. 27.
73. Josephson, p. 444.
74. *Reveries of a Solitary*, p. 31.

a preference for the Ivory Tower, nonetheless hope through self-expression to impose themselves upon society, even if only the society of the "happy few" in some distant future. The mixture of defensiveness with self-exaltation is one of Rousseau's contributions to the stereotype of the "artistic temperament."

The religious aspect of Rousseau's withdrawal from society was apparently unnoticed by his contemporaries and followers. What struck them was the example of a romantic rebel who preferred picturesque solitude to participation in the activities of society, an exile who withstood persecution, both real and imagined. As a young musician Rousseau had been a sort of wandering gypsy, hence one of the first Bohemians. Matthew Josephson has suggested that Rousseau's characteristic costume during his later years, the Armenian robe "which, in view of his particular disorder of frequent, painful urination, he found nicely suited to his convenience," helped to establish informality of dress among artists.[75] Rousseau helped too in destroying the tradition of anonymity in the arts. The fact that he insisted upon signing his works shocked many of his contemporaries, but as Rousseau said in the Preface to *Julie*, every honest man ought to acknowledge his own offspring. It goes without saying that the artist who concealed himself behind a veil of anonymity could not be much of a hero.

Nor can we overlook Rousseau's importance in helping to establish the value of sensitivity as the artist's claim to distinction. Although Rousseau himself, as we have seen, often considered sensitivity the root of his misfortunes, it was this aspect of his character which most appealed to those who viewed him as a romantic ideal. M. B. Ellis has shown that the passionate and sensitive Saint-Preux of *La Nouvelle Heloise*, though autobiographical, does not represent Rousseau's personal ideal, which is to be found rather in the more balanced character of Julie, and that Rousseau was actually opposed to the immoral passion represented by his hero.[76] But in spite of the conservative moral of the story, its championing of the family and the norms of a good society, it has usually been read as if Saint-Preux were the central character. The *Julie* of literary tradition is the book described by Ernst Cassirer: "In individual pictures and scenes of the novel we immediately perceive the breath of a new era —as in that farewell scene in which Saint-Preux, compelled to leave his mistress and seized by the presentiment of eternal separation, sinks down in tears on the stairs which he has just descended and

75. Josephson, p. 412.
76. *Julie ou La Nouvelle Heloise: A Synthesis of Rousseau's Thought* (Toronto: University of Toronto Press, 1949), *passim*.

covers the cold stone with kisses. Here a new figure is born in literature: Goethe's Werther rises before us."[77]

For all his influence on the emergence of a new kind of hero—one who was to become the characteristic hero of the artist-novel—Rousseau, we must remember, did not work out in art his solution to the conflict between the individual and society, between temporal existence and dissociated consciousness. Rather, he sought his personal solution in contemplation and reverie and came eventually to regret his own writings, to feel that, because they were misunderstood, they had done more harm than good. As the products of action, they were tainted. The *Confessions* was an attempt to achieve a triumph over the self, and we may say that, to a degree, he succeeded, for it takes detachment from the ego to confess one's pettiness, to say nothing of one's sins, as candidly as Rousseau did. But his frequent attempts to justify himself to society indicate that the success was not complete. He was one of "the most sociable and loving of human beings," but his desire to be at ease in society was always in conflict with a personal ideal so high that neither he nor society could attain it. If Rousseau came too late, at a time when the "type of the holy man . . . was no longer permitted to exist," he came also too early, before art was exalted as a holy calling that required no justification.

IV   *"J" As Hero: The Confessional Novel, 1785–1869*

THE combined influence of Goethe's *Werther* and Rousseau's *Confessions* resulted in a host of imitators. These novels are similar enough to be recognized collectively as a special genre of fiction, though scholars call it by different names: "the psychological novel," "the personal novel," or "the confessional novel."[78] This genre, which flourished on the Continent, especially in France, from the late eighteenth century to about 1870, includes such works as *Anton Reiser*, by the German writer Carl Philipp Moritz; Senancour's *Obermann*, Chateaubriand's *René*, Constant's *Adolphe*, William Hazlitt's *Liber Amoris*, Sainte-Beuve's *Volupté*, Stendhal's *Life of Henry Brulard*, Musset's *Confession of a Child of the Century*, Lamartine's *Raphael*, Turgenev's *Diary of a Superfluous Man*,

77. Cassirer, p. 89.
78. Studies of this type of novel include Joachim Merlant, *Le Roman Personnel de Rousseau à Fromentin* (Paris: Hachette, 1905); N. H.

Clement, *Romanticism in France* (New York: Modern Language Association, 1939), pp. 295–299; F. C. Green, *French Novelists from the Revolution to Proust* (London: Dent, 1931), pp. 21–88.

Fromentin's *Dominique,* and Flaubert's *Sentimental Education.* Although only some of the heroes are identified as artists, all are obvious surrogates for their authors, and all are men of artistic temperament. The cumulative effect of these novels was to change the emphasis in fiction from outside the self to analysis of the hero's psychology. Thus they prepared the way for the artist-novel proper.

Of the confessional novels, one of the first and one of the last, *Anton Reiser* and *Sentimental Education,* seem to me more significant than the others. Thus I should like to look at *Anton Reiser* in search of hypotheses about the nature of the artist, test them through a consideration of the other novels, and finally show how Flaubert's novel summed up the tradition and brought it to a temporary halt.

A classic in Germany, *Anton Reiser* has remained little known elsewhere. P. E. Matheson's translation in 1926 for a World's Classics edition (now out of print) was the first rendition in English, and though some English and French writers knew the book in its German version, there is little evidence that it had much influence outside of Germany. If, however, we take *Anton Reiser* from out of the shadow of *Werther* and the *Confessions,* we discover that in its emphasis on specific details as revelations of character and its penetration into the psychology of a morbidly sensitive artist, it is surprisingly modern. In parts of *Anton Reiser* Moritz seems an early Proust.

Although *Anton Reiser: A Psychological Novel* is obviously and frankly modelled upon *Werther* in its analysis of character, it has the distinction of anticipating *Wilhelm Meister* in its form. Whereas *Werther* deals with a brief period, *Anton Reiser* is a *Bildungsroman* which takes its hero from childhood to maturity and traces his efforts to find a suitable vocation. Like Wilhelm, Anton tries unsuccessfully to become a poet and an actor, but, unlike Wilhelm, he never repudiates art. The novel in which he appears ends before Anton has found himself; but that Anton (who is Moritz) did eventually become an artist is shown by the accomplishment of this book, just as Joyce's *Portrait* is itself a demonstration of Stephen's fulfillment as artist. If *Anton Reiser* is a more significant portrait of the artist than *Wilhelm Meister,* however less influential, it is partly because the lack of an arranged conclusion and of intervention by the author leaves the hero at the point where he is ready to write the book we have finished reading. Thus Moritz announces in a prefatory note to Part II:

> To obviate further misdirected criticisms, such as have already been passed on this book, I find myself obliged to explain that

what, for reasons which may easily be guessed, I have called a psychological romance, is properly speaking a biography, and is as nearly as possible a true and faithful presentation of a human life, down to its smallest details. Any one who is interested in such a faithful presentation will not take offence at what seems at first insignificant and unimportant, but will bear in mind that human life is a complex web in which an infinite number of tiny threads are interwoven, all of which, insignificant as they may appear, have the greatest importance in the whole structure.

A man surveying his past life is at first inclined to see in it mere aimlessness, broken threads, confusion, night and darkness; but as he fixes his gaze more closely, the darkness vanishes, the aimlessness gradually disappears, the broken threads rejoin, order appears in place of confusion and disorder, and discord is resolved into harmonious melody.[79]

The ordered arrangement is not, however, fully explained in the novel itself, as it is through the almost supernatural unraveling of the mysteries in *Wilhelm Meister;* instead, the pattern must be discovered by the reader.

Anton Reiser is the child of an unhappy marriage between a neurotic, self-martyring mother and a father whose religion holds that "to kill all passions and eradicate all individuality" is the sign of true piety.[80] Forced to make his own pleasures, Anton turns to books: "Through reading a new world was opened up for him once for all, in the enjoyment of which he could compensate himself in some degree for all that was unpleasant in his actual world." [81] Like Rousseau, Anton moves from reading to daydreaming, then still further into introversion: "What was most singular was that his continual reflection and immersion in his own thoughts led him into an egoism which might almost have made him lose his reason. For as his dreams were in general very lively and almost seemed to border on reality, he began to fancy that he was dreaming in broad daylight, and that the people about him, with all that he saw, might be creatures of his imagination." [82] With no one to show him affection, the butt of his schoolmates' scorn, Anton next takes refuge in the world of the theater, where "he could be everything for which he had no opportunity in the real world, and which yet he so often longed to be—generous, beneficent, noble, steadfast—raised above all that was humiliating and debasing." [83] It is natural that after

79. *Anton Reiser: A Psychological Novel,* trans. P. E. Matheson (London and New York: Oxford University Press, 1926), p. 107.

80. *Anton Reiser,* p. 2.
81. *Anton Reiser,* p. 10.
82. *Anton Reiser,* p. 31.
83. *Anton Reiser,* p. 174.

he has failed as a student and as a hatter's apprentice, he should join a wandering troupe of actors. He soon learns, however, that the theatrical life is less romantic than he had anticipated, and his personal difficulties—his shyness, his arrogance, and his impetuous, unstable character—make it difficult for him to make headway in this or any other profession that depends on others. He becomes an outsider.

The thought came to him that from childhood up his fate had been to be crowded out. If he wanted to look on at anything, when it was a case of putting oneself forward, every one else was quicker than he and got in front of him. He thought one day he would find an empty place where he could fit in without jostling any one, but he found none, and retired, and now was looking at the throng from a distance, as he stood lonely there. And as he stood lonely there, the thought that he could look on the throng so quietly without mingling in it, made up somewhat for the loss of what he missed seeing: alone he felt himself nobler and more distinguished than lost among the crowd. His pride, which came to the fore, overcame the vexation that he felt at first, because he could not join the crowd, it drove him back on himself and ennobled and exalted his thoughts and feelings.[84]

Although there may be something pitiful about "this complete outsider" who in a crowd presses close to strangers in an attempt to "penetrate the dividing-wall" which separates their thoughts from his,[85] there is a positive side to Anton's alienation, for detachment leads him to something approaching omniscience. He acquires the gift of second sight. From the beginning Anton had lived "a double life, inward and outward, quite distinct from one another," [86] but as the inner life comes to dominate the outer man, Anton learns that he can think himself into the lives of others, can turn the chaos of fluid perceptions into a kind of harmony unified by his own imaginative insight. Moritz does not tell us so, but it is this ability which will turn Anton into an artist as skillful as his author. Not immersion in self, but alienation carried to the extent that Anton is capable of standing apart and seeing himself as if he were a stranger is what gives him that "distance" to which Moritz attributes artistic ability. This general principle is stated in the novel when Anton steps outside the gates of Brunswick, where he has served a year's apprenticeship, and suddenly understands the meaning of his life there: "In order to obtain a distinct view of his present life

84. *Anton Reiser*, pp. 246–247.   86. *Anton Reiser*, p. 219.
85. *Anton Reiser*, p. 177.

as a whole, it was necessary that all the threads, so to say, should be cut off which fastened his attention on what was momentary, every-day and fragmentary, and that he should be put again at the point of view, from which he regarded his life in Brunswick before it be-gan, when it still lay before him in the twilight of the future. To this point of vision he was now transported, when he came by chance out of the Gate through which about a year and a half before he had come in along the broad willow-planted high road and had seen the sentinel walking to and fro on the rampart." [87]

In his prefatory note to Part IV, Moritz sums up the basic themes of his novel:

> The earlier Parts of this story show clearly that Reiser's irre-sistible passion for the stage was simply a result of the circum-stances of his life. From childhood up he found himself thrust out from the real world, and conceiving a bitter disgust for it lived more in his imagination than in reality. Hence the stage as the true world of imagination was his natural refuge from all the diffi-culties and sufferings, he felt that here alone he could breathe freely, and move in his true element.
>
> At the same time he had a certain sense of the real objects which surrounded him in the world and did not wish entirely to give them up, because like other men he had a sense of life and existence. This led to a perpetual struggle within him. He was too serious to give himself up entirely to the suggestions of his fancy and be content with himself: on the other hand he had not the strength of character resolutely to pursue any complete plan which conflicted with his fanciful imagination.
>
> In him, as in countless others, there was a conflict between truth and illusion, dream and reality, and which was to prevail was undecided: this sufficiently explains the peculiar states of mind into which he fell.
>
> Contradictions from within and without had so far been his whole life. The question is, how these contradictions are to be re-solved.[88]

Although the inner and outer man in Anton never blend, he at least learns to accept the split in himself. Resolution of the contra-dictions, merely hinted at in the final sections of the novel, comes about when his complete detachment brings him the compensation of "distance." Through this he attains a double vision which enables him both to see himself objectively—hence to write his novel—and

87. *Anton Reiser*, p. 81.   88. *Anton Reiser*, pp. 343–344.

to feel himself into the thoughts and emotions of others. Sitting in an inn, Anton studies an old woman until "he thought himself by degrees into the thoughts and ideas of this old woman so completely that he forgot himself and fell into a kind of waking dream." [89] The gift of second sight may be mere illusion, but it could also be another name for the artistic imagination.

THE related themes of the divided self, art as compensation, and the principle of distance appear frequently in succeeding confessional novels. Most of the heroes are so self-absorbed that they have difficulty getting outside themselves and hence are naturally at odds with their environment. Turgenev's hero says, "As I am a superfluous man and have imposed an internal constraint on myself, it is fearful for me to express my thoughts, especially as I know in advance I shall express them very badly. I sometimes wonder how people can talk, and so simply, so easily. . . . What audacity, you know!" Lonely and shy people, he says, see everything through "tinted spectacles. Their own thoughts and observations hinder them at every step." [90] Obermann feels himself "condemned ever to wait for life," because "I am alone. . . . I am here in the world, a wanderer, solitary in the midst of people for whom I care nothing; like a man, deaf for many years, whose eager eyes gaze upon the crowd of silent beings who move and pass before him. He sees everything, but everything is withheld from him; he suffers the silence of all things in the midst of the noise of the world." [91] René characterizes himself as a "young man without strength and without courage, who finds torment within himself and yet can barely find words to complain of the evil he does to himself. . . . Mine was an impetuous temperament and an unstable character. By turns noisy and happy, silent and sad, I gathered about me young comrades; then, abandoning them suddenly, I would go and sit apart from them to contemplate the fugitive clouds or listen to the rain falling on the leaves of trees." [92] The editor of Dominique's papers sums up the character not only of his subject but of a half-century of introspective heroes:

89. *Anton Reiser,* pp. 349–350.
90. "The Diary of a Superfluous Man," in *The Borzoi Turgenev,* trans. Harry Stevens (New York: Knopf, 1950), pp. 761, 770.
91. Étienne Pivert de Senancour, *Obermann: Selections from Letters to a Friend,* trans. and ed. Jessie Peabody Frothingham (Cambridge,

Massachusetts: Riverside Press, 1901), I, 63, and I, xii–xiii.
92. François René de Chateaubriand, "René," trans. George K. Anderson, in Anderson and Robert Warnock, eds., *The World in Literature* (Chicago: Scott-Foresman, 1951), II, 400–401.

A great concentration of mind: a habit of intense and active self-observation; the instinct to reach ever greater heights: an endlessly vigilant self-control: the enthralling changes that life brings, and determination to recognize the same self intact in each new phase: the voice of nature, never silenced: the birth of emotions which soften the young heart feeding with callow egoism on its own substance; the name entwined with another name, the verses that slip from the sheath like a flower opening in springtime; frantic flights towards the lofty summits of the Ideal; last of all, peace descending on this heart, so stormy, perhaps so ambitious, and certainly tormented by the desire of the unattainable.[93]

As may be expected of books in the *Werther* tradition, the ideal sought by the self-absorbed hero usually takes the tangible form of a woman who is unattainable or who proves to be very different in the realization from what she seemed to be in anticipation. Most of the confessional novels are love stories—or, to be more accurate, stories of frustrated love. Fromentin's Dominique, Flaubert's Frederic Moreau, and Turgenev's superfluous man, among others, abandon their will-to-life when they fall in love with women they cannot have. Stendhal's Henry Brulard pursues woman after woman in search of the ideal mate-mother. Sainte-Beuve's Amaury in *Volupté* can never reconcile spiritual with carnal love. Constant's Adolphe and Musset's "I" secure the love of the desired woman, but like Proust's Marcel with Albertine, their unfounded jealousy, revealing their egoism, drives them to torture themselves and their mistresses. Hazlitt's *Liber Amoris* is a painful confession of love for his landlady's daughter. Whether the love is thwarted or consummated, the artist is somehow annihilated. Thus Lamartine's Raphael says of his loved one, "Had I lived long with her, I should never have read or written poetry. She was the living poem of Nature and of myself; my thoughts were in her heart, my imagery in her eyes, and my harmony in her voice." [94] Chauteaubriand's René thinks that he might have been happy if he had found a woman to love, but, just as Raphael's mistress was "the living poem . . . of myself," René wants a woman like Adam's, "taken from myself." [95] The critic who thinks it probable that Anton Reiser's morbid inclinations may be attributed to his lack of sexual outlet should consider the fate of

93. Eugène Fromentin, *Dominique*, trans. Edward Marsh (London: Cresset Press, 1948), pp. 27–28.
94. Alphonse de Lamartine, *Raphael*, or *Pages of the Book of Life at Twenty* (Boston: L. C. Page, 1906), p. 81.
95. "René," p. 405.

those heroes who are like Anton in temperament, but who succeed in finding a sexual outlet: they become more miserable and morbid than ever because of their love.[96] Perhaps the explanation is to be found in their self-centered nature: like the legendary Narcissus, they are incapable of finding genuine love outside themselves. For them the Sacred Fount is dry.

Frustrated in their attempt to secure the ideal in the real world, many turn to the dream world of art as a refuge. P. Mansell Jones, in his study of French introspectives, finds that most of them suffered from poor health, and he suggests the almost inevitable presence of a physical affliction or a mental obstruction, the overcoming of which is the main purpose of the introspection.[97] Like the Goethe of *Werther*, they write to cure themselves. Musset's "I" admits this purpose openly; [98] Dominique's poetry, an effort to compensate for the love he cannot have, is "like an overflow from my heart, which felt a gradually growing relief as the level subsided"; [99] and Obermann, after he has come finally to reject all "willful weaknesses" and to accept his aloneness, decides that his "only sphere is that of an author." [100]

It is significant that though the autobiographical heroes of these novels almost invariably fail, the books in which they appear are nonetheless artistic performances of merit. If, then, we distinguish between the heroes and the authors, we may see a difference between the mediocre art that seems to derive only from the need for compensation and the more significant art that comes with greater detachment and distance. Ramon Fernandez, comparing *Henry Brulard* with *The Red and the Black*, has argued convincingly that the projection of the personality into a work of art offers a means of self-knowledge superior to direct introspection.[101] The fact that the "I" is analyzed through fiction rather than through autobiography suggests at least a degree of removal that we do not find in the spontaneous lyric outbursts by the characters portrayed in the works. Dominique's poetry, the fruit of emotional inspiration, is commonplace; yet, when the editors of a Paris newspaper in 1952 asked sixteen distinguished critics to select the best French novels of the nine-

96. William Rose, *From Goethe to Byron: The Development of "Weltschmerz" in German Literature* (London: Routledge, 1924), p. 96.
97. *French Introspectives from Montaigne to André Gide* (London: Cambridge University Press, 1937), p. 92.
98. *Confession of a Child of the Century,* trans. Kendall Warren (Chi-

cago: Charles H. Sergel and Co., 1892), p. 7.
99. Fromentin, *Dominique,* p. 73.
100. Senancour, *Obermann,* II, 189.
101. "Autobiography and the Novel: The Example of Stendhal," in his *Messages,* trans. Montgomery Belgion (New York: Harcourt, Brace and Company, 1927), pp. 89–136.

teenth century, Fromentin's novel rated sixth.[102] The short lyric of romantic yearning which Stephen Dedalus in Joyce's *Portrait* composes almost spontaneously is mediocre at best, but the novel in which Stephen appears is a modern classic partly because Joyce, like the authors of the confessional novels, achieved detachment from self in his treatment of his autobiographical hero.

As in *Anton Reiser,* the concept of distance seems to be related psychologically to the idea of a second self. "The compulsion to consider oneself over and over again as one unknown, as an uncannily remote stranger," as Arnold Hauser has put it, is an *idée fixe* among the Romantics.[103] The conflict between the instinct to act in a direct, uninhibited manner and the tendency to observe the self acting often paralyses the character into a modern Hamlet, torn between opposing purposes. Hence, Dominique describes "the cruel gift of the power to look on at one's own life as if it were a play staged by someone else" which afflicts him: "This continually and mercilessly critical eye turned inwards upon myself, now friendly, now hostile, irksome as an ever-present eye-witness and suspicious as a judge, this perpetual eavesdropping on my own simplest actions at an age when action is mostly instinctive and self-scrutiny rare—all this threw me into a state of successive depressions, agitations, stupors and excitements in which I was heading straight for a crisis." [104] In some cases —René and the superfluous man come to mind—the crisis is never passed and the self, either incapable of detaching itself from the man or of accepting the split, leads only to self-destruction, as in the legend of Narcissus or the story of Werther. Carried far enough, however, as *Anton Reiser* shows us, this ability to observe the self can lead to a feeling of god-like omniscience, in which the artist emerges from the man.

In many of the novels under consideration, removal from the self is represented objectively through the device of a "frame" which separates the admittedly autobiographical character—the "I" who was—from the author—the "I" who is. In *Werther, René, Adolphe, Liber Amoris,* and *Dominique* the first-person confessions of the heroes are presented in the form of notes or journals which, often posthumously, are arranged, edited, or introduced by another. The "editor," I would suggest, is equivalent to the second, observing self who "frames" the suffering, acting counterpart. Often too the fact that we know from the beginning that the journal or the notes are

102. *Le Figaro Littéraire,* December, 1952.
103. *The Social History of Art,* trans.

Stanley Goodman (New York: Knopf, 1951), II, 669.
104. Fromentin, *Dominique,* pp. 67–68.

completed, the story ended, imposes the illusion of a circlelike frame similar to the sensation Anton Reiser experiences when he steps outside the gates of Brunswick.

As far as fictional form is concerned, those books which are thus framed seem to be superior to those which are not; in fact, there is some question as to whether or not works like *Obermann* (a collection of letters) or *Henry Brulard* (random autobiographical notes) may be considered works of fiction at all, so close are they to direct introspection and autobiography. In general, there seems to have been a progression from the subjective earlier works in the tradition, like *Obermann* and *René,* to more objective analyses of the hero's psychology. According to N. H. Clement, "the advent of realism after 1850 hastened the decline of the personal novel, which in its later stages is already strongly realistic, as in *Dominique*." [105] Although in even the later books of the tradition, the heroes are usually presented with little suggestion of deliberate irony, there are passages in Turgenev's *Diary of a Superfluous Man* which hint at a conscious parody of the Werther type of hero. And in the final version of Flaubert's *Sentimental Education* we have an objective depiction of an introspective hero.

So far removed is Flaubert from Frederic Moreau, the hero of *Sentimental Education,* that Frederic seems to stand for only one of Flaubert's many selves. Frederic is the passive, self-indulging dreamer incapable of the strength which Flaubert's life and art reveal: the firm self-control and willingness to take pains that is exhibited in both his way of living and his manner of writing. But apparent strength is often a disguise of inner weakness, and we know from biographers of Flaubert that he had always to fight against those tendencies in himself that make Frederic a failure in both life and art.

From all accounts, Flaubert was a manly, handsome person attractive to women and not without the usual instincts of the normal man. Acting as a check against this aspect was "another personality inside him who observed his acts and emotions with sardonic interest and mockingly checked any tendency to self-abandonment." [106] Both his nervous seizures and his celebrated love of Madame Schlesinger, a woman he knew he could not have, seem to have been self-imposed psychic "wounds" which, like Rousseau's malady, gave him excuses for remaining detached from the usual duties and responsibilities of life. And just as Rousseau's aloofness seems rooted in his temperament, so Flaubert was detached long before he met

105. *Romanticism in France,* p. 299.   *ography* (London: Faber and Faber,
106. Philip Spencer, *Flaubert: A Bi-*   1952), p. 51.

Mme. Schlesinger or had the first of his attacks. "Beneath my youthful exterior lies a strange senility," he wrote to Louise Colet, "I do not know what it was that made me old from my cradle, and disgusted me with happiness even before I had tasted it. Everything about life repels me; everything that draws me into its abyss appals me." [107] The main function of Flaubert's double wound was to allow him to remain uncommitted to life, even though he picked up prostitutes—for "physical hygiene"—and kept up a long affair with Louise Colet. That he did these things and that he felt compelled always to battle against the philistines toward whom he considered himself indifferent suggest, however, that the separation of the man from the artist was never complete.

Flaubert's personal ideal is to be found in *The Temptation of Saint Anthony*, that romantic portrait of a voluntary exile who remains firm against worldly temptations and finally attains a vision of all-embracing unity. If this is Flaubert's own romantic dream, his failure to achieve it completely accounts in part for both *Madame Bovary* and *Sentimental Education*, clinical analyses of romantics caught by the disparity between dream and reality. Flaubert himself could find no evidence of a divine plan in the world around him, but instead of indicting romantic illusion and praising everyday reality, he came to feel that everything must be illusion and that all any individual can do is choose among the illusions.

There was a time, though, when people could accept the illusion for the truth. Realizing that his age was a period of intellectual and spiritual chaos, Flaubert blamed the times for the suffering of the individual. Like Emma Bovary, who rationalized her downfall by attacking the inadequacy of life in a provincial village, Flaubert condemned the nineteenth century for its failure to meet the ideal envisioned by men of imagination and insight. It is for this reason that society is more important in *Sentimental Education* than in the earlier confessional novels, with the exception of Musset's *Confession of a Child of the Century*, in which the uncertainty of the "I" is attributed to the uncertainty of the times:

> Three elements entered into the life which offered itself to these children: behind them a past forever destroyed, moving uneasily on its ruins with all the fossils of centuries of absolutism; before them the aurora of an immense horizon; the first gleams of the future; and between these two worlds—something like the Ocean which separates the old world from Young America, something

107. *Letters*, ed. Richard Rumbold,   denfeld and Nicolson, 1950), p. 39.
trans. J. M. Cohen (London: Wei-

vague and floating, a troubled sea filled with wreckage, traversed from time to time by some distant sail or some ship breathing out a heavy vapour; the present, in a word that separates the past from the future, which is neither the one nor the other, which resembles both, and where one cannot know whether, at each step, one is treading on a seed or a piece of refuse.

It was in this chaos that choice must be made; this was the aspect presented to children full of spirit and audacity, sons of the Empire and grandsons of the Revolution.[108]

The uncertainty of Musset develops into the despair of Flaubert, who in 1852 wrote to Louise Colet: "I believe that . . . rules of all kinds are breaking down, that barriers are tumbling, and the earth falling to a dead level. . . . Broad construction itself is becoming more and more impossible, with our limited and precise vocabulary and our vague, confused and fugitive ideas. All that we can do then is, out of sheer virtuosity, to tighten the strings of the overstrummed guitar and become primarily virtuosi, seeing that simplicity in our age is an illusion." [109]

The action of *Sentimental Education* occurs before and after the Revolution of 1848—"the turning point at which modern history failed to turn." [110] Young artists at the beginning of the nineteenth century were optimistic that they would live to see the emancipation of the individual from the old absolutes: the "common man," who for most of the Romantics was the "natural man" and thus basically good, would come to power under the leadership of men capable of subordinating individual ambition to the general welfare. In view of the early nineteenth-century conviction that the poet is the proper leader of mankind, it is significant that in both France and Italy Romantic poets played leading roles in the revolutions of 1848—Lamartine in France, Mazzini in Italy. Unfortunately, the common man failed to respond to their leadership and, after a brief flurry of revolutionary ardor, settled back into worship of state authority and material prosperity. Lamartine was spurned by the French people, who demanded Louis-Napoleon, and the disillusioned Mazzini came "to hate the masses everywhere." Thus, though history failed to turn in 1848, that year was an important turning point for the artist. After 1848, says Albert Guerard, "the sudden exaltation, the brief, confused, inglorious struggle, the abrupt irremediable

108. *Confessions of a Child of the Century*, p. 14.
109. *Letters*, p. 73.
110. George Macaulay Trevelyan, *British History in the Nineteenth Century* (London: Longmans, Green and Co., 1937), p. 292.

fall created in Europe a new state of mind. For some, the collapse of idealism was an encouragement to seek pleasure, the one thing as certain as death, and to conquer wealth, as the sure means to purchase pleasure. For others, impassivity was a refuge: a frigid mask covering equally indifference or despair. The wounded survivors of Romanticism clung to art when all else had perished." [111] After 1848 the worship of art seemed to demand contempt for the common man, and from that time dates the philistine-baiting so conspicuous in Flaubert, Baudelaire, and other writers of the second half of the nineteenth century.

Frederic Moreau is a typical hero of a confessional novel in that he is sensitive, introspective, and egoistic. Being passive, easily roused and embittered, he is at the mercy of the forces around him. At a time and in a place more congenial to his temperament, he might have fared well. Living in the early nineteenth century and reaching manhood at the time of the 1848 revolution, he is a victim of the times: the collapse of his romantic dreams coincides with the collapse of ideals after the revolution. "If we ask at what point in the sentimental plot the Revolution occurs in the history," Paul Goodman has noted, "we find that it is just at the moment that Frederic finally comes to possess a woman, a moment marked by the ending of Part II, and then Part III opens in an atmosphere of fulfilment and joy. But alas! the woman is not the Ideal Marie, who did not keep the appointment, but Rosanette, whom he brings to the room prepared for the other. Again, if we look at the moment of complete frustration of all his desires, the end of Part III, chapter v, we find that it is the moment when Dussadier, crying 'Vive le République!' is shot dead." [112] Like the other young French intellectuals of his time, Frederic had hoped that the revolution would give him a chance to perform social service; but he discovers that the ones he would serve—"what dolts, what morons!" [113]—are more suspicious of idealism than the aristocrats they have overthrown. His attempt to set himself up as a candidate is rejected by the workers. "He had knocked at the gates of Democracy, had offered his pen, his oratory, his energy, for her service; everywhere he had been rejected." [114] At the conclusion of the novel Frederic and his friend Deslauriers compare notes on their failure. The one dreamed of love, the other

111. *Art for Art's Sake* (Boston: Lothrop, Lee and Shepard, 1936), p. 33.
112. *The Structure of Literature* (Chicago: University of Chicago Press, 1954), pp. 155–156.
113. *Sentimental Education*, trans. Anthony Goldsmith (Everyman's Library, 1941), p. 288.
114. *Sentimental Education*, p. 342.

of power; and Deslauriers comments, "I suffered from excess of logic, you, of emotion." [115] Neither the rationalism of a Deslauriers nor the idealism of a Frederic can lead to success in a world which prefers mediocrity. If one is to attain success, he must, like Homais in *Madame Bovary*, be without personal ideals and thus ready to shift allegiances in accord with what the age deems expedient.

Although there is undoubtedly something of Flaubert in Frederic, the author differs from the hero as success differs from failure. Flaubert's personal solution was to take the way of art. "Life is such a hideous business," he wrote, "that the only method of bearing it is to avoid it. And one does avoid it by living in Art, in the ceaseless quest for Truth presented by Beauty." [116] And elsewhere: "If it is an illusion I am pursuing, at least I prefer the highest illusions." [117] In an earlier version of *Sentimental Education*, Flaubert let the character Jules serve as a spokesman for the author: Jules finds comfort from uncertainty in the creation of art for his own pleasure. In the later version, however, Flaubert achieves further detachment from his story by withholding from his hero the solution he had found. Frederic is defenseless against the collapse of his dreams because, though he is a would-be artist, he is weaker than his creator. Frederic's failure, like that of Emma Bovary, is one of character as much as of the times in which he lives. His dream may have been false, but if he had remained as firm in his quest of it as Saint Anthony did, then the illusion at least might have been retained. Not only circumstances and accidents, but also his own hesitancy and his willingness to accept the solace offered by Rosanette frustrate his hopes of attaining Madame Arnoux, just as his counterpart, Deslauriers, betrays his ideal of pure logic by trying to take advantage of his friend. The same betrayal is evidenced in Frederic's aspirations as an artist. Instead of subordinating all else to art, Frederic, essentially a dilettante, turns to art only as a means to something else. His attempted novel, *Sylvio, the Fisherman's Son*, is in imitation of the popular literature of his day and is written to appease his romantic longing. When he realizes that his novel is a failure, he has difficulty deciding what art he is to practice, knowing only that he is an "artist." He composes German waltzes and, most tellingly, "he wanted to write a history of aesthetics—a result of his conversations with Pellerin—. . . and to compose a grand comedy, through the indirect influence of Deslauriers and Hussonet." [118] But when he tries to work, the face of the loved Marie passes before his

115. *Sentimental Education*, p. 395.   117. *Letters*, p. 67.
116. *Letters*, p. 108.   118. *Sentimental Education*, p. 138.

eyes and he yields to the vision. The same passivity that dooms
Frederic's sentimental hopes makes it impossible for him to find success either as artist or man of action. Even during the uprising, "the
wounded falling, and the dead lying stretched out, did not look as if
they were really wounded or dead. He felt as if he were watching a
play." [119] Frederic keeps waiting to be called on stage, but must remain in the audience. "I belong to the tribe of the disinherited," he
says, "and I shall go to my grave with a treasure hidden within me,
and I shall never know if it is diamonds or paste." [120] The reader
comes to suspect that the treasure is paste.

Flaubert's detachment is evident even in the structure of his novel.
When he made a personal religion of art, he saw his mission not
as that of a passive disciple, such as was Saint Anthony, but as a
creator of reality. Because Flaubert could see no evidence of divine
unity and control in the world, he made his artist-god "invisible and
all powerful . . . everywhere felt, but nowhere seen." [121] Whereas
Madame Bovary is unified and aesthetically controlled, *Sentimental
Education* is faithful to Flaubert's later, disillusioned view of reality.
To this fidelity he attributed the later book's popular failure: "It is
too life-like and, aesthetically speaking, it lacks the illusion of perspective. The plan has been so well co-ordinated that it disappears.
Every work of art should have a point, a peak, should be shaped like
a pyramid, or have the light strike it on the tip of the dome. Now
there is nothing like that about life." [122] For the sake of his convictions, Flaubert sacrificed even the illusion of auctorial control, though
this is itself an illusion. *Sentimental Education* is a peculiarly flat
novel, not only in its structure but also in the depiction of its hero.
Whereas the earlier writers of the confessional novels would have
exalted the character of a Frederic and made him seem a noble exception, a poor Chatterton perhaps, Flaubert turns him into the
just anybody of an age which could not believe in heroes. Flaubert's
unsentimental analysis of a sentimentalist helped to bring the tradition of the self-expressing novel to a temporary halt.

When, however, the tradition was revived through the Stephen
Dedaluses and Marcels of modern fiction, Flaubert's counter-portrait
of the artist proved an important influence. The method of the novel
—practically everything is seen through the eyes of Frederic, who is
described in the third person—may have suggested to writers like
James and Joyce a means of balancing the subjective and the objective. To describe the romantic through the eyes of the detached ob-

119. *Sentimental Education*, p. 268.   121. *Letters*, p. 98.
120. *Sentimental Education*, p. 17.   122. *Letters*, p. 228.

server—both of whom represent the split selves of the author—is to neutralize sentimental commitment and to achieve in actual form that "distance" which Anton Reiser grasps only in theory. In addition to this lesson in technique, Flaubert's example in his own person of the detached and dedicated artist provided a model for later inhabitants of the Ivory Tower.

CHAPTER TWO

ART AS EXPERIENCE

The Sacred Fount Tradition

THERE appears to be little historical progression in the concept of the artistic temperament. We may discover variations of the archetype described in the preceding chapter, but the main characteristics of the artist are unchanged from the first of the artist-novels to those of our own time. Among those characteristics, we have seen, is that ability to look on at the self from a distance which separates the man who acts from the man who observes and sets up a conflict between the urge to "live" and the temptation to seek solitude. I must emphasize this point strongly, because in this chapter and the next I wish to separate artist fiction into two distinct traditions—the Sacred Fount and the Ivory Tower—and it is necessary to realize that in novels of either tradition we find a contrary pull from the other. The artist-hero may move toward the Tower or the Fount, but it is seldom that he is not tempted to take both directions.

"The middle area from which the finest fiction comes," Mark Schorer tells us, ". . . is the crossroad of sensibility and social history, the point at which the two roads make one square, where each disappears into the other." [1] If for "sensibility," the individual vision of the novelist, and "social history," the life which he must use in his art, we substitute the Ivory Tower and Sacred Fount traditions, then the same principle may be applied to the portrait-of-the-artist

1. "Foreword: Self and Society," in *Society and Self in the Novel: English Institute Essays 1955* (New York: Columbia University Press, 1956), pp. ix–x.

novel. In the "finest fiction," as I hope to show in my chapters on individual novelists, the two traditions are successfully reconciled. Usually it is among the lesser talents that we find a strong preference for one direction or the other, and this may explain why most of the artist-heroes to be discussed in the next two chapters fall short of true greatness. When there is a war between art and life, one side may defeat the other, but the victory is usually pyrrhic.

The Sacred Fount tradition takes precedence here because it established itself first. There are early sources of the Ivory Tower concept of the artist, but the tradition did not achieve prominence until the late nineteenth century and then had to compete against a contrary belief already firmly entrenched. Eventually, in the first half of the twentieth century, the Ivory Tower concept of the dedicated artist secured dominance, and we became so accustomed to thinking of the artist as a recluse or a detached observer that writers like Lawrence, the artist as man of passion, or Hemingway, the artist as soldier and athlete, seemed out of step with their time. Because they insisted on their right to love and adventure, Lawrence and Hemingway are closer in spirit to Byron and the early Romantics than to writers like Flaubert and James, who set the critical temper of their age. To find the beginnings of the Sacred Fount tradition, we must look back to the art novels of the Romantic period.

I   *Romantics*

BECAUSE there are conflicting varieties of romanticism in the early nineteenth century, there are also different concepts of the artist. The Romantic artist is typically both an outcast from society and a teacher of his fellowmen, but in either case he is considered a superior kind of person. We may distinguish two main ideal types of romantic artist-heroes: one is the Chatterton image, the sensitive plant too delicate to feel at ease in a material world; the other is Byronic, the guilt-cursed rebel whose intensity of purpose and appetite for passionate experience alienate him from a society that prefers mildness to intensity and the usual to the unique. The first type is the Shelley of Matthew Arnold's famous, if inaccurate description: "beautiful and ineffectual angel, beating in the void his luminous wings in vain." [2] It is "The Poet" described by Keats:

> Sometimes, above the gross and palpable things
> Of this diurnal sphere, his spirit flies

2. *Essays in Criticism: Second Series*   203–204.
(London: Macmillan, 1911), pp.

On awful wing; and with its destined skies
Holds premature and mystic communings:
Till such unearthly intercourses shed
A visible halo round his mortal head.[3]

Or it is the genius portrayed by Jean Paul Richter: "Above his dreamy, enthusiastic eye rose a smooth, peaceful, guiltless forehead, which the fortieth year left as unruled and unmarked as the fourteenth. He bore a heart which vices, as poisons do precious stones, would have crumbled to pieces; even another's face ploughed or sowed with sins oppressed and stifled his breast, and his inner man turned pale in the presence of filthy souls, as the sapphire on the finger of the unchaste man is said to lose its azure glow."[4] It is this type of romantic artist that we may expect to find in the Ivory Tower —and we shall—but he is so spiritually refined that he hardly needs to seek a retreat from life. Divine grace has made him from birth an angelic innocent, innately detached from the affairs of men, carrying his own Ivory Tower with him wherever he goes.

The other type of artist has tremendous capacity for experience. Like the genius Lombroso in Melville's *Mardi,* he has "primus and forever, a full heart—brimful, bubbling, sparkling; and running over."[5] Because he feels more intensely than others, he is tempted to explore the extremes of experience, and if it is a sense of guilt that forces him into exile, it is also guilt that gives him the right to offer lessons to those who have not gone so far as he. He may be like Shelley's "Adonais," who

Had gazed on Nature's naked loveliness,
Actaeon-like, and now he fled astray
With feeble steps o'er the world's wilderness
And his own thoughts, along that rugged way,
Pursued, like raging hounds, their father and their prey.[6]

Or Coleridge's "Kubla Khan":

And all should cry, Beware! Beware!
His flashing eyes, his floating hair!
Weave a circle round him thrice,
And close your eyes with holy dread,

3. *Poetical Works,* ed. H. W. Garrod (London: Oxford University Press, 1939), p. 528.
4. *The Invisible Lodge,* trans. Charles T. Brooks (New York: Henry Holt, 1883), p. 22.
5. Quoted by Henry A. Murray in his Introduction to Melville's *Pierre; or The Ambiguities* (New York: Hendricks House, 1949), p. xix.
6. *Works,* ed. Harry Buxton Forman (London, 1880), III, 20–21.

> For he on honey-dew hath fed,
> And drunk the milk of Paradise.[7]

As Robert Penn Warren points out in his brilliant reading of *The Rime of the Ancient Mariner*, Wordsworth's image in *The Prelude* of the "innocent bird, hath goadings on/That drive her as in trouble through the groves" is a less compelling artist-surrogate than Coleridge's mariner, "who passes like night from land to land," but both derive from the same conception of the artist as an agonized messenger of the divine vision.[8] For Coleridge, as for most of the early Romantics, the guilt-cursed artist seeks redemption by passing on to others his vision of the absolute. For a later Romantic like Melville, the artist may set himself up as equal to God. "Exiled for aye from God and man," the hero of *Pierre* declares, "I shall declare myself an equal power with both." [9] The first type of romantic artist is an angelic innocent; the second, a diabolical rebel.

Lord Byron gives his name to this second type of artist. More notorious than the other Romantic poets, he succeeded in stamping his own likeness on the public's image of the poet, and because he was as well known as a lover and a man of action as a poet, it is to him more than to any other individual that we may attribute the equation of art with experience throughout much of the nineteenth century.

> I have not loved the world nor the world me;
> I have not flatter'd its rank breath, nor bow'd
> To its idolatries a patient knee,
> Nor coin'd my cheek to smiles,—nor cried aloud
> In worship of an echo; in the crowd
> They could not deem me one of such—I stood
> Among them, but not of them. . . .[10]

Lines like these served as the keynote for much of the philistine-baiting of the nineteenth century and helped to link in the popular imagination the poet with the aristocratic rebel. Passionate, misanthropic heroes like those of *Lara* and *The Corsair* became stereotyped figures in Victorian sensation fiction, and scarcely a writer of the period escaped a Byronic phase in his youth. A minor source of the artist-novel may well have been the half-dozen novels published by 1837 whose heroes were based upon the life and character

7. *The Complete Poetical Works*, ed. E. H. Coleridge (Oxford University Press, 1912), I, 298.
8. "A Poem of Pure Imagination: An Experiment in Reading," in his *Selected Essays* (New York: Random House, 1958), pp. 260–261.
9. *Pierre*, p. 126.
10. *Works*, ed. E. H. Coleridge (London, 1922), II, 286.

of Byron.[11] Add to these admittedly biographical novels the many other literary works which utilized the Byronic hero, and it is not difficult to see how Byron helped to establish the type of the poet as rebel.

Yet Byron was as much a teacher of his fellowmen as an outcast from them, and in him, as in others of his type, guilt was the link between the oposing roles. For a man who claimed "I have not loved the world nor the world me," he seems to have spent a great deal of time in the world. He preferred politicians and men of action to writers and artists; and *Lara,* he tells us, "was written amidst balls and fooleries, and after coming home from masquerades and routs, in the summer of the sovereigns." [12] Here is the antithesis of the Ivory Tower. Yet, why would a man write a work like *Lara* after coming home from a ball if it were not that revelry seemed not enough, the masquerade only playacting, and real drama to be found only in the realm of the imagination? Perhaps Byron's ambition from youth on "to carve myself the passage to Grandeur" [13] was rooted in his sense of guilt, for a man does not have to keep proving himself unless he is insecure. His accomplishments as poet and lover, according to Herbert Read, were attempts to escape from himself: "To withdraw *myself* from *myself* (oh that cursed selfishness!) has ever been my sole, my entire, my sincere motive in scribbling at all." [14] This self-disgust, reflected even in the reference to his "scribbling," apparently goes back to his fear that the precocious sexual experiences of childhood had made him anticipate life. *Childe Harold,* he states in his preface, teaches that "early perversion of mind and morals leads to satiety of past pleasures and disappointment in new ones." [15] Against those early experiences he opposed always a dream of the "First Kiss of Love" never to be realized because the first kiss had come too early to be a kiss of love and no other kiss could ever be first. Hence Byron had to keep searching for the greater love, the wilder passion, the new first emotion. Recurrent hope and disillusionment is the pattern of both his poetry and his life. Experience never quite meets the ideal, but there is always hope. *Childe Harold* and the other subjective writings are filled with alternating self-pity and self-exultation, and the loneliness which domi-

11. See Samuel C. Chew, *Byron in England, His Fame and After-Fame* (London: John Murray, 1924), pp. 141–168.

12. *A Self-Portrait: Letters and Diaries, 1798 to 1824,* ed. Peter Quennell (New York: Scribner's, 1950), II, 699.

13. *A Self Portrait,* I, 10.

14. *The True Voice of Feeling: Studies in English Romantic Poetry* (London: Faber and Faber, 1953), p. 297.

15. *Works,* ed. Thomas Moore (London: John Murray, 1832), VIII, 6–7.

nates these works implies not only the need to escape from self, but the intense desire to find the companion or the cause which could take him away from that "cursed selfishness." Byron may have found the means in the last moments of his glorious end, but we seek it in vain in his poetry. The cynical detachment of Byron's best satirical verse suggests a removal, but we know that Byron's satires, like Swift's, are the products of a disillusioned idealist whose unusual capacity for affection and experience made him bitter at the failure of life to meet his personal standards of intensity.

Not the satires, but *Childe Harold* and the subjective verse dramas seemed truly "Byronic" to his contemporaries. His main appeal, like that of D. H. Lawrence in a later day, was to women and adolescents, and the appeal was primarily a challenge to live life to the full. After Byron, art became a glamorous vocation, because the artist now was seen to be a person of intense appetites and powers capable of living at a sustained level of exuberance, excitingly wavering between passionate exhilaration and melancholic despair.

Both the innocent and the rebel are to be found among the artists of fiction during the Romantic period. Even in the nonartist heroes of the historical novels, the Gothic romances, and the novels of manners which dominated the literary scene—in, for instance, the apocalyptic geniuses of Fanny Burney's stories; the proud and shy introvert Darcy of *Pride and Prejudice;* the dandies of Disraeli's and Bulwer-Lytton's novels; Cooper's solitude-loving Leatherstocking— we find examples of both kinds of heroes, alienated either by sensitivity or insight and quite different from the heroes committed to action and the conventional values of society found in earlier fiction. The new hero may be likened to the protagonist of Hawthorne's first novel, *Fanshawe,* a pale young scholar who seems to "others and to himself, a solitary being, upon whom the hopes and fears of ordinary men were ineffectual." [16] When he rides out to rescue the fair Ellen, he is almost overcome by "a longing for rest, for his old retirement, that came at intervals so powerfully upon him, as he rode on, that his heart sickened of the active exertion on which fate had thrust him." [17] Scott's *Waverley* provides a more unexpected example of a passive hero. As a child Edward Waverley had a "vivid power of imagination and an ardent love of literature"; [18] in fact, his "habit of abstraction and love of solitude" worried his elders

16. *The Complete Novels and Selected Tales of Nathaniel Hawthorne,* ed. Norman Holmes Pearson (New York: Modern Library, 1937), p. 14.

17. *The Complete Novels . . . ,* p. 70.

18. (Boston: Houghton Mifflin, 1923), I, 21.

and increased his "dislike of society." [19] Forced by accident into serving with the army of the Pretender, Waverley is never convincing as a military man, though he proves brave enough when the need arises. As his name suggests, he is troubled by a "wavering and unsettled habit of mind" [20] which makes it difficult for him to decide where his true loyalties lie or even which of two young women he loves. The girls solve the problem for him, the one by spurning him, the other by accepting. The first, Flora Mac-Iver, says of him, "He would never have been his celebrated ancestor Sir Nigel, but only Sir Nigel's eulogist and poet." [21]

Flora is herself a poet, and undoubtedly her ode on the hero of an earlier rebellion was the major influence on Waverley's decision to serve the Pretender. Although the patriotic Flora yearns for a lover more heroic than Waverley, she proves to be too high-minded and romantic to bring herself down to the level of mundane love. In his depiction of Flora, Scott seems to have been strongly influenced by Madame de Staël's popular *Corinne*. The two heroines share much the same fervor for the good of humanity, and though both are beautiful as well as brilliant, they are unhappy in love. Because their exalted ideals unfit them for reality, they are the true ancestresses of the Emma Bovarys and Carol Kennicotts of more recent fiction.

Corinne deserves brief attention as the first of the "art novels" to achieve wide recognition and to serve as a model for the genre. Less portraits of the artistic temperament than guidebooks to the art capitals of Europe presented in the guise of sentimental romances, these books—which include such later representatives as Hawthorne's *Marble Faun* and James's *Roderick Hudson*—usually include artists among the leading characters. Like Byronism, these novels helped to make the artist seem romantic; and just as Byronism was more an appeal to live intensely than to create art dispassionately, these books make it clear that being an artist is an exciting way to live.

Corinne is alienated by her sensitivity and spiritual insight. Half-Italian, half-British (a combination of dark and blond nationalities which was to become a stereotype in later artist-heroes, as we note in "Tonio Kröger" and other stories by Thomas Mann), Corinne is educated in Rome, where she develops her artistic sensibilities, but is then forced to live in Scotland with her father and his second wife. Corinne finds herself poorly attuned to the philistine society of the Scottish village, and just as the local gentry are made uncomfortable by her enthusiasms and raptures, so is she miserable in the

19. *Waverley*, I, 25–26.   21. *Waverley*, II, 140.
20. *Waverley*, I, 55.

company of people whom she considers dullards. When her father dies, she takes advantage of her new independence to drop her last name, return to Italy, and launch a career which makes her famous as "the most celebrated woman of Italy, Corinne, poetess, writer, improvisatrice, and also one of the loveliest women in Rome." [22]

Corinne's art is emotional, admittedly inspired, didactic in purpose, rhapsodic in form. "I feel myself a poet," she says, "not only when a happy choice of rhymes or of harmonious syllables, a happy blending of images, dazzles my hearers; but when my soul is elevated, when it looks down with disdain on selfishness and meanness; in short, when a beautiful deed would be easiest to me, then my verses are at their best. I am a poet when I admire, when I scorn, when I hate, not for personal feeling, not for my own sake, but for the dignity of humanity, the glory of the world." [23] Although Corinne's unhappy love affairs would seem to indicate that artistic temperament may be in natural conflict with womanly desires and duties, Madame de Staël tries to show through her heroine that art is rooted in experience and that the person who lives most intensely is the best artist.

In the succeeding art novels more emphasis is placed on the conflict between life and art, though life usually triumphs. For example, one of the few art novels of the early nineteenth century that remain readable is Hans Christian Andersen's *The Improvisatore; or, Life in Italy*. Even a brief synopsis reveals the conflict between life and art. Orphaned as a child, the shy and dreamy Antonio is raised in a peasant's cottage in the Campagna. Under the protection of a rich nobleman, Antonio receives a sound education and appears to be destined for a career in the Church, a vocation appropriate to his temperament. However, he falls in love with a beautiful singer, Annunciata, wounds his best friend accidentally, and flees to Naples, where he makes an impressive debut as a Corinne-like improvisatore. Through a series of misadventures he leaves Naples just before Annunciata arrives and hence fails to learn of her love for him. He is persuaded by the family of his benefactor to return to his scholarly studies, and seven years pass before he again escapes back into life. In Venice, again an improvisatore, he finds personal fulfillment in marriage with the beautiful and wealthy Maria, who proves to be the once blind girl, Lara, whom Antonio as a child had idolized. It is significant that after Antonio marries Maria, we hear no more of his art.

Four women in the novel play symbolic roles: the beautiful Santa,

22. *Corinne; or, Italy*, trans. Emily Baldwin and Paulina Driver (London: George Bell and Sons, 1888), p. 17.

23. *Corinne*, p. 43.

Annunciata, Lara-Maria, and the Madonna. When Santa tries to seduce the young Antonio, he runs away, trusting in the protection of his beloved Madonna—action which suggests the conflict between passion and spirit which is eventually reconciled. Annunciata and Lara-Maria represent the false and the true blend of the carnal and the spiritual. Dramatic art, personified by Annunciata, is an improper goal because it can only be transitory: the rapidly aging Annunciata "discovered already that which I myself perceived only afterwards, that my love for her had misled me in placing her art, and she who exercised it, within the range of immortality, which it could never reach. Dramatic art is like a rainbow, a heavenly splendor, a bridge between heaven and earth; it is admired, and then vanishes with all its colors." [24] As improvisatore, Antonio too is a dramatic artist, and if he ceases to practice his art after his marriage it is because he has found the woman who is both "soul's ideal," Lara, and the womanly Maria, a madonna with physical graces as striking as those of the beautiful Santa.

In story, hero, theme, and technique The Improvisatore is similar to Wilhelm Meister, and just as one cannot feel that Wilhelm's rejection of a career as actor for a life of social service means much of a loss to art, we should have to agree that for Antonio art is but a means to an end. Like Wilhelm, he is too self-engrossed to see beyond his own interests. He tells us that as a child, "I lived quietly in my own self-created dream-world"; [25] his benefactor "thought that I was too much occupied by my own peculiar individuality—I did not come sufficiently out of myself—did not let the radius of the mind intersect the great circle of the world." [26] His art, which seems to rely on inspiration and emotions, is effective only when he can "bring himself in." [27] Thus he is chastised by one of his teachers: "Feeling, and feeling! that is not all which makes the poet! What a combating with fancies,—now one is here! now one is there! Neither is it thought, no, discretion, golden discretion! The poet must not let himself be run away with by his subject. He must be cold—ice-cold, must rend to pieces the child of his heart, that he may understand every single portion of it; it is only thus that a work of art can be put together. Not with all this driving and chasing, and all this wild inspiration!" [28] This speech sounds like the sculptor Gloriana lecturing the emotional Roderick Hudson in James's novel, and the two books are not unlike in other respects. But whereas for Andersen Antonio graduates from a false career as improvisatore to

24. Translated by Mary Howitt (Bos- 26. The Improvisatore, pp. 83–84.
ton: Houghton Mifflin, n.d.), p. 109. 27. The Improvisatore, p. 262.
25. The Improvisatore, p. 7.   28. The Improvisatore, p. 68.

fulfillment as man and husband, James implies that the talented Roderick *descends* from art to life when he turns from the ideal beauty symbolized by his statues to the worldly appeal of Christina Light. Between the publication of *The Improvisatore* in 1832 and the appearance of *Roderick Hudson* in 1876 a gradual change of emphasis in artist-novels was such that by the 1870's a writer could argue convincingly that art was a sufficient end in itself.

Of George Sand's many novels with artists among the leading characters, *Consuelo* was probably the most popular and hence the most influential on the public's conception of the artist. Art novel, historical romance, and *Bildungsroman, Consuelo* includes a gallery of artist types. Like Andersen, Hawthorne, and many other writers of the early nineteenth century, George Sand was convinced that art forms a bridge between the physical and the spiritual and, like them, she classifies her artists in terms of their relation to life and spirit. The conflict in the novel is not only between the woman and the artist in Consuelo, but also between worldly, transitory glory and the "divine breath" which can triumph over death. Thus just as Andersen's story of Antonio is concerned with the artist-hero's relation to four women who symbolize varying balances between life and spirit, so Consuelo's story is symbolically dependent on three men: the passionate young singer Anzoleto, the dedicated old composer Porpora, and the mystic Count Albert Rudolstadt. Although all three are artists, their attitude toward art differs so widely that they seem to stand, roughly, for life, art, and spirit. Anzoleto, "artist even to the bones, that is, seeking and feeling life with a frightful intensity," [29] is eager to accept the worldly rewards and the feminine favors that come with artistic recognition. Porpora, on the other hand, would sacrifice all for art, which he feels is a "rage" and a "combat" against "vulgar mortals." [30] Count Albert, who knows little about musical theory or technique, nonetheless has a "revelation of the true, the grand music," and can play the violin beautifully when "prostrate in spirit before the Divinity." [31]

Consuelo as complete and true artist combines the traits personified by the three men. The child of a wandering, gypsy-like mother, Consuelo is "as calm as the water of the lagunes, and at the same time as active as the light gondolas which incessantly furrow its surface." [32] She has the power of concentrating to the level of abstraction, and is blessed with both a lovely natural voice and sufficient dedication to develop her talent. Matter-of-fact in her attitude

29. *Consuelo*, trans. Francis G. Shaw (Boston: William D. Ticknor, 1846), I, 21.

30. *Consuelo*, II, 278ff.
31. *Consuelo*, I, 415.
32. *Consuelo*, I, 11.

toward her gift, natural in her personal manner, she represents what her master, Porpora, considers the highest type of genius. When she makes her successful debut, "her forehead seemed to swim in a celestial fluid, a soft languor still bathed the delicate and noble outlines of her generous and serene features. Her calm countenance indicated none of those small passions which seek for and covet ordinary success. There was in her something grave, mysterious, and profound, which commanded respect and tenderness." [33]

Consuelo learns that the life of the artist is one of suffering. Compelled to sing in spite of her sorrow when she hears that Anzoleto has been unfaithful to her, she feels that the audience which calls her back for an encore is composed of "savage, ferocious, wild beasts," and there is more lament than triumph in her vow, "Ah! far from me, . . . far from me all love, all caresses, and all sweet words! no love! no husband! no lover! no family for me! my master has said it! liberty, the ideal, solitude, glory!" [34] We are hardly surprised therefore when Consuelo temporarily abandons her career. Fleeing Venice, with its unhappy memories of Anzoleto, she takes a position as companion in the old castle of the Rudolstadt family of Bohemia.

There she finds the son of the family, Count Albert—as pale, as gloomy, and as mysteriously stricken as Poe's Roderick Usher—suffering from spiritual delusions and his own uncanny powers. Gifted with second sight, convinced that he has lived before, and likely at any moment to fall into a cataleptic trance, Albert seems to be warring with diabolic spirits. Through the agency of the spiritually pure Consuelo, he is saved from his apparent doom and, in gratitude, offers her his love and his hand in marriage. Although she loves Albert, Consuelo realizes that his parents are opposed to their only son's marrying a gypsy singer. Fleeing the castle, she meets the boy Joseph Haydn on the road, and after a series of picaresque adventures with him, eventually finds her way back to Venice, where she again meets Porpora and resumes her career as singer. Now, though, she realizes even more than before the conflict between fulfillment as artist and fulfillment as woman:

What a strange destiny was mine! . . . Heaven has given me faculties and a soul for art, the need of liberty, the love of a proud and chaste independence, but at the same time, instead of giving me that cold and ferocious selfishness which insures to artists the strength necessary to clear their way through the difficulties and temptations of life, that celestial Will has placed in my bosom a tender and sensitive heart, which beats only for

33. *Consuelo*, I, 71–72.   34. *Consuelo*, I, 158–159.

others, and cannot live except in affection and devotedness. Thus divided between two opposing forces, my life is wasted, and my aim constantly fails to be realized.[35]

Only when Count Albert is on his deathbed does Consuelo agree to marry him, and then, when he dies, instead of taking advantage of her new title and wealth, she leaves the castle to once again resume her career. Young Haydn had told her, "You were born an artist, therefore you must be one, and whoever prevents you from being one will kill you or give you a life worse than the grave." [36] In the sequel, *The Countess of Rudolstadt,* the emphasis, however, is not on Consuelo's artistic career, but on her attempts to reunite mystically with the dead Albert, who symbolizes the true, celestial music, intimations of which have made Consuelo the great singer of her time.

Obviously, *Consuelo* is dated, but the importance of the novel in establishing the artist as a suitable hero of fiction is apparent. Few other books, earlier or later, ascribe a more exalted role to the artist. Even the extravagance of the supernatural element and the ecstatic sentimentality help George Sand convey her belief in the role of the artist as intermediary between life and spirit. In the Count Albert strain of the novel, with its idealized concept of art and the not quite successful attempt to fuse dream with reality, *Consuelo* follows a tradition that began with the mystical artist romances of Richter and Novalis and led, as we shall see in the next chapter, to the Ivory Tower esthetes of the late nineteenth century.

But in addition to this strain, *Consuelo* follows also the romantic view of the artist as one whose art is based on experience, even though the transcending of such experience for the sake of art must inevitably lead to suffering. The novel reflects another romantic tradition, that of the artist as wanderer, gypsy, or Bohemian free from the restraints of social convention. If we could remove the pseudo mysticism and the sentimentality, we should have a novel that is romantic in incident but realistic in its depiction of the life of the artist. The sections dealing with Consuelo and Anzoleto as poor children of the Venetian streets and those recounting the adventures of Joseph Haydn and Consuelo on their journey to Venice have a lightness and a charm which are lacking once the scene shifts to the Rudolstadt castle. At this point the novel becomes overburdened with George Sand's mystical philosophy. Yet, significantly, the castle is in Bohemia, and Consuelo, whose ancestry is unknown, has the feeling that she is returning home. Although she is ap-

35. *Consuelo,* II, 262.   36. *Consuelo,* II, 371.

parently Spanish rather than Bohemian by nationality, she and her mother knew the wandering, gypsy-like way of existence traditionally associated with the Bohemians, and she is more than once called a "Bohemian" girl. If we keep in mind too that Count Albert represents the true source of art, his castle Consuelo's spiritual home, then it may not be too fanciful to suggest that *Consuelo* is one of the founders of the Bohemian tradition in artist fiction.

Henry Murger, however, was chiefly responsible for starting the vogue of Bohemia. Whereas George Sand used the term "Bohemian" in its old sense of the wandering artist-gypsy, Murger had in mind the "Bohemia" of the Latin Quarter, a place and a designation which existed long before Murger brought them into fashion. Prior to Murger, the Latin Quarter seems to have been considered a disreputable area inhabited by impoverished students and artists only because they could not live so cheaply elsewhere. Murger's contribution in his series of sketches, *Scènes de la vie de Bohème* (which began to appear in 1845), in his stage adaptation of them with Théodore Barrière in 1849, and in the use of his *Scènes* for Puccini's popular opera of 1896, was to turn Bohemia into a mecca for bourgeois visitors and art-loving exiles.

Those who know Murger's Bohemia largely through Puccini's sentimentalized version are likely to be surprised to discover in Murger's sketches "predominantly a book of laughter and high jinks." [37] Just as the wandering Bohemians moved from adventure to adventure free of all social restraint, so the young students, artists, and grisettes of Murger's stories follow a disordered, day-to-day mode of living. Attachments, residences, and love affairs are fleeting. If the young Bohemians have to struggle to survive, at least they have company in the struggle. The antithesis of the Ivory Tower, Bohemia is the most sociable of colonies, and though a few of the inhabitants maintain a hermitage in their garrets, the majority prefer the gay company of the café. The loudly-proclaimed freedom and spontaneity of the Bohemians is largely the making of a virtue of necessity. When they can rent an apartment in a bourgeois milieu, they leave the Latin Quarter in the comfortable assurance that Bohemia is a way-station to success and a fitting domain only for young people. Just as Murger himself abandoned the Latin Quarter after his depiction of the scene brought him fame and fortune, so his characters eventually grow tired of irregularity and an inadequate diet. Says one of them: "For my part, I've had enough of it. Poetry is not to be found in disorder—in improvised pleasures—in love affairs

37. Michael Sadleir, "Introduction," Cameron (London: Hamish Hamil *Vie de Bohème,* trans. Norman ton, 1949), p. x.

that last as long as a candle—in more or less eccentric rebellions against the prejudices that will eternally rule humanity. It is easier to overthrow a dynasty than an established custom, even a ridiculous one. To wear a spring coat in December is not a sufficient proof of talent. One can be a poet or a true artist, and still keep one's feet warm and eat three meals a day." [38]

Not such sober words as these, but the merriment which precedes them is what impressed the first readers of Murger's *Scènes*. The painter Whistler, for example, was so taken by his reading of Murger that he hurried from Washington, D. C., to Paris, scorning the American Bohemias which had sprung up after Murger made such living respectable, and thus helped to set off the second wave of Bohemianism a half century later by serving as the model for Joe Sibley in George du Maurier's *Trilby*, a novel which had an impact on American and British readers which can scarcely be overemphasized. The third major wave of popularity came in the 1920's, and books like Ernest Hemingway's *The Sun Also Rises* kept the tradition of the Latin Quarter alive for a new generation of aspiring artists. That the Bohemian tradition is still powerful is shown by the "beatnik" vogue of our time which, like all previous manifestations of Bohemianism, seems rooted in the Romantic concept of art as experience. The beatnik rebels against the standards of the multitude and goes " on the road," but he is seldom a hermit, and what he looks for primarily is people of his own sort, a new experience, sensual excitement. With their beards and characteristic costumes, the beatniks prove themselves to be conformists, and much of their literature, like that of the Byronic and Bohemian traditions, is but a form of self-publicity.

A retreat to Bohemia is a mild form of revolt. The potential artist, in rebellion against the standards of middle-class society, goes to the Latin Quarter or Greenwich Village not only to develop his art but also to find convivial companions, to join coteries, and to establish an environment congenial to his temperament. Thus the Bohemian, instead of alienating himself from society, substitutes one kind of society for another and usually stops short of the detachment of those who follow the ideal of the Ivory Tower. As one of Murger's characters comes to realize, "True freedom consists in being able to do without others and live on one's own resources." [39]

Because of its popularity, however, the literature of Bohemia helped to assure an audience for more genuine portaits of the artist. Through the influence of Murger and his successors, the artist came

38. *Vie de Bohème*, p. 302.   39. *Vie de Bohème*, p. 301.

to seem a romantic, attractive, sometimes eccentric but usually amusing fellow. The literature of Bohemia had also a negative effect in that it supported the middle-class conception of the artist as a naughty, sometimes even dirty "foreigner" and thus provided ammunition for strait-laced Victorian parents who did all they could to dissuade their children from following a vocation that was not quite respectable. Lady Agnes in James's *Tragic Muse,* like the relatives of Clive Newcome, would be a less formidable enemy of her son's aspiration to become a painter if Bohemianism had not helped to form her notion of an artist.

II   *Apprentices to Art*

ALTHOUGH we have seen that the artist was an established hero in Continental novels by 1800, it was not until the 1830's that English novelists began to write portrait-of-the-artist novels. Perhaps the chief reason for the belated appearance of the artist-novel in England may be found in the paucity of major novelists during the early decades of the nineteenth century. *Wuthering Heights* was perhaps the first really significant Romantic novel, and that most uncharacteristic of English novels was not published until 1847. Jane Austen and Sir Walter Scott were major novelists, of course, but neither had the introspection that we associate with authors of artist-novels. We cannot visualize either of them writing *The Prelude,* and it is a *Prelude* in prose that is conspicuously lacking in English literature of the Romantic period.

Another reason may be found in the impact of the *Bildungsroman,* the apprentice-novel, which, because of the peculiar circumstances of its importation, exerted a binding influence on those novelists who otherwise might have produced more original portraits. Goethe's *Wilhelm Meister* had little influence on British fiction until Carlyle's translation of 1824, but then it inspired a type of novel which has remained popular ever since. In her excellent study of the English *Bildungsroman,* Susanne Howe outlines the usual pattern of apprenticeship: "The adolescent hero of the typical 'apprentice' novel sets out on his way through the world, meets with reverses usually due to his own temperament, falls in with various guides and counselors, makes many false starts in choosing his friends, his wife, and his life work, and finally *adjusts himself in some way to the demands of his time and environment* by finding a sphere of action in which he may work effectively." [40] In the itali-

40. *Wilhelm Meister and His Eng-*   (New York: Columbia University
    lish Kinsmen: Apprentices to Life   Press, 1930), p. 4.

cized phrase there is perhaps a clue to the belated appearance of the apprentice in art. Wilhelm Meister, we have seen, is an artist of sorts throughout most of Goethe's novel, but he finally decides to devote his life to humanitarianism not necessarily because social values are more important than artistic ones, but because he eventually realizes that he lacks the ability to be a true artist. In his translation of Goethe's novel, Carlyle tended to distort the main theme —what Miss Howe calls "the ideal of deliberate, harmonious self-culture"—and emphasized instead his own doctrine of work—the necessity for "acting as well as suffering." [41]

Spiritual mentor in his own right as well as Goethe's translator, Carlyle exerted a double influence on his young followers. The result is that most of the apprentice heroes follow the path laid down in *Sartor Resartus*: almost invariably they pass through the "Everlasting No" and the "Centre of Indifference" to attain eventually an "Everlasting Yea," which is usually an affirmation of social values. If they happen to be artists, they will ultimately become reconciled to the necessity of subordinating their art to some form of social purpose. The Carlylean "hero as poet" is not a conformist; he is superior to the average man, but instead of separating himself from mankind, he feels that his mission is that of the prophet who leads his neighbors out of the wilderness.

Although most of the apprentice-novels are autobiographical, only a few of the heroes are permitted to find their proper "sphere of action" in an artistic vocation, and of the few, most assume a role in public affairs as well. Art in itself is suspect, but art conceived as a form of social duty is the noblest mission of the man of genius. Thus, even among the group-within-a-group with which we are here concerned, the apprenticeships are as much to life as to art. That the sensitive individual may meet with "reverses usually due to his temperament" is acknowledged, but the goal of these books is to bring the "I" of the artist into harmony with the "others" of society. A few of the early apprentices to art retreat to an Ivory Tower, but they are not allowed to remain there. It is no coincidence that the same novelists who introduced the artist to English fiction introduced also the novel of social purpose.

First of the artist-apprentice novels in England is Benjamin Disraeli's *Contarini Fleming*, which appeared in 1832. To write "an ideal and complete picture of the development of the poet" [42] was Disraeli's alleged intention, and he succeeded to an extent. Contarini

41. *Wilhelm Meister and His English Kinsmen*, p. 88.
42. *Contarini Fleming: A Psycholog-* *ical Romance* (New York: Knopf, 1926), p. ix.

Fleming, as his name suggests, is burdened from the start with a mixed nationality not unlike that of Madame de Staël's Corinne. Son of a Scandinavian father and an Italian mother—hence troubled by a conflict between "duty" and "passion"—Contarini finds himself uncomfortable in the northern country to which his father has returned after the death of his first wife. Contarini is an impulsive, sensitive boy given both to visionary dreams and mischievous exploits, such as his thwarted attempt to form a "Secret Union for the Amelioration of Society" devoted to robbing the rich in order to feed the poor. Of the plot of the story it is sufficient to say that it traces Contarini through early love affairs, his first efforts as a poet (including a book on the nature of the poetic temperament), a brief period of political glory, marriage to his beautiful Venetian cousin, her death, his despair, his wanderings in the East, and, finally, his decision to build himself a palace of art to which he can retreat. Here, it would seem, is an artist-hero who finds the culmination of his personal quest in art rather than social mission, and a statement by Contarini at the beginning of his memoirs gives us the right to expect such a conclusion: "Some exemption from the sectarian principles that embitter life may surely be expected from one who, by a curious combination of circumstances, finds himself without country, without kindred, and without friends; nor will he be suspected of indulging in the delusion of worldly vanity, who, having acted in the world, has retired to meditate in an inviolate solitude, and seeks relief from the overwhelming vitality of thought in the flowing spirit of poetic creation." [43] But this turns out to be a premature hope, for the novel concludes with the assurance that Contarini has not put entirely behind him his hopes for the amelioration of society: "Here let me pass my life in the study and creation of the beautiful. Such is my desire; but whether it will be my career, is, I feel, doubtful. My interest in the happiness of my race is too keen to permit me for a moment to be blind to the storms that lour on the horizon of society. Perchance also the political regeneration of the country to which I am devoted may not be distant, and in that great work I am resolved to participate." [44]

Similarly undecided whether to be "man of books or a man of deeds" is Ernest Maltravers, titular hero of a two-part novel by Edward Bulwer-Lytton that seems to have been more influential on subsequent artist-novels than was Disraeli's pioneer study. The career of Ernest Maltravers follows the usual Byronic pattern of Bulwer and Disraeli's heroes. He is introduced as a young man proud

43. *Contarini Fleming*, p. 4.   44. *Contarini Fleming*, p. 363.

and haughty, yet buoyant and gracious. When he loses his first love, Alice, he attempts to forget by plunging into politics and letters, but soon becomes disillusioned with both. "He had commenced life too soon," we are told, "he was disappointed, he found some persons he could admire, some whom he could like, but none with whom he could grow intimate, or for whom he could feel an interest. Neither his heart nor his imagination was touched; all appeared to him like artificial machines; he was discontented with things like life, but in which something or other was wanting." [45] Retaining his proud and idealistic respect for the "people," he becomes contemptuous of the "public," withdraws from political life, and determines to find solace in the creation of works for his personal pleasure. Bulwer, however, makes it obvious that this is an evil course of action. As Ernest pursues his "haughty and lonesome way" through the Alps and the Orient, he loses not only his sympathy with others, but even the solace of art. The true poet, Bulwer lectures us, "must have intimate knowledge of men as well as mountains, if he desires to become the CREATOR," [46] and "the difference between talent and genius lies rather in the heart than the head." [47] Fortunately, when Ernest has returned from his Byronic wanderings, he discovers to his dismay that he still retains the "vain madness" of his youth, "the haunting susceptibility to love." He falls in love with a young girl, who he is later led to believe is his own daughter. Thinking that he has narrowly escaped incest, Ernest undergoes a fall from pride which "restores him to his race" and, as if in reward, to the arms of the long-lost Alice, his first love and the true muse of his poetry. According to Bulwer's theory, this should enable Ernest to resume his artistic career with new sureness. But it is not at all clear whether Ernest turns back to art or to politics. We know only that

Maltravers once more entered upon the career so long suspended. He entered with an energy more practical and steadfast than the fitful enthusiasm of former years; and it was noticeable amongst those who knew him well, that while the firmness of his mind was not impaired, the haughtiness of his temper was subdued. No longer despising Man as he is, and no longer exacting from all things the ideal of a visionary standard, he was more fitted to mix in the living World, and to minister usefully to the great objects that refine and elevate our race. His sentiments were,

45. *Complete Works of Edward Bulwer-Lytton* (New York and San Francisco: Wheeler Publishing Company, n.d.), XI, i, 193.
46. *Complete Works*, XI, i, 122.
47. *Complete Works*, XI, ii, 23.

perhaps, less lofty, but his actions were infinitely more excellent, and his theories infinitely more wise.[48]

As if the story of Ernest Maltravers did not offer a clear enough indictment of the man who presumptuously removes himself from human sympathy, Bulwer included two foils to Ernest who represent the extremes of the conflict within him between action and sentiment. One is Lumley Ferrars, who represents the evil of the man of action who lacks sentiment. Bulwer apparently intended the Italian poet Castruccio Cesarini to represent the evil of the man dominated by his feelings. Lacking in talent but burdened with an excess of artistic temperament not unlike that of Goethe's Tasso, from whom he seems to derive, Cessarini personifies an image of the "artist" that was a stereotype even in Bulwer's time.

> Signor Cesarini returned their salutations with a mixture of bashfulness and hauteur, half-awkward and half-graceful, and muttering some inaudible greeting, sank into a seat and appeared instantly lost in revery. . . . He was extremely slight and thin, his cheeks hollow and colourless, with a profusion of black silken ringlets that almost descended to his shoulders. His eyes, deeply sunk into his head, were large and intensely brilliant; and a thin moustache, curling downwards, gave an additional austerity to his mouth, which was closed with gloomy and half-sarcastic firmness. He was not dressed as people dress in general, but wore a frock coat of dark camlet, with a large shirt-collar turned down, and a narrow slip of black silk twisted rather than tied round his throat; his nether garments fitted tight to his limbs, and a pair of half-hessians completed his costume.[49]

Although Cesarini affects the softest sentiments in his verse, his vanity prevents him from demonstrating his affection: "From the children, the sister, the friend, the whole living earth, he fled to a poem on Solitude, or stanzas upon Fame." [50] We are not surprised therefore that when Cesarini does fall in love he is so maddened by jealousy of Ernest that he enters into a plot with Ferrars which brings about the death of the young woman, drives Ernest into exile, and leads to Cesarini's commitment to an insane asylum. Years later he escapes, murders Ferrars, and throws himself into the Seine. Some "wild, incoherent verses" found in his pocket identify *le poète manqué* led to disaster by vanity, inadequate talent, and a tendency

48. *Complete Works*, XI, ii, 445.   50. *Complete Works*, XI, i, 128.
49. *Complete Works*, XI, i, 111–112.

"to pamper every unwholesome and unhallowed feeling as a token of the exuberance of genius." [51]

In Charles Kingsley's *Alton Locke, Tailor and Poet*, the old Carlylean bookseller Sandy Mackaye, hands a copy of *Ernest Maltravers* to his young protegé with the advice to "read, mark, learn, an' inwardly digest the history of Castruccio Cesarini; an' the gude God gie ye grace to lay the same to heart." [52] Although Alton Locke is half-angry at what he feels is a pointed allusion to his aspirations as poet, he is actually in little need of the lesson. Unlike Cesarini, Alton is a humble young man who, in spite of the opportunity to rise socially, devotes himself to improving the lot of his own class. "I do not complain that I am a Cockney," he says. "That . . . is God's gift. He made me one, that I might learn to feel for poor wretches who sit stifled in reeking garrets and workrooms, drinking in disease with every breath—bound in their prison-house of brick and iron, with their own funeral pall hanging over them, in that canopy of fog and poisonous smoke, from their cradle to their grave. I have drunk of the cup of which they drink. And so I have learnt —if, indeed, I have learnt—to be a poet—a poet of the people." [53] But if this early Hyacinth Robinson is a Cockney tailor, a Chartist, and a disciple of the philosophical Sandy Mackaye, he is also gifted with some poetic talent, an instinctive gentility, and a yearning for beauty that belies his zeal as social reformer. He tells us that "I could not control my daydreams; they swept me away with them over sea and land, and into the bowels of the earth. My soul escaped on every side from my civilized dungeon of brick and mortar into the great free world from which my body was debarred. . . . And as the self-indulgent habit grew on me I began to live two lives— one mechanical and outward, one inward and imaginative." [54] The two sides of Alton's character force him to choose between two ways of life. He falls in love with a genteel young lady, whose father holds out some encouragement, but advises the young man to spurn political opinions of any kind. When his fashionable connections and his love of art begin to alienate Alton from his Chartist friends, he forces himself to remember his social mission, preaches rebellion in a provincial village, and spends three years in prison. Upon his release, he lingers in England long enough to witness the fall of the Chartist hopes, then sails off to Texas in an attempt to restore his lost health. He dies on the evening of his arrival in the New World,

51. *Complete Works*, XI, ii, 240.   53. *Alton Locke*, p. 4.
52. *Alton Locke, Tailor and Poet*   54. *Alton Locke*, p. 97.
(London: T. Nelson & Sons, n.d.),
p. 293.

but leaves some inspirational verses—"Up, up, up, and up,/Face your game, and play it!"—that reveal not only his continued devotion to social reform, but also the fact that poor Alton was possibly less gifted a poet than Kingsley intended him to be.

Even less satisfactory as a portrait of the artist is George Henry Lewes's *Ranthorpe*, an overplotted novel which contains a number of high-flown comments on the nature of the artist, but fails to demonstrate them. Percy Ranthorpe is introduced as a young man with a "weak, wayward, and somewhat womanly nature. . . . [His] mouth was very remarkable: it was voluptuous, and yet refined; full, yet delicate—the mouth of a poet. The eyes were of a deep blue; long and somewhat languishing, and shaded with the sweetest fringe imaginable. The forehead was delicately cut; the chin weak and faltering." [55] This young man becomes estranged from his father when he gives up a safe and respectable position as a clerk to seek a precarious living as a journalist and poet. Percy's first book, *The Dreams of Youth*, is a fashionable success, and he finds himself lionized. Spoiled by the attentions he receives, he jilts Isola Churchill, the friend of his youth and "a true artist," for Florence Wilmington, a wealthy flirt. When the latter rejects him, his second book of verse is a failure, and his first tragedy is hooted off the stage, Percy flees abroad, "self-exiled from his native land." Gradually he learns humility, subordinates his ego both to others and to art, seeks a reconciliation with his dying father and all that the father represents, and—since "the artist cannot live wholly for his art: human affections and human infirmities irresistibly chain him to the world from which he would flee" [56]—marries the long-patient Isola. Lewes sums up the development of this Stephen Dedalus in reverse: "He has won his spurs. His genius has begun to take its magnificent flight far above the reach of other wings. He is in his twenty-fifth year, and his genius is free to operate untrammelled upon the materials afforded him by experience. He has felt, and he has thought; he has dreamed, and he has suffered. He is now to "preach from the text of his own errors"—to make his experience incarnate in song." [57]

Although the authors of apprentice-novels at midcentury subscribed to the Romantic notion that an artist must depend on his experiences, they were also aware of what Bulwer-Lytton called the "terrible disconnection between the author and the man." [58] If these writers accepted also the Romantic concept of art as a sacred calling,

55. *Ranthorpe* (New York: William S. Rottsberger, 1881), p. 4.
56. *Ranthorpe*, p. 175.
57. *Ranthorpe*, p. 326.
58. *Complete Works*, XI, i, 393.

if they felt that a true artist is one "possessed" not *of* genius but *by* it, nonetheless in their fiction man usually triumphed over genius. To give but one additional example from the fiction of this period, Bianca Piazzi, the actress-heroine of Geraldine Jewsbury's *The Half-Sisters,* says: "You don't know what it is to be devoted to an art; it possesses one like a demon; it is a sacred calling laid upon me, which I cannot help obeying." [59] Like her prototypes Corinne and Consuelo, however, Bianca is woman as well as artist. The passionate and mobile temperament that helps Bianca become a good actress also tempts her away from the stage to the life of a wife and mother:

> She endeavoured to give her whole soul more and more to her art; tried to make herself believe that to live a calm, self-sustained existence, dedicated like that of a priestess, cold, strong, and pure, to the utterance of the oracle confided to her, was indeed the noblest and highest vocation she could embrace. But it would not do, she needed some more human motive to sustain her. . . . She had acquired a fortune amply sufficient for all her wants; but her whole being was drooping in the glare of her success; her heart was aching with desire for that common blessing, which yet is more precious than life—the natural affection of friends and kin-folk; which comes from God, and is given when men enter on this weary life, to be a rest and refreshing for them, and that they should not walk through the desert alone.[60]

At the end of the novel the woman in Bianca triumphs over the actress, and she abandons the stage for marriage. It is clear that for Miss Jewsbury, friend of the Carlyles, art may be a noble calling, but when it conflicts with one's duty as wife and mother, it must be sacrificed.

If life comes out better than art in the apprentice-novels of the minor writers, they nonetheless agree that art is a sacred vocation when devoted to the good of one's fellowmen. In Thackeray and Dickens, the two major novelists of the midcentury, claims for the divine calling of art and the exalted stature of the artist are almost invariably ridiculed. Art is a trade like any other, Thackeray would have us believe, and of all the kinds of vanity in Vanity Fair none seems more preposterous than that exhibited by the posturing cranks who claim to be writers and painters. No doubt Thackeray wrote with tongue in cheek when he made fun of literary men and painters —"such odd-looking, hairy men as those young artists" [61]—and, in

59. (London: Chapman and Hall, 1866), p. 101.
60. *The Half-Sisters,* pp. 271–272.

61. *The Newcomes,* in *The Works,* Cornhill Edition (New York: Scribner's, 1923), V, 298.

the person of Arthur Pendennis, was capable of holding up his own weaknesses to affectionate ridicule. Nonetheless, Thackeray's portraits of writers and artists are so devastating that he was accused by John Forster and others of vilifying his own profession in order to court the nonliterary class. His reply to this charge was that it is a writer's duty "to practise regularity and sobriety, to love his family, and to pay his tradesmen." [62] Thus, when the self-indulgent Pendennis says, "We must deal kindly with the eccentricities of genius, and remember that the very ardour and enthusiasm of temperament which makes the author delightful often leads the man astray," his friend Warrington replies, "A fiddlestick about men of genius! I deny that there are so many geniuses as people who whimper about the fate of men of letters assert there are. . . . If an author fuddles himself, I don't know why he should be let off a headache the next morning." [63]

Arthur Pendennis and Clive Newcome are like their creator in that they turn to art only after other means of courting public favor have failed. Both are sensitive, imaginative young men who think well of themselves, but they are also gregarious, genial men, quite at home in the world. After a romantic stage represented by his "Leaves from the Life-Book of Walter Lorraine," a Wertherian psychological novel which Thackeray spoofs pleasantly, Pendennis undergoes the usual fall from pride of the Victorian artist-hero and emerges as a successful reviewer for the quarterlies and a writer of fashionable novels. Clive Newcome fights to overcome his family's opposition to his becoming a painter only to discover that he has just enough talent to become a successful illustrator and portrait-painter, but not enough to be taken seriously as a true artist. The gentleman in Thackeray was always a little ashamed of having to turn to writing for a living, and there is in his attitude toward the professional writer or artist much of the attitude of the eighteenth-century man of fashion toward the menial trades. "The Muse of Painting," Thackeray writes in *The Newcomes*, "is a lady whose social station is not altogether recognized with us as yet. The polite world permits a gentleman to amuse himself with her, but to take her for better or worse! forsake all other chances and cleave unto her! to assume her name! Many a respectable person would be as much shocked at the notion, as if his son had married an opera dancer." [64] But Thackeray's novels scarcely helped to improve the status of the artist in society, and

62. John W. Dodds, *Thackeray: A Critical Portrait* (Oxford University Press, 1941), p. 143.
63. *The History of Pendennis: His Fortunes and Misfortunes, His* Friends and His Greatest Enemy (Oxford University Press, 1908), p. 450.
64. *The Newcomes*, V, 433–434.

much of the Victorian view of the artist as a fellow at best amusing and clever, at worst irresponsible and immoral may be traced to such acidulous sketches as Thackeray's description of Becky Sharp's father: "Miss Sharp's father was an artist, and in that quality had given lessons of drawing at Miss Pinkerton's school. He was a clever man; a pleasant companion; a careless student; with a great propensity for running into debt, and a partiality for the tavern. When he was drunk, he used to beat his wife and daughter; and the next morning, with a headache, he would rail at the world for its neglect of its genius." [65]

Dickens too was leery of those who professed to be "artists," but in *David Copperfield,* one of his several apprentice-novels, he wrote the first portrait of the artist in English fiction that stands up in its own right as a major work of art. According to Bernard Shaw, "When Dickens introduced in his stories a character whom he intensely disliked he chose an artistic profession for him. Henry Gowan in *Little Dorrit* is a painter. Pecksniff is an architect. Harold Skimpole is a musician. There is real hatred in his treatment of them." [66] Although this statement, like many of Shaw's pronouncements, must be qualified—Henry Gowan, for example, may be a satirized portrait of Thackeray, who had annoyed Dickens by belittling the importance of the novelist—there can be little doubt that Dickens held a view of his profession that was modest in comparison with the attitude of the Romantics who preceded him or the esthetes who followed. Like Trollope, he seems to have considered writing to be a matter of craftsmanship and self-discipline, of setting to work in the fashion of any other kind of skilled worker. If he took pride in his artistic ability, it was for his ability to make a plot "work" and his usefulness as a social commentator and reformer. His characters often appear to be alienated in that they are solitaries, but they do not want to be alone any more than Dickens did. If we had only Dickens' opinions, if we could piece together his philosophy, we would no more expect him to be capable of writing great fiction than was David Copperfield. But we know that men sometimes create better than they realize.

There is general agreement that *David Copperfield* is the most autobiographical of Dickens' novels. In 1849, shortly before beginning the novel, he started to write a formal autobiography, but could not get past his twelfth year, the year when his father was imprisoned for debt and he was put to humiliating work in a blacking

65. *Vanity Fair,* in *The Works,* Cornhill Edition (New York: Scribner's, 1923), I, 15.

66. "Foreword," *Great Expectations* (London: Hamish Hamilton, 1947), p. xi.

factory. Reluctant to make public confession of his private shame, Dickens nonetheless felt the need to exorcise the past and to attempt self-understanding in a deliberate search of time past. In the novel that took the place of the autobiography, the personal experiences are disguised, though so thinly that scholars have had no difficulty in finding numerous parallels between the lives of Dickens and David.[67] Their dates nearly coincide, and David has Dickens' initials in reverse order. Obvious parallels include their favorite childhood pleasures; their estrangement from parents who, once loving and protecting, seemed to become cruel and indifferent; their attendance at inadequate schools; their degrading work in factories; their careers that begin in law offices and proceed through shorthand reporting to journalism to the writing of fiction. Dickens' biographers, especially those who utilize psychoanalysis, have been as struck by the divergences from reality as by the parallels. If Dickens' love of Maria Beadnell is similar to that of David's for Dora, it differs too in that David marries his Dora and discovers the union a blessing and a curse—as if Dickens wanted both to retain an illusion and destroy it. The dissemination of his own parents among the many surrogate parents of the novel—Mrs. Copperfield, Murdstone and his sister, Mr. and Mrs. Micawber, and Aunt Betsey Trotwood—reveals an even greater ambivalence of concealment and exposure. The "ideal" education at Dr. Strong's school and David's flight from the warehouse undoubtedly had their parallels, not in reality but in the daydreams of the unhappy young Dickens.

After the dream flight from the factory and after David has found refuge with Aunt Betsey, the "fairy godmother" of the novel, the divergences between David and Dickens are more significant than the resemblances. Surely, the later, mature David—calm, self-effacing, troubled only for others—does not fit the image of the mature Dickens that we derive from his biographers—the quarrelsome, excitable, self-exhibiting, often bitter man fighting with his wife and seeking the one impossible woman who could combine the virtues of wife, mistress, and mother. After the first two hundred pages of the novel, the emphasis changes from David to those he knows and, as in *Wilhelm Meister*, the plot is suddenly overburdened with incidents that have no direct relation to David's own story. With the discovery of the godmother, David's character is set in such a way that everything moves smoothly for him. Even adversity—the loss

67. See, for example, Edgar Johnson, *Charles Dickens: His Tragedy and Triumph* (New York: Simon and Schuster, 1952), II, 677–686; and Leonard F. Manheim, "The Personal History of David Copperfield," *American Imago*, IX (April, 1952), 3–25.

of his aunt's fortune and the inadequacy of Dora as homemaker—
tends to work for his benefit. After the dream flight David ceases to
be the Dickens of reality and becomes the Dickens who might have
been. "God help me," David says at the height of his childhood misfortunes, "I might have been improved for my whole life, I might
have been made another creature perhaps, for life, by a kind word
at that season." [68] Aunt Betsey stands for that "kind word," and from
the moment that David receives her blessing, Dickens departs from
disguised autobiography and lets the fictive world of his imagination
take over.

"Whether I shall turn out to be the hero of my own life . . .
these pages must show"—so David begins his story. Most readers
have answered David's question in the negative; and to say that
David is the least vivid character in the novel, a passive reflector
who links the stories of others into a single narrative, is to repeat a
commonplace of criticism. Perhaps because David as a person is too
placid to be thoroughly credible, we find it difficult to think of him
as the successful artist he is said to be by the time the novel ends.
Somerset Maugham speaks for many readers when he writes, "I
cannot persuade myself that in the end he became the successful
novelist we are told he did. If he wrote novels, I suspect they were
more like the novels of Mrs. Henry Wood than the novels of Charles
Dickens." [69] But this is the trap we fall into if we confuse the private
self of the artist with the public man. Few readers would consider
the autobiographical Philip Carey capable of writing *Of Human
Bondage*. Dickens himself recognized the distinction between man
and author when he had David write: "In pursuance of my intention of referring to my own fictions only when their course should
incidentally connect itself with the progress of my story, I do not
enter on the aspirations, the delights, anxieties, and triumphs of
my art. That I truly devoted myself to it with my strongest earnest-
ness, and bestowed upon it every energy of my soul, I have already
said. If the books I have written be of any worth, they will supply
the rest. I shall otherwise have written to poor purpose, and the rest
will be of interest to no one." [70] Among those books, we must remember, is *David Copperfield* itself, and though David claims that
the book is for his eyes alone, we must assume that it is a representative example of his art. Elsewhere David says of his writings, "They
express themselves, and I leave them to themselves," [71] but the

68. *David Copperfield* (New York: Company, 1948), p. 180.
    Modern Library, 1950), p. 49.   70. *David Copperfield*, p. 889.
69. *Great Novelists and Their Nov-*   71. *David Copperfield*, p. 727.
    els (Philadelphia: John C. Winston

statement is an invitation to discover what is expressed through the façade of a novel which fuses everything through an "I" but takes the "I" for granted and spurns direct self-analysis.

"Nature and accident had made me an author," [72] says David. If we read the novel casually, the development of David as artist seems dependent more on an accident of circumstance than on nature. As a child David has no conscious desire to be a writer, and he might well have followed the gentlemanly career as proctor which his aunt envisioned for him if the loss of her money had not forced David to supplement his income by becoming first a secretary to Dr. Strong, then a shorthand reporter, then a news reporter, and finally a writer of fiction. The chain from secretary to author is a likely one, but if the first step is simply a matter of David's responding to opportunity, the others seem to involve deliberate choices. Accident will not explain why David developed from copyist to creator.

If, however, we read the novel against the background of other portraits of the artist, we discover in David most of the traditional characteristics of the artistic temperament, and his development as artist seems almost a classic example of the norm. David assures us that he "was a child of close observation." [73] A gift for objective observation suggests the potential scientist but in David, as in most potential artists, close observation merges with imaginative reverie. He describes a typical Sunday in church:

> It's a dreadful thing to gape, but I must do something. . . . I look up at the monumental tablets on the wall, and try to think of Mr. Bodgers, late of this parish, and what the feelings of Mrs. Bodgers must have been, when affliction sore, long time Mr. Bodgers bore, and physicians were in vain. I wonder whether they called in Mr. Chillip, and he was in vain; and if so, how he likes to be reminded of it once a week? I look from Mr. Chillip, in his Sunday neckcloth, to the pulpit, and think what a good place it would be to play in, and what a castle it would make, with another boy coming up the stairs to attack it, and having the velvet cushion with the tassels thrown down on his head. [74]

Even in the process of observation the things observed, such as the wording on the tablet, "affliction sore," are mingled with imaginative speculation: "what the feelings of Mrs. Bodgers must have been."

David has also that ability to abstract himself from his surroundings and to concentrate upon a single object which we have found

72. *David Copperfield*, p. 727.   74. *David Copperfield*, pp. 15–16.
73. *David Copperfield*, p. 14.

to be characteristic of the "totality" type of artist. "I never could have done what I have done," he says in one of his few comments on his writing, "without the habits of punctuality, order, and diligence, without the determination to concentrate myself on one object at a time, no matter how quickly its successor should come upon its heels. . . . Never to put one hand to anything on which I could throw my whole self, and never to affect depreciation of my work, whatever it was, I find now to have been my golden rules." [75]

If David seems to lack at least one quality of the typical artist-hero—egotism—it is perhaps because he has an excess of another—passivity. A more aggressive boy would hardly have taken as much abuse from Murdstone as David did before he finally struck back. Later, when David leaves the factory and makes his bid for freedom, it is again only because he has been driven to desperation. For a boy as passive as David, adversity so extreme that it forces him to act is a positive stimulus to his personal development.

The abilities that nature gives—to observe, imagine, and concentrate—are common to many children, David himself assures us, and are not sufficient to make an artist. The young David is almost inseparable from his surroundings, unaware of his individuality, until he becomes estranged by the alteration in his domestic situation. When his mother remarries and has Murdstone's child, David becomes increasingly aware of his alienation. His desperate need for a "kind word at that season," a word not given, reminds us of Proust's Marcel overwhelmingly conscious of his aloneness on the night when his mother refused to give him the usual goodnight kiss. David, formerly a bright, responsive child, becomes increasingly "sullen, dull, and dogged. I was not made the less so by my sense of being daily more and more shut out and alienated from my mother. I believe I should have been stupefied but for one circumstance." [76] The circumstance is the usual one in portraits of the artist—the retreat to the dream-world of books. David, like other artists from Anton Reiser to Proust's Marcel, discovers *The Arabian Nights* and other stories of romantic adventure. Through reading and imaginative reverie David is able to move from the real world of pain and loneliness into a private "great good place."

Once we recognize the temperament which nature gives to David, the estrangement which makes him aware of his individuality, and the retreat into imagination, his later development as an artist seems inevitable. From reading stories in the attic at home to telling stories to Steerforth and the other boys at school—"What ravages I com-

75. *David Copperfield*, pp. 638–639.   76. *David Copperfield*, p. 58.

mitted on my favourite authors in the course of my interpretation of them" [77]—is a likely progression, and it stems partly from David's need to establish himself as a person, to communicate—if not with others, then with himself. "I was alone in the world," he says of his first days in London, "and much given to record that circumstance in fragments of English versification." [78] This verse writing precedes the loss of his aunt's money and helps us realize that his turning to reporting and writing is not entirely accidental. Without that adversity, though, David would presumably have remained an amateur poet. The loss of the money forces David to overcome his passivity and to find his own way in the world, armed with the temperament and the talent of the artist.

That we find in David the usual components of the artistic temperament and in his life a typical progression to an artistic vocation may help to persuade us that David is capable of becoming a successful author. It does not, however, assure us that *David Copperfield* is a superior portrait of the artist nor explain what makes Dickens' novel a more distinguished work of art than the other artist-novels of its time. We recognize the temperament and the development of David as typical of the contemporaneous view of the artist, because the same concepts of the artist are stated explicitly in books like *Contarini Fleming* and *Ernest Maltravers*. Dickens' distinction is that, unlike the other writers of the period, he does not impose a theory of the artist upon his hero, but lets the vocation emerge as the result of David's unique experiences—does not, in fact, consciously write a portait-of-the-artist novel until, writing his own life story in symbolic form, he discovers that his hero, like himself, has become an artist almost unawares.

Much of the distinction of *David Copperfield* may be attributed to Dickens' approach to his material, for this is the first truly introspective novel in English fiction and thus, by one definition, the first modern novel. In the early chapters of the novel Dickens, speaking through David, tries to evoke a lost time through a deliberate recall of things past:

> The first objects that assume a distinct presence before me, as I look back into the blank of my infancy, are my mother with her pretty hair and youthful shape, and Peggotty with no shape at all, and eyes so dark that they seemed to darken their whole neighbourhood in her face, and cheeks and arms so hard and red that I wondered the birds didn't peck her in preference to apples.
>
> I believe I can remember these two at a little distance apart,

77. *David Copperfield,* pp. 98–99.   78. *David Copperfield,* p. 406.

dwarfed to my sight by stooping down or kneeling on the floor, and I going unsteadily from the one to the other. I have an impression on my mind which I cannot distinguish from actual remembrance, of the touch of Peggotty's forefinger as she used to hold it out to me, and of its being roughened by needlework, like a pocket nutmeg-grater.[79]

What is observed through memory is colored by the sensuous impressions which the objects aroused in the child. Peggotty's arms and cheeks are objectively round and hard; another novelist would perhaps use the simile "like apples," but Dickens somehow makes it clear that they seemed *to the child* so round and hard that they might be mistaken for apples by the birds. At their best, these passages of reminiscence have a reverie- and dream-like fluidity. The attempt to recapture particular objective features of the past breaks down continually because David must, in maturity as in childhood, see things imaginatively. Objects are of little interest in themselves; it is as impressions that they must be recaptured. The curious statement, "I have an impression on my mind which I cannot distinguish from actual remembrance," suggests the way in which memory is fused through sensuous impressions. The elder David, seeing Peggotty's finger in his memory picture, actually feels her work-roughened finger on his forehead. When the child David falls asleep, the elder David becomes drowsy—

Once more the little room, with its open cupboard, and its square-backed chairs, and its angular little staircase leading to the room above, and its three peacocks' feathers displayed over the mantel-piece—I remember wondering, when I first went in, what the peacock would have thought if he had known what his finery was doomed to come to—fades from before me, and I nod, and sleep. The flute becomes inaudible, the wheels of the coach are heard instead, and I am on my journey. The coach jolts, I wake with a start, and the flute has come back again, and the Master at Salem House is sitting with his legs crossed, playing it dolefully, while the old woman of the house looks on delighted. She fades in her turn, and he fades, and all fades, and there is no flute, no Master, no Salem House, no David Copperfield, no anything but heavy sleep.[80]

In fact, much of the dreamlike mood evoked by these opening chapters is the result of the wearying effort to remember, to keep

79. *David Copperfield*, p. 13.   80. *David Copperfield*, p. 80.

the memory centered on the object, and the continual breaking down. "I had reached that stage of sleepiness when Peggotty seemed to swell and grow immensely large." [81]

Some things David remembers clearly; others, such as the name of an inn where he stops on his journey to school, he confesses that he cannot recall—"I forget whether it was the Blue Bull, or the Blue Boar; but I know it was the Blue Something, and that its likeness was painted upon the back of the coach." [82] Passages like this trick us into trusting the honesty of David's exercise in voluntary memory. We have to remind ourselves that he also relates many specific details about things which he could not possibly remember. The first chapter describes the visit of Aunt Betsey to David's mother before David's birth—for example, "Miss Betsey, looking around the room, slowly and inquiringly, began on the other side, and carried her eyes on, like a Saracen's Head in a Dutch clock, until they reached my mother. Then she made a frown and a gesture to my mother, like one who was accustomed to be obeyed, to come and open the door." [83]

Of course, David, waiting to be born, cannot observe this glance any more than he can hear the dialogue that follows. Blending the deliberate, painstaking act of memory and the sensuous imaginativeness that recaptures the past are the numerous passages in which David is the omniscient author. The point of view is thus not only "double," as E. K. Brown has described it,[84] but triple: we have the David of the past as seen through the vision of the David of the present, and we have also the David who, as omniscient artist, can see both selves at once and transform actuality into the stuff of art.

When David's memory is most successful, he recaptures the past in such a way that he does not have to see it mellowed and modified by the intervening events.

> Can I say of her face—altered as I have reason to remember it, perished as I know it is—that it is gone, when here it comes before me at this instant, as distinct as any face that I may choose to look on in a crowded street? Can I say of her innocent and girlish beauty, that it faded, and was no more, when its breath falls on my cheek now, as it fell that night? Can I say she ever changed, when my remembrance brings her back to life, thus only, and, truer to its loving youth than I have been, or man ever is, still holds fast what it cherished then? [85]

81. *David Copperfield*, p. 16.
82. *David Copperfield*, p. 75.
83. *David Copperfield*, p. 4.

84. "Introduction," *David Copperfield*, p. v.
85. *David Copperfield*, p. 26.

In recapturing such moments, David feels that he is himself outside the range of time and back in the period when "we had no
future." [86] Remembrance itself is a "dim and stale oppression" [87]
until it succeeds and the act of memory may be forgotten in the
reliving what memory has evoked. Obviously, Dickens is here dealing with something less clearly formulated than Proust's theory of
the "unconscious memory," but, as in Proust, the attempt is not only
to remember the past, but to re-experience it and thus win a victory
over the time that destroys.

In the illusion of timelessness, in the sensuousness of his impressions, David is faithful to what we know of childish sensitivity.
In the mind of the child everything is alive: "I felt the words of
my lessons slipping off, not one by one, or line by line, but by the
entire page. I tried to lay hold of them; but they seemed, if I may
so express it, to have put skates on, and to skim away from me with
a smoothness there was no checking." [88] The letters of the alphabet
are transformed into people—"the easy good-nature of O and Q
and S" [89]—and David, not yet conscious of his uniqueness as a
person, thinks of himself as an object—"the clerk . . . presently
slanted me off the scale, and pushed me over to him, as if I were
weighed, bought, delivered, and paid for." [90] This quality of childlike sensitivity is one that Dickens retained; it is, as Dorothy Van
Ghent and others have shown,[91] a distinguishing characteristic of
Dickens' vision, his special aura. David, seeking to recapture the
child's world, seems thus to be seeking his essential self. He attempts
to justify the accuracy of his memory pictures: "I think the memory of most of us can go further back into such times than many of
us suppose, much as I believe the power of observation in numbers
of very young children to be quite wonderful for its closeness and
accuracy. Indeed, I think that most grown men who are remarkable
in this respect, may with greater propriety be said not to have lost
the faculty, than to have acquired it; the rather as I generally observe such men to retain a certain freshness, and gentleness, and
capacity of being pleased, which are also an inheritance they have
preserved from childhood." [92] The artist in Dickens retains the
child's vision of life. If this explains some of his weaknesses as a
novelist—his philosophical naiveté, his inability to write of sexual
love, his sentimentality—it explains also some of his unique powers.

86. *David Copperfield*, p. 40.
87. *David Copperfield*, p. 61.
88. *David Copperfield*, p. 60.
89. *David Copperfield*, p. 55.
90. *David Copperfield*, p. 77.

91. See, for example, Dorothy Van
Ghent, *The English Novel: Form
and Content* (New York: Rinehart,
1953), pp. 127–128.
92. *David Copperfield*, p. 13.

Seeming actuality distorted by the imagination, numerous images of sentient things, grotesque characters swelling larger and deflating smaller than life, a technique of "signatures," a compulsive imagery of retreats that resemble a child's attic or treetop "castle," a constant fluidity of time and space—these are the things that make Dickens' art childlike. The artist in Dickens is always an Alice in Wonderland.

What I have been saying of *David Copperfield* applies only to the first quarter of the book, when the attempt to evoke the lost world of the child's imagination, to achieve self-justification, has not yet given way to the objectivity of experience. David, like the artist in Dickens if not the man, is allowed to retain the child's vision. Once David meets his fairy godmother, that vision is protected. His character as artist is already set; it requires no further demonstration. What happens after may be seen as an illustration of his skill. Once the validity of the observer has been demonstrated, the external world dominates the action, as it does in *Moby-Dick, Madame Bovary, The House of the Seven Gables,* or those other novels in which the first-person narrator gives way to the third person while continuing to pin actuality to individual impressions. Unlike the other artist-apprentice novels of the mid-century, *David Copperfield* reveals the artistry of its hero; it does not merely talk about it. It is a portrait of the artist seen from within. The process is similar to that in James's "The Birthplace." We cannot know the artist by talking about him, any more than the hero of James's story can justify his attempts to provide specific details of Shakespeare's life. A compromise is somehow dishonest, and the only solution is for the commentator himself to become an artist. Art takes over—and that, essentially, is what happens in *David Copperfield*. And if David seems to become the least vivid character in the novel, it is because the artist in David is equated with his experiences.

III   *Tapping the Sacred Fount*

PERHAPS one reason why many readers find the mature David Copperfield an unconvincing artist is that he is happily married. In the artist-novels that followed in abundance during the late nineteenth and early twentieth centuries, the artist is often forced to choose between woman and vocation, and only rarely does he achieve fulfillment as both artist and lover. In spite of the Hollywood myth that behind every great man stands a loyal woman, most portraits of the artist assume that sexual love and artistic creation are in conflict.

In the later apprentice novels that flourished in England and America from about 1880 to 1920, the hero is often a gifted young man who is ultimately defeated by passion. In such novels as Samuel Butler's *The Way of All Flesh,* Hardy's *Jude the Obscure,* and Somerset Maugham's *Of Human Bondage,* a sensitive young man who seems destined for better things finds himself entrapped by a woman who is unworthy of him. Occasionally—as in Compton Mackenzie's *Sinister Street*—the hero passes successfully through the experience and finds himself the better for it, but more often the discovery of his human bondage destroys whatever artistic aspirations or ability he may have. Several of George Gissing's novels reflect the situation of his own life, and in the enslavement of such heroes as Arthur Golding of *Workers in the Dawn* and Edward Reardon of *New Grub Street* to their prostitute wives he represented his acceptance of a common myth of the late nineteenth century, woman as the *femme fatale,* the destructive element capable of destroying a man's career.[93] The painter Logan in Gilbert Cannan's *Mendel: A Story of Youth* falls in love with a voluptuous girl whose vitality is so much greater than his own that she ruins both his manhood and his art. The heroes of Arnold Bennett's *A Man from the North* and J. D. Beresford's Jacob Stahl trilogy [94] decline in artistic aspirations in direct ratio to their declining taste in women: after unhappy love affairs with ladies of the upper class and women of the middle class, the one hero marries a restaurant cashier, the other settles down to a common-law relationship with a boardinghouse keeper; both find "happiness," but lose their artistic ambitions in the process. A reverse decline is to be found in Wyndham Lewis' *Tarr.* As the novel opens, Frederick Tarr, a young English painter, defends his relations with Bertha Lunken, a German girl as earthy as her name:

> "Why am I associated sexually with that irritating nullity? First of all, I am an artist. With most people, who are not artists, all the finer part of their vitality goes into sex if it goes anywhere: during their courtship they become third-rate poets, all their instincts of drama come out freshly with their wives. The artist is he in whom this emotionality normally absorbed by sex is so strong that it claims a newer and more exclusive field of deployment . . . one by one his powers are turned away from the usual

93. On artist-novels of the period by Gissing and others, see Bernard Bergonzi, "The Novelist as Hero," *Twentieth Century,* CLXIV (November, 1958), 444–455.

94. *The Early History of Jacob Stahl* (1911), *A Candidate for Truth* (1911), and *The Invisible Event* (1915).

object of a man's personal poetry or passion and so removed from the immediate world. One solitary thing is left facing any woman with whom he has commerce, that is his sex, a lonely phallus." [95]

In time, though, Tarr grows weary of Bertha and "in the interests of his animalism he was about to betray the artist in him: for he had of late been saying to himself that he must really endeavour to find a more suitable lady-companion, one he need not to be ashamed of. 'Life' would be given a chance." [96] He finds the more suitable companion in Anastasya Vasek, who is not only more intellectual and presentable than Bertha, but "in the sex department, . . . a Juggernaut." [97] From this point on we hear little of Tarr's art, for he has come back into life and, as he knew all along, "Surrender to a woman was a sort of suicide for the artist." [98]

The promising musician in Henry Handel Richardson's *Maurice Guest* kills himself, Werther-like, when the woman he loves marries another. But judging from the stories in which the artist-heroes possess the women they love, frustration is better for artistic productivity than attainment. Jocelyn Pierston, the sculptor-hero of Thomas Hardy's strange romance *The Well-Beloved: A Sketch of a Temperament,* finds the key to artistic success in an unattained ideal. At twenty he loves Avice Caro; at forty, her daughter; at sixty, her granddaughter. Desiring but never capturing "the migratory, elusive idealization he called his Love who, ever since his boyhood, had flitted from human shell to human shell an indefinite number of times," [99] Jocelyn remains a young man for more than sixty years while the ideal, which is simply mortal "life," passes from generation to generation until, his work completed, the spell is broken and he finds "his sense of beauty in art and nature absolutely extinct." [100]

Several of the artists in fiction of the period pass beyond their need for "life" by becoming thoroughly dedicated to their art. When Thea Kronborg in Willa Cather's *The Song of the Lark* is reproached for not having enough private life, she replies, "I don't have any. Your work becomes your personal life. You are not much good until it does. It's like being woven into a big web. You can't pull away, because all your little tendrils are woven into the picture. It takes you up, and uses you, and spins you out; and that is your life. Not much else can happen to you." [101] But there are also those

95. *Tarr* (London: Methuen, 1951), pp. 11–12. The text used in this edition of the novel is that of Lewis's 1928 revision.
96. *Tarr,* p. 220.
97. *Tarr,* p. 344.
98. *Tarr,* p. 221.

99. *Works,* Wessex Edition (London: Macmillan, 1912), XIII, 7.
100. *Works,* XIII, 213–214.
101. *Novels and Stories of Willa Cather,* Library Edition (Boston: Houghton Mifflin, 1937), II, 546.

who seem to achieve success through their ability to "fearlessly accept or reject what life offered." [102] Even as most of Henry James's artists manage to make the best of two worlds, so Romain Rolland's Jean-Christophe assimilates a variety of experiences and emerges as a true master.

Just as frequently, though, the artist who thinks that he has triumphed over life finds that life has a way of taking its revenge. A sensuous nature that has remained long dormant suddenly awakens, as in Thomas Mann's *Death in Venice*. Frank Norris' Vandover tries desperately to find refuge in art, but as the "brute" in him becomes stronger than his higher nature, he deteriorates to the point where he crawls naked on the floor and howls like a wolf. In his quest of art and self-development, Jack London's Martin Eden passes beyond his need for love, society, and fame, but grows indifferent even toward art and self and, a complete nihilist, drowns himself. The implication in such works is that the artist who separates himself from life carries a burden of guilt which he must eventually expiate. Theories of the artist as a criminal or a neurotic and hence art as disease were prominent around the turn of the century: Cesar Lombroso offered scientific "proof" of the alliance of the genius and the criminal; Max Nordau used it as the basis for his attack on modern art in *Degeneration,* and Émile Zola adapted the notion in his genealogy of the Rougon-Macquart family by making his artist the brother of a homicidal maniac. Thomas Mann never tired of dealing with the artist-criminal paradox, and in *Doctor Faustus* brought the theme to its fullest dramatic realization. Adrian Leverkuhn's pact with the devil is made on the literal level when he voluntarily has sexual relations with a young prostitute he knows to be venereally diseased. By thus separating himself from normal, healthy mankind, Adrian is enabled to become a great composer, and it is thoroughly consistent that the unknown benefactress who helps him in his later years should be the prostitute who started him on the road to greatness.[103] If, as usually interpreted, *Doctor Faustus* is a social and political allegory as well as a portrait of the artist, and if Adrian represents Nazi Germany, the implication is that art, which manifests itself in detachment, and "life," which manifests itself in aggression, are intimately related and must share guilt. Adrian must sin to be an artist, and he does so by tapping a Sacred Fount which he knows to be polluted.

102. Compton Mackenzie, *Sinister Street* (London: Martin Secker, 1923), p. 630.
103. See Victor A. Oswald, Jr., "The Enigma of Frau von Tolna," *Germanic Review*, XXIII (December, 1948), 249–253.

TO realize that the cult of art as experience remains alive in the twentieth century, we have only to think of Ernest Hemingway, the French Existentialists, and the contemporary Bohemians we call beatniks. However, if there is one major modern novelist who best represents the tradition, it is D. H. Lawrence; and just as *David Copperfield* is the best exemplum of the early apprentice-novel—a novel which both typifies the group and goes beyond it—so we may find in *Sons and Lovers* a "life" novel that not only seems based on the theory of the Sacred Fount, but also shows how the true artist may make use of life without being destroyed in the process.

Readers who object to what has been called Lawrence's "unrestrained emotionalism over glandular matters" [104] overlook the fact that for Lawrence sex is not just something to put into a novel or leave out. In *Fantasia of the Unconscious* he described his novels and poems as "pure passionate experience," [105] and in a letter to a friend confessed that "work is produced by passion with me, like kisses." [106] A character in *Lady Chatterley's Lover* proclaims, "Renior said he painted his pictures with his penis. . . . He did too, lovely pictures." [107] Because "sex is a creative flow," Lawrence frequently exalts it as a source of creative renewal and describes coition as an exploratory searching that "enables man and woman to go to the deepest sources of their natures, and thus to understand themselves," [108] which is precisely what Lawrence seems to have attempted in his art. When near the end of *Sons and Lovers* Paul Morel says to himself, "you can go on with your painting, . . . or else you can beget children," [109] Lawrence asserts that sexual and artistic creativity offer two ways out of despair; and in spite of the "or else" which separates painting from begetting children, Lawrence treats them as equivalents. I see in this a clue to one of the fundamental themes of *Sons and Lovers,* for if that novel is about

104. Van Ghent, *The English Novel,* p. 245.
105. (New York, 1922), p. xiv.
106. *Letters,* ed. Aldous Huxley (New York: Viking Press, 1932), p. ix. Compare with the following statement from his Foreword to *Women in Love:* "In point of style, fault is often found with the continual, slightly modified repetition. The only answer is that it is natural to the author; and that every natural crisis in emotion or passion or understanding comes from this pulsing, frictional to-and-fro which works up to culmination"—Compass Books Edition (New York: Viking Press, 1960), p. viii.
107. (New York: Grove Press, 1959), p. 44.
108. Frederick J. Hoffman, "Lawrence's Quarrel with Freud," in Hoffman and Harry T. Moore, eds., *The Achievement of D. H. Lawrence* (Norman: University of Oklahoma Press, 1953), p. 122.
109. *Sons and Lovers* (New York: Modern Library, n.d.), p. 481. Quotations from *Sons and Lovers* are made with the permission of Viking Press.

love, as everyone agrees that it is, then it is also about art—not merely because Paul is an artist as well as a son and a lover, but, more importantly, because Lawrence sees the sexual act as similar to the creative process.

Lawrence's insistence on art as experience, a corollary of which is his likening of the artistic process to the sex act, puts him in the tradition of those writers who feel that the richness of a work of art may be measured by the completeness and intensity of the felt life manifested in the work. Believing this, Lawrence was eager to recruit the assistance of those who had shared his experiences, as when he drew upon Jessie Chambers and Frieda Lawrence for the writing of *Sons and Lovers*. The more viewpoints represented in the work, the more felt life. "Form for him," Graham Hough has written, "was the embodiment of an experience, and a form not lived through in experience was impossible to him." [110] This conception of art places Lawrence outside the tradition represented by such writers as James, Flaubert, and Joyce, writers who held that the artist must remain detached from life in order to see it clearly and who produced static works of art dealing often, it is true, with personal experience, but experience somehow finished, exhausted, and thus subject to the artist's deliberate control and manipulation. Lawrence's art is more kinetic; the experience is lived in the process of writing as Lawrence, like Melville in *Moby-Dick,* explores a situation which he does not fully understand. The poem or novel becomes a purgation and works out its fulfillment, so that the artist is liberated from *that* experience and released for others which, in turn, will be lived through both progressively and destructively until they also are turned into art. Each successful work of art—like each successful sexual union, Lawrence would say—represents a creative renewal.

In the final version of *Sons and Lovers* the artist theme is scarcely the dominant one. Paul Morel's relationship to himself and his art is less apparent to the reader than his relationship to the women in his life, his mother, Miriam Leivers, and Clara Dawes. Presumably the two earlier versions of the novel (which Lawrence called *Paul Morel*) were closer to the *Bildungsroman* tradition than is the finished version, and it is probable that in the early drafts Paul's development as an artist received more emphasis. Perhaps because Frieda Lawrence's enthusiastic adoption of Freudian theory helped Lawrence to alter the emphasis from Paul as an individual to his representative role as son and lover, the artist theme tends to be subordinated. Nonetheless, an understanding of the artist theme helps to

110. *The Dark Sun: A Study of D.*   lan, 1957), p. 41.
H. *Lawrence* (New York: Macmil-

clear up some of the mysteries of the novel which have not yet been satisfactorily explained by the more obvious themes.

These themes are identified in Lawrence's letter to Edward Garnett, and no interpretation of *Sons and Lovers* can afford to ignore the author's own statement of intention:

> It follows this idea: a woman of character and refinement goes into the lower class, and has no satisfaction in her own life. She has had a passion for her husband, so the children are born of passion, and have heaps of vitality. But as her sons grow up she selects them as lovers—first the eldest, then the second. These sons are *urged* into life by their reciprocal love of their mother—urged on and on. But when they come to manhood, they can't love, because their mother is the strongest power of their lives, and holds them. . . . As soon as the young men come into contact with women, there's a split. William gives his sex to a fribble, and his mother holds his soul. But the split kills him, because he doesn't know where he is. The next son gets a woman who fights for his soul—fights his mother. The son loves the mother—all the sons hate and are jealous of the father. The battle goes on between the mother and the girl, with the son as object. The mother gradually proves stronger, because of the tie of blood. The son decides to leave his soul in his mother's hands, and, like his elder brother, go for passion. He gets passion. Then the split begins to tell again. But, almost unconsciously, the mother realizes what is the matter, and begins to die. The son casts off his mistress, attends to his mother dying. He is left in the end naked of everything, with the drift towards death.[111]

Two related themes are suggested by Lawrence's précis. The dominant one is that of the Oedipus complex. This leads to Paul's repression, an aspect of which is the second theme: loving his mother too deeply, Paul cannot get body and soul together in his relations with other women. Therefore, Paul is "split," and the novel itself, according to Mark Schorer,[112] is also split between the sections describing Paul's love of his mother and those describing his relations with Miriam and Clara. I believe that the stalemate between these two themes is ultimately overcome through the emergence of a third theme: the liberating force of artistic creativity. Unless there is some such resolving theme, we would have to agree with Schorer that the novel is split not only between intention and performance, but also

111. *Letters,* pp. 78–79.
112. "Technique as Discovery," in John W. Aldridge, ed., *Critiques and*

Essays on Modern Fiction, 1920–1951 (New York: Ronald Press, 1952), pp. 74–75.

between idea and form, and we should have to agree in turn with those critics who feel that the last part of the novel is a failure.

As many commentators have pointed out, Lawrence's account of the novel is an unreliable description of the story we read. If the book ended with the death of the mother and the defeat of Paul, the formula would work generally if not in all details. However, Paul is eventually regenerated and, far from drifting toward death —at least in its conventional meaning—seems at the end of the story to be liberated and redeemed so that he can move on to life. The obvious inadequacy of Lawrence's understanding of the book he had written lends support to the view that *Sons and Lovers* contains a buried theme that enabled Lawrence subconsciously to resolve conflicts which are unsolvable on the conscious level. Paul is once described as "producing good stuff without knowing what he was doing." [113] So with Lawrence.

It seems to me apparent that neither the Freudian reading nor one which emphasizes the concept of a split answers some of the questions raised by a close reading of the novel. If it is intended to illustrate the case of a young man defeated by an Oedipus complex, how do we explain the fact that Paul becomes a friend and protector of the father-surrogate, Baxter Dawes, that he deliberately kills his mother, or that, with Clara at any rate, there is little evidence of sexual inhibition? Similarly, if we see the novel primarily in terms of the "split" theme, which would have Clara represent physical love and Miriam cerebral love, how do we justify the befogging of this theme through Paul's physical intimacy with Miriam? Mark Spilka asks another key question—who defeats Miriam and Clara? —and answers it by saying not the mother, as the Freudian commentators would have it, but their own inadequacies.[114] Just as important, I would say, is that hard core of aloneness in Paul which none of his women can share.

Paul Morel is sensitive, shy, and introverted—traits associated with the stereotype of the artistic temperament. He is an intent observer of things, and has the "impersonal, deliberate gaze of an artist." [115] He has the faculty of concentrating on his work to the exclusion of everything around him; and though he has misgivings about everything else, "he believed firmly in his work, that it was good and valuable. In spite of fits of depression, shrinking, everything, he believed in his work." [116] That, however little we may hear directly of his art in *Sons and Lovers*, Paul Morel is clearly a true artist is

113. *Sons and Lovers*, p. 451.   versity Press, 1955), p. 74.
114. *The Love Ethic of D. H. Law-*   115. *Sons and Lovers*, p. 220.
     rence (Bloomington: Indiana Uni-   116. *Sons and Lovers*, p. 354.

shown not only by such internal evidence, but also by the fact that
to the extent any fictional character may be equated with its living
model, Paul is a self-portrait of Lawrence. We are told that Paul
"loved to paint large pictures, full of light, but not merely made up
of lights and cast shadows, like the impressionists; rather definite
figures that had a certain luminous quality, like some of Michael
Angelo's people. And these he fitted into a landscape, in what he
thought true proportion. He worked a great deal from memory,
using everybody he knew." [117] This description of Paul's art—one
of the few given in the novel—would apply to Lawrence's fiction as
well as his painting. Paul is supposed to be a painter, not a writer,
but in one passage Lawrence makes a telling slip: "Often he could
not go on with his work. The pen stopped writing." [118]

Paul has innately the temperament and the talent that are the
essential qualities of the artist. However, these are not enough in
themselves. The artist-to-be must also be motivated. The artist theme
blends with the Oedipus theme when we are told that Paul's first
motivation was simply his desire to please his mother: "When she
was quiet so, she looked brave and rich with life, but as if she had
been done out of her rights. It hurt the boy keenly, this feeling
about her that she had never had her life's fulfillment: and his own
incapability to make up to her hurt him with a sense of impotence,
yet made him patiently dogged inside. It was his childish aim." [119]
Gift offerings to the mother-queen Gertrude provide a running
motif throughout the novel. In the climax of the first scene, William's gift of two egg cups, a feminine symbol as the Freudian interpreters make clear, is received gratefully, while the father's gift
of a coconut, "a hairy object," is accepted begrudgingly: "A man
will part with anything so long as he's drunk," said Mrs. Morel." [120]
Later William brings his athletic trophies to his mother, like a knight
to his lady, and Paul offers her his early drawings, like a court painter
offering pictures to his queen. When Paul wins two first prizes in an
exhibition, his mother is as exultant as if she had herself produced
them: "Paul was going to distinguish himself. She had a great belief in him, the more because he was unaware of his own powers.
There was so much to come out of him. She was to see herself fulfilled. Not for nothing had been her struggle." [121] Even at the end
of the novel, when Paul is fighting against the despair caused by
his mother's death, his justification for going on by painting or by
begetting children is that "they both carry on her effort." [122]

117. *Sons and Lovers*, p. 354.
118. *Sons and Lovers*, p. 452.
119. *Sons and Lovers*, p. 80.

120. *Sons and Lovers*, p. 10.
121. *Sons and Lovers*, p. 217.
122. *Sons and Lovers*, p. 481.

The struggle between Gertrude Morel and Miriam Leivers is not simply the vying of two women for Paul's love, but the jealous struggle of two patronesses for the homage of the artist and the right to control him. Miriam, in fact, often seems to be a muse—a "shy, wild, quiveringly sensitive thing" [123] who "always looked so lost and out of place among people." [124] No wonder then that Paul thinks that "she could scarcely stand the shock of physical love, even a passionate kiss." [125] Yet, because for Lawrence the artist's muse cannot be dissociated from his sexuality, Paul uses Miriam to bring forth his art in a way that Lawrence describes in obviously sexual terms: "There was for him the most intense pleasure in talking about his work to Miriam. All his passion, all his wild blood, went into this intercourse with her, when he talked and conceived his work. She brought forth to him his imaginations. She did not understand, any more than a woman understands when she conceives a child in her womb." [126] In view of this, it is not surprising that Paul's possessing her physically should become a dramatic necessity for the novel. Only then does Paul realize that even as muse she is false. She gives herself to him as a kind of sacrifice, but her aim is to possess by giving, without realizing that she must either keep her distance like a true muse or really be sacrificed if Paul is to move from one phase of his artistic development to another. She is "always most interested in him as he appeared in his work" [127] and essentially indifferent to him physically. Like his mother, therefore, she is not jealous of Clara Dawes, for she thinks that after Paul has "achieved his baptism of fire in passion," he will return to her, "for he would want to be owned, so that he could work." [128] Like his mother, too, she is not repudiated even after she has been sacrificed, for she has become assimilated into Paul and made use of, just as Jessie Chambers, by her own account, was used, then sacrificed for the writing of *Sons and Lovers*.[129] In keeping with Miriam's function as muse, it is her visit to Paul's apartment in the last chapter which reawakens his interest in his art and enables him to realize that "work *can* be nearly everything to a man." [130]

Clara Dawes has happened to Paul in the meantime, and if the main trouble with Miriam is that "she could not take him and relieve him of the responsibility of himself," [131] it is partly because Paul has already discovered through Clara the liberating force

123. *Sons and Lovers*, p. 170.
124. *Sons and Lovers*, p. 483.
125. *Sons and Lovers*, p. 211.
126. *Sons and Lovers*, p. 239.
127. *Sons and Lovers*, p. 485.
128. *Sons and Lovers*, p. 373.

129. *D. H. Lawrence: A Personal Record* (London: Jonathan Cape, 1935).
130. *Sons and Lovers*, p. 486.
131. *Sons and Lovers*, p. 489.

which frees him from himself at the very moment when he becomes self-fulfilled. Clara, too, is presented in symbolic terms: she is Big Blonde Woman, sensuous and coarse, yet—as befits the mother-surrogate in the novel, also withdrawn and dignified. If she is a queen mother, she is also a Molly Bloom or a Eula Varner, and the contradictions in her make-up are those that we expect to find in the earth-moon-sea goddess who appears in so many guises throughout literature. Whereas Paul first possesses Miriam in bed, he takes Clara on the ground, after a compulsive, symbolic ordeal which brings them from the highway down a difficult riverbank so that their first physical intimacy may occur as close to the river as possible. Clara is associated with water—like the girl standing in midstream at the moment of consecration in Joyce's *Portrait of the Artist* —and the strongest image of Clara is when she stands naked and outlined against the immensity of the sea. But when, in this moment of realization, the moon disappears and Paul sees her "dazzled out of sight by the sunshine," she appears to grow smaller, to change from sea goddess to mere woman to "just a concentrated speck blown along, a tiny white foam-bubble, almost nothing among the morning";[132] and it is at this moment that Paul realizes that he no longer needs her.

Because of Paul's Oedipal situation, he can be liberated and fulfilled, made whole as a man, only through a full sexual initiation. To the extent that Clara, like Miriam, is a surrogate for Paul's mother, Paul's intimacy with Clara carries overtones of incest and thus follows closely the archetypal "solution" to the Oedipal situation in literature.[133] Whereas with Miriam in the sex act, Paul remained self-conscious, fumbling, guilt-stricken—partly at least because the similarity between Miriam and his mother was apparent to him—with Clara he finds himself carried away from self through passion. Lawrence's description of the sex act sounds like accounts by poets of the creative process in moments of true inspiration when the afflatus descends upon the artist and carries him along in spite of himself:

> As a rule, when he started love-making, the emotion was strong enough to carry with it everything—reason, soul, blood—in a great sweep, like the Trent carries bodily its back-swirls and intertwinings, noiselessly. Gradually, the little criticisms, the little sensations, were lost, thought also went, everything borne along in one flood. He became, not a man with a mind, but a great instinct.

132. *Sons and Lovers,* p. 420.
133. See William Wasserstrom, "In Gertrude's Closet," *Yale Review,* XLVIII (Winter 1959), 245–265.

His hands were like creatures, living; his limbs, his body, were all life and consciousness, subject to no will of his, but living in themselves. Just as he was, so it seemed the vigorous, wintry stars were strong also with life. He and they struck with the same pulse of fire, and the same joy of strength which held the bracken-frond stiff near his eyes held his own body firm. It was as if he, and the stars, and the dark herbage, and Clara were licked up in an immense tongue of flame, which tore onwards and upwards. Everything rushed along in living beside him; everything was still, perfect in itself, along with him. This wonderful stillness in each thing in itself, while it was being borne along in a very ecstasy of living, seemed the highest point of bliss.[134]

Just as inspiration comes to the artist involuntarily and cannot be forced, so Paul and Clara discover that their lovemaking becomes less satisfactory when they begin to experiment in an attempt to bring back lost glamor: "And afterwards each of them was rather ashamed, and these things caused a distance between the two of them." [135]

Ultimately, though, Paul and Clara draw apart simply because she demands too much of him. She wants to love all the time—during the day, in broad sunlight, at work—whereas Paul is for Lawrence typically masculine in that he is interested in love only sporadically, taking the conventional view that there is a right time and place for everything. For man, Lawrence implies, sex is not the end, but a means. According to Frederick Hoffman's synopsis of Lawrence's philosophy of sex, "man should go beyond the crucial union of egoes which is the act of coition. For him it is the source of renewal, which should serve to drive him forward into creative group life. Woman offers the nucleus of further renewal, and supplements her husband's life by turning him back from time to time to the fountain source of his strength." [136] The battle between the sexes is largely the result of this fundamental difference, for with woman love is the center of life; the creative act; for men it is only a bridge to creation. Thus Paul lectures Miriam:

"A woman only works with a part of herself. The real and vital part is covered up."
"But a man can give *all* himself to a work?" she asked.
"Yes, practically."
"And a woman only the unimportant part of herself?"
"That's it."

134. *Sons and Lovers*, pp. 426–427.   136. Hoffman, p. 122.
135. *Sons and Lovers*, p. 427.

The trouble with Miriam is that as an intellectual she would deny this—

> She looked up at him, and her eyes dilated with anger.
> "Then," she said, "if it's true, it's a great shame." [137]

Clara, on the other hand, exults in her womanhood and offers Paul the dignity of a man-woman struggle as she strives to possess him completely and he fights to retain his independence. Because they are opposites, his satisfactory unions with her resolve all differences and give him a feeling of wholeness, of utter stasis in the midst of movement, if only momentarily.

Whereas Clara offers Paul the chance for a genuine struggle for dominance between a man and a woman, both his mother and Miriam assume that he "would want to be owned so that he could work." What they fail to realize is that there is a side to Paul which can never be owned—that side which shows itself in those moments of work when he is abstracted, "producing good stuff without knowing what he was doing." Even while his mother lies dying, he finds it possible to abstract himself and to work on his pictures, oblivious to all around him. This trait also parallels the successful lovemaking, for when Clara protests,

> "But you've never given me yourself."
> He knitted his brows angrily.
> "If I start to make love to you," he said, "I just go like a leaf down the wind."
> "And leave me out of count," she said.[138]

In this inability to give himself completely, Paul is very much like Aaron Sisson of *Aaron's Rod*, and the later novel deals openly with an aspect of Lawrence's character that is only dimly presented in *Sons and Lovers*. Aaron has "a hard, opposing core in him," [139] and "his very being pivoted on the fact of his isolate self-responsibility, aloneness." [140] Thus: "He never gave himself. He never came to her, *really*. He withheld himself. Yes, in those supreme and sacred times which for her were the whole culmination of life and being, the ecstasy of unspeakable passional conjunction, he was not really hers. He was withheld. He withheld the central core of himself, like the devil and hell-fiend he was. He cheated and made play with her tremendous passional soul, her sacred sex passion, most sacred

137. *Sons and Lovers*, pp. 486–487.   mann, 1954), p. 18.
138. *Sons and Lovers*, p. 426.   140. *Aaron's Rod*, p. 158.
139. *Aaron's Rod* (London: Heine-

of all things for a woman. All the time, some central part of him stood apart from her, aside, looking on." [141] Aaron, too, is an artist, and his flute, with its obvious phallic connotation, is not only the means of his art, but also a symbol of his aloneness. It is significant that Lawrence represents art by means of a strongly masculine symbol, for it is only such a conjunction that enables us to understand the leading thesis in *Sons and Lovers* that a man's work, his art, is something that can never be fully shared with women.

In the typical portrait-of-the-artist novel, the hero, blessed from the beginning with talent and the right temperament, becomes motivated through allegiance to some kind of "master," often represented by a father, mother, or lover, then after a period of apprenticeship involving commitment to the standards of his chosen master finds it necessary to break away in order to become master in his own right. I have pointed out that Paul has the talent and temperament of the true artist and that he is motivated through a mother-worship represented dramatically in terms of his relations with the two mother-surrogates, Miriam and Clara. It remains necessary to consider the process of liberation.

In his phase of apprenticeship, Paul tries to deny the existence in himself of the qualities which he associates with his father. Walter Morel, for all his apparent sociability, is "an outsider," [142] thoroughly masculine in his interests and abilities. A good workman and skillful craftsman who sings when absorbed in his work, he too is an incipient artist, the best dancer in the village and once master of a dancing school. He breaks away from his wife, in much the same fashion and for basically the same reasons as did Aaron Sisson, for he too has a hard core of aloneness and finds it impossible to submit to his wife's domination. His realm is the black pit of the mine, and throughout the novel he is associated symbolically with the forces of night and darkness. Just as Aaron is compared to "the devil and hell-fiend," so Walter Morel "had denied the God in him." [143]

Paul begins to free himself from the oppression of his mother when he assumes the role of the father. Thus when he makes love to Clara he reverts unconsciously to the speech of Walter Morel. But the return of the father is best represented in terms of Paul's relationship with Baxter Dawes, Clara's estranged husband. As Daniel Weiss has pointed out, Baxter is physically similar to Walter Morel and, like him, works with his hands and is the rejected husband of an educated woman. [144] In the beginning there is natural

141. *Aaron's Rod*, p. 156.
142. *Sons and Lovers*, p. 77.
143. *Sons and Lovers*, p. 77.

144. "Oedipus in Nottinghamshire," *Literature and Psychology*, VII (August, 1957), 36.

hostility between Baxter and Paul, similar to that between Paul and
his father, but whereas the physical fights which threaten to occur
between Paul (and William) with the father are always stopped
by the mother's intervention, Paul and Baxter finally come together
in actual battle. Significantly, the fight takes place at night, in mine-
like darkness, and there can be little doubt that it is seen by Lawrence as a symbolic ordeal by which Paul proves his masculinity,
even though in suddenly submitting to the other man and taking a
beating he does so unconventionally. The growing friendship between Paul and Baxter after the fight is less mysterious than it seems
on the surface, for now the two men are more alike than different.
To some extent, Paul shares Baxter's illness and recuperation—
traditional symbols of death and rebirth in the *Bildungsroman*.
Finally, Paul, who already realizes that Clara is a bridge for him
rather than his goal, engineers a reconciliation between Clara and
Baxter. If Gertrude Morel suggests Hamlet's mother, so Paul is like
Hamlet in that he stages a drama, with Clara and Baxter as player-
queen and player-king, that represents his own internal conflict.
When he plays thus the artist, he is already a long way on the road
to emancipation. He has admitted the father in himself.

It remains necessary for Paul to destroy his dead self. This, I
think, is represented in the novel by Mrs. Morel's death. Paul kills
his mother by giving her an overdose of medicine. The ethics of
euthanasia aside, this form of death is not dramatically necessary in
the novel; in fact, if the novel were intended only to show the defeat
of Paul, it would be better for Mrs. Morel simply to die. Instead,
she clings desperately to life, fearing to the end the forces of darkness. The conflict of man-will and woman-will culminates in Paul's
giving her—fitting climax to the gift-offering motif in the novel—
the bitter cup of poison which kills her and a part of himself, but
which frees him for a new life.

After the death of Mrs. Morel, it is natural that Paul should
undergo a period of despair in which the feeling of emptiness which
engulfs him is so strong that he ceases even to practice his art. He is
derelict now, truly alienated in that he feels a barrier between himself and the life around him: "He could not get in touch." [145] Like
his father, he too is now an outsider. But this is a period of symbolic
death for Paul, necessary if he is to be liberated from the restrictions
of his apprenticeship, and he waits to be reborn into a new life. The
visit from Miriam makes him realize that the past which she represents is now dead for him—"and they went out talking together, he
talking, she feeling dead." [146] After he has left her, however, he

145. *Sons and Lovers*, p. 482.   146. *Sons and Lovers*, p. 490.

suddenly experiences a moment of consecration very similar to that experienced by Stephen Dedalus in Joyce's *Portrait:*

> Whatever spot he stood on, there he stood alone. From his breast, from his mouth, sprang the endless space, and it was there behind him, everywhere. The people hurrying along the streets offered no obstruction to the void in which he found himself. They were small shadows whose footsteps and voices could be heard, but in each of them the same night, the same silence. He got off the car. In the country all was dead still. Little stars shone high up; little stars spread far away in the flood-waters, a firmament below. Everywhere the vastness and terror of the immense night which is roused and stirred for a brief while by the day, but which returns, and will remain at last eternal, holding everything in its silence and its living gloom. There was no Time, only Space. . . . On every side the immense dark silence seemed pressing him, so tiny a spark, into extinction, and yet, almost nothing, he could not be extinct. Night, in which everything was lost, went reaching out, beyond stars and sun. Stars and sun, a few bright grains, went spinning round for terror, and holding each other in embrace, there in a darkness that outpassed them all, and left them tiny and daunted. So much, and himself, infinitesimal, at the core a nothingness, and yet not nothing.[147]

Stephen Dedalus and Paul share in their moments of baptismal consecration the feeling of complete aloneness, the sensation that they are outside time, and the awareness of perfect stasis even in the midst of movement. Stephen, though, almost immediately feels triumphant. With Paul there is as much terror as triumph. Twice he whimpers "Mother!," then suddenly knows that "she was gone, intermingled herself." [148] The novel concludes: "But no, he would not give in. Turning sharply, he walked towards the city's gold phosphorescence. His fists were shut, his mouth set fast. He would not take that direction, to the darkness, to follow her. He walked towards the faintly humming, glowing town, quickly." [149] The ending is ambiguous, though most readers would agree that it appears to be more affirmative than negative. He will not follow his mother into death, though if Lawrence really meant to leave him "with the drift towards death," as he wrote to Garnett, he must have meant that Paul cannot leave his mother entirely behind, that he and she and everything are now "intermingled" and that he carries this

147. *Sons and Lovers*, pp. 490–491.   149. *Sons and Lovers*, p. 491.
148. *Sons and Lovers*, p. 491.

realization into a new phase of life.[150] If "quickly" suggests life (the quick and the dead), as Harry Moore has argued,[151] Paul is committing himself to the "faintly humming, glowing town" just as Stephen shouts "Welcome, O life" at the same time as he rejects the dead life of his past. Joyce's description of Stephen at the moment of consecration—"His soul had arisen from the grave of boyhood, spurning her grave-clothes"[152]—could apply to Paul as well. Both Joyce and Lawrence conclude their portraits of the artist with the heroes, having tested and found wanting the claims of love and family, poised for exile, but an exile which is to lead to creative renewal.

Seymour Betsky has said that "*Sons and Lovers* is a purgation become the successful work of art."[153] The novel itself thus stands for the transformation of life into art. Lawrence has tapped the Sacred Fount and used up the life which finds its way into the novel. Having done so, he, like Paul, is both dead and reborn. Lawrence's next novel, *The Rainbow*, reveals a new and different Lawrence, though it is the same Lawrence too in that the author of *Sons and Lovers*, having lived through that eperience and killed it by transforming it into art, is now "intermingled"—like Paul's murdered mother.

150. Lawrence's poem "The Virgin Mother" would seem to substantiate this interpretation. See *Complete Poems* (London: Heinemann, 1957), I, 83–85.
151. *The Life and Works of D. H. Lawrence* (New York: Twayne Publishers, 1951), p. 105.

152. *A Portrait of the Artist as a Young Man* (New York: Modern Library, 1928), p. 197.
153. "Rhythm and Theme: D. H. Lawrence's *Sons and Lovers*," in Hoffman and Moore, eds., *The Achievement of D. H. Lawrence,* p. 143.

CHAPTER THREE

ART AS RELIGION:

The Ivory Tower Tradition

WE have seen that the typical artist-hero of the Sacred Fount tradition finds the source of his art in experience. If he is superior to the average man, it is largely because he lives more intensely, feels more deeply, and is more aware of the world about him. He exults in his humanity, but sees mankind as a part of nature. He may rebel against society, but when he does, he usually flees to high mountains or ocean shores so that he may commune directly with nature, become rejuvenated at the fountain source of his being, then return to the society of men. The artist of the Ivory Tower tradition, on the other hand, cares little for humanity or nature. Far from wanting to live more fully, he resents his carnal appetites and natural instincts, and yearns for release from human bondage. His Ivory Tower, like a monastic cell or Faust's chambers, is often without windows; and if he looks out at all, it is not so much *at* the world as *down* upon it. As the Ivory Tower tradition gains momentum, we shall see a new emphasis on internal consciousness, a predilection for the unnatural, a striving for the unknown and the unseen. The artist tries to become a saint, like Flaubert's Anthony in the desert, strong enough to withstand all worldly temptations. Dissatisfied with the way in which he was made, he tries to create himself anew, thus becoming a dandy or an esthete. Life is replaced by art, and art becomes a sacred ritual.

This new view of art has its roots in what may be considered a secondary romanticism. Counterbalancing the social romanticism which dominated the early years of the nineteenth century—a romanticism which exalted life, accepted both reason and inspiration, and believed in progress—was a spiritual romanticism which insisted that there are no real barriers between heaven and earth, that all is one, and that life is not a chain linking the lowest, inorganic forms to the Absolute, but an organic growth developing and circling outward from itself. For many of the later romantics, such as Poe, Nerval, and Rimbaud, the absolute is not something out there, to be searched for. Heaven, they would insist, is within themselves; they are at once God and Satan, saint and sinner, agent and object. To create totality, they must create themselves.

The new religion of art owes much to magic and occultism. Reaction from the inadequacies of this world turns many artists to otherworldliness. In its most respectable form, the reaction takes the form of platonic idealism, religious mysticism, or transcendentalism, but if the psychology of the artist is of a particular sort, the reaction is strong enough, and the artist has no conventional religion, the otherworldliness is likely to take the direction of magic, alchemy, and satanism.[1] One strain of spiritual romanticism could be traced from Plato to Leibnitz to Berkeley to Swedenborg to the German idealistic philosophers to Coleridge and Carlyle to Poe to Baudelaire to Mallarmé to the Symbolists. Another would lead from the beginnings of the Hermetic tradition to the cabalists to the illuminists, who flourished in France and Germany in the years just before the French Revolution, to the occult researches of a half-mad Gerard de Nerval to the Rosicrusianism of Villiers de l'Isle-Adam to the satanic decadence of *fin de siècle* writers like Huysmans, Baron Corvo, and Aleister Crowley. Many writers of the late nineteenth and early twentieth centuries, we shall see, owe much to both strains of this tradition. But anyone who seeks to trace specific lines of influence in this area must soon become embarrassed by an abundance of riches. One discovers so many sources in the philosophy, science, and art of the period that he is forced to conclude that otherworldliness, whether it took the form of a respectable transcendentalism that could be reconciled with Christianity or a diabolic occultism that represented only an inverted Christianity, was simply *there*, an atmosphere of the times. During much of the early romantic period, however, it was subterranean, manifesting itself not so much

1. Good treatments of this relationship are to be found in Albert Béguin, *L'Ame Romantique et le Rêve: Essai sur le Romantisme Allemand et la Poésie Française*, Nouvelle Edition (Paris: Librairie Jose Corti, 1946) and John Senior, *The Way Down and Out: The Occult in Symbolist Literature* (Ithaca, New York: Cornell University Press, 1959).

in art or literature as in independent visionaries or secret fellowships. Not until Poe and Baudelaire, who join occultism with idealism, did this otherworldliness become prominent in imaginative literature.

Against social romanticism, then, we have the pervasive counter-movement of a spiritual romanticism that branches into two related movements: mysticism and occultism. Goethe's *Wilhelm Meister* is the key artist-novel reflecting romanticism of the first type, and to see the differences between the two, we have only to compare the function of Lothario's castle and the secret fellowship in Goethe's novel with the castles of art and the masonic leagues favored by the spiritual romanticists. There is a suggestion of the occult in the castle and the fellowship in *Wilhelm Meister,* but it is largely through their influence that Wilhelm renounces his profession as artist and his spiritual yearnings. The fellowship is composed of superior men who have learned from experience; their alliance may be said to stand for worldly wisdom. The code of the fellowship causes its members to seek justification in active participation in the affairs of society; like modern-day Masons, they easily reconcile their rituals and indentures with Christianity, and they consider social service one of their main functions. The supernatural is brought down to earth and harnessed to man's energy: we are reminded of the promises of worldly power offered to us today in advertisements of the Rosicrucians or similar groups. In contrast to Lothario's castle we have in early portraits of the artist such retreats as Jean-Paul Richter's invisible lodge, the mountain mansion in Balzac's Swedenborgian romance, *Seraphita,* and Count Rodolphe's Bohemian castle in George Sand's *Consuelo.* Goethe's heroes retreat to the castle, learn divine wisdom there, and then return to the real world armed with the knowledge that may serve mankind. Far from harnessing spiritual energy to physical energy, the heroes of Richter, Balzac, and Sand would serve the divine will; and their retreats are gateways to the spiritual realm, jumping-off places for ascending to heaven.

Perhaps the first portrait-of-the-artist novel to reflect the doctrine of spiritual romanticism is Novalis' *Henry von Ofterdingen,* which was conceived as a direct answer to *Wilhelm Meister* and published in 1799. Whereas Wilhelm renounced art for social service, Novalis' unfinished story was to have made the artistic calling seem the most noble vocation open to man. Novalis does not imply that art is better than life, but insists that the two are fused, and through his novel tries to reflect the alliance between matter and spirit. According to his friend Tieck, Novalis intended to write a book in which "the partition between Fiction and Truth, between the Past and the Present has fallen down. Faith, Fancy, and Poetry lay open the internal world." [2] Rich in mythological allusions, allegorical identifications, characters who become other characters, extensive use of dreams, and an attempt to exhaust all life, the book is not unlike an early, aborted *Finnegans Wake*. There is a prevision of Proust, too, in that the story was to have concluded with an old song exciting "long forgotten recollections" and leading Henry to a solution of the mysteries he has encountered; in fact, as in Proust, Henry at the end of the novel was to have been ready to tell the story already narrated. It would be an error, though, to assume that a completed *Henry von Ofterdingen* would be another *Finnegans Wake* or *Remembrance of Things Past*. Apparently one reason why Novalis could not finish the work was that he was unable to resolve a conflict in his own thinking, a yearning for mystic idealism versus acceptance of conventional religious belief. Too, Novalis was a typical child of his time in that he felt that art was dependent upon experience, for "Henry having . . . lived through and observed nature, life, and death, war, the East, history and poetry, turns back into his mind as to an old home. From his knowledge of the world and of himself arises his impulse for expression." [3] For all its limitations, however, *Henry von Ofterdingen* was not only a valiant answer to *Wilhelm Meister* but also a novel far in advance of its time.

If we look in fiction for artists' residences representing the occult tradition to compare with Lothario's castle and the gateways of spiritual romanticism, we may find partial prototypes in the alchemic chamber of Faust, the tower of Merlin, or the scientific laboratory of Dr. Frankenstein. The Ivory Tower concept owes something at least to the haunted castle of Gothic fiction; and the new artist derives in part from the type of the mad scientist in that both invoke magic and ritual as a means of penetrating to a secret that will result in their mastery over the universe.

Edgar Allan Poe belongs to the Gothic tradition, and my first example of the Ivory Tower artist is his Roderick Usher, who lives in an isolated mansion, "has a passionate devotion to the intricacies . . . of musical science," and paints pictures that are "pure abstractions" notable for their "intensity of intolerable awe." [4] As Allen Tate has commented, Roderick Usher's "want of moral energy" and hypertrophy of sensibility and intellect place him among the an-

2. *Henry of Ofterdingen: A Romance* (Cambridge: John Owen, 1842), p. 224.
3. *Henry of Ofterdingen*, p. 224.
4. "The Fall of the House of Usher," in *Selected Poetry and Prose of Edgar Allan Poe*, ed. T. O. Mabbott (New York: Modern Library, 1953), pp. 115–131. I have not attempted to identify specific page references for the many quotations from the short story cited in my discussion.

cestors of Monsieur Teste, Gabriel Conroy, John Marcher, J. Alfred Prufrock, and all the other "poor, sensitive gentlemen" who cannot function in the ordinary world, the unheroic heroes who dominate modern literature.[5] But if he serves as a convenient prototype for later artist-heroes, he also sums up much of what preceded him in the history of romanticism. He may well stand as our spokesman for spiritual romanticism.

1   *The Universe of Roderick Usher*

TO understand "The Fall of the House of Usher," it is necessary to know something of Poe's cosmology.[6] Although he did not sum up his philosophy until near the end of his life, when he wrote *Eureka*, Poe had long been attracted to philosophical and scientific works on the nature of the universe.[7] What the story of 1839 reveals through symbolic drama, the treatise of 1848 states through direct exposition; hence, an understanding of *Eureka* helps to clear up many of the ambiguities in a baffling story.

The universe, Poe says in *Eureka*, derives from a tiny particle of perfect oneness, matter in its utmost conceivable state of simplicity. From this initial unity are diffused spherically in all directions "a certain inexpressibly great yet limited number of unimaginably yet not infinitely minute atoms."[8] The agency of diffusion is radiation. The material-spiritual universe consists of tense relationships between the radiated particles—a continual struggle between attraction and repulsion, contraction and expansion. The law of gravity demon-

5. "Three Commentaries: Poe, James, and Joyce," *Sewanee Review,* LVII (Winter, 1950), pp. 1–5. Reprinted in Caroline Gordon and Allen Tate, *The House of Fiction: An Anthology of the Short Story with Commentary* (New York: Scribner's, 1950), pp. 114–117.

6. Allen Tate has said of Poe's symbols in general that they "refer to a known tradition of thought, an intelligible order, apart from what he was as a man, and are not merely the index to a compulsive neurosis."— "The Angelic Imagination: Poe as God," in his *The Forlorn Demon: Didactic and Critical Essays* (Chicago: Henry Regnery, 1953), pp. 59–60. In another essay, "Our Cousin, Mr. Poe," Tate analyzes "The Fall of the House of Usher"

in relation to the vampire theme in Poe's fiction and, without developing the idea, states in passing that the catastrophe of the story illustrates the central thesis of *Eureka.—The Forlorn Demon,* pp. 86–89.

7. Poe is presumably the author of a series of articles on the solar system published in *The Southern Literary Messenger* during 1838 which anticipate the ideas later elaborated in *Eureka.* See Margaret Alterton, *The Origins of Poe's Critical Theory, Iowa Humanistic Studies,* II, No. 3 (Iowa City, 1922), 144.

8. *Eureka: An Essay on the Material and Spiritual Universe.* In *The Complete Works of Edgar Allan Poe,* ed. James A. Harrison (New York: Thomas Y. Crowell, 1902), XVI, 208.

strates the desire of all things to return to their initial unity. Against attraction or gravitation is the power of repulsion, or what Poe calls radiation. Since matter can be perceived only through its properties of attraction and repulsion and therefore *is* only attraction and repulsion, a finally consolidated, completely *attracted* universe would be a realm of no-matter or nothingness. The diffusing, radiating, repulsing agency, Poe believes, grows progressively weaker. When it can no longer withstand the power of attraction, all particles will return to oneness and the universe will disappear. The process of expansion and contraction may, however, be renewed again and again—"a novel Universe swelling into existence, and then subsiding into nothingness, at every throb of the Heart Divine." [9]

Poe equates the Heart Divine with the artist, and there is a close analogy between his cosmology and his theory of the short story. The artistic imagination is for Poe a creative power which disperses elements previously ordered by God and reassembles them into new unities or totalities. In his discussion of the short story, Poe says: "In the whole composition there should be no word written of which the tendency, direct or indirect, is not to the one pre-established design." [10] In *Eureka*, which was composed at about the same time as his theory of the short story, he says: "In the construction of *plot* . . . we should aim at so arranging the incidents that we shall not be able to determine, of any one of them, whether it depends from any one other or upholds it. In this sense, of course, *perfection* of *plot* is really, or practically, unattainable—but only because it is a finite intelligence that constructs. The plots of God are perfect. The Universe is a plot of God." [11]

The universe is the perfect plot of God because, since everything derives from the same basic oneness, each particle attracts each other particle. Cause is virtually indistinguishable from effect. If matter sprang from nothingness, it had to be created: a God exists to create a single particle which is the central core from which all other matter is diffused. Yet, Poe implies elsewhere in *Eureka*, the agent is not really distinct from the substance: the things in the universe are "really but infinite individualizations of Himself"; [12] and "God— the material *and* spiritual God—*now* exists solely in the diffused Matter and Spirit of the universe." [13] Thus cause becomes effect, and effect, cause.

Poe's use of the term "plot" to describe the creation of the universe is in agreement with his theory of the short story. The tale, Poe says,

9. *Eureka,* p. 208.   12. *Eureka,* p. 314.
10. *Selected Poetry and Prose,* p. 381.   13. *Eureka,* p. 313.
11. *Eureka,* p. 292.

derives from a central core of *single effect* to which all elements must be related. The writer first determines the end of his story, the climax or catastrophe or solution which links and resolves all the earlier details. Then, working backward, he builds upon this central core increasingly diffuse, though always relevant, details. The writer's task is analogous to the cosmic process of expansion through radiation. The reader—who, Poe insists, must contemplate "with a kindred art"—begins at the level of greatest expansion and, linking detail to detail, reaches the climactic oneness which was, for the artist, the beginning of the story. The reader's task is analogous to the cosmic process of contraction through attraction.

The completed short story, like the completed universe, remains unified in that every element depends on the others. "Bear in mind," Poe says in the concluding sentence of *Eureka*, "that all is life—life —life within life, the less within the greater, and all within the Spirit Divine." From the initial unity of singleness comes the unity of mutual relationship. In the ideal short story, like the universe, everything is related and nothing is irrelevant. "The Fall of the House of Usher," many critics have found, is a nearly perfect illustration of Poe's theory of totality. That there are no collateral lines of the Usher family, that the name "House of Usher" signifies to its neighbors both the mansion and the family, that there is a barely perceptible crack running from roof to base of the house, that Roderick Usher has a particularly acute sense of hearing—all such details contribute to the single effect of the story and play a part in the final catastrophe.

The house of Usher is like the universe not only in that everything is related but also in that it is limited. In *Eureka* Poe insists that the universe we know is not infinite and that there may be many neighboring universes each with its own god. As a result, our universe could conceivably be entered and left again. The same is true of the house of Usher, and Poe permits us to crack the shell with the narrator, who comes from outside, travels the "whole of a . . . day" through "a singularly dreary tract of country," arrives at "an atmosphere which had no affinity with the air of heaven," enters the house, walks "through many dark and intricate passages," meets Roderick Usher in what appears to be the central apartment, is a reluctant observer of all that occurs, and finally leaves—a rounded process which in itself suggests the circle-like unity of the story. The emphasis on the isolation of the house of Usher helps the impression of a self-contained world, a totality.

Within the unity of the house of Usher are many diffusions in the form of mirrored or echolike correspondences. The house is reflected in the tarn. Roderick and Madeline are twins between whom "sympathies of a scarcely intelligible nature" had always existed. Roderick's painting suggests Madeline's vault. The sounds described in "Mad Trist" are echoed by the noises which accompany Madeline as she seeks her revenge. The storm outside the window reflects the storm within Roderick's mind. His song, "The Haunted Palace," relates symbolically the union between the "radiant palace" and the mind of its tenant, and—a key element in the structural unity—it is Poe's story in capsule form.

The main line of diffusion runs chainlike from the tarn to the house to Roderick to Madeline. The narrator, arriving before the "mansion of gloom," is immediately conscious of the isolated and self-contained atmosphere of the place: "It was possible, I reflected, that a mere different arrangement of the particulars of the scene, of the details of the picture, would be sufficient to modify, or perhaps to annihilate its capacity for sorrowful impression; and, acting upon this idea, I reined my horse to the precipitous brink of a black and lurid tarn that lay in unruffled lustre by the dwelling, and gazed down—but with a shudder even more thrilling than before—upon the remodelled and inverted image of the gray sedge, and the ghastly tree-stems, and the vacant and eye-like windows." One feature of the house is the "barely perceptible fissure, which extending from the roof of the building in front, made its way down the wall in a zigzag direction, until it became lost in the sullen waters of the tarn." The "unruffled" tarn may be interpreted as the oneness or nothingness from which all has emerged and to which all must return.

The next link of diffusion is the correspondence between the house of Usher and Roderick. In addition to several analogies described in "The Haunted Palace," many details in the story express the relationship. The "eye-like windows" and doors like "ponderous and ebony jaws" are the most obvious. The "minute *fungi* . . . hanging in a fine tangled web-work from the eaves" is equivalent to Roderick Usher's hair "of a more than weblike softness and tenuity." The "wild inconsistency" between the house's "perfect adaptation of parts, and the crumbling condition of the individual stones" is the "inconsistency" which arises from Roderick's "feeble and futile struggle to overcome an habitual trepidancy." The crack in the building corresponds to Roderick's struggle against insanity, his effort to maintain his composure against what may be called the "kingdom of inorganization."

The fissure in the building also corresponds to the diffusion split between Roderick and Madeline. Just as the house and Roderick are included within the range and influence of the tarn, the house is equal to both the Ushers. In a sense, however, Madeline is sub-ordinate to her brother. Poe tells us that there had always been an "undeviating transmission, from sire to son, of the patrimony with the name." This would imply that there has been but one surviving male Usher in each generation and that the daughters, who need not have appeared in every generation, have either failed to marry or to survive. The "sympathies of a scarcely intelligible nature" between the twins would suggest that, like the two William Wilsons, the one must always suffer with the other. But, as far as most of Poe's narrative is concerned, it is Roderick who affects, Madeline who is affected. Her mysterious illness appears to be the reflection of his mental affliction. The relation between brother and sister is not unlike that of Dumas's Corsican brothers, one of whom responds to the other's actions and emotions. In Poe's story this is true only along the line of expansion; when the contraction begins, the relationship is reversed.

In the story, as in *Eureka,* the force of diffusion is radiation. Roderick Usher "was enchained by certain superstitious impressions in regard to the dwelling which he tenanted, and whence, for many years, he had never ventured forth—in regard to an influence whose supposititious force was conveyed in terms too shadowy here to be re-stated—an influence which some peculiarities in the mere form and substance of his family mansion, had, by dint of long sufferance, he said, obtained over his spirit—an effect which the *physique* of the grey walls and turrets, and of the dim tarn into which they all looked down, had, at length, brought about upon the *morale* of his existence." The power of the mansion and the tarn to influence the mind of Roderick is, in part, explained by his belief in the sentience of things. The narrator scoffs at this "superstition," but lists in a footnote four authorities for the idea. It was not so much the novelty of animism as the "pertinacity" with which Roderick Usher held the conviction that made it important: "in his disordered fancy, the idea had assumed a more daring character, and trespassed, under certain conditions, upon the kingdom of inorganization." Evidence of this sentience Roderick found in "the gradual yet certain condensation of an atmosphere of their own about the waters and walls." The narrator, too, has noticed the "pestilent and mystic vapour, dull, sluggish, faintly discernible, and leaden-hued" which apparently "had reeked up from the decayed trees, and the grey wall, and the silent tarn." "An atmosphere of their own" suggests that the house and its domains have not only sentience but also the power to transmit it—that is, to radiate.

Poe's own philosophy was as animistic as Roderick Usher's.

Throughout *Eureka* he makes no distinction between vegetable or biological life and inanimate matter. Matter, he says, is but attraction and repulsion: "The former is the Body; the latter the Soul: the one is the material; the other the spiritual, principle of the Universe. *No other principles exist*." [14] And "thus the two Principles Proper, *Attraction* and *Repulsion*—the material and the spiritual—accompany each other, in the strictest fellowship, forever. Thus *The Body and The Soul walk hand in hand*." [15] The Divine Being, Poe says, "now feels his life through an infinity of imperfect pleasures—the partial and pain-intertangled pleasures of those inconceivably numerous things which you designate as his creatures, but which are really but infinite individualizations of Himself. All these creatures—*all*—those which you term animate, as well as those to whom you deny life for no better reason than that you do not behold it in operation —*all* these creatures have, in greater or less degree, a capacity for pleasure and for pain. . . . These creatures are all too, more or less conscious Intelligences." [16] A belief in the sentience of things is a necessary corollary of Poe's insistence on unity. Because the heart divine is "our own," each soul "is, in part, its own God—its own Creator." [17]

Poe's equating of agent with substance permits us to understand how Roderick Usher, presumably a created being, can influence his environment as well as be affected by it. While his *morale* is affected by the *physique* of his surroundings, his own mind helps to determine the character of the house and tarn. Roderick Usher is the dramatic center of the story, and we must see the chain from his point of view. When the narrator arrives before the house of Usher, "a sense of insufferable gloom" pervades his spirit. When he enters Roderick's studio, "an air of stern, deep, and irredeemable gloom hung over and pervaded all." The mystery of this recurrently mentioned gloom is solved when the narrator perceives "the futility of all attempt at cheering a mind from which darkness, as if an inherent positive quality, poured forth upon all objects of the moral and physical universe, in *one unceasing radiation of gloom*."

Roderick's power to radiate is intensified by his art. We have seen that if the universe is a plot of God, a story resembles the universe and the artist resembles God. The peculiarity of the Usher family is "a passionate devotion to the intricacies, perhaps even more than to the orthodox and easily recognizable beauties, of musical science." Music is the most appropriate art for the Ushers because waves of sound, particularly from stringed instruments, suggest the process

14. *Eureka*, pp. 213–214.   16. *Eureka*, p. 314.
15. *Eureka*, p. 244.   17. *Eureka*, p. 313.

of radiation. "The Haunted Palace," a sample of Roderick's musical gift, is sung to the accompaniment of a guitar, and the song itself is significant because it expresses Roderick's awareness of his own dilemma. He is also a painter. One of his pictures is described in detail: "A small picture presented the interior of an immensely long and rectangular vault or tunnel, with low walls, smooth, white, and without interruption or device. Certain accessory points of the design served well to convey the idea that this excavation lay at an exceeding depth below the surface of the earth. No outlet was observed in any portion of its vast extent, and no torch, or other artificial source of light, was discernible; yet a flood of intense rays rolled throughout, and bathed the whole in a ghastly and inappropriate splendour." We are told just before this description that "if ever mortal painted an idea, that mortal was Roderick Usher," and of his paintings that "an excited and highly distempered ideality threw a sulphureous lustre over all." As one of the many mirrorlike diffusions in the story, the picture represents Madeline's vault. (On a different level, it is Poe's short story.) The fact that there is no visible outlet suggests a totality, and the "flood of intense rays" implies the "sulphureous lustre" that radiates from Roderick's (or Poe's) mind.

Roderick's artistic activities are closely related to his sanity. It is significant that after Madeline has been buried, "his ordinary occupations were neglected or forgotten." As long as Roderick continues the diffusive power symbolized by his music and his painting, he can maintain the delicate balance between repulsion and attraction and save himself from annihilation. Yet, it is his awareness of his tense situation that finally drives him mad. The first step toward insanity is his acceptance of animism and his sense of intimate relationship with the objects about him. Any movement, Poe says in *Eureka*, sets off a chain reaction that affects every part of the whole: "If I venture to displace, by even the billionth part of an inch, the microscopical speck of dust which lies now upon the point of my finger, what is the character of that act upon which I have adventured? I have done a deed which shakes the Moon in her path, which causes the Sun to be no longer the Sun, and which alters forever the destiny of the multitudinous myriads of stars that roll and glow in the majestic presence of their Creator." [18] It is not difficult to see that such a belief could lead to a morbid sensitivity. Roderick "suffered much from a morbid acuteness of the senses; the most insipid food was alone endurable; he could wear only garments of a certain texture; the odours of all flowers were oppres-

18. *Eureka*, p. 218.

sive; his eyes were tortured by even a faint light; and there were but peculiar sounds, and these from stringed instruments, which did not inspire him with horror." Some years after the story was first published, Poe added as a motto the appropriate heart-lute image from De Béranger:

> Son cœur est un luth suspendu,
> Sitôt qu'on le touche il résonne.

As used here, the lute is an intermediary. While Roderick maintains the balance between reception and transmission, he is sane. When he only receives, he becomes a passive prey to the "kingdom of inorganization." In "The Haunted Palace," built on contrasting images of reason-order and madness-disorder,

> Spirits moving musically
> To a lute's well-tuned law

become

> Vast forms that move fantastically
> To a discordant melody.[19]

The problem of motivation has perplexed many critics of "The Fall of the House of Usher." To the extent that Roderick's actions may be attributed to insanity, the question of motivation is beside the point. And, at any rate, whether or not Roderick wills his fate is less important than that the fate does occur. In line with *Eureka,* however, Roderick Usher is both the agent of his fate and its object. There is sufficient internal evidence in the tale to suggest that Roderick deliberately buried his sister alive. He paints the picture of Madeline's vault before he places her there. Poe emphasizes the screwing down of the coffin lid. After the burial, "there were times, indeed," says the narrator, "when I thought his unceasingly agitated mind was labouring with some oppressive secret, to divulge which he struggled for the necessary courage." He would have known that while he lives, Madeline is not dead. When, in the climax of the story, he hears her approaching, he cries, "Is she not hurrying to upbraid me for my haste?" And, certainly, there is every appearance of vengeance about Madeline when she appears at the door of the room. Madeline is Roderick's "tenderly beloved sister," but his realization that her terrible illness is the product of his mental afflic-

19. A more complete discussion of the reason-order and madness-disorder symbols is to be found in Darrel Abel, "A Key to the House of Usher," *University of Toronto Quarterly,* XVIII (January, 1949), 176–185.

tion leads him to what could be described as a mercy killing—and a suicide.

Roderick's motivation may be explained in terms of *Eureka*. The general proposition of Poe's treatise is: *"In the Original Unity of the First Thing lies the Secondary Cause of All Things, with the Germ of their Inevitable Annihilation."* [20] Once diffused, every particle desires to return to the initial singleness: "A diffusion from unity," Poe says, "involves a tendency to return into unity—a tendency ineradicable until satisfied." [21] Inevitably, the diffusing agency becomes weakened. Roderick is apparently a deterioration of his ancestors, and the presence of the narrator implies that Roderick was stronger in the past than in the present. When he can no longer stand to be a tense, suffering creature, attracting and repulsing, attracted and repulsed, he seeks a return to the unity of no-attraction-repulsion, no-matter, nothingness. He is like Ethelred, the hero of "Mad Trist," who, "having sought in vain for peaceable admission into the dwelling of the hermit [aloneness, oneness], proceeds to make good an entrance by force." By burying his sister alive, Roderick tries to halt the diffusion. The totality symbolically presented in his picture of Madeline's vault implies, in a sense, the completion of expansion, the attempt to become independent of the diffused portion of himself by isolating it. The Divine Being, Poe says in *Eureka*, "passes His eternity in perpetual variation of Concentrated Self and almost infinite Self-Diffusion." [22] Godlike Roderick's action is the peak of the self-diffusion, the beginning of a return to a concentrated oneness, which, as we have seen, is nothingness and annihilation. After Madeline is placed in the tomb, Roderick's "ordinary manner had vanished . . . the luminousness of his eye had utterly gone out."

We can better understand Roderick's motivation if we recognize its parallel in Poe's life. Many students of Poe have considered him a virtual suicide. A few months before his death he wrote to Mrs. Clemm: "It is no use to reason with me *now*; I must die. I have no desire to live since I have done 'Eureka.' I could accomplish nothing more." [23] His almost triumphant despair is expressed in the conclusion of his treatise. Every creature, person, and thing, he says, is a conscious intelligence—"conscious, first, of a proper identity; conscious, secondly, and by faint indeterminate glimpses, of an identity with the Divine Being of whom we speak—of an identity with

20. *Eureka*, pp. 185–186.
21. *Eureka*, p. 207.
22. *Eureka*, p. 314.
23. *The Letters of Edgar Allan Poe,*   ed. John Ward Ostrom (Cambridge, Mass.: Harvard University Press, 1948), II, 452.

God." [24] The first consciousness, Poe says, will grow weaker as the latter becomes stronger, and when the sense of individual identity has been merged in the general consciousness, man "will at length attain that awfully triumphant epoch when he shall recognize his existence as that of Jehovah." [25] Shortly before this prediction appears a revealing passage: "In this view, and in this view alone, we comprehend the riddles of Divine Injustice—of Inexorable Fate. In this view alone the existence of Evil becomes intelligible; but in this view it becomes more—it becomes endurable. Our souls no longer rebel at a *Sorrow* which we ourselves have imposed upon ourselves, in furtherance of our own purposes—with a view—if even with a futile view—to the extension of our Joy." [26] The evil "sorrow" refers, I assume, to Poe's self-imposed tortures, particularly his drinking and drugtaking. He now recognizes such activity as a projection from the self, a form of diffusion not unlike the creating of art. No longer rebelling at the sorrow which accompanies it, he solaces himself with the conviction that such activity, carried to its furthest extent, may annihilate an identity that has become repugnant to him. Like Roderick Usher, he seeks a return to *oneness*. Before the burial, Roderick's voice had "that leaden, self-balanced and perfectly modulated guttural utterance, which may be observed in the lost drunkard, or the irreclaimable eater of opium, during the period of his most intense excitement." After the burial, "the once occasional huskiness of his voice was heard no more." No longer self-balanced, the diffusion has been carried to the point of annihilation.

Although the radiation from Roderick's consciousness ceases with the burying of his sister, the diffused particles remain and begin their return. They must now return because there is nothing to hold them back. The "gradual yet certain condensation of an atmosphere of their own about the waters and walls" becomes, in the climactic scene, "the unnatural light of a faintly luminous and distinctly visible gaseous exhalation which hung about and enshrouded the mansion." The narrator says, "The exceeding density of the clouds (which hung so low as to press upon the turrets of the house) did not prevent our perceiving the lifelike velocity with which they flew careering from all points against each other, without passing away into the distance." The narrator, trying to comfort his disturbed friend, unwittingly tells him a truth that could well increase the terror: " 'These appearances, which bewilder you, are merely electrical phenomena not uncommon—or it may be that they have their ghastly origin in the rank miasma of the tarn.' "

24. *Eureka*, p. 314.   26. *Eureka*, p. 313.
25. *Eureka*, p. 315.

Roderick is linked as closely in one direction to his sister as, in the other direction, to the house and the tarn. And, of course, Madeline must return upon him also. The supernatural—the lid of the coffin was screwed down—has a philosophical, if not a natural, explanation. When the movement reaches the end of the chain of expansion, it must return along the line of contraction. Roderick, who formerly acted upon his sister, has now become the passive victim. With the destruction of the part occurs the annihilation of the whole.

The house should be destroyed simultaneously with the death of the last of the Ushers, but Poe has to let the narrator escape to tell his story. As a result, the last paragraph not only concludes the tale but also repeats, in concentrated form, the unity-radiation-diffusion-return-to-unity process which has determined the ideological structure of the story. In a marginal revision of *Eureka* Poe said of a passage on the act of diffusion, "Here describe the process as one instantaneous flash." [27] The House of Usher splits first into two parts, corresponding to the many delicately balanced diffusion-correspondences in the story. The crack widens, suggesting Roderick's insanity, his inability to maintain balance, and hence his desperate effort to become independent of the diffused matter. The two parts split into many fragments as the peak of diffusion occurs. The last sentence suggests a return to the original unity: "My brain reeled as I saw the mighty walls rushing asunder—there was a long tumultuous shouting like the voice of a thousand waters—and the deep and dank tarn at my feet closed sullenly and silently over the fragments of the 'House of Usher.' "

Many of Poe's stories demonstrate his strictures on the unity of single effect, but if my analysis of "The Fall of House of Usher" is valid, it follows that the complete relevance of details in this story—a fact long acknowledged by critics—is not simply a matter of careful plotting in terms of a theory of esthetic unity. Because the literary theory behind the story is actually religious in essence and because here content and form are one, we find in Roderick Usher an ideal and complete prototype of the artist-as-God. Roderick is not depicted as a person in the universe; he is himself his universe. The power to create is the power to destroy, and his most triumphant creation is the obliteration of his suffering, diffused self in a return to that oneness which is nothingness. His French followers also sought to create themselves, and some of them at least realized that to do so would mean annihilation of self in *le néant*.

27. *Eureka*, p. 326.

II   *Demons, Dandies, and Divines*

POE'S influence on subsequent literature owes much to his French translator, Charles Baudelaire, who himself may be considered the representative figure in a further development of the Ivory Tower concept of the artist. Baudelaire never got around to writing the "portrait de l'artiste, en géneral" which he listed among future projects in his journal.[28] Although he came close to it in his essays on Delacroix and Constantin Guys, and though the poet-hero of *La Fanfarlo,* one of his few works of prose fiction, is a thinly disguised self-portrait, it is Baudelaire the personality who, Byron-like, came to serve as the prototype of a new kind of artist. Therefore his personal writings—in particular his *Intimate Journals* and the letters recently selected and gathered under the title *Baudelaire: A Self-Portrait*—may serve as my major texts.

Many critics have wondered what Baudelaire saw in Poe that caused him to devote almost half of his literary output to translations of a writer whom many consider inferior to his translator. "Do you know why I translated Poe so patiently?" Baudelaire wrote. "Because he resembled me. The first time I opened one of his books, I saw with astonishment and delight not only subjects I had dreamed of, but SENTENCES which I had framed in my thoughts and which he had written twenty years before." [29] To the extent that this claim is justified, Baudelaire's translations are original compositions expressing himself. Poe, who was fascinated by the idea of the *doppelganger,* was to find his own double in the French dandy. The temperamental and situational affinities between Poe and Baudelaire cannot be attributed solely to the fact that Baudelaire took Poe for a model. Without a strong initial affinity Baudelaire would not have felt "incredibly drawn" to his *alter ego* in the first place.

Baudelaire says of the poet-hero Samuel Cramer of *La Fanfarlo* that "un des travers les plus naturels de Samuel était de se considérer comme l'égal de ceux qu'il avait su admirer; après une lecture passionnée d'un beau livre sa conclusion involontaire était: violà est assez beau pour être de moi!—et de là à penser: c'est donc de moi,—n'y a que l'espace d'un tiret." [30] Thus Samuel tends to become every

28. J. Mitchell Morse, "Baudelaire, Stephen Dedalus, and Shem the Penman," *Bucknell Review,* VII (March, 1958), p. 187.

29. *Baudelaire: A Self-Portrait,* trans. and ed. Lois Boe Hyslop and Francie E. Hyslop, Jr. (New York: Oxford University Press, 1957), p. 208.

30. *Oeuvres Complètes,* Édition définitive (Paris: Calmann-Lévy, n.d.), IV, 388.

artist he studies. He fits perfectly in the class of "gens absorbants," [31] those who can never go half way, but must enter completely. Such men tend to become what they see, or to see only what they are—a trait which we associate with the "totality" type of artist—and to create themselves by assimilating others.

Poe's "Man of the Crowd" can find self-identity only by merging himself with others, and in the prose-poem "Crowds," which was undoubtedly influenced by Poe's story, Baudelaire says:

> The poet enjoys the incomparable privilege of being, at will, both himself and other people. Like a wandering soul seeking a body, he can enter, whenever he wishes, into anyone's personality. For him alone all seats are vacant; and if some places seem to be closed to him, it is because in his eyes they are not worth the trouble of a visit. . . .
>
> What men call love is a very small, restricted and weak thing compared with this ineffable orgy, this holy prostitution of a soul that gives itself utterly, with all its poetry and charity, to the unexpectedly emergent, to the passing unknown.[32]

According to Joseph D. Bennett, Baudelaire himself assumed the role of the "Man of the Crowd": "When this exquisite man went abroad in the city, it seemed that he gave himself out, prostituted himself, exhausted his energy in facing every visage he saw. Crowds exhausted him; by the furious intoxication caused him through mingling with them, they drained him of all vigor. Each face was an obstacle that must be surrounded, dissolved, and assimilated by his consciousness, which, like an insatiable sphere, consumed everything within its ardent periphery."[33] Baudelaire defined genius as *childhood rediscovered*, by which he meant that the artist-genius attempts to face life with the "animally ecstatic gaze of a child confronted by what is new," to recover the child's sense of oneness with the universe.[34] Such an artist seeks not solitude, but assimilation with the crowd: "To the perfect spectator, the impassioned observer, it is an immense joy to make his domicile amongst numbers, amidst fluctuation and movement, amidst the fugitive and infinite. To be away from home, and yet to feel at home; to behold the world, to be in the midst of the world, and yet to remain hidden from the world—these are some of the minor pleasures of such independent, impassioned and impartial spirits, whom words can only clumsily

31. *Oeuvres Complètes*, IV, 394.
32. *The Essence of Laughter, and Other Essays, Journals, and Letters,* ed. Peter Quennell (New York: Meridian Books, 1956), pp. 139–140.
33. *Baudelaire: A Criticism* (Princeton, New Jersey: Princeton University Press, 1946), p. 10.
34. *The Essence of Laughter,* pp. 27–28.

describe." [35] Merging with the crowd, yet remaining alone; in the midst of the world, yet hidden from it—such a paradox may be resolved only if we recognize that for Baudelaire what is outside the self is "a forest of symbols which correspond to his various states of mind or feeling." [36] As he proclaimed most tellingly in the sonnet "Correspondences," there is no separation, ideally, between self and cosmos. Hence Baudelaire does not retreat to an Ivory Tower; like Roderick Usher's, his Ivory Tower is a projection of self.

An ideal is one thing, reality another. In practice, Baudelaire sought assimilation, but seldom achieved it. In defining genius as childhood rediscovered, he probably had in mind his childhood "conversations with God." [37] In later years he was at best a would-be mystic seeking to lose selfhood in oneness, but remaining chained to his suffering ego. Whereas a true mystic would subordinate self to cosmos and either accept reality or remain indifferent to things as they are, Baudelaire tried to bring the cosmos within himself and, failing, came to detest reality. Like most unsuccessful mystics, however, Baudelaire has frequently been mistaken for the real thing. To many of his followers he seemed a genuine *voyant* who could point the way to a place where he had been.

It is Baudelaire's attempt to achieve an impossible ideal that distinguishes him from the writers of the Sacred Fount tradition. The earlier romantics, he said, sought spiritual reality outside themselves, "but it was only to be found within." [38] They worshiped nature as a manifestation of God, but Baudelaire cared little for nature:

> You ask me for some verses for your little anthology, verses about *Nature*, I believe, about forests, great oak trees, verdure, insects—and perhaps even the sun? But you know perfectly well that I can't become sentimental about vegetation and that my soul rebels against the strange new religion which to my mind will always have something shocking about it for every *spiritual* person. I shall never believe that the *souls of the Gods live in plants*, and even if they did, I shouldn't be much concerned and I should consider my own soul of much greater value than that of sanctified vegetables.[39]

Nature, he said elsewhere, is a dictionary: "The whole visible universe is but a storehouse of images and signs to which the imagination will give a relative place and value; it is a sort of pasture

35. *The Essence of Laughter*, p. 29.
36. *Baudelaire: A Criticism*, p. 28.
37. *Intimate Journals*, trans. Christopher Isherwood (Boston: Beacon Press, 1957), p. 53.
38. *The Mirror of Art: Critical Studies*, trans. and ed. Jonathan Mayne (Garden City, New York: Doubleday Anchor Books, 1956), p. 43.
39. *Self-Portrait*, p. 96.

which the imagination must digest and transform." [40] Nature is a proper subject for art only when it is subjectively re-created by the artist, as in Poe's peculiarly unnaturalistic landscape descriptions, for "that which is created by the Mind is more living than Matter." [41] Whereas the early romantics believed in an ideal of progress, Baudelaire detested the very idea of progress, not only because he believed that "there cannot be any Progress . . . except within the individual and by the individual himself," [42] but also because progress is dependent on time, which for Baudelaire was the enemy, the great destroyer, to be forgotten through drugs and drunkenness, mastered only through the use of it creatively. Whereas the early romantics exalted feeling, Baudelaire distrusted it: "I know nothing more stupid than *pure feeling*, which is the sole inspiration of women and children.—Feeling impels a child, if he is very energetic, to kill his father for a pot of jam or, if he is 18, to buy lace for a prostitute; it impels a woman to kill her husband in order to buy jewels or to support a rascal—exactly as it impels a dog to push everything aside in order to seize a piece of meat." [43]

Whereas the early romantics worked for society, even when they rebelled against it, Baudelaire felt that the poet is inevitably at war with the society in which he lives. "To be a useful person has always appeared to me something particularly horrible" [44]—thus the poet is indifferent to all things worldly. When the poet is born, his mother cries to Heaven that she would rather have borne a nest of vipers than such an "absurd abomination," [45] but if the world despises him, the true poet remains sublimely indifferent, aware that his kingdom is not of this world.

Baudelaire the visionary attempts to see beyond the surface to a deeper reality that will cause him to forget the physical degradation of existence, the chaos of appearances, the tyranny of time. A second means of defense is to cultivate dandyism. Baudelaire never wrote his proposed book on *Le Dandyisme literaire ou la Grandeur sans conviction*, but his essays and journals show that he made many attempts to define what he meant by the dandy, a personal ideal which he had greater hope of attaining than his dream of visionary fulfillment. That the two ideals are both similar and incompatible is shown by the subtitle of his projected book, "La Grandeur sans conviction." [46] When the man of sensitivity fails in his search for a

40. *The Mirror of Art*, p. 241.
41. *Intimate Journals*, p. 3.
42. *Intimate Journals*, p. 29.
43. *Self-Portrait*, p. 187.
44. *Intimate Journals*, p. 27.
45. *Poems of Baudelaire: A Transla-* tion of *Les Fleurs du Mal*, trans. Roy Campbell (New York: Pantheon Books, 1952), p. 3.
46. Margaret Gilman, *Baudelaire the Critic* (New York: Columbia University Press, 1943), p. 157.

sublime reality that may be consistently maintained, when all nature, including his own human nature, begins to seem chaotic and corrupt, when he can take no solace in conventional religion, he must either submit to his degradation and become a demon or war against it and become a dandy. If he chooses the latter course, he assumes responsibility for himself by attempting to suppress the innate corruption of his nature by creating himself anew from a self-determined pattern. The romantic naturalist considers any pose bad to the extent that it is unnatural. Baudelaire considered dandyism magnificent simply because it is a pose.

"Dandyism is an institution as strange and obscure as the duel," Baudelaire explains in "The Painter of Modern Life," his essay on Constantin Guys. "It is very ancient, for Caesar, Catilina and Alcibiades were amongst its most brilliant representatives; and it is very widespread, for Chateaubriand has found it in the forests and on the lake-shores of the New World." [47] Baudelaire considered Chateaubriand the father of modern dandyism, but referred also to Sheridan, Brummel, and Byron as English examples of the type; in fact, an allusion to the English novel of "high life" would suggest that a main source of Baudelaire's concept of the dandy may well have been the heroes of novels by Bulwer-Lytton and Disraeli, the Pelhams and Vivien Greys who derived from such real life dandies as Count D'Orsay and such fictional dandies as D'Albert of Gautier's *Mademoiselle de Maupin*. But in taking over what was already an established label for a recognized character type, Baudelaire made it clear that while "dandyism, an institution above laws, has laws to which all its representatives . . . are strictly subject," it is the mark of the true dandy that he be unique.[48] The dandy ought to have sufficient money so that he may follow his fancy, and his dress ought to be a visible symbol of his aristocratic superiority; but neither wealth nor material elegance is an end in itself for the true dandy. He wants nothing in excess, he "would be content to be allowed to live indefinitely on credit," and he knows that "the perfection of personal appearance consists in complete simplicity." [49] What distinguishes the dandy from other men is neither his wealth nor appearance, but his "burning need to acquire originality, within the apparent bounds of convention." [50] In other words, the dandy is an artist of life who makes of himself an artistic creation.

Although the dandy prides himself on doing nothing useful and "aspires to indifference," [51] he is not simply a man of leisure bent

47. *The Essence of Laughter*, pp. 46–47.
48. *The Essence of Laughter*, p. 47.
49. *The Essence of Laughter*, p. 47.
50. *The Essence of Laughter*, p. 48.
51. *The Essence of Laughter*, p. 28.

upon personal cultivation alone. More damned even than the natural
man in Baudelaire's eyes was the man who

> never gambols,
> Nor crawls, nor roars, but, from the rest withdrawn,
> Gladly of this whole earth would make a shambles
> And swallow up existence with a yawn . . .[52]

Baudelaire knew that the best way to escape the ennui and *acedia*
which afflicted him throughout his life was to immerse himself in
work. His dandy is dedicated to disinterested work and usually serves
as poet, priest, or soldier:

> There are no great men save the poet, the priest, and the sol-
> dier.
> The man who sings, the man who offers up sacrifice, and the
> man who sacrifices himself.
> The rest are born for the whip.[53]

All other human activities are trivial, locked in time, and it is the
mission of the dandy to "combat and destroy triviality." [54] He remains aloof from distraction, reads no newspapers, and wears gloves
for fear of the itch; nonetheless, he burns with something not unlike
Pater's "hard, gem-like flame": "The characteristic beauty of the
dandy consists, above all, in his air of reserve," Baudelaire explained,
"which in turn, arises from his unshakable resolve not to feel any
emotion. It might be likened to a hidden fire whose presence can
be guessed at; a fire that could blaze up, but does not wish to do
so." [55]

The stoicism of the dandy, his adherence to a rigid code, and his
aloofness from worldly concerns make him a religious type that
"borders on spirituality." [56] Although dandyism "is a sort of cult of
oneself, which can dispense even with what are commonly called
illusions"—that is, *Grandeur sans conviction*—it is a "sort of religion" in that it exacts strict obedience and imposes terrible formulas
upon its devotees.[57] The dandy, W. H. Auden has remarked, is the
"religious hero turned upside down." [58]

Among the monastic rules of dandyism is that of chastity. Applied to the artist, Baudelaire's strictures on the advisability of chastity are historically important, for he was one of the first writers to
express himself on the subject. Whereas the Sacred Fount artists find

---

52. *Poems of Baudelaire*, p. 2.
53. *Intimate Journals*, p. 41.
54. *The Essence of Laughter*, p. 48.
55. *The Essence of Laughter*, p. 50.
56. *The Essence of Laughter*, p. 48.
57. *The Essence of Laughter*, p. 48.
58. "Introduction" to *Intimate Jour-*
nals, p. xix.

their motivation in the pursuit of love and often confuse artistic inspiration with erotic stimulation, Baldelaire insisted that art and sex are irreconcilable. "The more a man cultivates the arts the less he fornicates," he wrote in his journals, for "to fornicate is to aspire to enter into another; the artist never emerges from himself." [59] Baudelaire admired keenly Delacroix's passion for work. "The truth is that during his later years everything that one normally calls pleasure had vanished from his life, having all been replaced by a single harsh, exacting, terrible pleasure, namely *work*, which by that time was not merely a passion but might properly have been called a rage." [60] As a result of this absorption in his art, Delacroix "regarded woman as an object of art, delightful and well suited to excite the mind, but disobedient and disturbing once one throws open the door of one's heart to her, and gluttonously devouring of time and strength." [61] In his dandy stage, Samuel Cramer of *La Fanfarlo* feels that love ought to be less a matter of the senses than of the intelligence. He considers the sexual act a corruption of love and yearns for the hermaphroditic status of the angels. But when he falls in love with the beautiful dancer, La Fanfarlo, he learns differently and from that moment is destroyed as an artist. As the story ends, the former poet is even considering the founding of a political journal.

Therefore, for Baudelaire, woman is the anti-dandy:

> Woman is the opposite of the Dandy. Therefore she should inspire horror.
> Woman is hungry, and she wants to eat; thirsty, and she wants to drink.
> She is in rut and she wants to be possessed.
> What admirable qualities!
> Woman is natural, that is to say abominable.
> Thus she is always vulgar; the opposite, in fact, of the Dandy.[62]

As J. Mitchell Morse has remarked, Baudelaire's conception of woman as anti-dandy is an anticipation of Joyce's lusty, earthy Molly Bloom and Anna Livia.[63] Baudelaire, like Joyce, also saw the obverse of the coin and realized that all women, partaking as they do of the universal earth-mother, may be closer to the ultimate mysteries of life and death than any man. Woman may be a natural brute, but she is also "a divinity, a star that presides over all the

59. *Intimate Journals*, p. 49.
60. *The Mirror of Art*, p. 331.
61. *The Mirror of Art*, p. 334.
62. *Intimate Journals*, p. 25.

63. "Baudelaire, Stephen Dedalus, and Shem the Penman," pp. 192–193.

parturitions of the male brain" [64]—and we are reminded of that moment, just before Molly's soliloquy in *Ulysses,* when Leopold Bloom, standing on his porch, gazes at the heavens and reflects on the nature of moon and woman. In the poem "The Giantess" we have clearly a suggestion of the earth-mother:

> Of old when Nature, in her verve defiant,
> Conceived each day some birth of monstrous mien,
> I would have lived near some young female giant
> Like a voluptuous cat beside a queen;
>
> To see her body flowering with her soul
> Freely develop in her mighty games,
> And in the mists that through her gaze would roll
> Guess that her heart was hatching sombre flames;
>
> To roam her mighty contours as I please,
> Ramp on the cliff of her tremendous knees,
> And in the solstice, when the suns that kill
>
> Make her stretch out across the land and rest,
> To sleep beneath the shadow of her breast
> Like a hushed village underneath a hill. [65]

Baudelaire, though, never managed to come to terms with woman any more than he did with the absolute. If the seer in his make-up made him seek platonic idealizations of a divine muse or to see woman as a "divinity," he knew too that though woman may be that being who is "as terrible and incommunicable as God," there was this essential difference: "the Infinite does not communicate because it would blind and overwhelm the Finite, whereas the Being of whom we speak is perhaps incomprehensible only because she has nothing to communicate." [66] Insofar as the artist is concerned, only cooks and harlots serve him a useful purpose; and the dandy may well emulate Baudelaire's Don Juan in Hell:

> Showing their hanging breasts and their open gowns,
> Women writhed under the dark firmament,
> And, like a large flock of offered victims,
> Their long roaring dragged along behind him. . . .
> But the calm hero, leaning on his rapier,
> Looked at the wake of the boat and did not deign to
>   notice anything. [67]

64. *The Essence of Laughter,* p. 50.   66. *The Essence of Laughter,* p. 50.
65. *Poems of Baudelaire,* p. 25.   67. *Baudelaire: A Criticism,* p. 7.

The life which Baudelaire led—particularly the years of his bondage to the coarse harlot Jeanne Duval—enables us to understand not only the source of his disgust for women, but also the fact that for him the dandy was as unattainable an ideal as the seer. What is remarkable, again, is not the attainment but the attempt. We may be struck by the irony of the contrast between Baudelaire's belief in dandyism and his untidy existence, but we cannot help but admire him for the difficulty of the task he set himself. Surely, no one has ever had to work harder at being a dandy than Baudelaire, and there is something commendable in the fact that he never entirely gave up the effort. "As for your fears about my personal degradation in the midst of poverty," he wrote to his mother, "be assured that all my life, whether I was in rags or living decently, I have always spent two hours in grooming myself." [68] With all this effort, he achieved only the effect, in the eyes of the Goncourt brothers, of "une vraie toilette de guillotiné." [69]

The guillotine image probably came naturally to the Goncourts, for if Baudelaire seemed primarily a *voyant* to his successors and a dandy to himself, he seemed more like a demon to his contemporaries. He was the condemned poet of *Les Fleurs du Mal,* a known experimenter in vice and drugs, a profligate whose family considered him incapable of taking care of his own money, a Poe-like haunted man who seemed at times to be possessed by a devil. Again, we find the inevitable reaction from the ideal—the *either-or* attitude, the unwillingness to compromise, of the "totality" artist. When he could not escape his selfness by losing his ego in universal oneness, he deliberately cultivated his personal being and became a dandy; when the pull of the flesh became too strong for him to resist, he sought degradation by means of a deliberate descent to vice. W. H. Auden describes the process in this way: "Logically, the Dandy should remain chaste: if, like Baudelaire, he lacks the will-power to do so, he can at least partially assert his freedom from natural desire by choosing to be debauched, i.e., by yielding deliberately to what he despises and making it as despicable as possible, until every pleasure in love has been eliminated except the knowledge that he is deliberately doing evil." [70] There is much to be said for Sartre's thesis that Baudelaire deliberately chose to suffer.[71] The artist, Baudelaire said, is a perpetual convalescent, and to be convalescent one must

68. *Self-Portrait,* p. 86.
69. Peter Quennell, *Baudelaire and the Symbolists* (2d. rev. ed.; London: Weidenfeld and Nicolson, 1954), p. 4.
70. "Introduction" to *Intimate Journals,* p. xix.
71. Jean-Paul Sartre, *Baudelaire,* trans. Martin Turnell (Norfolk, Conn.: New Directions, 1950), pp. 26–27 and *passim.*

have been ill. Thus he could write, "J'ai cultivé mon hystérie avec jouissance et terreur." [72] In his quest of sin and illness, Baudelaire is a real-life counterpart of Mann's Adrian Leverkuhn.

From childhood, Baudelaire said, he felt the conflicting sensations of "the horror of life and the ecstasy of life." [73] The combination is characteristic of many writers of the latter half of the nineteenth century, though few of his imitators and spiritual followers felt the conflict as passionately as did Baudelaire. It is his intensity which justifies T. S. Eliot's statement that Baudelaire "was man enough for damnation." Much of his Satanism, Eliot said, was "an attempt to get into Christianity by the back door." [74] And it is clear from such works as the essay on "The Poem of Hashish" that Baudelaire's motivation for demonism was essentially the same as that for being a seer and a dandy. "How sad," he wrote, "that man's vices, however horrible we may conceive them to be, themselves contain the proof . . . of his longing for the Infinite." [75] In describing the sensations of one who has taken opium, he compares the process to poetic inspiration and speaks of the "monstrous expansion of time and space" to the point where the opium eater not only begins to feel godlike but can proclaim "I am God." [76] There is the ecstasy, followed by the horror of the aftereffects, the realization of the fatal skin, the inevitable destruction of life in the effort to use it.

Baudelaire's three masks as divine, dandy, and demon are incompatible. Yet they derive from the same impulse, and they balance one another. When he pushed any one of the roles to its limit, it tended to merge with the others. Always there was the same urge to alternating self-extension and self-contraction, the desire to overpower the universe. He summed up the meaning of his existence in the opening lines of the "My Heart Laid Bare" journal: "De la vaporisation et de la centralisation du *Moi*. Tout est là." [77] The capital letter and the italics suggest that Baudelaire meant by *"Moi"* something in addition to his selfhood—perhaps something like world soul, group ego, Coleridge's "the infinite I AM." As for what he meant by "vaporisation" and "centralisation," we have only to think of the diffusing and contracting tendencies of Poe's artist-god. Then we may well agree that "tout est là"; everything does indeed depend on that.

72. Quennell, p. 25.
73. *Intimate Journals,* p. 50.
74. *Selected Essays, 1917–1932* (New York: Harcourt, Brace and Co., 1932), pp. 335–345.
75. *The Essence of Laughter,* p. 67.
76. *The Essence of Laughter,* p. 96.
77. Quoted on the title page of Martin Turnell, *Baudelaire: A Study of His Poetry* (London: Hamish Hamilton, 1953). (See *Intimate Journals,* p. 24.)

ALTHOUGH Baudelaire blankets his literary age in France in the same way that Rousseau contained within himself the romantic movement of the first half of the century, Baudelaire's influence was dependent upon those contemporaries and literary heirs who provided a cultural climate in which the seeds planted by Baudelaire could flourish. The Ivory Tower concept in Vigny, Saint-Beuve, and Gerard de Nerval; the beginnings of art-for-art's-sake in Gautier and Flaubert; the cultivation of poetry as incantation and ritual in Mallarmé, Rimbaud, Laforgue, and other poets of the Symbolist movement; the diabolic rebellion of a Rimbaud or a Lautreamont; Villiers de l'Isle-Adam's *Axël*, a ritualistic drama which became the bible of the Symbolists in the last part of the century; the progression from dandy to esthete and the researches in diabolism and religion of J.-K. Huysmans—these are but a few of the steps in the progressive dissociation of art from life which, joining with a similar development in England, culminated in the decadence of the *fin de siècle*.

Although Baudelaire's literary heirs thought of themselves as solitaries and, with several exceptions, had difficulty appreciating and understanding each other, literary historians have had no trouble in grouping them. When we think of French literature since 1850, we think of schools and cults—the Parnassians, the Symbolists, the art-for-art's-sake movement, the Decadents, the Surrealists, and so on. Because there is considerable harmony and overlapping among the various groups, the same writers may belong to several movements. And what separates individual from individual, group from group, seems in retrospect less important than what they share—the dehumanization of art, the indifference to reality, the contempt for society, the conventionalization of alienation as pose, and the scorn for audience reflected in willful obscurity and experimentation.

The harmony may be attributed only in part to the fact that most of the writers of the later nineteenth century had a common source in Baudelaire. It was not until the 1880's that he was enshrined as the patron saint of a new cult of art worshipers, though his influence upon the individual writers who helped to found the cult had been strong. Nor would it be correct to say that these writers were simply imitators. Rimbaud and Mallarmé certainly must be considered innovators who went beyond Baudelaire in their intentions and in their art. With their help and through mutual effort, others succeeded in not merely prolonging but intensifying each of the three roles assumed by Baudelaire: the dandy becomes an esthete; the demon is no longer an experimenter in vice, but a Gilles de Rais or Marquis de Sade; and the visionary in Baudelaire, so easily reconciled with Christianity and the Hermetic tradition, is carried beyond the search for a hidden spiritual reality which is outside him to the point where he achieves a descent into *le néant* which is both within and beyond the "I." The major difference is that whereas Baudelaire wore all three of the masks, few of his followers were able to combine more than two.

Compared with such *voyants* as Gerard de Nerval, Rimbaud, and Mallarmé, Baudelaire the visionary seems conservative. The half-mad Nerval is Balzac's Louis Lambert come to life—the "desdichado" or outcast who wanders through life never quite sure where reality stops and *le rêve* begins. His autobiographical short novel *Aurélia* was for Nerval the record of his painful "descent into hell," which he seems to have taken for the spirit world, and is for modern readers a vivid record of insanity. In this strange work the poet walks through Paris accompanied by his own double, talks to the dead, files down a ring belonging to his mistress and sees blood flow from it, and, like Roderick Usher, is terrorized by the realization that "nothing is unimportant, nothing powerless in the universe; a single atom can dissolve everything, and save everything! What terror!" [78] and that "we are the gleams of that central fire which gives life and which is already growing weaker." [79] The poet-hero tries to establish universal harmony by means of cabalistic arts and occult powers, and much of the pain of his ordeal he attributes to the revenge of God. Whereas Baudelaire pursued a *chimera* and knew it for that, Nerval captured his *chimera* but was never quite sure it was the real thing. In any case, the effort cost him his sanity, and he died in an asylum.

Mallarmé too goes beyond Baudelaire. In his work we often seem to be safely within the realm of the Poe-Baudelaire *correspondances,* as in the poem "Les Fenêtres" with its characteristic lines:

> I flee, and cling to every casement window
> Turning my back on life and, blessed,
> In their panes washed by eternal dews
> And gilded by the chaste morning of the infinite
> I look upon myself and see myself an Angel! [80]

or the prose poem, "The White Water-Lily," in which "the silvery mist chilling the willow trees" becomes "the limpid glance" of the

---

78. *Selected Writings of Gerard de Nerval,* trans. and ed. Geoffrey Wagner (New York: Grove Press, 1957), p. 167.

79. *Selected Writings,* p. 125.

80. Marcel Raymond, *From Baudelaire to Surrealism* (London: Peter Owen, 1957), p. 24.

poet's mistress.[81] "The poet," Mallarmé wrote, "must find and establish hidden identities through a kind of equivalence which will gnaw and reduce physical reality, and always strive for a central state of purity." [82] The true function of literature is the "orphic explanation of the Earth," [83] and "Man's duty is to observe with the eyes of the divinity." [84] Wallace Fowlie has shown at length how for Mallarmé the writing of a poem was a spiritual exercise in which the experience of religion was completely merged with that of art.[85] But Mallarmé goes beyond Baudelaire and most of his contemporaries in several significant ways. First, he turns the work of art itself into a sacred object. Whatever is sacred, he said, ought to be clothed in mystery, and he regretted the fact that poetry, unlike music, must be expressed in language which is accessible to everyone. As a result, any fool thinks that he can understand poetry, and it is taught in schools "to all alike, democratically. For it is difficult to tell in advance which tousled head contains the white sibylline star." [86] Mallarmé's experiments in typography, as in *Un Coup de dés*, may be explained by his desire to make poetry more sacred by making it so mysterious and deliberately obscure that only the initiate may confront it with the proper humility. In "The Book: A Spiritual Instrument," Mallarmé describes even the physical aspects of a book in religious terms: "The foldings of a book, in comparison with the large-sized, open newspaper, have an almost religious significance. But an even greater significance lies in their thickness when they are piled together; for then they form a tomb in miniature for our souls." [87]

The tomb image occurs again in another essay: "A poet today, in the midst of this society which refuses to let him live, is a man who seeks out solitude in order to sculpture his own tomb." [88] Baudelaire was unable to get away from himself, and his dandy is an artist of life. "When the artist sits down to write," Mallarmé says, "he *makes himself*"; [89] and the implication is that he does so only when he writes, that the artist, not the man, is the true dandy. The personal life of the poet—whatever he may be socially and professionally—is of little account: Mallarmé the ineffectual schoolteacher is another being from Mallarmé the poet. It was the poet who set the programme for his life in a letter of 1866:

81. *Selected Prose Poems, Essays, and Letters,* trans. and ed. Bradford Cook (Baltimore: Johns Hopkins Press, 1956), p. 5.
82. *Selected Prose Poems,* p. 103.
83. *Selected Prose Poems,* p. 15.
84. *Selected Prose Poems,* p. 25.
85. *Mallarmé* (Chicago: University of Chicago Press, 1953), pp. 231–249.
86. *Selected Prose Poems,* p. 10.
87. *Selected Prose Poems,* p. 25.
88. *Selected Prose Poems,* p. 22.
89. *Selected Prose Poems,* p. 84.

I have laid the foundations for a magnificent work. Every man has his own special secret. Many men die without having discovered it, and they will not discover it because, when they are dead, neither they nor their secret will remain. I died, and I have risen from the dead with the key to the jewelled treasure of my last spiritual casket. Now I shall open it far from all borrowed inspiration, and its mystery will spread through the most beautiful of heavens. For twenty years I shall take monastic refuge in myself, shunning all publicity, except for private readings with my friends. I am working on everything at once; I mean that everything is so well ordered in me that each sensation is transformed at birth and simply pigeon-holed in a given book or poem. When a poem is ripe, it will fall. You can see that I am imitating the natural law.[90]

The poet is the dead self, his poetry its tomb. When we are told that "one of Mallarmé's most original rites . . . called for a Hamlet-'hero'—simultaneously actor and priest—appearing alone on an evanescent stage, reading from 'the book of himself,' " [91] we are given a glimpse of the ultimate in portraits of the artist.

Mallarmé went beyond self-worship in his ideal of the poet who, having to read from "the book of himself" since it is the only one he has, yet strives ultimately to efface himself. The poet should detach himself from the time in which he lives: "All he can do is work in mystery with an eye to the future or to eternity, and occasionally send his visiting card, a few stanzas, or a sonnet to the 'living,' so that they won't stone him, should they suspect him of realizing that they do not exist." [92] If "to create is to conceive an object . . . in its absence," [93] then the source of beauty is le néant: "After I had found Nothingness, I found Beauty." [94] Mallarmé's equation of music with silence is not unrelated to the belief developed by Villiers and Huysmans that to desire nothing is to possess everything. Joseph Chiari has summed up his aim in poetry: "Each poem is a new philosophical suicide of the poet's self, a kind of phoenix-like operation to rise from nowhere to nowhere." [95] According to Fowlie, his culminating ritual was that of the absent master who consecrates his work by his disappearance.[96] In abandoning himself to le néant, in becoming indifferent to self as well as to society, Mallarmé goes beyond Baudelaire and all artists who remain trapped in self. If the

90. *Selected Prose Poems*, p. 90.
91. Bradford Cook, in *Selected Prose Poems*, p. xvi.
92. *Selected Prose Poems*, p. 17.
93. *Selected Prose Poems*, p. 48.
94. *Selected Prose Poems*, pp. 89–90.
95. *Symbolism from Poe to Mallarmé: The Growth of a Myth* (London: Rockliff, 1956), pp. 146–147.
96. *Mallarmé*, p. 21.

ultimate form of alienation is suicide, then Mallarmé's poetry, dependent as it is on the disappearance of the poet and the effacement of objects so that only the idea remains, is a testimony from beyond the frontier of life.

Like Mallarmé, Rimbaud came to equate poetry with silence, but his main distinction is in extending Baudelaire's demonism to the point of nihilism. He hailed Baudelaire as the first true *voyant*, but felt that his predecessor placed undue emphasis upon the individual personality and soul, "the remains of an outworn and out-of-date egoism." [97] To become a true *voyant*, "a ravisher of the celestial fire," [98] one must obliterate self. Baudelaire cultivated his hysteria, but Rimbaud tried to deprave, degrade, and kill the self through the deliberate "dérèglement de tous les sens." [99] Baudelaire was moralistic enough to apologize for his experiments in drugs and other vice, and sensible enough to realize that opium dreams were after all delusions; the amoral Rimbaud felt that any means, including drugs, are good to the extent that they help the individual destroy his human reason and ego so that he may become the voice of the eternal. During the relatively short period when he was composing poetry, Rimbaud seems to have believed that he had acquired supernatural powers through magic and alchemy. Like Nerval, he thought of himself as a Faust, and came to believe that his sin of pride and arrogance was as great as Faust's and that what he had thought was absolute, selfless truth was only himself. It was then that he abandoned poetry to become not the romantic man of action he is sometimes depicted as being, but a neuter who had voluntarily cut himself off from his human *raison d'être*, retaining the capacity to suffer but no longer capable of transcending it. Fowlie has described him as "the one example of boy-poet-prophet who abandoned everything: his mother, his country, his God, his love, his poetry. He finally abandoned his mightiest sin: the desire to go too far in the order of creation." [100] We find in Rimbaud a continual conflict between the instinct for aggressive action and the temptation to detach himself from life. On the one hand, his "dérèglement de tous les sens," looking back to Sade and Barbey d'Aurevilly, helps to prepare the way for the diabolism of Lautreamont's *Maldoror*, in which the poet-hero finds his greatest moment in the rape of a female shark, and for later criminal-artists such as Aleister Crowley, Baron Corvo, Stanislaus de Guaita (who spoke of "le vertige extatique du Crime"),

97. Enid Starkie, *Arthur Rimbaud* (rev. and enl. ed.; New York: Norton, 1947), p. 14.
98. Starkie, p. 128.
99. Starkie, p. 129.
100. *Rimbaud: The Myth of Childhood* (London: Dennis Dobson, 1946), p. 33.

and Jean Genet. On the other hand, the development of Stephen Dedalus might have been different but for the pattern established by Rimbaud. The *Lettre du Voyant,* with its overtones of purification and secret initiation, is not unlike the esthetic theory and the consecration scene of Joyce's *Portrait.* It involves the renunciation of society, family, religion; the poet makes himself a stranger to the language of his people and discovers the language of his other self in "la plenitude du grand songe," the dream perhaps of a *Finnegans Wake.*[101]

As a literary artist J.-K. Huysmans hardly belongs in the same company with Mallarmé and Rimbaud, but as a novelist in an age of poets, he reflected most of the literary tendencies of his day and did much to popularize them. His most celebrated work, *A rebours* became a guidebook for esthetes, "the breviary of the decadence." [102] Whereas Mallarmé and Rimbaud extended the visionary and demonic aspects of Baudelaire in their writings, it is Huysmans who transforms Baudelaire's dandy from romantic aristocrat-rebel to the esthete of the *fin de siècle.*

The Duc Jean des Esseintes, hero of *A rebours,* is the dandy turned decadent. A composite figure, he owes much to Comte Robert de Montesquiou, who served also as a source of Proust's Baron de Charlus; much to Huysmans himself; and much to Roderick Usher. Like Poe's hero, des Esseintes is the sole surviving male descendant of a family once powerful which has steadily degenerated. He is introduced as "a frail young man of thirty, anaemic and nervous, with hollow cheeks, eyes of a cold, steely blue, a small but still straight nose, and long, slender hands." [103] He has a pointed beard of the palest blonde, and the expression of his eyes is at once languid and energetic. In childhood he had suffered persistent attacks of fever and certain "scrofulous affections." Orphaned at sixteen, when his mother, "a tall, silent, white-faced woman, died of general debility" and his father "succumbed to a vague and mysterious malady," [104] he found refuge in art and literature (the writers of the Latin Decadence were his early favorites), and though he engaged in unspecified perversities, he left vice behind him when he realized that his life was endangered by it. Nervous and hypersensitive, like Roderick Usher, he is pained by any contact with the

101. See Wallace Fowlie, *Age of Surrealism* (New York: Swallow Press and William Morrow, 1950), pp. 45–62.

102. Arthur Symons, *The Symbolist Movement in Literature* (London: Constable, 1911), p. 139.

103. *Against the Grain* (*A rebours*), with Intro. by Havelock Ellis (New York: Illustrated Editions, 1931), p. 78.

104. *Against the Grain,* p. 78.

normal and natural. He yearns for a "desert hermitage, combined
with modern comfort, an ark on dry land and nicely warmed, whither
he could fly for refuge from the incessant deluge of human folly." [105]
Insofar as *A rebours* has a story, it is the story of his discovering and
outfitting his ideal retreat.

Des Esseintes' house at Fontenay is the ultimate in Ivory Towers.
Located in an almost inaccessible spot, yet close enough to Paris
"to add a spice to his solitariness," [106] it is remodelled by its owner
in such a way that it becomes not only a retreat from which the in-
habitant may shut out the world, but an expression of his hyper-
esthetic character. Typical is the pink boudoir "where, amid dainty
carved furniture of the light-yellow camphor-wood of Japan, under
a sort of tent of pink Indian satin, the flesh tints borrowed a soft,
warm glow from the artfully disposed lights sifting down through
the rich material." [107] In the early days, while he is still in the habit
of inviting women to his house, he has suspended from the ceiling
of the boudoir a cage in which a cricket is kept prisoner to chirp
and remind des Esseintes of his wretched childhood until "roused
from his reveries by the movements of the woman he was fondling
mechanically at the moment . . . a sudden commotion would shake
his soul, a longing for revenge on dreary hours endured in former
times, a mad craving to befoul with base and carnal acts his recollections of bygone family life." [108] His dining room resembles a ship's
cabin, that the maritime atmosphere may sharpen his jaded appetite,
and while eating he "would rest his eyes by looking over the collection of chronometers and mariner's compasses, sextants and dividers,
binoculars and charts scattered about the table, whereon figured
only a single book, bound in sea-green morocco, the 'Adventures of
Arthur Gordon Pym,' specially printed for his behoof on pure linen-
laid paper, hand picked, bearing a sea-gull for water mark." [109] He
keeps a pet turtle the shell of which he has had glazed in gold and
set with jewels so that the movement of the creature may accentu-
ate the colors of his carpet. For a while he fills his house with artificial flowers that look real, then improves upon that by finding
natural flowers that look false.

The theme of des Esseintes' house is artificiality, for, like Baudelaire in the essay on cosmetics, he believes that "artifice was . . .
the distinctive mark of human genius." [110] But whereas Baudelaire
considered dandyism dependent upon simplicity, with Huysmans
the principle of adornment becomes increasingly complex, and

105. *Against the Grain*, pp. 83–84.   108. *Against the Grain*, p. 90.
106. *Against the Grain*, p. 88.   109. *Against the Grain*, p. 101.
107. *Against the Grain*, p. 89.   110. *Against the Grain*, p. 104.

eventually even des Esseintes begins to feel smothered by the intricate ornamentation surrounding him. He decides to leave his retreat and visit England. First he gets in the proper mood by reading Dickens and eating English foods. Then, having imagined the fulfillment, he realizes that there is no need to test the reality, and, like the lovers in Villiers' *Axêl*, discovers in renunciation the principle that to desire nothing is to possess all. He returns from the nearest railway station "feeling all the physical exhaustion and moral fatigue of a man restored to the domestic hearth after long and perilous journeyings." [111] Like Roderick Usher, though, des Esseintes begins to feel stifled by the oppressive weight of an atmosphere which is actually himself. On doctor's orders, at the verge of a nervous breakdown, he leaves Fontenay in a vain attempt to recover his health, and *A rebours* ends with a prayer of Christian humility: "Lord, take pity on the Christian who doubts, on the sceptic who would fain believe, on the galley-slave of life who puts out to sea alone, in the darkness of night, beneath a firmament illumined no longer by the consoling beacon-fires of the ancient hope." [112]

From this prayer and other evidence—the very extravagance of the descriptions, the occasional touches of satire, as when the pet turtle dies from the weight of its ornamentation, and the strong hints that des Esseintes is an abnormal person compensating for his inadequacies—it is clear that *A rebours* may be a portrait of the most extreme kind of esthete, but hardly a defense of the type. Like its British counterpart, Oscar Wilde's *The Picture of Dorian Grey*, it is actually a curiously moral depiction of vice and perversion. After all, Huysmans says, des Esseintes' "tendencies to artificiality, his longing for eccentricity" were "results of plausible studies, supraterrestrial refinements, semi-theological speculations: in ultimate analysis they amounted to the same thing as religious enthusiasms, aspirations towards an unknown universe, towards a far-off beatitude, just as ardently to be desired as that promised to believers by the Scriptures." [113] If des Esseintes is partly a portrait of his creator, we know what happened to the dandy-turned-esthete when he returned to society, for Huysman's four later novels dealing with the writer Durtal, a self-portrait, show first, in *Là-bas*, the turning toward demonism and Satanism through Research in black magic, and then, in the Catholic trilogy—*En Route, La Cathédrale* and *L'Oblat*—the turning toward religion. Whereas Baudelaire managed to be a religious visionary, dandy, and demon simultaneously, Huys-

111. *Against the Grain*, p. 242.   113. *Against the Grain*, p. 171.
112. *Against the Grain*, p. 339.

mans was one of the first writers to follow the now well-travelled route from dandyism to demonism to religious salvation.

III   *Aesthetes and Exiles*

THE growing dissociation of the artist from society in France during the later nineteenth century was paralleled by a similar development in England. Until the 1880's, when the French and English movements merged, the Aesthetic movement in England was for the most part an insular phenomenon not appreciably influenced by happenings on the Continent. Swinburne, deeply affected by Baudelaire, was almost alone in looking to French literature for direction. Ruskin, the Pre-Raphaelites, and William Morris looked to classic and medieval sources, and whereas Baudelaire in France broke sharply with the early Romantics, there is a more even progression from early to late romanticism in English literature. The early writers of the Aesthetic movement found their stimulus in Wordsworth, Shelley, and Keats (in whom they thought they recognized a pioneer champion of art-for-art's-sake), but overlooked William Blake, who could have been the Baudelaire of English literature. Blake did not come into his own until the last years of the century, when Yeats and his contemporaries rediscovered the nearest example of a *poète maudit* among their predecessors. Without a Blake or a Baudelaire to keynote rebellion, the Aesthetic movement in England was, not surprisingly, a tamer revolt than that which I have traced in French literature. Nonetheless, it produced in Oscar Wilde, Aubrey Beardsley, Baron Corvo, and other decadents of the *fin de siècle*, extremists who in many ways surpassed their French counterparts. More importantly, the Aesthetic movement served as part of the immediate background for Henry James and James Joyce; and when Proust sought a master, he turned not to his French predecessors for primary guidance, but to John Ruskin, one of the most eminently Victorian of Victorian writers.

Ruskin probably did more than any other writer of his time to enhance the prestige of the visual arts. We have only to compare the seedy Bohemian artists in Thackeray's novels with the artists of later fiction to realize that something must have happened in the interval to change the prevailing view of the artist. Although an exalted conception of the artist's mission was not unknown in England before Ruskin, he was the first really effective press agent for art. One would not expect a book like *Stones in Venice* to be a bestseller, but the surprising multitude of editions of that and other works by Ruskin testify to his effectiveness with the general public. He succeeded in removing art from the realm of entertainment and putting it safely into the area of religious and social endeavor, making the artist seem responsible and art respectable.

Ruskin's emphasis on the social and spiritual utility of art, his conviction that the artist can lead the way to a better world, is clearly a heritage from the artist-as-inspired-leader concept of the Romantic poets. Like Wordsworth and Shelley, he believed that the artist is the true leader of men because he is closer to the elementary forces of nature. Carlyle, we have seen, spoke in grandiose terms of the poet-prophet as hero, but distrusted the "dandiacal sect" and, on the whole, turned the path of reform away from both art and nature in favor of work and action for the good of society. Ruskin owed much of his sociological fervor to Carlyle and was certainly not averse to work (even Oscar Wilde pushed one of Ruskin's wheelbarrows at Oxford), but he helped also to restore the association between art and nature of the early romantics and to develop the idea beyond anything visualized by his predecessors. The nature that he championed in defending the painter Turner against charges of falsehood to life is not the same nature as that represented in the verse of the Lake poets. Ruskin, like the French Symbolists, insisted that underlying visible appearance is a deeper reality which the artist is capable of recognizing and transcribing, thus bringing a new vision to society and the desire for a world that is better than the apparent world because it is not only more beautiful, but closer to God's creation. His emphasis on the artist's unique powers of perception probably helped to bring about the conception of the artist as, above all else, a sensitive visionary, who sees things that are invisible to those ruled by habitual response. In a passage Proust-like in style and thought, Ruskin wrote:

When we begin to be concerned with the energies of man, we find ourselves instantly dealing with a double creature. Most part of his being seems to have a fictitious counterpart, which it is at his peril if he do not cast off and deny. . . . His false life is, indeed, but one of the conditions of death or stupor, but it acts, even when it cannot be said to animate, and is not always easily known from the true. It is that life of custom and accident in which many of us pass much of our time in the world; that life in which we do what we have not proposed, and speak what we do not mean, and assent to what we do not understand; that life which is overlaid by the weight of things external to it, and is moulded by them, instead of assimilating them; that which instead of grow-

ing and blossoming under any wholesome dew, is crystallized over
with it, as with hoar-frost, and becomes to the true life what an
arborescence is to a tree, a candied agglomeration of the thoughts
and habits foreign to it, brittle, obstinate and icy, which neither
bend nor grow, but must be crushed and broken to bits, if it stand
in our way. All men are liable to be in some degree frost-bitten in
this sort; all are partly encumbered and crusted over with idle
matter; only, if they have real life in them, they are always breaking this bark away in noble rents, until it becomes, like the black
strips upon the birch tree, only a witness of their own inward
strength.[114]

For Ruskin "the real life" which the best men discover in themselves is superior to that "life of custom and accident" which alone
is apparent to the casual spectator. So often are art and morality
associated in discussions of Ruskin's esthetic that it is sometimes forgotten that he was not urging a narrow sectarian ethic upon the artist.
While insisting that esthetic perception is a moral activity, he did
not think of morality as so much a question of right and wrong as
he did of the inevitable link between art and the whole man, of
whom the moral man is a part. Younger artists reacted against much
of Ruskin's evangelistic fervor, but most of them retained his conception of art as innately moral. And we must remember that by
exalting the superior moral perception of the artist and attacking
the ugliness of industrialized society, Ruskin actually encouraged
the alienation of the artist from the world in which he lives.

Perhaps the first work of prose fiction to express the concept of
art as an activity moral in itself and needing no justification is Dante
Gabriel Rossetti's short story "Hand and Soul," published in 1850.
Chiaro dell' Erma, an early Tuscan painter, is a young man thoroughly devoted to his art, "living entirely to himself. Sometimes,
after nightfall, he would walk abroad in the most solitary places he
could find; hardly feeling the ground under him, because of the
thoughts of the day which held him in fever." [115] A "feeling of worship and service" accompanies his painting: "It was the peace-offer-
ing that he made to God and to his own soul for the eager selfishness
of his aim. There was earth, indeed, upon the hem of his raiment,
but this was of the heaven, heavenly." Then one day, in a moment
of guilty apprehension, he realizes that "much of that reverence

114. *Works*, ed. E. T. Cook and Al-
exander   Wedderburn   (London,
1905), VIII, 191–192.
115. Quotations from this short story
have been taken from the text in

*Poems and Translations, 1850–1870,
Together   with   the   Prose   Story,
"Hand and Soul"* (London: Oxford
University Press, 1913), pp. 157–
172.

which he had mistaken for faith had been no more than the worship
of beauty." He decides that he will put his hand to no work except
that which reveals a moral purpose; instead of the action and passion
of human life, he will depict only "cold symbolism and abstract
impersonation." He loses his sense of irreverence and achieves serenity until on the day of a great feast at Pisa he witnesses a battle between two feuding families in the entry of a church where Chiaro
had painted a moral allegory on Peace—"there was so much blood
cast up the walls on a sudden, that it ran in long streams down
Chiaro's paintings." In revulsion, he says to himself, "Fame failed
me, faith failed me: and now this also,—the hope that I nourished
in this my generation of men,—shall pass from me, and leave my feet
and hands groping." But when Chiaro looks up, he finds a beautiful
woman in his studio, "and he knew her hair to be the golden veil
through which he beheld his dreams." She identifies herself as the
voice of his own soul and reproaches him for his presumption in
thinking that " 'I, in doing this, do strengthen God among men.'
When at any time hath he cried unto thee, saying, 'My son, lend
me thy shoulder, for I fail?' . . . Give thou to God no more than
he asketh of thee; but to man also, that which is man's." Chiaro's
mistake was in thinking that he could separate morality from art and
produce specifically didactic works. Art and morality, for Rossetti
as for Ruskin, are inseparable parts of the whole man, and the most
ethical art will be that in which the artist adheres to the truth of
his personal vision. Such an ethic is superior to the morality which
prevails outside the windows of the artist, who helps society best
by devoting himself to his art.

Walter Pater, like Ruskin and Rossetti, believed that great art,
which represents the quintessence of life, is ethical only to the extent
that it expresses human nature at its most ideally perceptive stage.
Like Rossetti in "Hand and Soul," he does not subordinate art to
ethics, but makes ethics a part of art: "He came to believe that art
actually enlarges and purifies the soul, by developing the emotions
and intellect and by holding up a vision of the ideal." [116] What separates him from both Ruskin and Rossetti is his inability to recognize
a divine unity behind the flux of appearance. Whereas Ruskin and
Rossetti believed that the artist could penetrate to reality by shedding
the layers of indifference and irreverence imposed on him by society,
thereby recognizing a Christian order beneath chaotic appearances,
Pater could discern no spiritual reality beyond the flux. His insistence

116. Ruth C. Child, *The Aesthetic*   millan, 1940), p. 10.
of Walter Pater (New York: Mac-

that the artist must create his own reality places him properly with the Ivory Tower writers.

If there is no true spiritual reality beyond the self, then the self becomes all that matters. One of Pater's contributions to the Aesthetic movement is his development of the esthete as a new kind of being, an artist of life, not unlike Baudelaire's dandy. *Marius the Epicurean,* Pater's symbolic autobiography, is the classic exposition of what Henry James was to describe as "the free brave personal way"—of the conviction that it is enough to *be* rather than to *do*. Young Marius after the death of his mother becomes a sceptic whose recognition of ceaseless flux is strengthened by his reading of Heraclitus, though, unlike Heraclitus, he cannot discern the divine order behind the flux. He settles then into Cyrenaicism, a modified form of hedonism, which consists of an appreciation of beauty in all of its forms in life, nature, and art, the totality of which perceptions leads to personal fulfillment. The later sections of the novel show Marius testing and discarding the other philosophies of his day. As he lies dying, a martyr to the Christianity he refused to embrace, he takes comfort in the realization that his life was not without value:

> Revelation, vision, the discovery of vision, the *seeing* of a perfect humanity, in a perfect world—through all his alternations of mind, by some dominant instinct, determined by the original necessities of his own nature and character, he had always set that above the *having*, or even the *doing*, of anything. For, such vision, if received with due attitude on his part was, in reality, the *being* something, and as such was surely a pleasant offering or sacrifice to whatever gods there might be, observant of him. And how goodly had the vision been!—one long unfolding of beauty and energy in things upon the closing of which he might gracefully utter his "Vixi!" [117]

This peculiarly Jamesian passage—it could be placed intact in the conclusion of *The Ambassadors*—expresses the conviction of a personal ethic that transcends hedonism: "Not pleasure, but fullness of life, and 'insight' as conducting to that fullness" [118] is what Marius earlier saw as the goal of his life. And the process of self-development calls for discipline of the faculties and rigid adherence to the personal vision: "As other men are concentrated upon truths of number, for instance, or on business, or it may be on the pleasures of appetite, so he is wholly bent on living in that full stream of refined sen-

117. *Marius the Epicurean, His Sensations and Ideas* (New York: Modern Library, n.d.), p. 378.
118. *Marius the Epicurean,* p. 125.

sation. And in the prosecution of this love of beauty, he claims an entire personal liberty, liberty of heart and mind, liberty, above all, from what may seem conventional answers to first questions." [119] Liberty leads to the final aloofness. As Marius reflects on the progression of his life, he realizes that "actually, as circumstances had determined, all its movement had been inward; movement of observation only, or even of pure meditation; in part, perhaps, because throughout it had been something of a *meditatio mortis,* ever facing towards the act of final detachment." [120]

Marius the Epicurean is a partial explanation of what Pater meant in the conclusion to *The Renaissance* when he wrote that "to burn always with this hard, gemlike flame, to maintain this ecstasy, is success in life." [121] He suppressed the "Conclusion" when he realized that several of his disciples had omitted the qualification "hard, gemlike" and that what he had intended as a plea for the losing of self in the consciousness of ecstacy was misunderstood as a plea for the enjoyment of sensual ecstasy for the sake of the self. That Marius is something other than the typical esthete is shown by his yearning for self-effacement, for "final detachment." The novel leaves him short of his goal, but in "Sebastian van Storck" of *Imaginary Portraits,* Pater clarified what he meant by "final detachment." The glorious youth Sebastian, who has naturally the beauty of appearance and refinement of intellect which the esthete tries to achieve artificially, is like Villiers' Axêl in his scorn of life. Coldly rejecting the girl who loves him, refusing even to have his portrait painted, Sebastian seeks only to lose himself in "the void, the *tabula rasa,* into which, through all those apparent energies of man and nature, that in truth are but forces of disintegration, the world was really settling." [122] He yearns for annihilation:

> Detachment: to hasten hence: to fold up one's whole self, as a vesture put aside: to anticipate, by such individual force as he could find in him, the slow disintegration by which nature herself is levelling the eternal hills:—there would be the secret of peace, of such dignity and truth as there could be in a world which after all was essentially an illusion. . . . One's personal presence, the presence, such as it is, of the most incisive things and persons around us, could only lessen by so much, that which really is. To restore *tabula rasa,* then, by a continual effort at self-effacment! Actually proud at times of his curious, well-reasoned

119. *Marius the Epicurean,* pp. 219–
220.
120. *Marius the Epicurean,* p. 370.
121. (New York: Modern Library,
n.d.), p. 197.
122. Library Edition (London: Macmillan, 1922), p. 108.

nihilism, he could but regard what is called the business of life as no better than a trifling and wearisome delay.[123]

In passages such as this we find a Pater who is closer in spirit to the French writers of his time than to his British contemporaries: he achieves for himself the Villiers-Huysmans realization that to desire nothing is to possess all, and surely his yearning for immersion in *tabula rasa* is equivalent to Mallarmé's exploration of *le néant*. No wonder then that Pater was misunderstood by his contemporaries, for there is much to be said for the theory that Pater, far from being one of the last of the romantics, was actually one of the first of the moderns.[124]

William Butler Yeats pondering sadly the thwarted ambitions, the scandalous lives, and the early deaths of what he called the "tragic generation" of the nineties—his fellows in the Rhymers Club, promising young poets like Ernest Dowson, Lionel Johnson, and John Davidson, as well as the better known Oscar Wilde and Aubrey Beardsley—placed some of the blame on Pater. "Three or four years ago," he wrote in 1922, "I re-read *Marius the Epicurean*, expecting to find I cared for it no longer, but it still seemed to me, as I think it seemed to us all, the only great prose in modern English, and yet I began to wonder if it, or the attitude of mind of which it was the noblest expression, had not caused the disaster of my friends. It taught us to walk upon a rope, tightly stretched through serene air, and we were left to keep our feet upon a swaying rope in a storm." [125] Pater had taught them to be ceremonious and polite, to speak their opinions in low voices, to maintain a calm exterior however raging the flame within; but many of them lived secret lives of disorder, and instead of shielding the flame, they fanned it and burned themselves out. On a cold winter night a friend of Aubrey Beardsley reproached him for going without an overcoat, "Aubrey, you will kill yourself!" "Oh, no," replied Beardsley, "I never wear an overcoat. I am always burning." [126] But the anecdote loses some of its point when we learn that Beardsley died at the age of twenty-five and, like so many of his contemporaries, failed to live out the century. It was as if the writers of the period took seriously their role in the *fin-de-siècle*, assumed that it was their histori-

123. *Imaginary Portraits*, pp. 110–111.
124. See James Hafley, "Walter Pater's 'Marius' and the Technique of Modern Fiction," *Modern Fiction Studies*, III (Summer, 1957), 99–109.
125. *The Autobiography of William Butler Yeats* (New York: Macmillan, 1953), p. 181.
126. Osbert Burdett, *The Beardsley Period* (London: John Lane, 1925), p. 98.

cal mission to be decadent, and strove to produce "a swan song and a death-bed repentance." [127]

In the fiction of the period there is more repentance than exaltation. The works which literary historians describe as the manifestos of estheticism and decadence turn out, like *A rebours,* to be not defenses, but repudiations. The esthetes may be lovingly described, as in Wilde's *The Picture of Dorian Gray* or Beardsley's *Under the Hill,* but we often sense the tongue in cheek, and we may well have difficulty in distinguishing the real thing from such satires as Robert Hichens' *The Green Carnation* and G. S. Street's *The Autobiography of a Boy. Under the Hill,* for example, after pages of richly ornamented prose ends abruptly with a two-word sentence when the hero, the Abbé Fanfreluche, a gentleman of lavish elegance, is taken by his hostess to see Adolphe, her pet unicorn: "Adolphe snorted." [128] Another example is John Davidson's *Earl Lavender,* which describes, among other representative fads of the time, the visits of fastidious young gentlemen and their ivory ladies to flagellation chambers. Beardsley provided a flagellation scene as the frontispiece for the volume, and we are assured solemnly in the novel that the characters find whipping each other a purifying, refreshing experience, much more stimulating and a good deal less untidy than fornicating. Davidson, however, was careful in his preface to denounce the practice of flagellation, which he attributed to "unfortunate people with no vital interest in life, ignorant of what to do with their health and strength," [129] and there is much cautious irony throughout the narrative.

The tragic generation's apologetic view of themselves, their concession to ironic double meanings, and their reluctance to take even themselves seriously may be explained only in part by their feeling that they represented not the beginning but the end of a movement. However, as shown by such of the time journals as *The Yellow Book* and *The Savoy,* their deliberate experimentation, their eager acceptance of foreign influences, and their desire to shock, they saw themselves also as the *avant-garde,* riding a swaying rope in a storm perhaps, but willing to wait out the storm in anticipation of a new earthly paradise. "Our whole age is seeking to bring forth a sacred

127. Holbrook Jackson, *The Eighteen Nineties: A Review of Art and Ideas at the Close of the Nineteenth Century* (Harmondsworth: Penguin Books, 1950), p. 60.
128. *Under the Hill, and Other Essays in Prose and Verse* (London: John Lane, 1928), p. 36.

129. *A Full and True Account of the Wonderful Mission of Earl Lavender, Which Lasted One Night and One Day: With a History of the Pursuit of Earl Lavender and Lord Brumm by Mrs. Scamler and Maud Emblem* (London: Ward and Downey, 1895), p. x.

book," Mallarmé had said, and Yeats added, "Some of us thought that book near toward the end of the last century, but the tide sank again." [130] Afflicted by their sense of living in an "age of transition," which made them feel transitory, many of them tried to hasten the end of the century. But was living in an age of transition responsible for the contrast between their search for purity in art and their lives of disorder, Yeats asked, "or did we but pursue antithesis?" [131]

The artist's sense of a split self is, we have seen, a pervasive theme in portraits of the artist of all times. At the end of the century, though, this acceptance of duality, pursuit of antithesis, and cultivation of a double life became an obsession. In his discussion of the phenomenon, Richard Ellmann has pointed out that the *doppelganger* notion is central to works as varied in type as Stevenson's *Dr. Jekyll and Mr. Hyde*, Wilde's *The Picture of Dorian Gray*, Max Beerbohm's *The Happy Hypocrite* (in which Lord George Hell transforms himself into Lord George Heaven!), and Valéry's *Monsieur Teste*.[132] Ellmann finds further evidence of the obsession in the popularity of pseudonyms among Yeats's friends. W. K. Magee became "John Eglinton" to avoid the provincialism suggested by his too-Irish name; George Russell derived "AE" from Aeon, a heavenly personage who came to him in a vision; Oscar Wilde adopted the name "Sebastian Melmoth," perhaps after Maturin's hero, in the hope that it would eliminate "amiable, irrepressible Oscar" entirely; and so thoroughly did William Sharp become "Fiona Macleod" that "he wrote under her name books in a style different from his own, sent letters for her to friends in a feminine handwriting, complained to friends who wrote to her that they never wrote to him, and eventually almost collapsed under the strain of a double life." Rousseau, we have seen, shocked many of his contemporaries by signing his works and thus insisting upon a personal identity. By the middle of the century, anonymity had returned to fashion, as shown by the abundance of novels signed "by the author of," and Baudelaire praised Constantin Guys for refusing to sign his work. By the end of the century the fashion was pseudonymity, and many writers liked to think that it was not they, but the anti-selves of their pen names who actually produced their work.

For Yeats the concept of the dual man was more than a literary convention, for he made it the basis of his theory of art. His first book of fiction, *John Sherman and Dhoya*—signed "Ganconagh" and published in the Pseudonym Library—divides his own charac-

130. *Autobiography*, p. 189.
131. *Autobiography*, p. 182.
132. *Yeats: The Man and the Masks*, (New York: Macmillan, 1948), pp. 70–73.

ter into passive-active surrogates. When he joined the Hermetic Students of the Gold Dawn and was asked to choose an order name he, revealingly, took the phrase "Demon Est Deus Inversus." [133] Poetry, he wrote in *Per Amica Silentia Lunae*, derives from "the quarrel with ourselves," [134] and the successful poet is he who is capable of calling from the realm of the dead a Daemon most unlike himself who serves as the medium for those symbols and images which have their origin in a "great memory passing on from generation." [135] For a long time, he wrote elsewhere, he sought revelation outside himself, but came to realize that it derives from that "age-long memoried self, that shapes the elaborate shell of the mollusc and the child in the womb, that teaches the birds to make their nest; and . . . genius is a crisis that joins that buried self for certain moments to our trivial daily mind." [136] It is curious to note that Yeats anticipates at least two of Jung's main concepts—the *persona* and group memory.

In Yeats's early stories the poet is often presented as a man bewitched. The bewitchment may provide inspiration for the poet's songs, but it also makes him an outcast from society. Alienation is a major theme in the stories of *The Secret Rose*. In "The Crucifixion of the Outcast," for example, a wandering gleeman is nailed to a cross by a group of monks whom he has cursed for the poor accommodations they afforded him. Some beggars, in gratitude for the entertainment he has provided them on the way to his execution, linger about the cross for a time to keep wolves and carnivorous birds from the poet, but when the weather turns cold, they leave. "And presently the birds lighted all at once upon his head and the wolves began to eat his feet. 'Outcasts,' he moaned, 'have you all turned against the outcast?'" [137] Poet, priests, and beggars—here is not only a depiction of the poet as Christ, but an obvious parable of the situation of the artist in Ireland, with the priests representing the Church and the beggars the mass of men, an allegory which Joyce must have approved. In "The Wisdom of the King" a young ruler is loved and needed by his people, but he abdicates when he realizes that his wisdom is that of bewitchment. In "Out of the Rose," the dying last knight of the Fellowship of the Rose tells the secrets of the order to a simpleminded boy who cannot understand him. *Stories of Red Hanrahan* deals with a poet and schoolteacher who while attempting to make his way to his sweetheart is "touched" by the

133. *Yeats: The Man and the Masks*, p. 96.
134. (New York: Macmillan, 1918), p. 29.
135. *Per Amica Silentia Lunae*, p. 55.
136. *Autobiography*, p. 164.
137. *Early Poems and Stories* (London: Macmillan, 1925), p. 333.

emissaries of the great witch Sidhe and does not reawaken to reality for a year. Too late to claim his bride and her land, he becomes a wanderer, welcomed briefly for his inspired songs and entertainment, but always distrusted and never truly at home anywhere.

But the most significant of Yeats's early stories are the *Rosa Alchemica* group, comprising the story of that name, "The Tables of the Law," and "The Adoration of the Magi," in which Yeats describes his own dalliance with magic, alchemy, and mystical fellowships. In the first story, the narrator, who seems to have borrowed many of his characteristics from des Esseintes, is converted to the Order of the Alchemical Rose through the influence of Michael Robartes. As if under a spell, he accompanies Robartes to the temple of the order, located at the end of a pier, "between the pure multitude by the waves and the impure multitude of men." [138] In the midst of the initiatory ceremonies, the narrator realizes that the fellows of the order are actually demons. He escapes providentially when the temple is destroyed by a mob of angry fisherfolk. What had first attracted him to the order was its religion of art. Its gods were fictional beings such as Hamlet, Faust, Roland, and Lear—"The many think humanity made these divinities, and that it can unmake them again; but we who have seen them pass in rattling harness, and in soft robes, and heard them speak with articulate voices while we lay in deathlike trance, know that they are always making and unmaking humanity, which is indeed but the trembling of their lips." [139] Yeats's own worship of a religion of art is evident from much that he wrote—in his autobiography, for example, he confessed to a belief almost identical with that of the mystic order in *Rosa Alchemica* [140]—but in the stories of 1897 he made concessions and ended, like Huysmans, Wilde, and so many others of his generation, by repudiating the pursuit of esoteric doctrine. At the end of "The Adoration of the Magi" Yeats as narrator assures us, "I have turned into a path which will lead . . . from the Order of the Alchemical Rose. I no longer live an elaborate and haughty life, but seek to lose myself among the prayers and the sorrows of the multitude." [141] That Yeats failed to do so and continued his quest for a mystical communion of art is evident from the fact that *A Vision* appeared first in 1925 and was revised with additions in 1937, two years before his death. If Yeats was the only major literary artist before Joyce produced by the Aesthetic movement in the British Isles, it may be not only because he had more

138. *Early Poems and Stories,* p. 479. 141. *Early Poems and Stories,* pp.
139. *Early Poems and Stories,* p. 475.   525–526.
140. *Autobiography,* pp. 70–71.

talent and a better ear than his contemporaries, but also because he never gave up the attempt to produce a "sacred" corpus of art.

If Yeats is representative of the Ivory Tower writers in that the only religion possible to him was a uniquely personal one, he is different too in that he claimed no personal credit for it, insisting that it came in revelation from the anti-self. The concept of the double enabled him to achieve a balance between self and transcendence of self. The decadent writers of the nineties, on the other hand, found no means of escape from self and, unless they committed suicide, usually ended by capitulating to life. As I noted in the previous chapter, life has ways of taking revenge on those who would deny it; and it should not be surprising that the most decadent of the Ivory Tower writers actually find themselves before the Sacred Fount, for in confusing art with self, they fail to realize that whereas a work of art may defeat time, the physical self is always in decay, always mortal. By reversing this process in *The Picture of Dorian Gray,* Oscar Wilde shows that art and life may be mutually destructive.

Wilde's novel, like its French counterpart, *A rebours,* the "yellow book" which for Dorian provides a model of conduct, is a literary exercise which assimilates many of the conventions of romanticism. In addition to the *doppelgänger* theme, it draws upon such works as the Faustus dramas, Maturin's *Melmoth the Wanderer,* and Balzac's *Illusions perdues* in its use of the *pactum cum diabolo* theme.[142] The basic premise of *Dorian Gray,* however, is rooted in the tradition of the "romantic portrait," in which a model pines away as the portrait take on life, a tradition based on that romantic idea that spirit and matter are reversible which I have already related to the Sacred Fount concept.[143] A major source was Balzac's *Peau de chagrin,* from which Wilde may have derived the portrait idea in the "fatal skin" talisman which, in mirrorlike sympathy with its possessor, measures the expenditure of his life.[144] Still another supernatural tradition, the quest for an elixir of youth, was actually demonstrated in Wilde's day by some of his magician friends.[145] The estheticism of the novel draws upon *Mademoiselle de Maupin, Marius the Epicurean, A rebours, Là-bas,* and *Axêl;* and the character of Dorian

142. On sources of *The Picture of Dorian Gray,* see Aatos Ojala, *Aestheticism and Oscar Wilde: Part I —"Life and Letters"* (Helsinki: Annals of the Finnish Academy of Science and Letters, 1954), pp. 209–215.

143. Eino Railo discusses the tradition of the "romantic portrait" in his *The Haunted Castle: A Study of the Elements of English Romanticism* (London: Routledge, 1927), pp. 305–307.

144. Frances Winwar, *Oscar Wilde and the Yellow Nineties* (New York: Harper, 1958), p. 165.

145. See Yeat's *Autobiography,* pp. 112–115.

derives obviously from such early dandies and later esthetes as Disraeli's Vivien Grey (from whom Wilde probably drew the name of his hero), Balzac's Lucien de Rubempré, Gautier's d'Albert, Huysman's des Esseintes, and others. But in spite of the many sources revealed in the novel which make *Dorian Gray* seem to sum up an entire literary movement, the work is also peculiarly original and warrants more penetrating interpretation than it has received.

The Picture of Dorian Gray is a parable of art and life which, in spite of its reputation, is a surprisingly moral fable. We tread on dangerous ground, though, when we try to narrow its meaning, for the story is filled with paradoxes. Some of the contradictions may be deliberate, but others appear to be the result of Wilde's own confusion. For instance, one of the epigrams in the Preface is: "To reveal art and conceal the artist is art's aim," [146] but the painter Basil Hallward says, "Every portrait that is painted with feeling is a portrait of the artist, not of the sitter. The sitter is merely the accident, the occasion. It is not he who is revealed by the painter; it is rather the painter who, on the coloured canvas, reveals himself." [147] Then a few pages later Hallward proclaims, "An artist should create beautiful things, but should put nothing of his own life into them. We live in an age when men treat art as if it were meant to be a form of autobiography. We have lost the abstract sense of beauty. Some day I will show the world what it is; and for that reason the world shall never see my portrait of Dorian Gray." [148] One way of interpreting this assertion is to say that Hallward feels that he has failed in his portrait because he has put too much of himself into the picture; he has painted not the real Dorian, but his ideal conception of the young man. Dorian betrays the ideal self, the innocent soul, of the picture by seeking sensation for its own sake, but he must betray the ideal because it was a false conception in the first place. The real Dorian—that is, *life*—destroys the art of the painter and finally the painter himself. It is a dramatic necessity that Dorian murder the man whose creation of a false ideal has deluded him. But when he also destroys the picture, which would have kept the ideal, the anti-Dorian, free of time, he destroys himself as well.

For, Wilde seems to say, life always destroys art, and art destroys life. The artist who creates the actual Dorian is not Basil Hallward, but Lord Henry Wotton, the Wilde-like esthete and wit, who in conversation with Dorian in the painter's studio awakens the young

146. *The Picture of Dorian Gray* (New York and Cleveland: World Publishing Company, 1931), p. 9.
147. *The Picture of Dorian Gray*, p. 15.
148. *The Picture of Dorian Gray*, p. 21.

man's slumbering senses to the extent that his face takes on a new expression which the painter captures in a moment of inspiration. "The aim of life is self-development," Lord Henry tells the youth, "To realise one's nature perfectly—that is what each of us is here for." [149] And he sounds like Lambert Strether addressing Little Bilham when he urges Dorian to "Live! Live the wonderful life that is in you! Let nothing be lost upon you. Be always searching for new sensations." [150] Strether, though, would not have used the word "sensations," and it is with that word that Lord Henry tempts and traps the young man. Dorian, inspired by Lord Henry, tries to "gather up the scarlet threads of life, and to weave them into a pattern," [151] for "certainly, to him Life itself was the first, the greatest, of the arts, and for it all the other arts seemed to be but a preparation." [152] But the artist of life must work in the material of sensation, and in seeking new means of sensual stimulation in an effort to intensify the "life" which is his "art," Dorian comes to realize that each moment of living is measured in mortality, and the more intense the passion, the greater the cost, the more rapid the deterioration reflected in the portrait. That life destroys art is shown even more clearly in the Sibyl Vane episode. Dorian falls in love with the young actress because he is attracted to her genius, but when she responds to his love, she loses her talent:

> "Dorian, Dorian," she cried, "before I knew you, acting was the one reality of my life. It was only in the theatre that I lived. I thought that it was all true. I was Rosalind one night, and Portia the other. The joy of Beatrice was my joy, and the sorrows of Cordelia were mine also. I believed in everything. The common people who acted with me seemed to me to be godlike. The painted scenes were my world. I knew nothing but shadows, and I thought them real. You came—oh, my beautiful love!—and you freed my soul from prison. You taught me what reality really is. Tonight, for the first time in my life, I saw through the hollowness, the sham, the silliness of the empty pageant in which I had always played." [153]

But when she loses her art, Sibyl loses also her lover, who tells her coldly, "Without your art you are nothing. I would have made you famous, splendid, magnificent. The world would have worshipped

149. *The Picture of Dorian Gray*, p. 26.
150. *The Picture of Dorian Gray*, p. 33.
151. *The Picture of Dorian Gray*, p. 109.
152. *The Picture of Dorian Gray*, p. 144.
153. *The Picture of Dorian Gray*, p. 97.

you, and you would have borne my name. What are you now? A third-rate actress with a pretty face." [154]

We are told that during the nineties and later Oscar Wilde attempted to trace in his own life the fatal pattern which he created in the novel, in spite of the fact that the book provided a clear warning of the ultimate result of such procedure. Seen thus, *Dorian Gray* is an exposure of self and a veiled confession that Wilde recognized the fallacy of his own position. Dorian attempts to escape time, to remain ever youthful and beautiful, but the materials with which he works are mortal, and he comes to know the "ruin that Time brought on beautiful and wonderful things." [155] To attempt to turn one's own life into a work of art, Wilde admitted, was a sign that the real artist—the "abstract" artist who is not represented in the novel— had died in him. What do we make of the remarkable loquacity and the personal charm of Lord Henry or of Wilde himself when we learn that he wrote to a friend, "The greatest artists are stupid and tiresome men as a rule. Flaubert was certainly a stupid man. But bad poets and novelists are romantic and delightful"? [156] The same idea is put into the mouth of Lord Henry Wotton, who indicts himself and his creator thus: "Good artists exist simply in what they make, and consequently are perfectly uninteresting in what they are. A great poet, a really great poet, is the most unpoetical of all creatures. But inferior poets are absolutely fascinating. The worse their rhymes are, the more picturesque they look." [157] Most biographies of Wilde agree that for all his efforts to shape himself in the pattern of a dandy and esthete who is above the struggle, he was nonetheless oppressed throughout his life by remorse, guilt, and a sense of fatality. Much of that oppression he put into *The Picture of Dorian Gray*.

The Desire and Pursuit of the Whole, by Frederick Rolfe, the self-styled Baron Corvo, carries implications of decadence to an extreme unmatched in other fiction of the period. Although in many respects it is as original as we would expect from an eccentric like Corvo, and though it was not written until 1909 or published until 1934, due to the exigencies of the law of libel, it is nonetheless a representative work of the *fin-de-siècle*. The title derives from Plato's precept, "The desire and pursuit of the whole is called love," but for Corvo, as for the other Ivory Tower writers, love is self-love. Nicholas Crabbe, the solipsistic hero of the romance, seeks self-fulfillment

154. *The Picture of Dorian Gray*, p. 98.
155. *The Picture of Dorian Gray*, p. 154.
156. Ojala, p. 63.
157. *The Picture of Dorian Gray*, p. 68.

in love of the "whole," but the "whole" turns out to be merely an extension of himself: "All he did want was that ideal of his, that Other Half of him which he knew he lacked. He did not know whether that Other Half was a person or a position. He always thought it was priesthood, though he was not unprepared to find that it was a friend; and failure after failure (to find a friend with the faintest trace of faithfulness) had made him more and more convinced that priesthood was the one thing lacking to his happy completion." [158]

Nicholas Crabbe's name is symbolic. Like a crab, he is "hard as adamant—outside," but soft inside:

> Have you, o most affable reader, ever dissected a crab? If not, pray do so at once, if possible, plunging him first into boiling water to boil for five whole minutes and evitate unnecessary barbarity. Lift the lid of his shell, and look inside. You will find it filled with a substance like new cheese; and a magnifying-glass will shew you that this is held together by a network ramification infinitely closer and finer than spiders' webs. Under his shell, in fact, your crab is as soft as butter, and just one labyrinthine mass of the most sensitive of nerves. From which pleasing experiment you should learn to be as merciful as God to all poor sinners born between the twenty-first of June and the twenty-fourth of July: for they are born under the constellation Cancer; and their nature is the nature of a crab. They are the cleverest, tenderest, unhappiest, most dreadful of all men.[159]

Just as a crab prefers tranquillity in a crevice, Nicholas Crabbe tries to hold himself aloof: "He knew so well how to walk in the world without in the least being of the world." [160] Yet in spite of his vow of twenty years of chastity, now nearing the end of its term, Crabbe "did yearn to be wanted, to belong—if it could be plainly and unmistakably offered to and pressed upon him, on those conditions he did indeed yearn for an earthly home and for earthly human love." [161] The only salvation for men born under the sign of Cancer, Corvo tells us, is union with "a Saturnian, born between the twentieth of December and the twenty-first of January, who is their diametrical opposite and complement, soft outside, hard within." [162]

158. *The Desire and Pursuit of the Whole: A Romance of Modern Venice* (London: Cassell, 1953), p. 107.
159. *The Desire and Pursuit of the Whole*, pp. 11–12.
160. *The Desire and Pursuit of the*

Whole, p. 73.
161. *The Desire and Pursuit of the Whole*, p. 225.
162. *The Desire and Pursuit of the Whole*, p. 12.

The novel is an incongruous blend of dream fantasy with sordid experience derived from Corvo's own life. The idyllic dream involves the relation between Crabbe and the boy-girl Zildo or Zilda—a Saturnian, of course—whom he rescues from an earthquake and seems to revive from the dead. He allows her to live with him on condition that she disguise her sex and pass as his boy servant and gondolier. The "other world" of the novel deals with Crabbe's associations with a group of parasitical hypocrites in England who have gained control of his unpublished manuscripts and whose attempts to capitalize on his talent are revealed through correspondence,[163] as well as with a group of pious, interfering Britishers in Venice. Crabbe refuses all compromise with the former and all assistance from the latter ("I don't try to make friends now, just because I'm in violent danger of wanting friends soon" [164]), with the result that he is thrown out of his quarters and forced to live aboard his gondola. Starving, he wanders about Venice trying to avoid the devoted Zildo and deliberately seeking annihilation. At the last moment, Zildo rescues him from drowning in a storm—she seems to bring him back from death, just as he had rescued her—and the circle is complete. They embrace, and "the Desire and Pursuit of the Whole was crowned and rewarded by Love." [165] The dreamlike fantasy of the conclusion is enhanced by receipt of a letter from a British publisher offering the most favorable of terms for Crabbe's writings. "Give all, gain all" [166] seems to be the final moral.

But it is difficult to believe in the triumph of Nicholas Crabbe, for Corvo's failure to reconcile the two worlds of his fictional self, actuality and fantasy, is matched in the form of this strange work of art. The style varies from terse abruptness to orchidaceous richness. There are scenes of natural beauty interspersed with ugliest vituperation; and though an artificial quality in the narrative often makes it seem dehumanized, the reader can never forget the presence of the suffering, unbalanced man who wrote the novel. "He who would see as a god sees," Corvo tells us, "must hasten to mount upon his cross; and, there suspended, crucified in his own shrinking but unblenching flesh, raised higher even than angels, he will see and understand mysteries hidden from the worldly wise and stringently concealed from the squinting of the purely prudent." [167] By trying

---

163. Crabbe's earlier life in London is the subject of the long-suppressed *Nicholas Crabbe; or, The One and the Many: A Romance*, ed. Cecil Woolf (Norfolk, Connecticut: New Directions, 1958).

164. *The Desire and Pursuit of the Whole*, p. 162.

165. *The Desire and Pursuit of the Whole*, p. 299.

166. *The Desire and Pursuit of the Whole*, p. 298.

167. *The Desire and Pursuit of the Whole*, p. 221.

to crucify himself, Corvo is like many of his fellow decadents, but there is more paranoia than god-like detachment in this novel, and it fails to be a major work of art for the same reason that the author failed in life to reconcile Baron Corvo with Frederick Rolfe.

We know from A. J. A. Symons' *Quest for Corvo* that Rolfe's last years in Venice were crowned by no such fulfillment as he grants to Crabbe in the novel, that actually he allowed himself to be corrupted in his quest for beauty by an excess of homosexual vice. In fact, Thomas Mann's *Death in Venice* depicts a curious, accidental parallel with Rolfe's final days. Gustave von Aschenbach, the writer who serves as hero in Mann's story, has always held himself solemnly aloof from the pleasures of life: "Always, wherever and whenever it was the order of the day to be merry, to refrain from labour and make glad the heart, he would soon be conscious of the imperative summons . . . back to the high fatigues, the sacred and fasting service that consumed his days." [168] At the height of his fame, however, Aschenbach finds himself drawn to romantic Venice, where he falls in love with a young boy, Tadzio, and undergoes a rapid moral deterioration that ends mercifully in his death before he has even spoken to the boy. Tadzio stands as an image of mortal life—"Aschenbach thought. 'He will most likely not live to grow old.' He did not try to account for the pleasure the idea gave him." [169] But it is apparent that the beautiful youth is an ideal projection of Aschenbach himself. When, for once, Tadzio smiles at Aschenbach, we are told that "with such a smile it might be that Narcissus bent over the mirroring pool, a smile profound, infatuated, lingering, as he put out his arms to the reflection of his own beauty; the lips just slightly pursed, perhaps half-realizing his own folly in trying to kiss the cold lips of his shadow—with a mingling of coquetry and curiosity and a faint unease, enthralling and enthralled." [170] In a sense Aschenbach becomes enamoured of his own shadow as he follows the boy about Venice; and before his death he realizes what he has refused to acknowledge before—"that we poets cannot walk the way of beauty without Eros as our companion and guide. We may be heroic after our fashion, disciplined warriors of our craft, yet are we all like women, for we exult in passion, and love is still our desire —our craving and our shame." [171]

For Aschenbach, as for Nicholas Crabbe, life in the form of that otherness from self that is yet a part of the self may be held off

168. "Death in Venice," in *Stories of Three Decades*, trans. H. T. Lowe-Porter (New York: Knopf, 1951), p. 409.

169. "Death in Venice," p. 404.
170. "Death in Venice," p. 418.
171. "Death in Venice," pp. 434-435.

for a time through rigid self-discipline, but eventually the other self must return as surely as Madeline Usher returns to her brother. In all these stories, the return to oneness means annihilation. Thus Aschenbach is drawn to travel by a vision of life seen as a lush tropical landscape, where "among the knotted joints of a bamboo thicket the eyes of a crouching tiger gleamed." [172] Later we are told that the Asiatic cholera that kills Aschenbach has its source in "the hot, moist swamps of the delta of the Ganges, where it bred in the mephitic air of that primeval island-jungle, among whose bamboo thickets the tiger crouches, where life of every sort flourishes in rankest abundance." [173] We may well be reminded of Henry James's "The Beast in the Jungle." The hero of that story, John Marcher, also tries to deny the forces of life, but when the beast springs at last, Marcher knows that it has always resided in the jungle within himself.

Or we may be reminded of the setting of Joseph Conrad's *Heart of Darkness,* for there too the jungle is as much within the self as outside, and the moral decline of Kurtz is not unlike that of Aschenbach, though more extreme. Before he went to the Congo, Kurtz was known as a potential "universal genius"—a brilliant musician, painter, poet, journalist, orator—and in the eyes of the natives he becomes a king-god in whose honor "unspeakable rites" are performed. But according to most critics, Kurtz's final utterance—"The horror! The horror!"—reflects not only his realization that the darkness of evil is everywhere, but that it derives from within the self. When Marlow tells Kurtz's Intended that the last word spoken by her betrothed was her name, he does not tell a complete lie, for the final scene of the story shows that there is as much horror, as much darkness in the dark-eyed girl herself as in the depths of the Congo. *Heart of Darkness* is, I think, a bitter indictment of life, but we read the story superficially if we merely equate darkness with evil—it is not a matter of darkness out there and lightness here, but darkness forever corrupting the light. If Kurtz was man enough to be damned, it was because he had within himself a capacity for greatness that could never be satisfied with the middle way. Like Satan, he fell through pride—"exterminate the brutes!"—but he fell from a height, whereas the other exploiters in the Congo were mere agents of the "flabby devil" who ran their show. A third response is that of Marlow. If his trip up the Congo represented his "furthest point of navigation," it was because he discovered in Kurtz an aspect of himself which, once seen, forced him to assume the attitude of onlooker.

In Axel Heyst of *Victory* we have a Marlow-like hero whose de-

172. "Death in Venice," p. 380.   173. "Death in Venice," p. 427.

fense against life is "to drift without ever catching on to anything," for he believes that "he who forms a tie is lost. The germ of corruption has entered into his soul." [174] Before the crisis, Heyst, like Marlow before his Congo experience, has been fortunate in not having to test his detachment. "I don't know myself what I would do," he tells Lena, "what countenance I would have before a creature which would strike me as being the evil incarnate." [175] After Marlow faced the heart of darkness in Kurtz, he too retreated from all ties, lest he be corrupted, but in learning to transform his experiences—by, in fact, telling "benevolent lies" that are actually truths—he became a storyteller, like Conrad, affirming the vision of the artist even while indicting raw experience. Heyst, on the other hand, cannot retreat before the evil incarnate of the diabolic Mr. Jones, and *Victory*, like most of the other works with which I am here concerned, ends in the destruction of the hero. *Victory* appeared at the beginning of the first World War, and in its symbolic depiction of the detached man forced to commit himself in action, it provides a fitting climax to the Ivory Tower tradition.

If I am right in reading *Heart of Darkness* as an indictment of life and if the standard interpretations of *Victory* as an attack on detachment are also valid, we would have to assume that Conrad changed his mind radically between 1899 and 1914. Again and again we have been told that the meaning of *Victory* is summed up in the final words of Axel Heyst: "Ah, Davidson, woe to the man whose heart has not learned while young to hope, to love—and to put its trust in life!" [176] I find it hard to believe that so subtle an author as Conrad could have attached so simple a moral to the end of a complex story; and is that the lesson the story actually teaches? It makes more sense, I think, to read *Victory* as a tragedy of inadequate detachment, for if Heyst had not become involved with life, if he had resisted the impulse to play the rescuing knight, he would not have fallen. Then, too, if the author of this novel is on the side of participation as opposed to detachment, how do we explain the fact that the representatives of life depicted in the novel are so singularly unattractive? Jones says, "I am the world itself come to pay you a visit," [177] and later he and his confederates are identified as "the worthy envoys, the envoys extraordinary of the world." [178] Perhaps Jones, Ricardo, and Pedro are only "the embodied evil of

174. *Victory* (New York: Modern Library, n.d.), pp. 89, 188. I have taken the liberty of correcting several typographical errors in quoting passages from this edition of the novel.

175. *Victory*, p. 196.
176. *Victory*, p. 383.
177. *Victory*, pp. 354–355.
178. *Victory*, p. 327.

the world," [179] but which characters represent its goodness? The benevolent but blundering Morrison? The sympathetic but retreating Davidson? The victimized and scarred Lena? Surely not the Schombergs nor Zangiacomo? And, finally, if *Victory* demonstrates the evil of detachment, how do we reconcile this with the praise of detachment in the "Author's Note," where Conrad tells us that "the unchanging Man of history is wonderfully adaptable by his power of endurance and in his capacity for detachment," and that this "faculty of detachment born perhaps from a sense of infinite littleness . . . is yet the only faculty that seems to assimilate man to the immortal gods." [180]

Part of the difficulty in interpreting *Victory* comes from its inconsistent point of view. Because the author's voice in the novel is never clearly established, we are all too likely to let Heyst be the interpreter of his own story. In fact, the several narrators of the story seem to have an attitude toward life not unlike that of the sceptical Heyst. In the first paragraph of the novel the human narrator of the first part tells us that we are "camped like bewildered travellers in a garish, unrestful hotel"; and it is the later, omniscient narrator who tells us that "every age is fed on illusions, lest men should renounce life early and the human race come to an end." [181] If it is Heyst who says that "all action is bound to be harmful," the omniscient narrator echoes his opinion with the statement that action is "the barbed hook." [182] Because there is no Marlovian mask in this novel, the distinction between teller and hero is dangerously obscured, and we suspect that in this novel Conrad did not find it necessary to disguise himself.

The difficulty we have in determining the author's voice in *Victory* is matched by our difficulty in understanding Axel Heyst. At one level he is simply a man—like all men, made up of contradictions and caught, like Hamlet, in indecision: too sympathetic to remain entirely alone, too reserved to participate effectively. Much of his detachment seems unnatural, a heritage from an embittered father which was imposed upon him against his will. He is at once introverted and gregarious, and his many contradictory nicknames suggest that Conrad meant to make him represent all mankind. Symbolically, however, he carries an additional weight of meaning. First, he is an artist: he arrives in the islands with a portfolio of sketches, and though we hear nothing more about his art, his temperament is certainly that of the late nineteenth-century archetype of the artist. His name "Axel" may well have derived from the Axêl of Villiers'

179. *Victory*, p. 279.
180. *Victory*, pp. ix–x.
181. *Victory*, p. 91.
182. *Victory*, pp. 52, 164.

drama—that epitome of the artist-as-exile who was willing to leave his living to his servants. Conrad changed the last name from Berg to Heyst, perhaps to suggest "highest," perhaps because "Heyst" rhymes with "Christ," for in the early pages of the novel Conrad clearly attributes godlike qualities to this "strange being without needs." [183] He is out of everybody's way, yet conspicuous, and his most frequent visitors are shadows. To Morrison, he seems to come in answer to prayer, and for a man supposed to hold himself aloof, he does a remarkable amount of saving of other people. He saves Morrison, he saves Lena, he saves even Jones, Ricardo, and Pedro. Is it too much to suggest that in this single figure Conrad sought to sum up all his selves—the man, the artist, and that creative force which neither Captain Korzeniowski nor the respected British man of letters "Joseph Conrad" could fully understand? If so, it is only the man who utters the famous "moral" to Davidson, and it is only the man whom the critics seem to hear.

What may those other selves be saying? Perhaps because some critics find this novel, unlike most of Conrad's, too easy to understand, they have been harsh with it. We are told that the inconsistent point of view suggests Conrad's uncertainty, that the style is weaker than that of his earlier works, and that he could find no way to resolve the action except through coincidences. Yet Conrad is known to have taken pride in this work—to have felt that his reputation as a literary artist would stand on *Nostromo* and *Victory*. Perhaps he felt this so strongly that he retained the title because of its relevance for him. His explanation in his note to the first edition is weak. There he tells us that he realized the public would be likely to associate the word with the war that was raging when the novel was published and that "the word Victory, the shining and tragic goal of noble effort, appeared too great, too august, to stand at the head of a mere novel," but that he actually had decided to retain it because "Victory was the last word I had written in peace time. It was the last literary thought which had occurred to me before the doors of the Temple of Janus flying open with a crash shook the minds, the hearts, the consciences of men all over the world. Such coincidence could not be treated lightly. And I made up my mind to let the word stand, in the same hopeful spirit in which some simple citizen of Old Rome would have 'accepted the Omen.'" [184] I prefer to take more seriously the first paragraph of this note—"The last word of this novel was written on the 29th of May, 1914. And that last word was the single word of the title"—for if we like coin-

183. *Victory*, p. 190.   184. *Victory*, p. vii.

cidences, we must be struck by the fact that actually the last word of the story is "nothing."

> Davidson took out his handkerchief to wipe the perspiration off his forehead.
> "And then, your Excellency, I went away. There was nothing to be done there."
> "Clearly," assented the Excellency.
> Davidson, thoughtful, seemed to weigh the matter in his mind, and then murmured with placid sadness:
> "Nothing!"

The novel seems to exist between poles of nothingness and victory, and is therefore more complex, ironic, and ambivalent than is generally assumed. If so, it is in the total balancing of a pure work of art that the artist's victory is to be found, for ultimately the poles merge. Perhaps, in fact, there is an affirmative progression from an acceptance of the horror at the heart of existence to the realization, as in Poe and Mallarmé, that when the darkness pervades everything a oneness is achieved that is equivalent to nothingness. There is a precedent in Conrad for the equation of victory with final insight. Of Kurtz's last utterance, Marlow said, "It was an affirmation, a moral *victory* paid for by innumerable defeats, by abominable terrors, by abominable satisfactions. But it was a *victory!*" [185] As Conrad completed his story of Axel Heyst, life at its most evil and violent welled up around him in the form of a world war, and the creative spirit in him may have clung to the title because it knew that it was superior to life, for it could see clearly the evil at the heart of life, yet transform it into a strange, artistic beauty.

As a surrogate for the artist who wrote *Victory*, Axel Heyst also triumphs by acknowledging the nothingness at the heart of existence. In most interpretations of the novel the final victory is accorded to Lena, for she "breathed her last, triumphant, seeking his glance in the shades of death." [186] But if her motive was to balance the scales by saving Heyst, as she had been saved, she is victorious only in achieving a proud martyrdom, and Heyst makes it a pyrrhic victory when he voluntarily destroys the self she has saved. The real victory is Heyst's. Some critics feel that he achieves a partial triumph in the self-awareness of his final statement to Davidson, but even before the trio arrived on the island, he knew and regretted his in-

185. Bruce Harkness, ed., *Conrad's Heart of Darkness and the Critics* (San Francisco: Wadsworth Publishing Company, 1960), p. 63.
186. *Victory*, p. 380.

capacity to let himself go. No new insight is reflected here. Another possibility is that he discovers courage in himself when he learns to be afraid. As long as he scorned life, it was easy to be brave, but when he formed a tie, "all his defenses were broken now. Life had him fairly by the throat." [187] With something at stake now, he finds himself weaponless and hesitant until, with the girl dead and, with her, everything that was at stake, he takes his revenge upon the world.

In one of his symbolic roles, we have seen, Mr. Jones represents "the world itself." One of the unsolved mysteries of *Victory* is the manner of Jones's death. Davidson says, "I suppose he tumbled into the water by accident—or perhaps not by accident." [188] One possibility is that Jones killed Heyst, as he killed Ricardo, then set fire to the cottage and committed suicide. But in another of his symbolic roles, Jones is the devil, and because the devil ought to die in a fiery blaze, it seems wrong for Jones to leave the cottage to end his life on the wharf. Did he shoot himself, then jump into the water? It is equally difficult to visualize his drowning, accidentally or intentionally, in shallow water within easy reach of the wharf. Perhaps Wang, the Chinese house servant, killed Jones as he killed Pedro, but we are told that it was Wang who discovered the body. This leaves Heyst as the most likely killer. Earlier, Conrad drew a connection between killing and loving. Heyst told Lena, "I've never killed a man or loved a woman—not even in my thoughts, not even in my dreams," and a moment later, "To slay, to love—the greatest enterprises of life upon a man! And I have no experience of either." [189] The repetition suggests that Conrad wanted us to assume that if Heyst could learn to love a woman, he could also learn to kill.

But why would he kill Jones? One reason is that he sees in Jones a double of himself. Just as Jones represents the world—even his name suggests Everyman—Heyst has to acknowledge that there is much of the "original Adam" in himself. Heyst and Jones are both exiles, but whereas Heyst's aloofness was the result of his temperament and his father's lessons in scepticism, Jones had been "hounded out of society," and having been "ejected . . . from his proper social sphere because he had refused to conform to certain usual conventions he was a rebel now, and was coming and going up and down the earth." [190] With his effeminate eyebrows and his perverse hatred of women, Jones is apparently homosexual—an Oscar Wilde turned outlaw—whereas we can only assume that Heyst was not sexual at all until he met Lena. Nonetheless, Jones perceives an

187. *Victory*, p. 209.　　　　189. *Victory*, p. 200.
188. *Victory*, p. 384.　　　　190. *Victory*, pp. 357, 297.

affinity between himself and Heyst, and recent critics of the novel have had no difficulty documenting the similarities.[191] Driven by his perverted love for Ricardo, Jones tries to kill his secretary rather than lose him to a woman, but the shot goes astray and wounds Lena. Actually, Heyst is partly responsible for her death, not only because he failed to defend her against "the world itself," but because, "towering in the doorway," he failed to heed Jones's request that he "stoop a little" as Jones took aim at Ricardo.[192] But if to learn to love is to learn to kill. Heyst balances the scales when he admits to himself his love for Lena, then finds the means somehow to destroy Jones. After that he must kill himself, just as the original Axel thought that he could retain a pure love only by killing himself and his beloved. From Roderick Usher to the two Axels, the artist of the Ivory Tower tradition seeks annihilation of the suffering, human self in order to free the creative spirit that represents the God in man. It is appropriate that at the moment of her death Lena receives a vision of "divine radiance" as she imagines Heyst "ready to take her up in his firm arms and take her into the sanctuary of his innermost heart—for ever!" [193] By voluntarily accepting oblivion, she and Axel Heyst achieve at last a complete detachment—"the only faculty," we recall from Conrad's preface, "that seems to assimilate man to the immortal gods."

191. See, for example, Frederick R. Karl, *A Reader's Guide to Joseph Conrad* (New York: Noonday Press, 1960), pp. 258–260.
192. *Victory*, pp. 376, 368.

2.   Four Masters

CHAPTER FOUR

HONORÉ DE BALZAC:

The Novelist As Creator

"THE crossroad of sensibility and social history," we have seen, is the area from which the finest fiction comes.[1] Because the greatest novelists achieve a balance between individual vision and the life which they must use in their art, they seem to reside midway between the Ivory Tower and the Sacred Fount. Such a novelist was Honoré de Balzac. When we consider his total work after his early apprenticeship as a hack writer, we must be impressed by its evenness of quality: some of the novels and stories in the *Comédie humaine* are, of course, better or worse than others, but it is impossible to discover a clear pattern of improvement or deterioration in Balzac's literary career. It is as if he had from the beginning a vision so complete that it could never be exhausted and so balanced that it need never be rejected. He had only to draw upon that total vision as long as he lived.

Because Balzac's fiction falls within the middle area, both realists and romantics claim him as their own. Ferdinand Brunetière argued that "if romanticism consists especially in the display of the writer's ego, or, further, in the systematic reduction of the spectacle of the vast world to the range of the poet's or novelist's personal vision, who will deny that the whole work of Balzac is, on the contrary, a perpetual effort to subordinate his individual manner of viewing things . . . to the restraint of a reality which, by its very definition, is ex-

1. See above, p. 65.

175

terior, anterior, and superior to it?" [2] Much of the more recent criticism of Balzac, however, sees him as a romantic and uses as its starting point Baudelaire's assertion, "I have often been astonished that the great glory of Balzac was to pass for an observer. It has always seemed to me that his principal merit was to be a visionary and a passionate visionary." [3] That to this day much of the criticism of Balzac assumes the unnecessary task of trying to classify him as either a realistic chronicler of his world or a romantic visionary creating a private world and that convincing cases can still be made for both classifications seems to me sufficient proof that Balzac was both a realist and a romantic, an observer and a visionary. Perhaps it is time for criticism to call a truce between the opposing camps and to investigate that "middle area" in Balzac where sensibility and history blend.[4]

THE blending occurs in the vision of the artist. There is *one who sees,* and there is *something seen;* but what really distinguishes one artist from another is the *way of seeing.* Of the important aspects of the art of fiction which distinguish it from other forms of literature, none has been more neglected by critics than what Henry James described as

> the projected light of the individual strong temperament—the color of the air with which this, that, or the other painter of life . . . more or less unconsciously suffuses his picture. . . . This is of the nature of the man himself—an emanation of his spirit, temper, history; it springs from his very presence, his spiritual presence, in his work, and is, in so far, not a matter of calculation and artistry. All a matter of his own, in a word, for each seer of visions, the particular tone of the medium in which each vision, each clustered group of persons and places and objects, is bathed.[5]

For want of a better term, we may substitute *aura* for "projected light": *aura,* the dictionary assures us, is "a distinctive air, atmos-

2. *Honoré de Balzac,* trans. R. L. Sanderson (London: Lippincott, 1906), pp. 129–130.

3. Quoted by Martin Turnell, *The Novel in France* (London: Hamish Hamilton, 1950), p. 213.

4. Herbert J. Hunt in his *Balzac's Comédie Humaine* (London: University of London Athlone Press, 1959), published after this chapter was written, takes a similar view—

e.g., "Balzac the scrutinizing observer is supported and transformed by the *voyant* whose intuitive apprehension of reality transcends mere experience and enables him, to use his own expression, to 'invent truth'" (p. 14).

5. "The Lesson of Balzac," in his *The Future of the Novel: Essays on the Art of Fiction,* ed. Leon Edel (New York: Vintage Books, 1956), p. 108.

phere, character"; "a subtle emanation proceeding from a body and surrounding it as an atmosphere." Aura is the *-ian* in "Dickensian," "Jamesian," or "Balzacian."

James had little difficulty describing the characteristic aura of Dickens, Hawthorne, George Eliot, and Charlotte Bronte; but of Balzac's he could say only, "It is rich and thick, the mixture of sun and shade diffused through the *Comédie humaine*—a mixture richer and thicker and representing an absolutely greater quantity of 'atmosphere,' than we shall find prevailing within the compass of any other suspended frame." [6] As James's borrowing of images from the art of painting suggests, aura derives from the individual artist's unique way of seeing and is conveyed primarily through images of what is seen; hence, it is visual and, unlike those aspects of fiction more frequently discussed of late, closer to the plastic arts than to poetry or music. Like a painting, aura is spatial and static. Borrowing "color of the air" from the times of day or seasons of the year favored by the novelists (Dickens is an early-morning novelist, Hawthorne a late-afternoon novelist), it captures time and transforms it into something that may be perceived visually. The action of the *Comédie humaine* ranges in time from 1308 to 1846, but Balzac's aura varies little from work to work; and in spite of his painstaking documentation of his historical backgrounds, the world of his novels seems universal and timeless.

We are more conscious of aura in Balzac than in many other novelists because he took the trouble to create a fictive world which, however similar to the real world it may seem to be, is nonetheless uniquely personal. A private world at once better (more logically controlled) and worse (more evil and distorted) than the real world, it is not depicted in its entirety in the novels Balzac lived to write; but whereas many novelists give us recognizable fragments of the world they and we know only in part, Balzac's novels are fragmentary reflections of a world which we feel he knew in its entirety, a world which was somehow within him before he created it in fiction. Thus for any one work of Balzac the author has, in the other books of his series, a readymade frame of reference. Characters reappear naturally from book to book, and, in spite of the artificiality of a scheme which was imposed after many volumes of the series were already written, the novels complement one another in a remarkably consistent way. Balzac, faithful to his vision, *had* to be consistent.

Although Balzac's aura gains much from his private world, it is not entirely dependent upon it. (James, Dickens, Dostoevsky

6. "The Lesson of Balzac," p. 110.

have their characteristic auras without using recurring characters or imposing a private sociology.) Aura may be discerned in the individual works of the *Comédie humaine,* though we cannot be sure that it is characteristicly Balzacian unless we are familiar with many of the other works as well. How often we are struck by the casual way in which Balzac warms up to his subject, how, in a typical novel, he begins by describing a scene in exhaustive detail, brings on to this setting an individual with an obviously dominant trait, describes him physiologically (sometimes even phrenologically), pauses to analyze his personality, and yet, in spite of this mechanical progression, manages to convey the illusion of life. In a good Balzac novel things suddenly come into focus. When the light is not working, the picture of life is blurred.

Ramón Fernandez wisely remarked that the reader of Balzac never knows "precisely if the feeling which he has of the *reality* of a scene is not an illusion due to the *truth* of the abstract commentary framing it." [7] Although it is usually assumed that Balzac began with a generalized type in mind, then illustrated it, I suspect that he did just the opposite. He began with elaborate descriptions because only by first visualizing his characters was he able to interpret and understand them. Just as he proceeded almost always from physical appearance to moral nature, he seems to have determined the type only after he had *seen* the individual. His approach was inductive, a deliberate observing of something already within his vision. Many details in his descriptions are irrelevant to the context; usually his inserted essays on such topics as the manufacture of paper or the legal procedure of bankruptcy are like the cetological chapters in *Moby-Dick* in that they give us more information than we really need to understand the action in the story. Yet these descriptions and digressions are never entirely irrelevant, for they are the means by which Balzac keeps us aware of his posted presence in his works, his control over the materials of his fictive world. Unity in a Balzac novel depends not on the complete dramatic relevance of detail, but on our awareness of the creator in whom every detail has its source and who brings all details into relation.

Balzac's well-known method of working—the hours from midnight to eight in the morning, the monkish robe, the black coffee made from a special oriental formula, the precise ordering of his working tools, and his trancelike state—constituted a ritual whereby, isolated from the world and free from distractions, he could be-

7. *Messages,* trans. Montgomery Belgion (New York: Harcourt, Brace & Co., 1927), p. 72.

come completely absorbed in the visional world of his creating. According to Stefan Zweig, the "monk's robe unconsciously reminded him that he was in service to a higher law and bound, so long as he wore it, to abjure the outside world and its temptations." [8] At times he undoubtedly felt not only monklike, but godlike—else he would not have allowed one of the characters in *Albert Savarus* to say of another, "While all the world is sleeping, he is awake—like God!" [9] As early as 1830 in an essay on "Les Artistes," he set up Christ as the supreme type of the artist: "As he was despised and rejected, so are all artists hated, because they are the apostles of some truth hateful to the multitude." [10] In another work Balzac anticipated Flaubert and Joyce in comparing the novelist to God: "The true poet . . . ought to remain hidden, like God, in the centre of his universe, and be visible only in his creations." [11] The world of the *Comédie humaine* is, as Albert Thibaudet remarked, "l'imitation de Dieu le Père." [12] It is a kind of divine comedy as well as a human one and, since Balzac is playing at being a god, it is also what he originally intended to call it, a diabolical comedy. Like the Shakespeare-as-God of Stephen Dedalus' Hamlet theory in *Ulysses*, Balzac's creative self is diffused through all his characters. "He is not so much hidden, mysteriously intact, deep in the center of his work, like Stendhal or Flaubert," Samuel Rogers has written, "as diffused all through it, identified equally with every part and yet distinct from every part. He is himself both the one and the many." [13]

Like Anton Reiser and other solitaries, Balzac believed that solitude led to loss of self and the gift of second sight, the ability to enter the lives and thoughts of others.[14] But if Balzac was able to enter the selves of others, he brought to them much of himself. His power of self-absorption within the personages of his fictional world explains what Baudelaire, another "Man of the Crowd,"

8. *Balzac*, trans. William and Dorothy Rose (New York: Viking Press, 1946), p. 136.

9. Translated by Ellen Marriage, in *Novels of Balzac*, Centenary Edition (Philadelphia: Gebbie Publishing Co., 1899), VI, ii, 306.

10. Quoted in the unpublished dissertation by Mary Winfield Scott, "Art and Artists in Balzac's Comédie Humaine" (University of Chicago, 1936), p. 34.

11. *Modeste Mignon* in *The Works of Honoré de Balzac*, trans. Ellen Marriage and others, University Edition (Philadelphia: Avil Publishing Co., 1901), VI, ii, 57.

12. Quoted by Albert Béguin, *Balzac visionnaire* (Geneva: Éditions Albert Skira, 1946), p. 81.

13. *Balzac and the Novel* (Madison: University of Wisconsin Press, 1953), p. 3. For a brilliant exposition of Balzac's godlike relation to his fictive universe, see Georges Poulet, *The Interior Distance*, trans. Elliott Coleman (Baltimore: Johns Hopkins Press, 1959), pp. 97–152.

14. On Balzac's "second sight," see Hunt, pp. 47–50.

meant when he said, "Bref, chacun, dans Balzac, a du génie." [15]
Although not only his celebrated monomaniacs, but all of Balzac's
characters have something of his genius, the many artists in his
fictional world provide perhaps the most direct means of determining the sources of that visual aura which pervades the *Comédie
humaine*. Not any one artist stands as the surrogate for Balzac's
creative self, but all together; considered as a group, they enable
us to understand how Balzac was able to maintain a balance between observable reality and visionary insight.

so strong is our image of Balzac in his monkish cell that we
are likely to forget that he was capable of flinging himself into
the world of reality—into business, politics, love, treasure hunts—
with the same intense passion and absorption he revealed in the
creation of his fictional world. Long before James and Proust, Balzac recognized the disparity between the public and the creative
lives of the artist and realized that a man may be "completely out
of tune with the products of his mind." [16] Stefan Zweig's biography
of Balzac is one of the most convincing of all literary portraits
in part because of the biographer's awareness of the ironic difference between the two Balzacs: "Yet again and again we find in
Balzac's career the paradoxical phenomenon, repeated with uncanny
precision, that the brain which was able to pierce unerringly to
the heart of every situation in the fictitious world of its own creation, functioned in the world of reality with a naive and childlike
credulity." [17] After months of intense creative activity, Balzac would
plunge once again into society not only to replenish his store of
impressions, but also to bring about those frustrations and failures
that would send him back to the secluded life of his study and
the strict regimen that enabled him to pay for the life he had just
spent. In his fiction Balzac is obsessed by the conflict between art
and life, and he expressed the conflict more convincingly than
most other writers of his century because art and life held equally
powerful appeals for him.[18]

Le Chef-d'oeuvre inconnu and *La Peau de chagrin*, both published
in 1831 near the beginning of Balzac's career as a serious novelist,
serve as complementary warnings to their author of the fate which

15. Quoted by Béguin, p. 9.
16. *Modeste Mignon*, VI, ii, 52.
17. Zweig, *Balzac*, p. 274.
18. "Laure, Laure," he wrote to his
sister as a young man, "my two immense and sole desires,—*to be fa-*

mous and to be loved,—will they ever
be satisfied?"—Katherine Prescott
Wormeley, *A Memoir of Honoré de
Balzac* (Boston: Roberts Brothers,
1892), p. 44.

awaits the artist who fails to maintain the precarious balance between the Ivory Tower and the Sacred Fount. The pattern revealed by these two early stories is repeated again and again in the
later works.

Le Chef-d'oeuvre inconnu opens with the visit of Nicolas Poussin
and Frenhofer to the studio of François Porbus. Frenhofer criticizes a recent painting by Porbus, remarking that the throat seems
a "dead" thing. Porbus replies that he studied the throat with great
care in the model, and Frenhofer responds indignantly, "The
mission of art is not to copy nature, but to give expression to it!
You are not a base copyist, but a poet! . . . We have to grasp
the spirit, the soul, the features of things and beings." [19] Frenhofer
then demonstrates that he can make a painting seem alive, for he
takes one of Porbus' brushes and, with "passionate ardor" but
few strokes, makes the necessary alterations in the throat. Intrigued
and curious, the young Poussin learns from Porbus that Frenhofer,
though little known, is the greatest of living painters and that for
years he has worked on a painting of Catherine Lescault which he
will permit no one to see. However, when Poussin and Porbus
finally gain access to the old man's studio, they see on his canvas
only a conglomeration of colors and a mass of chaotic lines. "On
drawing nearer," though, "they spied in one corner of the canvas
the end of a bare foot standing forth from that chaos of colors,
of tones, of uncertain shades, that sort of shapeless mist; but a
lovely foot, a living foot! They stood fairly petrified with admiration before the fragment, which had escaped that most incredible
gradual, progressive destruction." [20] Overhearing the two painters
discuss his work, Frenhofer realizes that what is in his mind's eye
is not on his canvas. That night, after burning all his paintings,
the disillusioned Frenhofer dies.

The perfect foot suggests, however, that Frenhofer is not a false
visionary. For a time at least he did grasp an ultimate reality, and
Balzac leaves little doubt that he believes in the validity of Frenhofer's quest, in the existence of an ideal which may be captured.
The perfect foot is a typical touch of Balzacian irony, similar to
that in La Recherche de l'absolu, in which another of Balzac's
visionaries, Balthazar Claes, returns to his ancestral home after
years of exile imposed because his experiments to discover the
secret of matter had brought his family to the brink of poverty
and destruction. He finds his children on the eve of good mar-

19. Pablo Picasso, Forty Nine Lithographs, together with Honoré Balzac's Hidden Masterpiece in the
Form of an Allegory (New York:
Lear Publishers, 1947), pp. 24–26.
20. Picasso, p. 82.

riages, the family fortunes restored, and the home as well-furnished as before he began his experiments. Here, we are likely to say, is the triumph of common sense, self-sacrifice, and hard work over the impractical ideals of the deluded visionary. But when Baltha-zar's servant goes up to the abandoned laboratory, he discovers that the chemicals left there have produced, by chance and with no one to observe the process, one perfect diamond. The one perfect foot, like the diamond, represents the validity of Frenhofer's ideal.[21]

Further evidence that Balzac believed in the reality of Fren-hofer's ideal is given in his repetition of the theme in several later stories. Frenhofer the painter and Balthazar Claes the alchemist are joined by Gambara the musician, Seraphita the religious mystic, and Louis Lambert in Balzac's gallery of visionaries. Just as Fren-hofer seeks the core of reality beneath appearance so that he can represent it in painting and Balthazar Claes seeks the basic ele-ment common to all things so that he can create matter, so Gam-bara would discover the celestial powers that cause the sensuous effects of music. Once he attains a vision of the ideal, however, his music seems only noise to earthbound mortals and he is forced to compose for himself alone. The closer Louis Lambert comes to understanding the secret of the universe, the more insane he ap-pears to be; and his ultimate insight, like Balthazar's cry of "Eu-reka!", is reserved for the moment of death. In a turgid chapter which Balzac claimed to have written under divine inspiration, Seraphita-Seraphitus, the angelic girl-boy of Balzac's Swedenborgian romance, ascends to Heaven, leaving behind her/him disappointed lovers, male and female. In all these works, the visionaries have a passion for unity which forces them to seek the link between spirit and matter, but once they learn the secret—as several do— they are unfitted for life. Balzac thought highly of these stories, and though he wrote them during the 1830's, the first of his two decades of serious effort, he placed them at the end of the *Comédie humaine* as if to illustrate a Dantean progression from the diabolical to the divine, from self-interest ("Scenes of Private Life" is the first grouping) to self-transcendence in a vision of absolute unity.

Just as the artist's vision of the ideal may unfit him for life, his

---

21. Although Balzac seems not to have intended such an interpretation, there is a possibility that Frenhofer was simply in advance of his day and did succeed in creating the mas-terpiece he thought he had painted —in everything, that is, except that "lovely," "living," and hence rather naturalistic foot. Thus it is both en-lightening and confusing to read the story in the edition previously cited (*Forty Nine Lithographs*) contain-ing lithographs by Picasso which show progressive and degressive stages in the treatment of the same subject.

love of mortal pleasures and worldly glory may unfit him for art. Such is the theme of *La Peau de chagrin*. The story deals with Raphael de Vallentin, an impoverished young writer who sets himself a three-year apprenticeship in a Parisian garret, much as Balzac did, where he writes the *Treatise on the Will* that Balzac is said to have composed as a schoolboy. The treatise completed, he falls in love with Fedora, a beautiful but cold lady of fashion who, Balzac states explicitly, symbolizes Society. After losing the remains of his small fortune in a gambling den, Raphael decides to kill himself. On his way to the Seine, he stops at a strange museum-like shop filled with artistic treasures, where he is offered the "fatal skin," a piece of shagreen, which will grant him anything he wishes, but only at a terrible cost. Each time he wishes for something the wish is granted, but with each wish the skin shrinks and the days of the possessor's life are proportionally shortened. Possession of Fedora, wealth, and glory, Raphael now realizes, can bring him no joy because the gratification of each desire carries with it a visible price tag. In order to avoid wishing, Raphael isolates himself and tries to live a vegetable-like existence. He falls in love with and marries Pauline, a symbol of true, selfless love, a now-beautiful heiress who had loved him during his days in the garret. At first there is no shrinking of the shagreen, for Pauline already loves Raphael and he need not wish for her love. But after the marriage the fatal skin becomes a little smaller each night he possesses her. Finally, in desperation, Raphael, prematurely aged and decrepit like the lovers who serve at the Sacred Fount in Henry James's stories, resorts to the scientists in a vain attempt to stretch the shagreen. The intensity of his desire for release from the fatal skin simply accelerates his death.

In his *Treatise on the Will* Raphael argues that "the human will was a material force like steam; that in the moral world nothing could resist its power if a man taught himself to concentrate it, to economize it, and to project continually its fluid mass in given directions upon other souls. Such a man . . . could modify all things relatively to man, even the peremptory laws of nature." [22] The inscription on the fatal skin reads "This is thy life," but it says also, "thy life is mine, for God has so willed it. . . . Wilt thou have me? Take me. God will hearken unto thee." [23] Thus divine will working through human will explains the power of the shagreen. The ageless old man who gives it to Raphael makes this

22. *The Fatal Skin,* trans. Cedar Paul   p. 9.
(New York: Pantheon Books, 1949),   23. *The Fatal Skin,* p. 27.

identification clear. " 'There,' he burst out vehemently, 'there are To Will and To have your Will, both together,' he pointed to the bit of shagreen; 'there are your social ideals, your immoderate desires, your excesses, your pleasures that end in death, your sorrows that quicken the pace of life.' " [24] We know from Balzac's other writings that he believed in the world-transforming power of the human-divine will; for him each person has a given quantity of will, magic fluid or fatal skin, the use of which determines his fate. Hence the vital power of Balzac's monomaniacs, who concentrate their will on a single object.

Opposing To Will and To have your Will, according to the old man, are To Know and To See:

> To Will consumes us, and To have our Will destroys us, but To Know steeps our feeble organisms in perpetual calm. In me Thought has destroyed Will, so that Power is relegated to the ordinary functions of the economy. In a word, it is not in the heart which can be broken, nor in the senses that become deadened, but it is in the brain that cannot waste away and survives everything else, that I have spent my life. . . . I have attained everything, because I have known how to despise all things.
>
> My one ambition has been to see. Is not Sight in a manner Insight? And to have knowledge or insight, is not that to have instinctive possession? . . . Troubles, loves, ambitions, losses, and sorrows, as men call them, are for me ideas, which I transmute into waking dreams; I express and transpose instead of feeling them; instead of permitting them to prey upon my life, I dramatise and expand them; I divert myself with them as if they were romances which I could read by the power of the vision within me.[25]

This speech sounds very much like Balzac expatiating on his vision as artist, and the old man would seem to represent Raphael's past Balzacian life in his garret, when he slept upon his solitary pallet "like a Benedictine brother" and "by sheer contemplation of the things about me discerned an expression and a character in each . . . as my soul bathed itself in the beams of an unknown light, hearkened to the awful and uncertain voice of inspiration, as vision upon vision poured from some unknown source through my throbbing brain." [26]

It is easy enough to say that if Raphael had remained in his

24. *The Fatal Skin*, p. 30.   26. *The Fatal Skin*, p. 79.
25. *The Fatal Skin*, pp. 28–29.

garret and dedicated himself to disinterested scholarship and artistic creation instead of falling in love with Society as embodied in Fedora and being driven to the brink of suicide, he could have escaped the fate of the shagreen. But Balzac's irony is broad, and the story is not so simple as that. Balzac, who suffered a nervous breakdown after writing his treatise exalting the power of mind over matter, realized that not to will would require a superhuman detachment like that of the old man who, indifferent to all things, "seemed to possess the tranquil luminous vision of some god before whom all things are open." [27] For Raphael, as for Balzac, sometimes "natural propensities broke out like a fire long smoldered," [28] and there is always a carnal taint on any humanly conceived ideal. Thus Raphael's first wish with the shagreen is that the old man fall in love with an opera dancer and learn the pleasures of intemperance; and thus the fatal skin continues to shrink after Raphael has turned in revulsion from the soul-appropriating Fedora to the divine Pauline, for the unheroic Raphael wills to find escape in Pauline and would as a man possess what is sacred.

Balzac apparently chose the name Raphael for his hero to suggest his artistic nature. In the shop of the old man Raphael passes from several floors filled with historical relics and antiques to an upper gallery of art treasures. Of the many masterpieces collected there the greatest is Raphael's portrait of Christ, which is locked in a case for which only the old man has a key. "At the sacred names of Christ and Raphael," our Raphael shows curiosity, encourages the old man to open the case, then gazes in rapture at a picture which "breathed the spirit of prayer, enjoined forgiveness, overcame self; . . . [Raphael's] triumph was so absolute that the artist was forgotten." [29] On the opposite wall is the piece of shagreen with its artistically designed inscription. Thus if Raphael's name suggests the artist Raphael, who is said to have been a self-indulgent seeker of pleasure but who overcame self in his art, so the shagreen is a symbol large enough to include not only life and will, but also art. It is as if Balzac realized that in the creation of art as in the pursuit of pleasure one could use up life and sacrifice self to imaginative participation in the life of others. Inability to have his will drives Raphael to contemplate suicide; the shagreen gives him the power to realize whatever he wills, but that power, the story reveals, is but an alternate form of suicide. *La Peau de chagrin*, like Balzac's other literary works, was Balzac's own fatal skin.

27. *The Fatal Skin,* p. 22.   29. *The Fatal Skin,* p. 24.
28. *The Fatal Skin,* p. 80.

For after all, had Raphael simply remained in his garret and continued his search for the ultimate truth, his fate might have been that of Louis Lambert, who discovered the secret but lost his life in the process. *Louis Lambert* was published a year after *La Peau de chagrin* and shares the autobiographical overtones of its predecessor. The lives of Raphael and Louis coincide generally with the earlier life of Balzac. But while their lives are brought to an end within the works, Balzac's went on. On the one hand, *La Peau de chagrin;* on the other, *Louis Lambert* and *Le Chef-d'oeuvre inconnu*—here we find Balzac's concept of his alternate selves, the Balzacs who might have been. For the Balzac who maintained a perilous balance between the real and the ideal, we must turn to other artists in other works.

BALZAC was himself so balanced between the two extremes that he could work concurrently on the most ethereal of his philosophical tales and the most realistic of his social studies. Although he wrote works of both types, his best stories are those in which he combined the opposing strains. Such a work is the story of Lucien de Rubempré in *Illusions perdues* and its sequels. Of the many works in the *Comédie humaine* none is more central and inclusive, yet wide-ranging—and none presents a more convincing picture of the artist *in* society—than the Lucien series. The scene shifts between Paris and the provinces; the story includes a variety of character types, and ranges in social perspective from the criminal underworld through the Paris of the journalists and the courtesans, the world of business and finance, to the upper reaches of fashionable society. Many of the characters who play important roles in other novels make fleeting appearances in the series, which therefore provides a convenient focus on the whole world of the *Comédie humaine.*

When first introduced, Lucien de Rubempré is Lucien Chardon, a physically attractive, morally weak, and poetically talented young man. The first part, "Les deux poètes," set at Angoulème, contrasts Lucien with David Sechard, his friend and brother-in-law, a responsible, modest man with the talent of an inventor. While David works doggedly to find a cheaper method of manufacturing paper, Lucien seeks shortcuts to fame and fortune. His first step is to allow himself to become seduced and corrupted by Mme. de Bargeton, a great lady of the provinces, who encourages him to break with his family because "genius was answerable to no man." [30]

30. *Lost Illusions*, in *The Works of*   tion, VIII, i, 61.
Honoré de Balzac, University Edi-

Lucien next goes to Paris, where he lives with a group of high-minded young men, "Le Cénacle," and tries to achieve recognition as a poet and novelist. Failing, he abandons temporarily his high literary ambitions and becomes a journalist. At this point, Lucien "was standing at the parting of two distinct ways, between two systems, represented by the brotherhood upon one hand, and journalism on the other. The first way was long, honorable, and sure; the second beset with hidden dangers, a perilous path, among muddy channels where conscience is inevitably bespattered." [31]

Lucien has his moments of glory as a journalist, but continues to play for higher stakes: he would marry a wealthy lady of fashion, have his mother's noble name, de Rubempré, restored to him, and keep the actress Coralie as a mistress. Only the third of these ambitions is realized in "Un grand Homme de province à Paris." Lucien becomes enmeshed in journalistic conspiracies, falls from favor, and forges David's name to secure money. When Coralie dies, Lucien returns to Angoulème to confess his crime and make a fresh start. But his presence brings his sister and David only misfortune, and Lucien decides to kill himself. Instead, he meets Abbé Carlos Herrera, who offers a pact whereby Lucien will gain fortune and position in exchange for complete obedience to the Spanish priest, who we will soon learn is really the notorious criminal Jacques Collin, alias Vautrin. Just as Lucien in temperament and situation obviously derives from Raphael de Valletin, so Vautrin resembles the old man who is both God and Mephistopheles in La Peau de chagrin. When he offers the power of his will to Lucien, Vautrin is offering something very similar to the fatal skin.

The sequel, Splendeurs et misères des courtisanes, opens with Vautrin and Lucien, now de Rubempré, in Paris, where Lucien is already a social success and Vautrin is maneuvering to bring his disciple the fortune which will enable him to marry a lady of wealth and position. Again Lucien's native sensibility re-asserts itself, and, impractically, he falls in love with the beautiful courtesan Esther Gobseck. Esther in turn is coveted by the German millionaire Baron de Nucingen. At the suggestion of Vautrin, Esther, willing to do anything for Lucien, sells herself to the baron and serves as an instrument whereby Vautrin and Lucien can filch money from the financier. At the moment when Lucien is on the verge of total success, the plot is foiled by the police. Esther, like Coralie, dies; and the imprisoned Lucien commits suicide. As for Vautrin, he eventually joins the police and becomes the head of the Sureté.

Balzac assures us that Lucien has the talent and sensibility of a true poet. His bright, flashing eyes, his wild, curling hair, and

31. Lost Illusions, VIII, ii, 108.

his slight physique suggest the stereotyped artist of fiction, but if there is "divine graciousness" transfusing his white brows, there is also a short, weak chin which to Balzac the physiognomist signified not only "matchless nobleness" but also deficient will power. A friend of Lucien's reveals one of Balzac's sources for the type when he advises, "Read Goethe's *Tasso*,—the great master's greatest work, and you will see how the poet-hero loved gorgeous stuffs and banquets and triumph and applause. Very well, be Tasso without his folly." [32] But such folly is of the essence of the Tasso-type, and Lucien's tragedy is not so much that he is victimized by a money-hungry society, as Georg Lukàcs and other socially oriented interpreters of the novel suggest,[33] as that he is himself too weak to withstand temptation. "It should be observed," Balzac says, "that there are certain natures in which a really poetic temper is united with a weakened will; and these while absorbed in feeling, that they may transmute personal experience, sensation, or impression into some permanent form, are essentially deficient in the moral sense which should accompany observation." [34] Thus David Sechard is correct when he tells his wife, "Your Lucien is not a poet, he has the poetic temper; he dreams, he does not think; he spends himself in emotion, he does not create. He is, in fact . . . a womanish creature that loves to shine, the Frenchman's great failing. . . . He would not hesitate to sign a pact with the Devil tomorrow if so he might secure a few years of luxurious and glorious life." [35]

And that, of course, is just what Lucien does when he meets Vautrin. The archcriminal appears first in the guise of a Spanish priest whom he has murdered, but his speeches to Lucien, like those to Rastignac in *Père Goriot*, are paraphrases of the discourses of Satan to Christ, and the masses he celebrates are sacrilegious.[36] He is the fulfillment of the genius which Mme. de Bargeton had defined for Lucien: "It was the duty of a man of genius . . . to set himself above law; the man who is master of his age may take all that he needs, run any risks, for all is his." [37] In *Père Goriot* Vautrin tells Rastignac, "In every million of this higher class of cattle, there are ten fellows who rise superior to everything, even the laws; I am one of them." [38] And because Lucien's genius-ideal

32. *Lost Illusions*, VIII, ii, 81.
33. Lukàcs, *Studies in European Realism*, trans. Edith Bone (London: Hillway Publishing Co., 1950), pp. 47–64.
34. *Lost Illusions*, VIII, ii, 274.
35. *Lost Illusions*, VIII, i, 174.

36. Félicien Marceau, *Balzac et son Monde* (Paris: Gallimard, 1955), p. 283.
37. *Lost Illusions*, VIII, i, 61.
38. Translated by Jane Minot Sedgwick (New York: Rinehart Editions, 1950), p. 125.

is an artist, it is fitting that Vautrin should say of himself, "I am a great poet, but I don't write my poems; they consist of deeds and feelings." [39] A man of sensibility, like his disciple Svidrigailov in Dostoevsky's *Crime and Punishment,* a follower of Rousseau and what he calls the Anti-Social Contract, Vautrin even takes on the stature of a kind of god: "I take upon myself to play Providence and I will direct the will of God." [40] Balzac confessed in *Histoire des Treize* that he liked to play God; [41] and William Troy has noted

> In the Machiavellian oration he [Vautrin] delivers on the vices and follies of high society, on how much the young poet must sacrifice if he would be a success in it, it is the very voice of Balzac himself that we seem to hear; it is like the plot of one of his novels. And it is then that we are made aware of the parallel between the artist and the criminal, between the 'detached' observer of society and its detached enemy. Not only are both outside the pale but both are professionally given to the spinning of enormous plots. Vautrin is simply the artist functioning in the realm of action.[42]

If Vautrin is surrogate for Balzac in his role as spinner of plots and controller of a world, his existence in the *Comédie humaine* betrays the sense of guilt which Balzac as a pious Catholic must have felt: art is associated with crime as the archcriminal's attempt to replace God is associated with the playing at god of the world-creating artist. Balzac, like Hawthorne, realized that the artist may commit the sin of appropriating people from the world of observable reality for the sake of his controlling vision; the artist may violate the souls of others in making them adhere to his need for unity within his artistic structure. He may be guilty of the very sins with which he charges the society from which he keeps aloof. Thus Vautrin, when he is captured, is no longer artist, God, or Satan so much as he is simply "the type of a degenerate nation, of a people at once savage, logical, brutal and facile." [43] Vautrin, warring against society, becomes that which he hates, and it is entirely appropriate that the king of the criminal world should become the chief of the *Sureté.*

The opposite foil, counter to Vautrin and society, is represented

39. *Père Goriot,* p. 126.
40. *Père Goriot,* p. 129.
41. Harry Levin, *Toward Balzac* (Norfolk, Connecticut: New Directions, 1947), p. 19.
42. "On Rereading Balzac: The Artist as Scapegoat," in Stanley Edgar Hyman, ed., *The Critical Performance* (New York: Vintage Books, 1956), p. 212.
43. *Père Goriot,* p. 232.

by "Le Cénacle." This group is composed of seven regular members, plus Lucien de Rubempré and Louis Lambert, contrasting types who are only temporary associates. Although their interests and professions vary, the members have certain character traits which set them apart from the rest of society. "Genius," says Balzac, "is one and the same for all and resembles nothing so much as its self." [44] Each member of the Cénacle "bore the stamp of genius upon his forehead," and all of them were "gifted with the moral beauty which reacts upon the physical form, and, no less than work and vigils, overlays a youthful face with a shade of divine gold; purity of life and the fire of thought had brought refinements and regularity into features somewhat pinched and rugged. The poet's amplitude of brow was a striking characteristic common to them all; the bright sparkling eyes told of cleanliness of life." [45] All have the profound self-respect and dedication to vocation which enable them to accept poverty rather than compromise with society. Their hand-to-mouth existence in the Latin Quarter, good-hearted fellowship, and spirited arguments (for they share only a similar character, not the same philosophy) stamp them as perhaps the first Bohemians in fiction, though they are more serious, less attracted to women and other distractions, than the Bohemians of Murger and later writers. Perhaps the keynote of the group is best expressed by Daniel d'Arthez: " 'Genius is patience,' as Buffon said. And patience after all is a man's nearest approach to Nature's processes of creation. What is Art but Nature concentrated?" [46]

Only two of the regular group, Joseph Bridau, a painter, and the writer d'Arthez, are artists proper. Bridau, who is said to derive from Delacroix, plays a more important role in *La Rabouilleuse.* In this scathing indictment of a "society based on money values, on the glorification of success as an end to be obtained by fair means or foul," [47] Joseph Bridau is the only thoroughly sympathetic character, intended obviously to balance the scales against his older brother Philippe and the other scheming, selfish people who dominate the story. Among the reasons for Joseph's becoming a painter, we are told, were "the necessity of looking up at the sky to find consolation for the squalor of the dark, damp scene below, the spiritual quality . . . the enforced simplicity of living and the mother's preference for the older of her two boys coupled with her

44. *The Bachelor's House,* trans. Frances Frenaye (New York: Juniper Press, 1956), p. 40.
45. *Lost Illusions,* VIII, ii, 69.
46. *Lost Illusions,* VIII, ii, 64.
47. Balzac, "Preface," *The Bachelor's House,* p. 5.

disapproval of the tastes of the younger." [48] But that compensation in this case follows nature is shown by his complete absorption: "Because he was entirely wrapped up in his talent, the future artist did not bother with the details of everyday life; during his childhood this attitude was so close to sluggishness that it had been a cause of concern to his father." [49] When he is surrounded by an angry mob eager to revenge his alleged assault against a village hero, Joseph earns the praise of the arresting officer for his courage and calmness. Joseph explains: "My mind was on something far away. . . . An officer once told me about something of the same kind, which happened to him in Dalmatia. On his way back from an early morning walk, he found himself surrounded by the irate population. Comparing the two episodes in my mind, and examining the angry faces about me, I began to play with the idea of painting one of the great riots of 1793. And I began to think, 'Bad boy! That's what you get for chasing after an inheritance instead of sticking to the work you have to do in your own studio!' " [50] Often victimized by his brother and completely ineffective in his attempts to regain his rightful inheritance, Joseph Bridau "practises art for the sake of art," [51] and though he is indifferent to worldly success, the lottery of fate, which is the pervasive symbol of the novel, ultimately throws everything into his hands.

Somewhat less emotional than Joseph Bridau, Daniel d'Arthez is equally dedicated to his profession and similarly absorbed in his work. His "life was entirely devoted to his work. He saw society by glimpses only; it was a sort of dream for him. His house was a convent. He led the life of a Benedictine, with a Benedictine's sober rule, a Benedictine's regularity of occupation." [52] Blessed with second sight, he divines the misery of Lucien and helps him in every way possible—advising, protecting, financing, and even helping to write a derogatory review of his own work. We learn from *Les Secrets de la Princesse de Cadignan* that after years of poverty and hard work his books attain wide recognition and, though he has inherited money from a rich uncle, he continues to live a simple life. Then the Princesse de Cadignan, realizing that she has never been loved by a man of genius, sets about entrapping d'Arthez with all the cunning of the experienced woman. D'Arthez knowingly allows himself to be trapped. The woman of the world and the man of genius discover, to their mutual amazement, that

48. *The Bachelor's House*, p. 26.
49. *The Bachelor's House*, p. 28.
50. *The Bachelor's House*, p. 231.
51. *The Bachelor's House*, p. 77.

52. *The Secrets of a Princess*, in *La Comédie Humaine of Honoré de Balzac* (New York: Century Co., 1906), IV, 340.

they really love each other. By the end of this social comedy, the happy d'Arthez has reached a stage where he "very rarely publishes anything." It is clear, though, that, unlike Raphael or Lucien, he has not capitulated to life, and that he maintains his grip upon his talent, his self-respect, and the Princesse de Cadignan. If d'Arthez is, as usually assumed, an idealized self-portrait of Balzac, *Les Secrets* is Balzac's way of attaining in fancy the reconciliation of his two youthful ambitions, to be famous and to be loved.

Raymond Giraud has argued that Bridau and d'Arthez are introduced into the world of the *Comédie humaine* only to suggest the ideal of the uncommitted, singleminded artist which Balzac himself was not able to attain.[53] No doubt Balzac was more complicated than his Bridau or d'Arthez, but insofar as his life as an artist is concerned, these characters are recognizable self-portraits. What we know of Balzac's nature *as artist*—his dedicated attitude toward his work, his tremendous industry, his power of absorption, his kindliness, his indifference to contemporary opinions of his work, his childlike naiveté in worldly affairs—parallels the character of d'Arthez and Bridau. But the *Comédie humaine* itself, its scope and consistency and excellence, is the best testimony to the fact that Balzac as artist, if not as a man, had the power of self-absorption which we note in the members of the *Cénacle*.

THUS we have met the four main types of artist in Balzac's fiction: the men of sensitivity like Raphael de Valletin and Lucien de Rubempré, the visionaries like Frenhofer and Louis Lambert, the dedicated and singleminded men of genius like d'Arthez and Bridau, and the artist as world-controller and would-be God in Vautrin. If we ask which of the four stands for Balzac, we should perhaps have to admit that no one type explains his uniqueness. Balzac, it is clear, embodied traits of all four types, and it is only by considering their relationship to one another that we can discover the sources of that "projected light" which gives us the peculiarly Balzacian aura.

"My best inspirations," Balzac wrote, "have ever come to me in moments of anguish." [54] The Lucien type stands for the power of suffering, the suicidal impulse, which in Balzac took the form of self-imposed failures. Time after time, on the verge of success and financial independence, Balzac would leave his study and plunge

53. *The Unheroic Hero in the Novels of Stendhal, Balzac, and Flaubert* (New Brunswick, New Jersey: Rutgers University Press, 1957), p. 100.
54. Wormeley, p. 237.

into business projects, politics, and love affairs. Almost invariably he would fail and have to return, burdened with debts and frustration, to the sanctuary of his monastic cell where, in his absorption with work, he could forget his anguish. Then, after months of a strange calm in the midst of feverish activity, he would plunge again into the world of reality and the pattern would be repeated. Like other writers, Balzac worked best when he had to; if he had succeeded in his schemes to make a million or marry a wealthy heiress, we should not have had the *Comédie humaine*. Thus, Frenhofer is a failure as a painter—and he fails if for no other reason than that he destroys his masterpiece—because he was born rich and could afford to indulge his search for absolute perfection. The Lucien type stands also for an indispensable element in Balzac's psychological make-up, the need to suffer. Balzac's men of genius have to suffer because, as he wrote Madame Hanska, "observation is the result of suffering." [55] Louis Lambert "suffered at every point where pain could seize upon flesh or spirit" until "like martyrs who smile at the stake, he escaped to the heaven which thought opened to him." [56] More appropriately Balzac dramatized the link between suffering and observing in Lucien and Raphael, who are surrogates for Balzac's intense desire for glamor, social status, and the love of a beautiful woman; who, in other words, seek success not in their garrets but in that world which meant only anguish for Balzac. The Luciens do not, however, stand for something entirely negative. Adherence to what he had observed of the real world, in which he had suffered, was necessary if Balzac's writings were to achieve recognition, allow him as a man of honor to pay his debts, and keep him from the fate of a Frenhofer.

Balzac was saved too from the fate of a Lucien or a Raphael, who are entrapped by the world of observable reality. A part of Balzac knew that success and love in the real world, however desirable, are illusory and that "life is within us and not without us; that to rise above our fellows for the purpose of commanding them is only to magnify the career of a schoolmaster; and that men who are strong enough to lift themselves to the level at which they can enjoy the sight of worlds ought not to turn their gaze upon their feet." [57] *The sight of worlds*—the one physical trait which all Balzac's true men of genius have in common is the hawk eye. "As to the eyes, there were never any like them; they had a

55. Brunetière, p. 175.
56. *Louis Lambert*, in *La Comédie Humaine of Honoré de Balzac*, trans. Katherine Prescott Wormeley (Boston: Little, Brown & Co., 1896), XXIX, 35.
57. *Louis Lambert*, p. 91.

life, a light, an inconceivable magnetism; the white of the eye-balls was pure, limpid, with a bluish tinge, like that of an infant or a virgin, inclosing two black diamonds, dashed at moments with gold reflections,—eyes to make an eagle drop his lids, eyes to read through walls and into bosoms, or to terrify a furious wild beast, the eyes of a sovereign, a seer, a subjugator." This could be a passage from one of Balzac's more extravagant descriptions of a genius; actually, it is from Gautier's description of Balzac himself.[58] His worldly geniuses—the Luciens, Raoul Nathans, and Camille Maupins of his fiction—have flashing, penetrating eyes, but his more profound geniuses have eyes like those of Louis Lambert: "Some-times clear and wonderfully penetrating, at other times of heavenly sweetness, the eyes grew dull, deadened, colorless, when he yielded himself up to contemplation." [59] The first is the eye of the ob-server; the second, of the visionary. "When it pleases me to do so," Louis Lambert says, "I draw a veil before my eyes. I retire within myself and find a darkened chamber, where the events of nature reproduce themselves in purer forms than those under which they first appeared to my exterior senses." [60]

Balzac's visionaries often have the power of second sight. Facino Cane, an acknowledged self-portrait, says of himself:

> The faculty of observation had become intuitive with me; I could enter the souls of others, while still unconscious of their bodies,—or rather, I grasped external details so thoroughly that my mind instantly passed beyond them; I possessed, in short, the faculty of living the life of the individual on whom I exer-cised my observation, and of substituting myself for him, like the dervish in the Arabian Nights who assumed the body and soul of those over whom he pronounced certain words. . . . To what have I owed this gift? Was it second-sight? Is it one of those qualities the abuse of which leads to insanity? I have never sought to discover the causes of this power. I only know that I possess it, and use it; that is enough for me.[61]

In *Seraphita* and *Louis Lambert* Balzac calls this gift "specialism" and defines it as "a sort of inward vision which penetrates all things"; [62] "seeing the things of the material world as well as those of the spiritual world in their original and consequential ramifica-

58. Wormeley, pp. 205–206.
59. *Louis Lambert*, pp. 24–25.
60. *Louis Lambert*, p. 7.
61. *Facino Cane* in *La Comédie Hu-maine* . . ., trans. Wormeley, XXIX,

154–155.
62. *Seraphita* in *The Novels of Bal-zac*, trans. Clara Bell and R. S. Scott (Philadelphia: Gebbie, 1899), XIII, 77.

tions." [63] The divine and the physical worlds blend for the "specialist." Balzac hinted frequently at an undisclosed "secret" which would explain his creative power. Apparently the secret was concerned with his own uncanny powers of insight. He persuaded his sister that he could read her thoughts and often answered her before she spoke. He claimed to have "divined" a fortune in Sardinia. Curtius's explanation of Balzac's secret probably comes as close as any to Balzac's own belief: "Star and dream, objective and subjective, world and ego, had flowed together into one Vision; that is the secret of Balzac's childhood. It contains the secret of his life and of his art." [64]

For such a visionary, internal and external vision blend, and dreams become indistinguishable from realities. The numerous anecdotes about the extent to which Balzac accepted as real the people of the *Comédie humaine* testify that he shared this genial fault. When a woman in Venice said to him, "You always mistake your dreams for realities," he answered very earnestly, "In those few words you have hit upon the gravest secret of my life." [65] The desire for unity, his impatience with the fragment, his ambition for all-embracing possession help us to understand the philosophy expressed in *Louis Lambert*: "The Universe is, then, variety in Unity. Motion is the means, Number is the result. The end is the return of all things to Unity, which is God." [66] If this sounds like the Poe of *Eureka*, it is because both writers are in the tradition of romantic occultism which stretches from Goethe, Novalis, and Swedenborg to Blake to the American transcendentalist to the French Symbolists to the "religion of consciousness" of Henry James. To break down the barriers between world and ego, subject and object, is the aim of all these writers.

Balzac's desire for complete unity is equivalent to the single-mindedness which we have found best represented by d'Arthez and Bridau in his gallery of artists. But whereas these artists seek to remain aloof and uncommitted, Balzac had something of Raphael and Lucien as well, and could never completely separate society from his visional world. Balzac, for all his indictment of a world dominated by selfishness, was no champion of alienation. To deny any part of the whole would be a confession of failure, a denial of the all-pervading unity of things. It is perhaps Vautrin who best represents Balzac's own nature as a creative artist. The way

63. *Louis Lambert*, p. 143.
64. Quoted by Edwin Preston Dargan, *Honoré de Balzac, A Force of Nature* (University of Chicago Press, 1932), pp. 83–84.

65. Emil Ludwig, *Genius and Character*, trans. Kenneth Burke (New York: Harcourt, Brace and Co., 1927), p. 318.
66. *Louis Lambert*, p. 148.

in which the archcriminal manipulates people, spins plots, changes from pursued to pursuer, controls the lives of others but is himself vulnerable—this suggests something of the divine-human fusion, the artist as God and man creating worlds in which the subjective and the objective blend and cause becomes indistinguishable from effect, that lies behind Balzac's depiction of his artists and is responsible for the peculiar aura of the Balzacian world.

For all the greatness of Balzac's accomplishment, however, we must remember that, like Vautrin, he ultimately failed to subject real life to the power of his will and vision. He succeeded in molding his work and giving it the design of a systematic and generalized anatomy of society; nonetheless, life kept slipping from his grasp. Characters sometimes change from work to work as if they had a free will of their own in opposition to their creator's will. But even more important, Balzac had to spend himself in order to write at all, and he exhausted himself—his fatal skin—before he exhausted his materials. *The Comédie humaine,* in spite of its largeness, remains a fragment, for Balzac did not live to write the synthesizing work that would have done for his series of novels what *Le Temps retrové* does for Proust's *A la Recherche du Temps perdu.* Only a partial reflection of his total vision remains in the novels he left.

CHAPTER FIVE

HENRY JAMES:

The Ideal Of Detachment

HENRY James, it has been said, aspired to be the American Balzac.[1] We may well agree that he succeeded in this ambition, for in quantity and general level of excellence, his fictional output can stand comparison with that of his French master. But in other respects there are important differences between the two. Balzac, we have seen, achieved a balance between self and society by creating a uniquely personal fictive world very much like the real world. Balzacian aura is not essentially a matter of style—for Balzac was an indifferent stylist, clumsy or flamboyant at his worst, transparent at his best—but rather of something larger than style that may be called creativeness, the making of a universe. James, on the other hand, had a highly individualized style that derived from his uniquely discriminating way of *seeing* the world about him. We think of Balzac as preeminently a creator; of James, as primarily an observer.

The emphasis on observation in James's novels and stories may be attributed largely to his technique of the restricted point of view, the "center of consciousness," which is his main contribution to the technical advance of the novel, and the "figure in the carpet" which links the separate tales and helps to give them their peculiarly Jamesian aura.[2] By means of this characteristic technique,

1. Balzac's influence on James is discussed by Leon Edel in "The Architecture of James's 'New York Edition,'" *New England Quarterly,* XXIV (June, 1951), 169–178.

2. See Joseph Warren Beach, *The Method of Henry James* (New Haven, Connecticut: Yale University Press, 1918), pp. 145–161.

the seeing of the story through the eyes of an intelligent observer without his actually telling it, James attains balance between subjectivity and objectivity. As James's grasp of his art developed, he came more and more to place this center of consciousness in the person who has most at stake in the drama about him; actually, the narrative becomes the drama of his awareness in conflict with the world about him. If that world often seems different from the world we know, it is because of the special nature of the Jamesian lens.

Even when James's observers are not practising artists, they have most of the artist's characteristics—his detached curiosity, his faculty of observation and capacity for appreciation, and his devotion to an ideal—and lack only his "talent." Graham Fielder of *The Ivory Tower* is typical of what James called his "men of imagination." In his notes for the novel James wrote that he wished to "steer clear of the tiresome 'artistic' associations hanging about the usual type of young Anglo-Saxon 'brought up abroad,' " yet confessed that he envisoned Fielder "as more or less covertly and waitingly, fastidiously and often too sceptically, conscious of possibilities of 'writing.' " [3] In addition to this reason for his wishing to avoid the "artist" label, his natural reticence and his fear of exalting or incriminating himself by suggesting an autobiographical function for his writer-heroes explain why many of his artists appear as gentleman amateurs, enchanted expatriates, "heiresses of all the ages," or victimized children. One can add to these indirect representatives of the artistic temperament the heroes or minor characters explicitly identified as artists in more than fifty of James's stories. [4]

3. *The Novels and Tales of Henry James*, New York Edition (New York: Scribners, 1907–1917), XXV, 337–339. Unless otherwise specified, all subsequent references to James' fiction and prefaces are to this edition.

4. The importance of art and artists in Jame's fictive world may be gauged in part by the abundance of artists among the characters in his novels and stories. The following chronological list aims at completeness, but I have no doubt overlooked some minor characters in the other stories: "A Landscape Painter" (1866), "The Story of a Masterpiece" (1868), "Osborne's Revenge" (1868), *Gabrielle de Bergerac* (1869), "Travelling Companions" (1870), "The Madonna of the Future" (1873), "The Sweetheart of M. Briseux" (1873), "The Last of the Valerii" (1874), "Adina" (1874), "Professor Fargo" (1874), "Eugene Pickering" (1874), "Benvolio" (1875), *Roderick Hudson* (1876), "The Ghostly Rental" (1876), *The American* (1877), "Four Meetings" (1877), "Théodolinde" (1878), *The Europeans* (1878), *Confidence* (1879), "A Bundle of Letters" (1879), *The Portrait of a Lady* (1881), "The Author of 'Beltraffio,' " (1884), *The Bostonians* (1886), *The Princess Casamassima* (1886), *The Reverberator* (1888), "The Aspern Papers" (1888), "The Liar" (1888), "The Lesson of the Master" (1888),

Two other reasons help to explain why James preferred the indirect method: on the one hand, the intensity of his convictions on the importance of art may have made him hesitant of presenting them directly; on the other, his insistence that art be both hard and plastic made him distrust the lyricism and subjectivism of the autobiographical guise. After H. G. Wells parodied James in *Boon* and defended himself in a letter by saying that he considered himself a journalist rather than an artist and hence justified in subordinating art to "life," James replied sharply, "It is Art that *makes* life." [5] In an earlier letter to Wells, protesting against the latter's use of the autobiographical first person in *The New Machiavelli,* he indirectly defended his own method:

> I make remonstrance . . . bear upon the bad service you have done your cause by riding so hard again that accurst autobiographic form which puts a premium on the loose, the improvised, the cheap and the easy. . . . There is, to my vision, no authentic, and no really interesting and no *beautiful,* report of things on the novelist's, the painter's part unless a particular detachment has operated, unless the great stewpot or crucible of the imagination, of the observant and recording and interpreting mind in short, has intervened and played its part—and this detachment, this chemical transmutation for the aesthetic, the representational, end is terribly wanting in autobiography.[6]

Three comments in his letters to A. C. Benson are particularly important as revelations of his esthetic ideal: "Art should be as hard as nails—as hard as the heart of the artist—a person, who, *qua* artist, is an absolutely Roman father"; on the subject of the lyrical poem, James wrote, "When they have the lyric egotism and confidentiality

"Cousin Maria" (1889), *The Tragic Muse* (1890), "Brooksmith" (1891), "Nona Vincent" (1892), "The Private Life" (1892), "Collaboration" (1892), "Sir Dominick Ferrand" (1892), "The Real Thing" (1893), "Greville Fane" (1893), "The Middle Years" (1893), "The Death of the Lion" (1894), "The Coxon Fund" (1894), "The Next Time" (1895), "The Figure in the Carpet" (1896), "Glasses" (1896), *The Spoils of Poynton* (1896), "John Delavoy" (1898), "The Great Good Place" (1900), "The Real Right Thing" (1900), "The Tree of Knowledge" (1900), "The Abasement of the Northmeres" (1900), "The Tone of Time" (1900), "Broken Wings" (1900), "The Beldonald Holbein" (1901), *The Sacred Fount* (1901), *The Wings of the Dove* (1902), "Flickerbridge" (1902), *The Ambassadors* (1903), "The Story in It" (1903), "The Birthplace" (1903), "The Papers" (1903), *The Golden Bowl* (1904), "The Married Son" (1908), "The Velvet Glove" (1909), "Mora Montravers" (1909), *The Outcry* (1911), *The Ivory Tower* (1917), and *The Sense of the Past* (1917).

5. *The Letters of Henry James,* ed. Percy Lubbock (New York: Scribners, 1920), II, 490.

6. *Letters,* II, 181–182.

I want them to be hard and detached and impersonal—stony-hearted triumphs of objective form"; and, later, "I am also envious —envious of the lyric mood, the lyric *leak*. You can say the egotistical thing—I never." [7]

Such an ideal of art is shared by the most positive of James's artist-heroes. One should not suppose that because James distrusted the use of autobiography in fiction the artists and "men of imagination" in his stories are not, for the most part, self-portraits. James was once asked where he found his Neil Paradays, Ralph Limberts, Hugh Verekers, "and other such supersubtle fry." It is amusing to note the evasive way in which he replied. After saying that "few of them recall to me, however dimly, any scant pre-natal phase," he added somewhat impatiently that "if the life about us for the last thirty years refuses warrant for these examples, then so much the worse for that life," but that the occasional "symptoms of immunity" from the general infection of "the cheap and the easy" justify the use of "*signal* specimens." [8] If this is not enough evidence upon which to base the assumption that his artists are disguised self-portraits, there is his own precedent for making such an identification. In his biography of William Wetmore Story, James quotes several of Story's poems about painters and comments briefly, "Such passages in an artist's projection of another artist may mostly be taken as the revelation of the former's own emotion." [9]

In the Jamesian world, the artist is likely to be taken for granted as a person. His works may remain unsold—or if sold, unnoticed— but he will be invited to the best country homes. The typical Jamesian artist is polite, clean, witty; a cultivated person as much at home over the tea cups as at his desk or easel. Most of these artists could well echo the statement of the young painter Felix in *The Europeans*: "I have been a Bohemian—yes; but in Bohemia I always passed for a gentleman." [10] James's artists are indistinguishable in external manner from the people whose hospitality they accept. They may be more intelligent, sometimes more reserved, but a stranger would have difficulty in guessing their calling.

What, then, does distinguish the artists from the non-artists? Isabel Archer of *The Portrait of a Lady* has the intelligence, the sensitivity, the desire for independence of the artist, but "the girl had never attempted to write a book and had no desire for the laurels of authorship. She had no talent for expression and too little of the

7. *Letters to A. C. Benson and Auguste Monod,* ed. E. F. Benson (New York: Scribners, 1930), pp. 7, 14, 40.
8. XV, ix–x.
9. *William Wetmore Story and His Friends* (Edinburgh and London: Blackwood, 1903), II, 242.
10. (Boston: Houghton, Osgood and Co., 1879), p. 260.

consciousness of genius; she had only a general idea that people were right when they treated her as if she were rather superior." [11] *No talent for expression and too little of the consciousness of genius.* Insofar as talent is innate, the essential characteristic of the artist is a native gift, and James succeeded no better than most writers in explaining the source of the artist's talent. Sometimes he equated it with the "divine afflatus," but he usually implied that inspiration could come only to the person equipped to utilize it. The second requirement, the consciousness of genius, is something other than self-confidence; it may be defined as a heightening of vision, an awareness. Lambert Strether of *The Ambassadors* is "burdened . . . with the oddity of a double consciousness. There was detachment in his zeal and curiosity in his indifference." [12] What is this but disinterested interest? Strether, perhaps James's best example of the "man of imagination" and a conscientious editor in his own right, refuses to "get anything for himself." Nonacquisitive devotion to an ideal may be considered another Jamesian requirement of the artistic temperament. If Strether had also the "talent for expression," he may have been, like William Dean Howells, who supplied the "germ" of his character, a novelist as well as an editor. Ralph Pendrel of *The Sense of the Past* gains a "second consciousness" in London, but so long as he is immersed in his strange adventure, he cannot practise his art: "Detachment and selection, prime aids of the artist, were the sacred sparenesses menaced by a rank growth of material." [13] The tragedy of Isabel Archer is brought about primarily by her inability to detach herself. Her compulsion to duty is oddly at variance with her romantic, sensitive vision of life. "I'm absorbed in myself," she tells Ralph Touchett, "I look at life too much as a doctor's prescription." [14] Talent, disinterested curiosity, and detachment—these are the main essentials of the artist.

In two of his early stories James set forth a concept of the artistic nature which he was to retain for life. In "The Madonna of the Future"—a story influenced by Balzac's *Le Chef d'oeuvre inconnu*—two artists are depicted. One is Theobald, a romantic American who speaks with Ruskinian enthusiasm of the glories of art. Despite the extravagance of his character and speech, Theobald is no *poseur*. His talent is verified in his portrait of the dying son of the "sublime Serafina," and James lets him tell the narrator directly, "Whatever my limitations may be, I'm honest. There's nothing grotesque in a pure ambition or in a life devoted to it." [15] Theobald has sacrificed all

11. III, 67.
12. XXI, 5.
13. XXVI, 61.

14. III, 319.
15. XIII, 453.

promise of personal gain to his vision of an esthetic ideal, but vision is not enough. He prepares so long that his masterpiece cannot be painted. The second artist, Serafina's lover, is a manufacturer of satirical novelties of sculpture—obscene personifications of cats and monkeys. Theobald states the theme of the story: "I need only the hand of Raphael. His brain I already have. . . . I'm the half of a genius! Where in the wide world is my other half? Lodged perhaps in the vulgar soul, the cunning ready fingers of some dull copyist or some trivial artisan who turns out by the dozen his easy prodigies of touch!" [16] The artist as dreamer and the artist as craftsman: James was to imply throughout his fiction that the true artist must be both.

"Benvolio" is a thinly disguised parable on the artistic temperament. The main quality of Benvolio's character is his contrasting moods of expansion and contraction: love and literature, society and seclusion. One day Benvolio dresses in the highest fashion; the next, he is content with a "rusty scholar's coat." Now his conversation is light and gossipy; the next moment it is serious and metaphysical. Even his chambers reveal his split temperament: one is a luxurious room filled with valuable works of art; the other is as sparsely furnished as a monastic cell, containing only a bed and a little "ink-blotted table at which Benvolio did most of his poetic scribbling." Because he is both the man of fashion and the scholar, he is equally at home in the society of a countess who loves him and the bookish world of a neighborhood philosopher and his daughter. Benvolio, the handsome young poet, attempts to choose between the countess, who, like Balzac's Fedora, represents Society, and Scholastica, the daughter of the philosopher, who represents Knowledge. The final implication is that the poet requires both—or neither. When the countess tries to remove Scholastica by securing her a position as governess in a distant region, Benvolio tells her, "Don't you see—can't you imagine that I cared for you only by contrast? You took the trouble to kill the contrast, and with it you killed everything else. For a constancy I prefer this!" [17]—and he taps his brow much in the fashion of Shaw's Eugene Marchbanks bidding goodbye to Candida. Scholastica, befitting the representative of Knowledge, answers his question as to whether or not he should follow her father's suggestion that he make use of his aptitude for philosophical research:

> Her answer was very simple: "I believe you're a poet."
> "And a poet oughtn't to run the risk of turning pedant?"

16. XIII, 486–487. Thomas Seltzer, 1920), p. 280.
17. *Master Eustace* (New York:

"No," she replied, "a poet ought to run all risks—even that one which for a poet, perhaps is the most cruel. But he ought to evade them all!" [18]

Thus Benvolio makes use of everything without succumbing to anything. In the midst of society, he remains sufficiently detached to compose poetry. At the countess' country home, he amuses himself by turning out brilliant social comedies; at Scholastica's apartment, his genius is more lyrical. In moods of expansion he uses the world as material for his dramas; in moods of contraction, he accepts knowledge as the muse of his poetry. The element which unites these two interests is simply his poetic imagination:

> He did possess the magic ring, in a certain fashion; he possessed, in other words, the poetic imagination. Everything that fancy could do for him was done in perfection. It gave him immense satisfaction; it transfigured the world; it made very common objects seem radiantly beautiful, and it converted beautiful ones into infinite sources of intoxication. Benvolio had what is called the poetic temperament. It is rather out of fashion to describe a man in these terms; but I believe, in spite of much evidence to the contrary, that there are poets still; and if we may call a spade a spade, why should we not call such a poet as Benvolio a poet? [19]

Although the character of Benvolio was probably influenced by Turgenev's Schubin in *On the Eve*, who shares the expansion-contraction duality,[20] it seems more likely that in this early story, James was seeking to justify his own immersion in social life while defending his refusal to participate in its usual claims. To use the world rather than to be used by it was ever James's purpose.

The popular conception of James in his early years as a social prude, inordinately fond of country homes and aristocratic titles, may contain a degree of justice. He was fascinated by the social scene, particularly of the cultivated class, but even as a youth he was not taken in completely. His naturally detached temperament kept him aloof from too active a participation and made him aware of his proper function as a conscious observer. The quantity of his literary output over the years demonstrates that, like Benvolio, he had an

18. *Master Eustace,* p. 253.
19. *Master Eustace,* p. 205.
20. Schubin is an engaging young sculptor whose variability runs the gamut from platonic rhapsodies to chasing after servant girls, from tearful self-pity to ferocious self-castigation. James wrote, "Schubin, the young sculptor, with his moods and his theories, his exaltations and depressions, his endless talk and his disjointed action, is a deeply ingenious image of the artistic temperament."—*French Poets and Novelists* (London: Macmillan 1878), p. 227.

inner cell to which he could retreat; and his tremendous productivity is hardly that of a man willing to subordinate his art to gossip over the tea cups.

Nevertheless, James considered self-evident the truism that a writer must live before he can write. "Saturation" is his usual term for the collecting of experiences. "One can read when one is middle-aged or old," he wrote to his brother William in 1888, "but one can mingle in the world with fresh perceptions only when one is young. The great thing is to be *saturated* with something—that is, one way or another, with life; and I chose the form of my saturation." [21] As late as 1914, in his essay on "The New Novel," he grouped such writers as Conrad, Galsworthy, Wells, Bennett, and Lawrence because "they come together under our so convenient measure of value by *saturation.*" He defined this as a "closer notation, a sharper specification of the signs of life, of consciousness, of the human scene and the human subject in general, than the three or four generations before us had been at all moved to insist on." [22] In this essay he also, however, criticized the tendency of these writers to remain submerged too deeply in life: sometimes they failed to arrange their materials with the best possible economy and artistry. In his biography of Story, James accused the sculptor of too much saturation; he lacked "the proper detachment for full appreciation." [23] James as the small boy of *A Small Boy and Others* knew from his earliest years that his primary role in life was that of the observer: "I really believe I was already aware that one way of taking life was to go in for everything and everyone, which kept you abundantly occupied, and the other way was to be as occupied, quite as occupied, just with the sense and the image of it all, and on only a fifth of the actual immersion." [24] One-fifth immersion may be what James meant by "the form of my saturation." No doubt he was temperamentally detached from life, but he was hardly alienated from it—like Axel Heyst in Conrad's *Victory,* he was aloof from the beginning, but so fascinated by the spectacle of life that he could have earned the nickname "Enchanted."

"The novelist is a particular window, absolutely, and of worth in so far as he is one." [25] The window image appears frequently in James's works as a symbol of the importance of observation. The most famous example is the scene in *The Golden Bowl* when Maggie

21. *Letters,* I, 142.
22. *Notes on Novelists, with Some Other Notes* (London: J. M. Dent, 1914), pp. 253–254.
23. *William Wetmore Story and His Friends,* II, 225.
24. (New York: Scribners, 1913), p. 290.
25. *Letters,* I, 310.

Verver, standing on the terrace, looks through a window at the card players; thus "framed," they appear to her in a new light, for the window serves not only as the medium through which Maggie sees, but also as the barrier which separates her from what she sees. Henry St. George, the once distinguished writer of "The Lesson of the Master," is shut up each morning in a room which contains no windows. The absence of a window, he says, has saved him considerable time, but the implication is that this is one reason why St. George's novels have become increasingly artificial. Benvolio's desk, on the contrary, is placed in the embrasure of a wide window, and merely gazing through it absorbs much of his working time. But James implies that this is his proper work, for observation and inspiration are closely related: "It was here that his happiest thoughts came to him —that inspiration (as we may say, speaking of the poetic temperament) descended upon him in silence, and for certain divine, appreciable moments stood poised along the course of his scratching quill." [26] What Benvolio sees through the window is "a vast pictorial spectacle—the very stuff that inspiration is made of." [27]

During his early London years, James says in the Preface to *The Princess Casamassima,* he spent much of his time walking the streets: "One walked of course with one's eyes greatly open, and I hasten to declare that such a practice, carried on for a long time and over a considerable space, positively provokes, all round, a mystic solicitation, the urgent appeal, on the part of everything, to be interpreted and, so far as may be, reproduced." [28] Here is another "Man of the Crowd," and James shares with some of his predecessors—Moritz's Anton Reiser, Poe, Baudelaire, and Balzac—the conviction that observation leads to imaginative insight, the ability to go beyond mere observation to interpretation. James, as far as I know, never claimed the gift of second sight, but he seems to have felt that by means of a sympathetic response to the "mystic solicitation" of the observable world truths beneath the surface could be divined. It is this response, presumably, which links observation and inspiration. Miss Deborah, a kindly old maid in "The Ghostly Rental," sits almost continuously at her window. "When I asked her," says the narrator, "how she acquired her learning, she said simply, 'Oh, I observe!' 'Observe closely enough,' she once said, 'and it doesn't matter where you are. You may be in a pitch-dark closet. All you want is something to start with; one thing leads to another, and all things are mixed up. Shut me up in a dark closet and I will observe after a while, that some

26. *Master Eustace,* p. 208.   28. V, v.
27. *Master Eustace,* p. 267.

places in it are darker than others. After that (give me time), and I will tell you what the President of the United States is going to have for dinner.' " [29]

BUT there is danger in observation, for the artist who observes too closely may appropriate life for a selfish purpose. Like Nathaniel Hawthorne, from whom many of his ideas about art seem to derive, James made of the detached observer not only an esthetic ideal, but also an ethical one. Both Hawthorne and James insisted that the true artist must be detached in order to see clearly, and the really good observer, whether an artist or not, is sympathetically aware of the life about him without trying to appropriate it. Nothing is worse than the exploitation of a human soul: Hawthorne called it the "unforgivable sin," and in Jame's fiction it appears frequently as "emotional cannibalism," the worst of sins because it is the one most likely to blunt the freedom of the individual consciousness.[30] Both novelists recognized that the very purity and objectivity of the artist's vision makes him susceptible to the crime, for the intensity of his insight may "expose" reality and with it the sanctity of a soul. The painters in James's "The Story of a Masterpiece" and "The Liar" are akin to the artist in Hawthorne's "The Prophetic Pictures" in that they commit for the sake of art a sin as reprehensible as that of Roger Chillingworth, who would read the secrets of a human heart for personal revenge, or Gilbert Osmond, who would appropriate Isabel Archer for his collection of treasures. That the esthetic ideal of detachment can lead to the ethical crime of exposure is shown in Hawthorne's *The Blithedale Romance* and James's *The Sacred Fount*.

The thematic affinity between these two novels has apparently escaped notice. Both are told from the point of view of detached observers who are usually considered self-portraits of their creators. Hawthorne's Miles Coverdale and James's unnamed narrator both retire to an isolated gathering of intellectuals, Hawthorne's Blithedale and the country estate which James calls "a great asylum of the finer wit." [31] There they become interested in the mysterious relationships which seem to exist between their fellow guests; in both cases, what is observed is a situation of entangled dominances, the

29. *Eight Uncollected Tales of Henry James*, ed. Edna Kenton (New Brunswick, New Jersey: Rutgers University Press, 1950), p. 293.
30. Osborne Andreas traces this theme in *Henry James and the Expanding Horizon* (Seattle: University of Washington Press, 1948), pp. 22–53.
31. *The Sacred Fount* (New York: Grove Press, 1953), p. 98.

possession of one human soul by another. Both narrators attempt to solve the riddle of these relationships by observation and investigation, and their attempt to "play providence" is resented by the objects of their curiosity. Both begin by feeling intellectually superior to the people whom they scrutinize, and both ironically are defeated by a failure of detachment. By studying emotional cannibalism, they find themselves taking parasitical nourishment from the human puzzle upon which they have come to rely emotionally.

Most interpreters of *The Sacred Fount,* which is usually considered James's most baffling novel, make the mistake of assuming that James's hero is defeated because the premise upon which he bases his theory is false. The idea that in any romantic entanglement one party gains vigor in direct ratio to the depletion of strength in the other is perhaps as strange a belief for an intelligent person to hold as Hawthorne's half-serious conviction that he was "bewitched." But whether the concept of the Sacred Fount is psychologically valid or not, the earlier chapters of this book show that it is not peculiar to James's narrator alone. And there is enough evidence in James's own life and his other writings to suggest that it is not the falseness of the narrator's theory which leads to his defeat.

When Minnie Temple, the cousin whom James acknowledged as the original model for Milly Theale and whose significance in James's life has been established by his biographers,[32] died in 1870, the novelist wrote to his brother William: "I slowly crawling from weakness and inaction and suffering into strength and health and hope: she sinking out of brightness and youth into decline and death. . . . It's almost as if she had passed away—as far as I am concerned—from having served her purpose, that of standing well within the world, inviting and inviting me onward by all the bright intensity of her example." [33] Because the idea of the Sacred Fount appears in James's fiction as early as 1868, in "De Grey: A Romance," it is impossible to attribute the source of the idea, to Minnie Temple's death, but, as Leon Edel suggests,[34] James's letter clarifies the intensity of his lifelong obsession with the vampire theme, the sapping of life from one lover while the other flourishes. After "De

32. James devoted the last chapter of *Notes of a Son and Brother* (New York: Scribners, 1914), pp. 453–515, to his cousin Mary (Minnie) Temple. For her influence on his work, see F. O. Matthiessen, *Henry James: The Major Phase* (New York: Oxford University Press, 1944), 43–52; and Leon Edel, *Henry James: The Untried Years,* 1843–1870 (Philadelphia: Lippincott, 1953), pp. 323–333.

33. Quoted by Leon Edel in his edition of *The Ghostly Tales of Henry James* (New Brunswick, New Jersey: Rutgers University Press, 1948), pp. 27–28.

34. Edel, *Ghostly Tales of Henry James,* p. 27.

Grey," the theme is found most obviously in "The Last of the Valerii," "Longstaff's Marriage" and, of course, *The Sacred Fount*. But wherever love is depicted in his fiction, it seems tainted with vampirism, an emotional feeding on another's life. Particularly is this true of the stories of writers and artists. "The Lesson of the Master," for example, illustrates what could have happened to Benvolio if he had married the countess. Such stories imply that for the artist, love and marriage mean only the draining of creativity. The brilliant young sculptor in *Roderick Hudson* and the potential artist Hyacinth Robinson of *The Princess Casamassima* both succumb to the appeal of life held out to them by Christina Light, who in these two novels speeds the process of the fatal skin in much the same way that Fedora does in Balzac's *La Peau de chagrin*.

It is virtually impossible to summarize the intricate plot of *The Sacred Fount*, for, unlike *The Blithedale Romance*, it is so complex that it requires the same careful attention to detail that one would have to give to a mystery novel which lacked a final chapter and which the reader would have to solve for himself. Nonetheless, a synopsis of the narrator's theory is essential: On his way to Newmarch, he is struck by the manifest changes in several of his fellow guests. Gilbert Long, who previously seemed quite stupid, is now witty and charming; and Mrs. Brissenden, who before her marriage seemed prematurely aged, is now strikingly attractive and youthful. At Newmarch the narrator finds Mr. Brissenden who, though younger than his wife, now appears to be much older. Although the wife has drawn new life and nourishment from her marriage, "poor Briss" has sacrificed his energy to her transformation. To Ford Obert, a painter and hence a fellow observer, the narrator advances his theory of the Sacred Fount; in any love affair, one party gains at the expense of the other; one taps the Fount and grows stronger, while the other is depleted. Only the "author of the sacrifice" is aware of the change, and the measure of true love is the victim's ability to keep this awareness of his sacrifice from its recipient.

Not only is this change apparent in physical appearance, but it may affect the intelligence as well. If Gilbert Long has changed as much as Mrs. Brissenden, then he too must have found a Sacred Fount, and the narrator sets himself to discover the woman with whom Long is having an affair. She must meet three qualifications: she must be conscious of her sacrifice, she must keep nothing back, and she must, like Brissenden, make her sacrifice voluntarily and happily. The obvious candidate, Lady Jane, is ruled out because she remains as facilely charming as ever. Mrs. Brissenden, whom the narrator has taken into his confidence concerning Long's transformation without letting her see the analogy with her own condition, suggests that May Server must be Long's fount. She has a reputation for wit, but at Newmarch she seems as surprisingly stupid as Long appears intelligent. She is nervous and quite obviously depleted. The narrator, however, is reluctant to accept such a ready answer because he finds that Mrs. Server is anything but happy; unlike Briss, she seems conscious not of an ennobling sacrifice, but of abasement. It does not occur to the narrator that this could be attributed to the fact that whereas the Brissendens are united legally, the relationship between Gilbert Long and Mrs. Server is clandestine.

Our narrator begins to waver in his reluctance to identify the fount as Mrs. Server when he observes the increasing intimacy between her and Briss, a relation that suggests the mutual sympathy and understanding of the two conscious victims. The theory would now be rounded out if a similar relationship were to develop between Long and Mrs. Brissenden, but this cannot occur until the "objects of the sacrifice" are as conscious of it as the agents. And if this were to happen, all four parties would "change back" to their original state, and the narrator's "perfect palace of thought" would be revealed in its full symmetry.

On one occasion the narrator notices Mrs. Brissenden and Gilbert Long engaged in close conversation. The apparent discomfiture of Mrs. Brissenden and the worried appearance of Long would suggest that the two objects of the sacrifice are now aware of it. According to the narrator's theory, the four lovers should now revert to their original states; and he flatters himself that this is what has happened when he learns from Ford Obert that May Server has "changed back," that she is now the same brilliant and gracious woman whom he had painted several years before. However, "poor Briss" appears as antiquated as ever: "Things *had,* from step to step, to hang together," the narrator reflects, "and just here they seemed —with all allowances—to hang a little apart." [35]

The novel concludes with a long conversation between the narrator and Mrs. Brissenden, a verbal battle of wits that ranges over almost a fourth of the novel. Visibly weakening, she had gone upstairs with her husband, but sent down word that she wanted to talk with the narrator after the other guests were retired. When she appears, it is in the full height of her splendor. Just as her husband a few moments before had seemed a hundred years old, she now seems a somewhat "nervous twenty-five." She almost immediately takes

35. *The Sacred Fount,* p. 230.

the initiative by repudiating the theory of the Long-Server relationship which she had earlier helped to develop. She even denies that there has been a noticeable change in Long. She refuses to give any evidence for her change of mind, except to suggest that the narrator is "crazy." Her efforts amuse the narrator, though he is made somewhat uncomfortable by her "nervous" splendor. Her duplicity, he is convinced, is inspired by Long, and since it is really the narrator who has made them self-conscious, he is gratified by their bold attempt to live in a state of awareness. In the final chapter, though, Mrs. Brissenden admits that part of her previous approach has been deliberate duplicity. Irritated by the narrator's stubbornness, she gives her evidence: Lady Jane is clearly Long's lover; Mrs. Server, far from having a lover, is trying to find one and has even approached Brissenden. Both of these facts she learned from her husband. Finally, she tricks the narrator, who has been handicapped throughout the discussion by his reluctance to "give away" Mrs. Server, into repudiating his theory. When the narrator asks her what Brissenden has had to say about Mrs. Server, Mrs. Brissenden replies:

> "Why, that she's awfully sharp."
> I gasped—she turned it out so. "*She*—Mrs. Server?"
> It made her, however, equally stare. "Why, isn't it the very thing you maintained?"
> I felt her dreadful logic, but I couldn't—with my exquisite image all contrasted, as in a flash from flint, with this monstrosity—so much as entertain her question. I could only stupidly again sound it. "Awfully sharp?"
> "You after all then now don't?" It was she herself whom the words at present described! "Then what on earth *do* you think?" The strange mixture in my face naturally made her ask it, but everything, within a minute, had somehow so given way under the touch of her supreme assurance, the presentation of her own now finished system, that I dare say I couldn't at the moment have trusted myself to tell her.[36]

With this, the triumphant Mrs. Brissenden leaves the room, and the narrator decides that he had better leave Newmarch: "I *should* certainly never again, on the spot, quite hang together, even though it wasn't really that I hadn't three times her method. What I too fatally lacked was her tone." [37]

At the conclusion of the novel, the narrator gives every appearance of defeat. However, if one reads *The Sacred Fount* as a mystery

36. *The Sacred Fount*, pp. 317–318.　　37. *The Sacred Fount*, p. 319.

story and carefully weighs all the evidence, it becomes apparent that the facts which seem to refute the narrator's theory are out-weighed by those which substantiate it. The main clue is aware-ness itself. We must remember that a key point in the theory is the fact that only the one who makes the sacrifice is aware of it and that he is successful to the extent that he can keep this knowledge from his partner, for to profit knowingly from such a relationship would lead to a sense of guilt at having appropriated another human being for one's own self-fulfillment. Brissenden is happy and heroic in his sacrifice. May Server is not. With this in mind, we can under-stand what happened upstairs before the final interview between Mrs. Brissenden and the narrator. When Gilbert Long and Mrs. Brissenden begin to perceive the truth and thus to weaken in their self-assurance, May Server "changes back." Brissenden, however, in-sists on maintaining his renunciation, an act which James—as many other works testify—considered the most ethical and purest kind of love. He makes a further sacrifice and, perhaps fortified by the re-newed strength of May Server, prepares his wife for the interview with the narrator. The speeding of the aging process to the point where Brissenden appears a hundred years old and his wife be-comes still younger supports this interpretation. When Mrs. Brissen-den appears before the narrator, she has freshly tapped the Sacred Fount. So well has the heroic Brissenden succeeded that she can now see nothing in a theory which she had originally helped to develop. This, I think, is what the narrator means when upon her appearance he suddenly recognizes "the prodigious thing, *the* thing, I had not thought of." [38]

But in what sense is our narrator defeated? Certainly he is de-feated in that his assumption of the complete reversal, the final brick in his "perfect palace of thought," does not "come true." His own appropriation of living persons to his theory pales before the power of Brissenden. Then too he is defeated in his attempt to avoid exposing Mrs. Server. Reluctant to go all the way because he says that he puts his dignity before his curiosity, and aware of the dubious ethics of his detective work, he tries to avoid committing the sin of exposure only to be exposed himself. At the conclusion of the novel he stands revealed as a man who has attempted to compromise the sanctity of a human soul.

Like Miles Coverdale, the narrator is disturbed by the nature of his inquiry, but he receives some comfort from Ford Obert, who tells him that snooping into the lives of one's fellows is "positively

38. *The Sacred Fount,* p. 239.

honourable" when it relies on "the *kind* of signs that the game takes account of when fairly played—resting on psychologic signs alone, it's a high application of intelligence. What's ignoble is the detective and the keyhole." [39] There is, however, an important difference between Obert's observation and that of the narrator. As a painter Obert is satisfied in having May Server remain a picturesque mystery, being more interested in the effect than in the cause; the narrator, however, insists on knowing the whole story, and if he does not quite peek through keyholes, he does attempt to trick at least three of the parties to his theory into revealing their involvement. "It was absurd," he admits, "to have consented to such immersion, intellectually speaking, in the affairs of other people," [40] but he tries to justify himself on the grounds that "the general habit of observation" stems from his sympathetic interest in his fellow mortals— "My extraordinary interest in my fellow-creatures. I have more than most men. I've never really seen anyone with half so much. That breeds observation, and observation breeds ideas." [41] Hawthorne's Miles Coverdale could not understand Zenobia's resentment of his curiosity, but when he told her that he, for one, would be happy to feel himself followed everywhere by an "indefatigable human sympathy," she replied coldly, "We must trust for intelligent sympathy to our guardian angels, if any there be." [42] Lady Jane replies to a similar defense by our narrator, "You can't be a providence and not be a bore. A real providence *knows*; whereas you . . . have to find out." [43]

The wrong that Coverdale and the narrator compound is their presumption in acting not merely as God's spies but as providences. Speaking of his fantasies in childhood, the narrator says, "It was the coming true that was the proof of the enchantment, which, moreover, was naturally never so great as when such coming was, to such a degree and by the most romantic stroke of all, the fruit of one's own wizardry." [44] He is not content, in other words, with merely observing the mysteries about him; he insists on treating his fellows as pawns in a personal game of skill and wit. Coverdale says, "That cold tendency between instinct and intellect, which made me pry with a speculative interest into people's passions and impulses, appeared to have gone far towards unhumanizing my heart." [45] The narrator of *The Sacred Fount* says:

39. *The Sacred Fount*, p. 66.
40. *The Sacred Fount*, p. 89.
41. *The Sacred Fount*, p. 147.
42. Hawthorne, *Complete Works*, Riverside Edition (Boston: Houghton Mifflin, 1884), V, 505.
43. *The Sacred Fount*, p. 176.
44. *The Sacred Fount*, pp. 128–129.
45. Hawthorne, *Complete Works*, V, 495.

That I had done it all and had only myself to thank for it was what, from this minute, . . . was more and more for me the inner essence. . . . I know not what heavy admonition of my responsibility had thus suddenly descended on me; but nothing, under it, was indeed more sensible than that practically it paralyzed me. And I could only say to myself that this was the price—the price of the secret success, the lonely liberty and the intellectual joy. There were things that for so private and splendid a revel—that of the exclusive king with his Wagner opera—I could only let go, and the special torment of my case was that the condition of light, of the satisfaction of curiosity and of the attestation of triumph, was in this direct way the sacrifice of feeling. There was no point at which my assurance could, by the scientific method, judge itself complete enough not to regard feeling as an interference and, in consequence, as a possible check. If it had to go I knew well who went with it, but I wasn't there to save them. I was there to save my priceless pearl of an inquiry and to harden, to that end, my heart.[46]

But the narrator takes his detachment too soon for granted. In spite of the alleged "scientific method" of his inquiry, he not only formulates his "perfect palace of thought" for personal gratification, but also bases it partly upon vanity (Long appears brighter because he has recognized him) and he sacrifices May Server, to whom he is emotionally attached, because any suggestion of feeling would interfere with his "scientific method." But this is the crack in his "perfect palace." The irony of the story is to be found in that his theory is weakened by his compulsion to view Mrs. Server more emotionally than intellectually. His attraction to her, like Coverdale's romantic interest in Priscilla, represents the way in which the detached observer may succumb to life. If the Sacred Fount theory is true, and if the narrator falls in love with Life—which is, after all, what his "perfect palace" consists of—then there is no reason why he too may not be depleted. The life which he tries to control proves to be stronger than he. The final irony—another "prodigious thing"—is that the man who has flourished by unknowingly tapping the Sacred Fount suddenly becomes completely aware and "changes back." He must therefore leave Newmarch immediately and return to his previous finicky existence.

The Sacred Fount differs from *The Blithedale Romance* in that whereas Hawthorne sympathizes with his narrator and finds himself at the end at the same "idle pass," stalemated between art and

46. *The Sacred Fount,* pp. 295–296.

life, James treats his narrator with subtle irony throughout. That we are intended to see him as deluded, if not villainous, may be seen by comparing him with Lambert Strether of *The Ambassadors*. In both stories the hero goes to a "great asylum of the finer wit," notices the transformation of an old acquaintance, and attempts, by observation, to solve the mystery of the sudden blossoming.[47] But Lambert Strether, like Ford Obert, is more interested in the effect than in the cause. His method, as we have already seen, is one of disinterested interest. He is disinterested in that his truth-seeking is not motivated by selfishness, and his interest is benevolent, if non-participating. He invents no elaborate theory for his own gratification. He does intervene in the lives of others, but he realizes that his interference is ethical only to the extent that it is the product of his clear vision and only so long as it is disinterested. It is by placing himself in the position of others imaginatively, rather than by attempting a Caliban appropriation of them for self-exaltation, that he is able to emerge a victor. Strether adheres to all the rules of the game, takes no selfish advantage of others, and receives only the award of awareness.

Strether, however, is not an artist. If he were, he might perhaps find it more difficult to avoid using what he has observed and thus appropriating life. If the "palace of thought" created by the narrator of *The Sacred Fount* is equivalent to a work of art, then his art is life itself, and his method not so much creation as discovery. When real life revolts from his artificial control, as Wilson Follett pointed out in his sensitive reading of the novel years ago, his art is destroyed because it has been based on actuality rather than imagination.[48] James is not, however, writing a story of personal failure. The narrator is guilty because, for selfish reasons, he has meddled in the affairs of others. The implication is that this is ever the danger of any naturalistic-scientific theory of art as discovery rather than as creation of reality—that it will intrude upon the sanctity of life. As Quentin Anderson observes, "James found the artist *in* life a rather threatening figure. The artist who tries to work in life is arranging

47. One can find echoes of the Sacred Fount idea in the relationship between Chad Newsome and Madame de Vionnet. As Chad seems transformed physically and intellectually, Madame de Vionnet seems to fade and grow visibly older, partly because of her efforts to keep Chad from becoming aware of the sacrifice she has made for him.

48. "The Simplicity of Henry James," *American Review* I (May–June 1923), 315–325. A shorter, revised version of this interpretation is Follett's "Henry James's Portrait of Henry James," *New York Times Book Review*, (August 23, 1936), pp. 2, 16.

life itself—the lives, that is, of others so that they may compose a pattern for *him*." [49]

Although James emphasized the necessity of observation and included observers in most of his stories, he stressed the need for an imaginative transformation of reality. We know from the *Notebooks* that James often based his stories on actualities, but was impatient if told too much of what really happened. All he wanted for artistic inspiration were minute particles of life—"air-blown grains" or "germs":

> It at the same time amuses him again and again to know how, beyond the first step of the actual case, the case that constitutes for him his germ, his vital particle, his grain of gold, life persistently blunders and deviates, loses herself in the sand. The reason is of course that life has no direct sense whatever for the subject and is capable, luckily for us, of nothing but splendid waste. Hence the opportunity for the sublime economy of art, which rescues, which saves, and hoards and "banks," investing and reinvesting these fruits of toil in wondrous useful "works" and thus making up for us, desperate spendthrifts that we all naturally are, the most princely of incomes.[50]

IN acknowledging that an art based on observation requires knowledge of the world and that art and life may deplete each other, James appears to be on the side of the Sacred Fount. His correspondence shows that he found it easy to make friends, and he mingled in society with no apparent unease. Yet James is also a prime example of the Ivory Tower artist—a man who escaped most of the normal ties of life, who never married or had children or held a job, but simply devoted himself to his art with singleminded dedication. In his case, as in that of so many other writers, the road between the Sacred Fount and the Ivory Tower is a two-way route; and if being at once in the world and separated from it is a paradox, then James resolved the paradox by separating the man from the artist. He believed that every great artist *as an artist* is detached from society. There is an inevitable split between the social being and the creative personality, between the artist in society and the artist at work. Just as no art is entirely independent of life, so can

49. *The American Henry James* (New Brunswick, New Jersey: Rutgers University Press, 1957), p. 119.
50. X, vi. The relation of art to waste-ful reality is a frequent theme in James's fiction. See, for example, "The Sweetheart of M. Briseux," "The Real Thing," and "The Birthplace."

no artist entirely deny certain human functions. Yet the creative process is essentially subjective, and if the artist is to be more than a mirror of life or a passive receptor of external "inspiration," he must, in the act of creating, detach himself from life in order to see it clearly and to give his work the aura of his individuality. But since this detachment is necessary only in the creative process, the individual may participate actively in life without compromising the integrity of his vision as artist.

Recognition of this dualism is, as we have seen, the traditional solution to the conflict between art and life, but James is remarkable in that there appears to have been in his case virtually no conflict between his two selves. In spite of the efforts of Freudian-minded biographers and critics to show that James's detachment was a form of compensation for his inability to participate in life more actively —an inability usually attributed to that celebrated injury to his back, the "horrid even if an obscure hurt," which he experienced in 1861 —I believe that any fair appraisal of James's early years will show that he was a youth singularly free of repressions, that detachment was an innate characteristic of his temperament, and that the back injury served only as a convenient excuse for continuing to be what his nature insisted that he be.[51] The young James was more fortunate than most artists-to-be in that he had little domestic opposition to overcome and never had to alienate himself from his environment in order to develop as an individual; the essence of his domestic situation was complete freedom; and he remained for life, as his brother William said, "but a native of the James family, and [he] has no other country." [52] Too much has been written about his expatriation from America, for, as Edna Kenton pointed out years ago, he was never really *ex*patriated, only *dis*patriated from the beginning.[53]

James believed that detachment could not be attained artificially nor simulated, that it had to be an innate part of the nature of the true artist. Gilbert Osmond of *The Portrait of a Lady* reveals himself as an egotistic dilettante when he proudly proclaims that life has affirmed his indifference—"Mind you, not my natural indiffer-

51. The most influential psychoanalytic interpretation of James's injury is that by Saul Rosenzweig, "The Ghost of Henry James: A Study in Thematic Apperception," *Partisan Review*, XI (Fall, 1944), 435–455. For an attempted refutation, see my article, "The Turned Back of Henry James," *South Atlantic Quarterly*, LIII (October, 1954), 521–539.

Parts of this essay, in revised form, appear in this chapter.
52. F. O. Matthiessen, *The James Family* (New York: Knopf, 1947), p. 303.
53. "Henry James in the World," in F. W. Dupee, ed., *The Question of Henry James: A Collection of Critical Essays* (New York: Holt, 1945), pp. 132–133.

ence—I *had* none. But my studied, my wilful renunciation." [54]
This insistence that detachment be a natural characteristic of the
artist helps to explain James's impatience with those esthetes who
made a studied pose of greeting life with a yawn or the Bohemians
whose way of life seemed to him but a rationalization of necessity.
It explains also why James's fiction does not fit in the *épater les bourgeois* tradition so prominent during his lifetime. The artist throwing
stones at society seemed a contradiction of James's concept of the
dispatriated artist. Even Flaubert, James wrote, was guilty of betray-
ing his art when he attacked the philistines: "Why feel, and feel so
genuinely, so much about 'art,' in order to feel so little about its
privilege? Why proclaim it on the one hand the holy of holies, only
to let your behavior confess it on the other a temple open to the
winds? Why be angry that so few people care for the real thing,
since this aversion of the many leaves a luxury of space?" [55]

Such lapses in a Flaubert, James eventually came to realize, were
flaws of the man, not the artist. Although maintaining detachment
was never much of a problem for himself, James knew that other
artists had to live double lives which seemed to contradict each other.
When he visited England as a young man, he was frankly surprised
to find George Eliot domestic-minded.[56] Since there seemed no question but that she was a true artist, he concluded that external trap-
pings are unimportant and that the artist may live in any way he
pleases so long as he does not become so immersed in life that, like
Roderick Hudson, Frank Saltram of "The Coxon Fund," or Neil
Paraday of "The Death of the Lion," he can no longer produce his
art.

The sculptor Gloriani maintains an ideal balance between the
man and the artist. In *Roderick Hudson,* where he first appears,
Gloriani is one of several positive antitheses to the rhapsodical Roderick, for whom art is "a kind of safe somnambulism." [57] Gloriani,
unlike the young American, does not make the mistake of confusing
his social being with his genius. He lives fully—"when sometimes
he received you at his lodging he introduced you to a lady without
art of utterance whom he called Madame Gloriani—which she was
not" [58]—and also produced work of significance, perhaps because he
"had a definite, practical scheme of art, and he knew at least what
he meant." He felt that "the thing to aim at is the expressive and

54. III, 381.
55. *Essays in London and Elsewhere*
(New York: Harper, 1893), p. 149.
56. James describes these meetings in
his third volume of memoirs, *The*

Middle Years (New York: Scribners, 1917).
57. I, 26.
58. I, 108.

the way to reach it is by ingenuity" and that the prime function of a work of art is "to amuse, to puzzle, to fascinate, to report on a real aesthetic adventure." [59] Since esthetic adventure is a matter of vision, this statement prepares the reader for Gloriani's function in *The Ambassadors,* where, now an acknowledged master, he serves as the symbol of the kind of consciousness which Strether tries to attain:

> With his genius in his eyes, his manners on his lips, his long career behind him, and his honours and rewards all round, the great artist, in the course of a single sustained look and a few words of delight at receiving him, affected our friend as a dazzling prodigy of type . . . he [Strether] was to recall in espe- cial, as the penetrating radiance, as the communication of the illustrious spirit itself, the manner in which . . . he was held by the sculptor's eyes. He wasn't soon to forget them, was to think of them, all unconscious, unintending, preoccupied though they were, as the source of the deepest intellectual sounding to which he had ever been exposed. He was in fact quite to cherish his vision of it, to play with it in idle hours; only speaking of it to no one and quite aware that he couldn't have spoken without appearing to talk nonsense. Was what it had told him or what it had asked him the greater of the mysteries? Was it the most spe- cial flare, unequalled, supreme, of the aesthetic torch, lighting that wondrous world for ever, or was it above all the long straight shaft sunk by a personal acuteness that life had seasoned to steel? [60]

James often represented the separation of the artist from the man by the recurring image of a turned back. Psychiatrists would perhaps say that this image is James's acknowledgment of the contribution made by his own back in enabling him to maintain personal detach- ment without having to justify it to the world. But James knew that art is its own justification. In the Preface to *The Tragic Muse,* he apologized for his failure to make his hero, Nick Dormer, thor- oughly convincing as a practising artist: "It strikes me, alas, that he is not quite so interesting as he was fondly intended to be, and this in spite of the multiplication, within the picture, of his pains and penalties; so that while I turn this slight anomaly over I come upon

59. I, 107.
60. XXI, 196–197. In addition to appearing in *The Ambassadors,* Gloriani lends his studio as the set- ting of "The Velvet Glove." It is of interest that the only reappearing characters in James's "human com-

edy" are Gloriani and Christina Light, both of whom are introduced in *Roderick Hudson* and used later as contrasting symbols of the triumph of the artist and the roman- tic appeal of life.

a reason that affects me as singularly charming and touching. . . . Any representation of the artist *in triumph* must be flat in proportion as it really sticks to its subject—it can only smuggle in relief and variety. For, to put the matter in an image, all we then—in his triumph—see of the charm-compeller is the back he turns to us as he bends over his work." [61] This passage was written in 1906 or 1907. In at least three of his earlier stories of artists, as well as one published in 1908, are examples of the turned-back image. Although this may be mere coincidence rather than deliberate symbolism or compulsive association, the several appearances of the image are illustrative of a theory supported by a number of James's writings.

The image appears first in *Roderick Hudson*. The genius of the young sculptor is negated by his failure to achieve detachment. When Roderick falls in love with Christina Light and substitutes the pleasures of social intercourse for artistic creation—rather than, like Gloriani, keeping his art distant from his social and sexual lives—not only his productivity but even his ability as an artist declines. Shortly before his tragic death, Roderick and his friend Rowland Mallet see a figure on a distant hill which "in relief against the crimson screen of the western sky . . . looked gigantic." [62] The figure proves to be their friend Sam Singleton, a painter of miniatures and, the antithesis of Roderick in temperament, a patient plodder not given to talk of his art. The unsubtle symbolism of the giant on the horizon suggests the moral pointed up by the contrast between the two artists: "Roderick had said to Rowland at first that their friend reminded him of some curious insect with a remarkable instinct in its antennae; but as the days went by it was apparent that the modest landscapist's successful method grew to have an oppressive meaning for him. It pointed a moral, and Roderick used to sit and consider the moral as he saw it figured in the little painter's bent back, on the hot hillsides, protruding from beneath a white umbrella." [63] The moral, it should be clear, is simply the bent back.

When James met Tennyson in 1875, he flattered himself that he now understood the "true nature of the Bard." After describing Tennyson's un-Tennysonian reading of *In Memoriam*, James wrote in *The Middle Years*:

My critical reaction hadn't in the least invalidated our great man's being a Bard—it had only settled to my perception as not before what a Bard might and mightn't be. The character was just a rigid idiosyncrasy, to which everything in the man conformed,

61. VII, xxi.   63. I, 484.
62. I, 480.

but which supplied nothing outside of itself, and which above all was not intellectually wasteful or heterogenous, conscious as it could only be of its intrinsic breadth and weight. On two or three occasions of the after-time I was to hear Browning read out certain of his finest pages, and this exactly with all the exhibition of point and authority, the expressive particularisation, so to speak, that I had missed on the part of the Laureate; an observation through which the author of *Men and Women* appeared, in spite of the beauty and force of his demonstration, as little as possible a Bard.[64]

Nonetheless, Browning was a bard. Around this paradox James wrote in 1892 "The Private Life," in which Clare Vawdrey, as the author said in his notebooks, stands for the "idea of . . . R. B." [65] The narrator of the story is puzzled by Vawdrey, whose "talk suggested the reporter contrasted with the bard." [66] Actually, there are two Vawdreys: one, the disappointingly mundane gentleman of the social scene; the other, the true bard. "One goes out, the other stays at home," says the narrator. "One's the genius, the other's the bourgeois, and it's only the bourgeois whom we personally know." [67] The narrator discovers the split in Vawdrey's character when, confident that the great man is downstairs, he enters the poet's room and discovers another person already there: "His back was half turned to me, and he bent over the table in the attitude of writing, but I took in at every pore his identity." [68]

The turned-back image appears also in "The Great Good Place," a more important fantasy on the "private life" of the artist. George Dane is a celebrated author whom success has driven beyond the atmosphere in which he can work. Harried and frustrated by the invitations, requests, and obligations that accompany recognition, he is in danger of being submerged in life and losing his art. One morning when he is yearning more than usual for a "happy land" free of interruptions, a young writer whose book has impressed Dane arrives for breakfast. Almost immediately upon entering the room, the visitor guesses Dane's need. "I know what you want," he tells his host, "It exists—it exists." Then, "he suddenly sprang up and went over to my study-table—sat down there as if to write my prescription or my passport. Then it was—at the mere sight of his back, which was turned to me—that I felt the spell work. I simply sat and watched him with the queerest deepest sweetest sense in the world

64. *The Middle Years*, pp. 106–107.   University Press, 1947), p. 109.
65. *The Notebooks of Henry James*,   66. XVII, 227.
ed. F. O. Matthiessen and Kenneth   67. XVII, 244.
B. Murdock (New York: Oxford   68. XVII, 237.

—the sense of an ache that has stopped. All life was lifted; I myself was somehow off the ground. He was already where I had been. . . . He was already me." [69] Falling asleep while his counterpart works, Dane finds himself in the Great Good Place. Granted the setting of controlled form and arrangement, complete freedom from distractions, and aesthetic consciousness of the initiate, the result of a brief stay there is what Dane calls a return of "the vision and the faculty divine." [70]

My final example of the turned-back image is in "The Jolly Corner." Spencer Brydon is not identified as an artist, but he is usually considered a surrogate for James, and the story is often discussed as representing James's attempt to reconcile the self he had become with the self he might have been if he had remained in America. Brydon is surprised to discover in himself a business ability: "He had lived with his back so turned to such concerns and his face addressed to those of so different an order that he scarce knew what to make of this lively stir, in a compartment of his mind never yet penetrated, of a capacity for business and a sense for construction." [71] Brydon encounters his other self as a ghost, but just as the two Clare Vawdreys share the same body and the Great Good Place is actually Dane's study, both Brydons are within the same man. When he tells Alice Staverton that he will never consent to the desecration of the Jolly Corner property, she replies, "In short you're to make so good a thing of your sky-scraper that, living in luxury on *those* illgotten gains, you can afford for a while to be sentimental here!" [72] The compromise thus suggested is proof that Brydon is both the passive observer and the aggressive participant. He is taken aback by Alice's remark, but the story concludes with his reconciliation with his other self. The love of Alice, demonstrated by her willingness to accept both Brydons, permits him to overcome his horror and to recognize the other self.

> "He has been unhappy, he has been ravaged," she said.
> "And haven't I been unhappy? Am not I—you've only to look at me!—ravaged?"
> "Ah I don't say I like him *better*," she granted after a thought. "But he's grim, he's worn—and things have happened to him. He doesn't make shift, for sight, with your charming monocle."
> "No"—it struck Brydon: "I couldn't have sported mine 'downtown.' They'd have guyed me there."

69. XVI, 247.   71. XVII, 438.
70. XVI, 248.   72. XVII, 444.

"His great convex pince-nez—I saw it, I recognized the kind—
is for his poor ruined sight. And his poor right hand—!"

"Ah!" Brydon winced—whether for his proved identity or for
his lost fingers . . ."[73]

The emphasis on sight placed conspicuously in this concluding
passage is not, I think, accidental. If Brydon is a symbolic representation of James himself, the "poor ruined sight" of the other self is a
more important injury than the mutilated fingers. But the two go
together: the eyes that see, the hand that writes. It had occurred to
Brydon on facing a closed door that he could not have closed it because "it was against his whole policy . . . the essence of which
was to keep vistas clear. He had them from the first, as he was well
aware, on the brain." [74] The other self is, like the worldly Clare
Vawdrey, the nonartist half. "I don't say I like him *better*," says
Alice Staverton. "The Jolly Corner" certainly represents a confront-
ing of the rejected self, but it is less an attempt to rectify the past,
as it is sometimes interpreted, than to justify the present. And
Spencer Brydon discovers something that James had known for a
long time.

Five appearances of the turned-back image do not, of course, prove
that James used it always deliberately, but it seems significant that
the five turned backs represent almost the same thing in each instance. To repeat, it matters not what the artist does in the world,
how he dresses, what company he frequents; for when he creates, he
inevitably withdraws to a private realm. The detachment of the artist
is rooted in an innate consciousness that transforms and vitalizes normal perception, that actually "*makes* life." Thus James was able to
use the turned back of the artist to symbolize the "artist *in triumph*."

BUT what of that realm in which the artist finds himself after
he has turned his back on this world? As the Preface to *The Tragic
Muse* implies, this private world is truly revealed only in the artistic
products it sends back to the real world. The hero of that novel, Nick
Dormer, pursues his lonely way indifferent to publicity or glory because he has committed himself to the world of art itself. Looking
at some old portraits, he reflects:

These were the things the most inspiring, in the sense that while
generations, while worlds had come and gone, they seemed far
most to prevail and survive and testify. As he stood before them
the perfection of their survival often struck him as the supreme

73. XVII, 485.   74. XVII, 465.

eloquence, the virtue that included all others, thanks to the universal language of art, the richest and most universal. Empires and systems and conquests had rolled over the globe and every kind of greatness had risen and passed away, but the beauty of the great pictures had known nothing of death or change, and the tragic centuries had only sweetened their freshness. The same faces, the same figures looked out at different worlds, knowing so many secrets the particular world didn't, and when they joined hands they made the indestructible thread on which the pearls of history were strung.[75]

Such a vision of the grandeur of art seems to justify indifference to the "particular world." In accordance with the religious view of art and the ideal of detachment, the artist ought not to care whether or not his works are received and understood. But though James could afford to be more indifferent to success than most writers, he was human enough to desire recognition. He wanted to be read, he was convinced that he had something to say and, as his several attempts to write for the theater show, he was not above bending to public taste. As may be expected, his inability to produce a popu lar success led to some personal bitterness, which is occasionally reflected in his fiction. Particularly is this true of the stories he wrote during the 1890's. Leon Edel says that the dominant theme in James's fiction of this period is isolation; [76] it appears directly in the stories of writers and artists and indirectly in the "self-consolatory fables" in which the artist appears disguised as children victimized by society, as ghosts, or as sensitive "men of imagination." We can best understand James's personal version of the Ivory Tower by contrasting it with the world he knew, as that world is depicted in several artist stories of the nineties.

"The Death of the Lion" appropriately had the place of honor in the first issue of *The Yellow Book,* for it is a story that exalts the artist at the expense of society. When the little-known novelist Neil Paraday finally achieves a degree of fame, he is appropriated by Mrs. Weeks Wimbush, "wife of the boundless brewer and proprietess of the universal menagerie." [77] In spite of his poor health and the protests of his secretary, who narrates the story, he is made to sit for several of the young painters in Mrs. Wimbush's coterie and to visit her country home. His function is to provide entertainment for a gathering of light minded aristocrats by reading extracts from a new novel. The guests make much of Paraday, but no one in the party

75. VIII, 390–391.   *tiques* (Paris, 1931), p. 133.
76. *Henry James: Les Années drama-* 77. XV, 123.

gets beyond the twentieth page of his latest novel, and the notes for his next one are bandied about carelessly until they are lost. When the writer falls ill, he is placed in the most remote room of the house and abandoned to the care of his devoted secretary. Only the secretary, the doctor, and the servants are left in the cold house to preside at Paraday's death. The others have left the melancholy scene. Besides, two new "lions" have already appeared; they are Guy Walsingham, a popular novelist and champion of the "larger latitude," who turns out to be a pallid Miss Collop; and Dora Forbes, who proves to be a florid gentleman with a red moustache and bright knickerbockers. Describing his conception of "The Death of the Lion," James wrote, "It would have the merit, at least, of corresponding to an immense reality—a reality that strikes me every day of my life." [78]

The narrator has been virtually alone in his admiration for Paraday's writings until the day that one of his novels brings him a sudden and surprising fame.

> A national glory was needed, and it was an immense convenience he was there. . . . In a flash, somehow, all was different; the tremendous wave I speak of had swept something away. It had knocked down, I suppose, my little customary altar, my twinkling tapers and my flowers, and had reared itself into the likeness of a temple vast and bare. When Neil Paraday should come out of the house he would come out a contemporary. That was what had happened: the poor man was to be squeezed into his horrible age. I felt as if he had been overtaken on the crest of the hill and brought back to the city. A little more and he would have dipped down the short cut to posterity and escaped. [79]

Eight months after the publication of "The Death of the Lion" and just two weeks after the failure of James's play *Guy Domville*, the novelist wrote in his notebooks: "The idea of the poor man, the artist, the man of letters, who all his life is trying—if only to get a living—to do something *vulgar*, to take the measure of the huge, flat foot of the public: isn't there a little story in it, possibly, if one can animate it with an action; a little story that might perhaps be a mate to *The Death of the Lion*." [80] "The Next Time," the story thus suggested, is the counterpart to "The Death of the Lion" in that it depicts an artist who, unlike Paraday, never finds success. If Neil Paraday "had been overtaken on the crest of the hill and brought back to the city," Ray Limbert may be said to represent the writer

78. *Notebooks*, p. 148.   80. *Notebooks*, p. 180.
79. XV, 110–111.

who "dipped down the short cut to posterity and escaped."

In "The Author of 'Beltraffio' " and "The Lesson of the Master" James pointed out some of the dangers of marriage for the creative artist. Unfortunately, Ray Limbert is not only married, the father of several children, and domiciled with a contemptuous mother-in-law, but is also poor. He struggles desperately to write a popular success that will justify him in the eyes of the world and bring him enough money to support his family. Each time he is certain that "the next time" will be better, only to discover that he has again produced a masterpiece for the happy few. His one real appreciator, the narrator, adds to Limbert's bad luck by persisting, despite the pleas of his friend, in publishing serious reviews of each new book: "Mine was in short the love that killed, for my subtlety . . . produced no tremor of the public tail!" [81]

It is not until he is dying that Limbert, realizing that he cannot make "a sow's ear out of a silk purse," ceases to talk of "the next time." Working on *Derogation*, his last novel, "he had floated away into a grand indifference, into a reckless consciousness of art." [82] Some such state, a return to "the country of the blue," James himself appears to have attained shortly after the humiliating failure of *Guy Domville*. The idea for "The Next Time" is the first entry in the notebooks following his statement of rededication: "I take up my *own* pen again—the pen of all my old unforgettable efforts and sacred struggles. To myself—today—I need say no more. Large and full and high the future still opens. It is now indeed that I may do the work of my life. And I will. x x x x x I have only to face my problems. x x x x x But all that is of the ineffable—too deep and pure for any utterance. Shrouded in sacred silence let it rest." [83] Representative of the extent to which James drew upon his personal experience is the fact that the story written after this confession concerns a failure to measure "the huge, flat foot of the public." And representative too of his ability to transcend the personal is the fact that "The Next Time" contains satiric thrusts at the deluded Limbert. In the "Great Good Place" of artistic creation, James could afford to be amused at his own futile pursuit of lesser satisfactions.

"The Great Good Place," which appeared in 1900, shortly before what is considered the flowering of James's art, deals, as we have seen, with a writer who escapes to a distraction-free realm of ideal conditions for work. The story is best viewed against the background of James's theory of consciousness. In 1883, seven years before "The

81. XV, 161.   83. *Notebooks*, p. 179.
82. XV, 215.

Great Good Place" was written, James replied to a letter from Grace Norton, in which she, in a moment of spiritual despair, had asked him why we live. His answer contains one of his few statements of personal philosophy:

I don't know *why* we live—the gift of life comes to us from I don't know what source or for what purpose; but I believe we can go on living for the reason that (always of course up to a certain point) life is the most valuable thing we know anything about, and it is therefore presumptively a great mistake to surrender it while there is any yet left in the cup. In other words consciousness is an illimitable power, and though at times it may seem to be all consciousness of misery, yet in the way it propagates itself from wave to wave, so that we never cease to feel, and though at moments we appear to, try to, pray to, there is something holds one in one's place, makes it a standpoint in the universe which it is probably good not to forsake. . . . Don't melt too much into the universe, but be as solid and dense and fixed as you can.[84]

The implication here that consciousness is an "illimitable power" calling for personal awareness, is the essence of a philosophy that was to undergo very little change. The essay "Is There a Life after Death?," which James wrote in 1910, only expands his reply to Mrs. Norton. The question of immortality, he says, is significant in direct ratio to the questioner's awareness and appreciation of life; since it can be visualized only in a personal way, the vulgar concept of the hereafter as a communal spirituality, a realm of personal non-entity, offers little comfort for the artist. Living, which James defines as "feeling one's exquisite curiosity about the universe fed and fed, rewarded and rewarded—though I of course don't say definitely answered and answered," [85] is the highest conceivable good. It is as an artist that James most clearly recognizes the "consecrated" importance of consciousness, for the artist, "if he weren't constantly, in his commonest processes, carrying the field of consciousness further and further, making it lose itself in the ineffable, he shouldn't in the least feel himself an artist." Therefore:

The very provocation offered to the artist by the universe, the provocation of him to *be*—poor man who may know so little what he's in for!—an artist, and thereby supremely serve it; what do I take that for but the intense desire of being to get itself personally

84. *Letters*, I, 100–101.   85. Matthiessen, *The James Family*, p. 610.

shared, to show itself for personally sharable, and thus foster sublimest faith? If the artist's surrender to invasive floods is accordingly nine-tenths of the matter that makes his consciousness, that makes mine, so persuasively interesting, so I should see people of our character peculiarly victimized if the vulgar arrangement of our fate, as I have called it, imputable to the power that produced us, should prove to be the true one.[86]

"The creative awareness of things, . . . the artistic consciousness and privilege . . . thus shines as from immersion in the fountain of being." And since it is inconceivable that this "being" should be like a "sniggering little boy who makes his dog jump at a morsel only to whisk it away," a personal hereafter of extended consciousness appears highly probable.[87] If "immersion" and the "artist's surrender to invasive floods" suggest a passive role, it is overbalanced by the fact that James's "religion of consciousness" depends entirely on an individual quest of being. The result is a somewhat aristocratic heaven which omits all questions of divine grace, salvation, and equality, but it is democratic in that it grants to each individual the sole responsibility of attainment.

The mystic realm discovered by George Dane may be described as a dreamlike preview of the heaven postulated by James in "Is There a Life after Death?" Dane can find the land only through personal awareness, and the place seems to be "centred at the core in a consciousness" [88] which is apparently what James called "the fountain of being." Both George Dane and the young man, his "double," who provides the means of escape, know the place. We have seen that upon entering the room, the visitor guessed what Dane needs, and as the spell takes effect, Dane has the sensation that "he was already where I had been. . . . He was already me." And Dane is now where the young man came from. When Dane leaves the Great Good Place, one of the Brothers stands under a high arch and says, "Oh, it's all right!" Dane awakens and talks to the young man for a moment. Then,

Dane tried to take it all in, but was embarrassed and could only say weakly and quite apart from the matter: "I've been so happy!"

"So have I," said the young man. He positively looked so; seeing which George Dane wondered afresh, and then in his wonder read it indeed quite as another face, quite, in a puzzling

86. Matthiessen, *The James Family*, pp. 612–613.
p. 611. 88. XVI, 250.
87. Matthiessen, *The James Family*,

way, as another person's. Every one was a little some one else. While he asked himself who else then the young man was, this benefactor, struck by his appealing stare, broke again into perfect cheer. "It's all right." That answered Dane's question; the face was the face turned to him by the good Brother there in the portico while they listened together to the rustle of the shower. It was all queer, but all pleasant and all distinct, so distinct that the last words in his ear—the same from both quarters—appeared the effect of a single voice. Dane rose and looked about his room, which seemed disencumbered, different, twice as large. It *was* all right.[89]

The fact that the young man knows the solace of the Great Good Place, yet can enjoy doing Dane's work, shows the essential individuality of the happy land, reveals it as something different from an escapist paradise, and points up the ease with which Dane can return to his work without sacrificing the comfort he has found.

Like all mystical realms, the Great Good Place cannot be described in exact terms. Dane struggles for synonyms: "The sacred silent convent was one; another was the bright country-house. He did the place no outrage to liken it to an hotel; he permitted himself on occasion to feel it suggest a club. Such images, however, but flickered and went out—they lasted only long enough to light up the difference. An hotel without noise, a club without newspapers—when he turned his face to what it was 'without' the view opened wide." [90] He has no idea who the Host may be, "yet the wise mind was everywhere—the whole thing infallibly centred at the core in a consciousness. And what a consciousness it had been, Dane thought, a consciousness how like his own!" [91] This strangely personal atmosphere of the Great Good Place is found particularly in the library, where Dane recognizes "every dear old book that he had had to put off or never returned to; every deep distinct voice of another time that in the hubbub of the world, he had had to take for lost and unheard." [92] There are a number of friendly, but unobtrusive companions, but each seems to have a slightly different notion of his surroundings—"The thing's so perfect that it's open to as many interpretations as any other great work—a poem of Goethe, a dialogue of Plato, a symphony of Beethoven." [93] In other words, the Great Good

89. XVI, 247.
90. XVI, 249.
91. XVI, 250.

92. XVI, 253.
93. XVI, 257.

Place is a personal haven, a refuge for the dispatriated artist. It provides the conditions of discovery; it is not itself the Truth.

What happened was that in tranquil walks and talks the deep
spell had worked and he had his soul again. He had drawn in
by this time, with his lightened hand, the whole of the long line,
and that fact just dangled at the end. He could put his other hand
on it, he could unhook it, he was once more in possession. This,
as it befell, was exactly what he supposed he must have said to a
comrade . . .
"Oh it comes—comes of itself, doesn't it, thank goodness?—just
by the simple fact of finding room and time." [94]

The key to this happy land is "simply the cancelled list." Granted
these conditions, it is inevitable that Dane should experience again
"the vision and the faculty divine." He discovers that his genius
returns once "the mere dream-sweetness of the place was super-
seded" by the "world of reason and order, of sensible visible arrangement." [95] The artist's consciousness requires a setting of controlled
arrangement, not the oblivion and chaos of the traditional "inspired
state." Just as "he must arrive by himself and on his own feet," the
artist does not become a passive receptacle once he has attained this
Great Good Place of the higher consciousness. The main pleasure
there is that of observation and understanding. In "Is There a Life
after Death?" James wrote: "In proportion as we do curiously and
lovingly, yearningly and irrepressibly, interrogate and liberate, try
and test and explore, our general productive and, as we like to say,
creative awareness of thing . . . in that proportion does our function strike us as establishing sublime relations." [96] It is such an
interrogation and exploration that Dane enjoys. The price he pays
in this land where nothing is cheap is the friction of increased effort.
The young man would not have visited him at all if Dane had not
been the first man in ten years to perceive the special beauty of
his book. "I don't speak of the putting off of one's self," Dane says,
"I speak only—if one has a self worth sixpence—of the getting it
back." [97]

James's Great Good Place is, in a sense, his personal *Walden*.
The vision of a "consciousness" or "being" which links all life and
can be appreciated only through self-awareness and the absence of
materialistic distractions is similar to the philosophy of Thoreau.

94. XVI, 254–255.
95. XVI, 248.

96. Matthiessen, *The James Family*,
   p. 612.
97. XVI, 240.

Both Americans are spiritually minded—"transcendental" seems too strong a label to apply to James—to the extent that they accept a religious view of life, but they agree that this "being" does not call for oblivion or immersion so much as conscious control. Mental detachment from society is the first requisite of control. One of James's characters says:

> I note again how one has only to look at any human thing very straight (that is with the minimum of intelligence) to see it shine out in as many aspects as the hues of the prism; or place itself, in other words, in relations that positively stop nowhere. I've often thought I should like some day to write a novel; but what would become of me in that case—delivered over, I mean, before my subject, to my extravagant sense that everything is a part of something else? When you paint a picture with a brush and pigments, that is on a single plane, it can stop at your gilt frame; but when you paint one with a pen and words, that is in *all* the dimensions, how are you to stop? [98]

This character would immerse himself in life. But just as his individual consciousness shows him the links between all forms of being, he must as artist be "supreme master and controller." [99]

James's characteristic technique of the "center of consciousness" takes on new significance in relation to his full theory of consciousness. Not only are all aspects of art "one and continuous," as James says in "The Art of Fiction," but also the artist and his art may be seen as one, for subjectivity and objectivity are merged through James's device of the sensitive observer. The "man of imagination" provides a portal through which the reader of James's novels can share in the "process of vision" which, based on the "religion of consciousness," shows the relationship between all things without demanding a mystic surrender. The "process of vision" is simply the form.

James's Pater-like insistence that life, when it is most meaningful, is an "aesthetic adventure" and that art should reflect the awareness of the sensitive observer of life at its most significant level clarifies the particular relation to life represented by James. The artist is detached from one kind of life only that he may accept more fully and participate more completely in a different kind of life. The first is the life of *doing* and *getting;* the second, of *being* and *seeing.* The

98. "The Married Son," in *The Whole Family: A Novel by Twelve Authors* [W. D. Howells and others] (New York: Harper, 1908), p. 167. 99. *The Sense of the Past,* in XXVI, 354.

artist must be detached from the first if he is to be certain that his awareness is unqualified by selfish interest and acquisitive intent, for when so qualified, consciousness is impure. The artist convinced that life is an "aesthetic adventure" must deny many nonesthetic aspects of everyday life. His most "triumphant" response to society is therefore indifference: he turns his back on society to find in his art a realm where life *is* an esthetic adventure.

CHAPTER SIX

MARCEL PROUST:

The Quest For Self

MARCEL, the hero of Proust's *A la Recherche du Temps perdu*, meets at Balbec a young man named Octave in whom "the knowledge of everything that pertained to clothes and how to wear them, cigars, English drinks, horses, . . . had been developed in complete isolation, unaccompanied by the least trace of any intellectual culture." [1] Later, however, this frivolous young man produces several sketches for the theater which the best critics regard as "something of capital importance." Proust explains the paradox: "Who can say whether, seen from without, some man of talent . . . would not have appeared to anyone who met him at Rivebelle, at the hotel at Balbec, or on the beach there, the most perfect and pretentious imbecile. Not to mention that for Octave matters of art must have been a thing so intimate, a thing that lived so in the most secret places of his heart that doubtless it would never have occurred to him to speak of them." [2]

Most of the artists in Proust's novel illustrate his belief that "between what a person says and what he extracts by meditation from the depths where the bare spirit lies hidden and veiled, there is a world of difference. It is true that there are people superior to their

1. *Remembrance of Things Past,* trans. C. K. Scott Moncrieff and Frederick A. Blossom (New York: Random House, 1941), I, 660. Unless otherwise specified, all quotations from Proust are taken from this edition and reprinted by permission of Random House.
2. II, 807–808.

232

books, but that is because their books aren't *BOOKS*." [3] The writer
Bergotte, whose works had thrilled the young Marcel and excited
him with visions of a "long-lost father," proves to be in actuality "a
common thick-set peering person with a red nose curled like a snail-
shell and a black tuft on his chin." [4] Marcel and his family may
be forgiven for their failure to identify the prudish music master at
Combray as the Vinteuil whose daring music attains recognition in
the most advanced circles after his death; and Charles Swann could
not be expected to see in Monsieur Biche, who once emerged naked
and uttering fearful oaths from a hip bath in the Verdurin's drawing
room to frighten their guests as they returned from dinner, those
qualities which were to transform Monsieur Biche into the great
painter Elstir.

In stressing the disparity between what an artist appears to be in
person and what he is in his art, Proust was no doubt explaining
the paradox of his own achievement. The inability of Proust's
friends to conceal their astonishment at the artistry revealed in the
first parts of *A la Recherche du Temps perdu* was scarcely flattering.
Yet we can sympathize with these friends, for it is difficult to see in
the Proust depicted by his biographers—the sickly and neurotic youth,
the fastidious esthete of the nineties, the Jockey Club aristocrat, the
effeminate homosexual—the strength of character we would expect
to find in the author of what is not only one of the world's greatest novels, but one of the most massive. To understand Proust's
achievement we have to counter the image of the social man with
that of the author in his cork-lined study knowing that he was
dying but through sheer will power keeping himself alive long
enough to finish a novel which, though already nearly a million
and a half words in length, would be only a series of fragments
without the rounding off, the completing of the circle, which the
final volume supplies.

There is another reason why Proust stressed the dualism of the
artist. We have found the same idea expressed by many of the
other writers discussed in this book, but if the split between man
and artist seems more extreme in Proust than in James, for example,
it is because it enabled Proust to dramatize his conviction that art is
necessarily subjective, the reflection of a unique internal world.
Whereas James achieves a balance between the external and the
internal by fusing everything through a detached observer, Proust
confessed that "having no sort of power of detached observation,

3. *Letters of Marcel Proust*, trans.   Random House, 1949), p. 398.
  and ed. Mina Curtiss (New York: 4. I, 417.

never knowing what it was that I beheld," [5] he could find reality only within his own consciousness. As *A la Recherche du Temps perdu* appeared in its various parts, it seemed to many readers the last word in realism: in its meticulous accumulation of details, its picture of fashionable salons and the two "ways," its accurate historical settings and locales, and its analysis of the psychology of love, Proust's fictive world seems as realistic as Balzac's. Yet we can never forget that the world depicted is the world seen by the "I" whose story we are reading, and because this "I" is continually changing, so does the world he observes. The real is ever shifting, and the truth is somewhere beneath or beyond the visible surface:

> An hour is a vase filled with perfumes, with sounds, with moments, with changing moods and climates. Consequently, that literature which is satisfied to describe 'objects,' to give merely a miserable listing of lines and surfaces, is the very one which, while styling itself 'realist,' is the farthest removed from reality, the one that impoverishes and saddens us the most, for it sharply cuts off all communication of our present self with the past, the essence of which was preserved in those objects, or with the future, in which they stimulate us to enjoy the past anew. It is that essence which art worthy of the name must express and, if it fails to do this, one can even then draw a lesson from its failure (whereas one draws no lesson from even the successes of realism) namely, that this essence is in part subjective and cannot be communicated to others. [6]

Proust's spiritualized concept of art and his emphasis on subjectivity would seem to put him clearly on the side of the Ivory Tower. However, the essences which he feels that art must depict are sensory—sights, sounds, odors, tastes, and the feel of things—essences which can come to the artist only through emotive experience. The artist cannot help but tap the Sacred Fount—he must live, suffer, mingle with society—but his function as artist is to capture these essences and make them serve as unifying links in the work of art. If it is only through these essences that the artist can penetrate to the hidden country, it is their sum which makes up his ideal self. The *quest* for the ideal self demands the *conquest* of the suffering self; and the search for self becomes essentially a search for the form by which it can be expressed. Therefore every successful work of art is a metaphor representing the "unique world" of the artist.

Because *A la Recherche du Temps perdu* concludes with its hero

5. II, 648.   6. II, 1005.

now ready to write the novel which Proust has just completed, we are likely to confuse Proust with "Marcel" and to assume that the author, like his hero, is moving toward a solution as he writes. But if that were the case, the novel we read would be more like *Jean Santeuil* than *A la Recherche*. Now that Proust's earlier novel has been discovered and published, we can better appreciate the achievement of the later work, for while *Jean Santeuil*, which was written in the late 1890's, contains most of the ideas of the final version, and though it shows that Proust even at that early stage of his literary career could create a character, visualize a scene, and convey a mood, these are still but the raw materials which are not yet ready to be blended into a masterpiece. The secret of unity is the ideal self of the artist, and Proust had not yet discovered that self when he wrote *Jean Santeuil*. Although the book was meant to convey "the very essence of my life," [7] Jean fails to come to life. Partly because the story is told in the third person, partly because Proust is as yet reluctant to identify himself with his hero (hence the evasively indirect method: Proust meets the great writer C., who leaves a manuscript depicting the life of Jean Santeuil, who is actually Proust), and partly because Proust has not yet discovered the means of centering the work in the self, the emphasis falls upon society, upon Jean's "impressions," rather than upon Jean himself. Compared to Marcel, Jean is a transparent reflector still too immersed in reality to see his life as a totality.

"A book in which there are theories," Proust admits, "is like an article from which the price mark has not been removed." [8] Yet *A la Recherche du Temps perdu*, like *Jean Santeuil*, contains an abundance of theories. This raises a valid objection to the earlier work, for there the theories are not assimiliated into the dramatic action. In the later novel, however, the theories are justified as steps in Marcel's progression toward his discovery of the artist within himself. That *A la Recherche* is unified mainly by its central theme of the development of an artist should be obvious to any one who reads the seven books as one, but it is surprising how frequently one still encounters discussions of Proust's novel which imply that it is primarily a study of fashionable society, a psychological analysis of love, or a philosophical treatise on time. It is impossible in a chapter of this length to defend the essential unity of *A la Recherche* as a portrait of the artist to the same extent that F. C. Green achieves in his exhaustive *The Mind of Proust*, the main contention of which is that Proust's novel is basically "the narrative of

7. *Jean Santeuil*, trans. Gerard Hop-   Nicolson, 1955), p. 1.
kins (London: Weidenfeld   and   8. II, 1003.

Marcel's gradual spiritual evolution, the story of how his mind, by
a progressive extension in breadth and depth, finally acquired that
consciousness of existence which distinguishes the attitude or vision
of the artist from that of other men." [9] In this chapter I can show
only how Proust's masterpiece fits into the tradition of the artist-
novel, yet makes its own unique contribution. In order to do this, I
must first isolate from the total work the major stages in Marcel's
artistic development.

THE young Marcel fits the usual stereotype of the artist. Shy,
introspective, imaginative, he prefers solitary pleasures. From both
books and nature he experiences a spiritual sensation, as if by concentrated effort he can plunge to their hidden reality. He is determined to learn "the secret of Truth and Beauty, things half-felt by
me, half-incomprehensible, the full understanding of which was the
vague but permanent object of my thought." [10] But he finds it difficult to penetrate to the hidden reality:

> When I saw any external object, my consciousness that I was
> seeing it would remain between me and it, enclosing it in a
> slender, incorporeal outline which prevented me from ever com-
> ing directly in contact with the material form; for it would vola-
> tilise itself in some way before I could touch it, just as an in-
> candescent body which is moved toward something wet never
> actually touches moisture, since it is always preceded, itself, by
> a zone of evaporation. Upon the sort of screen, patterned with
> different states and impressions, which my consciousness would
> quietly unfold while I was reading, and which ranged from the
> most deeply hidden aspirations of my heart to the wholly external
> view of the horizon spread out before my eyes at the foot of the
> garden, what was from the first the most permanent and the most
> intimate part of me, the lever whose incessant movements con-
> trolled all the rest, was my belief in the philosophic richness and
> beauty of the book I was reading, and my desire to appropriate
> these to myself, whatever the book might be.[11]

Marcel's intense desire and adoration provide the first two requirements of the Proustian artist: an awareness of the immobility and
inadequacy of reason, and a conviction of the transcendent reality
beneath the surface of the visible world.

9. The Mind of Proust: A Detailed   Press, 1949).
Interpretation of "A la recherche du   10. I, 64.
temps perdu" (Cambridge University   11. I, 63–64.

It is natural that feeling this way about the grandeur of art, Marcel should wish to become a writer. In a characteristic daydream he imagines that the glamorous Mme. de Guermantes, taking a sudden fancy to him, "would make me tell her, too, all about the poems that I meant to compose. And these dreams reminded me that, since I wished, some day, to become a writer, it was high time to decide what sort of books I was going to write. But as soon as I asked myself the question, and tried to discover some subjects to which I could impart a philosophical significance of infinite value, my mind would stop like a clock, I would see before me vacuity, nothing, would feel either that I was wholly devoid of talent, or that, perhaps, a malady of the brain was hindering its development." [12] In this mood of despair, he tries to renounce literature; perhaps it, too, is illusion. But one day, returning from a ride, he experiences a strange vision which compels him to compose a fragment of prose.

At a bend in the road I experienced, suddenly, that special pleasure, which bore no resemblance to any other, when I caught sight of the twin steeples of Martinville, on which the setting sun was playing, while the movement of the carriage and the windings of the road seemed to keep them continually changing their position; and then of a third steeple, that of Vieuxvicq, which, although separated from them by a hill and a valley, and rising from rather higher ground in the distance, appeared none the less to be standing by their side.

In ascertaining and noting the shape of their spires, the changes of aspect, the sunny warmth of their surfaces, I felt that I was not penetrating to the full depth of my impression, that something more lay behind that mobility, that luminosity, something which they seemed at once to contain and to conceal.

. . . And presently their outlines and their sunlit surface, as though they had been a sort of rind, were stripped apart; a little of what they had concealed from me became apparent; an idea came into my mind which had not existed for me a moment earlier, framed itself in words in my head; and the pleasure with which the first sight of them, just now, had filled me was so much enhanced that, overpowered by a sort of intoxication, I could no longer think of anything but them. . . .

Without admitting to myself that what lay buried within the steeples of Martinville must be something analogous to a charming phrase, since it was in the form of words which gave me pleasure that it had appeared to me, I borrowed a pencil and some

12. I, 132–133.

paper from the Doctor, and composed, in spite of the jolting of the carriage, . . . the following little fragment. . . .[13]

Marcel's description of the steeples, too long to be quoted in its entirety, is noteworthy chiefly for its wealth of metaphors; the spires are now "three birds perched upon the plain, motionless and conspicuous in the sunlight," now "three golden pivots," now "three flowers painted upon the sky," and finally, "three maidens in a legend, abandoned in a solitary place over which night had begun to fall; and while we drew away from them at a gallop, I could see them timidly seeking their way, and, after some awkward, stumbling movements of their noble silhouettes, drawing close to one another, slipping one behind another, showing nothing more, now, against the still rosy sky than a single dusky form, charming and resigned, and so vanishing in the night." The significance of this experience is to be found in Marcel's realization that the essence of the steeples is to be captured through analogy, first through that "charming phrase" in which the idea appears to him, then through the artistic comparisons with which it is described. What can be the reality of appearances when the steeples never appear quite the same? They are always changing, never static, but they contain something which finds its counterpart in the perception of the observer. Art is the record of such awareness and response.

Unfortunately, Marcel forgets this experience, and not until many years later does he understand the secret behind the three spires. They have given him intense pleasure, and, inspired, he has been able to render them in a fragment of art. But must the artist rely upon such mystical and fleeting moments for the subjects of his art? If so, the prospect is discouraging, for such moments do not occur at will. It is not long before Marcel falls back into despair. He abandons his literary ambitions, though he is unable to find a more congenial vocation, and devotes himself to the pursuit of society. It is necessary to realize, however, that his climb up the social ladder is motivated more by the romantic, historical associations of old family names and traditions than by the mundane advantage of membership in the Jockey Club. It seems to him at this time that the Guermantes way represents the material of which art is made. It is not until later that he realizes his mistake.

He receives encouragement to become a writer from an unexpected source. M. de Norpois, an elderly diplomat, persuades Marcel's father that literature may well be as respectable an occupation

13. I, 138–139.

as diplomacy. Himself distrustful of the younger generation of states-men, Norpois asserts that it is "quite possible, by writing, to attract as much attention, to receive as much consideration, to exercise as much influence, and at the same time to preserve more independence than in the Embassies." [14] These, however, are not precisely the advantages which Marcel has hoped to gain from a literary career, and it is not surprising that in spite of Norpois' success in waiving parental opposition, Marcel is unsuccessful in his attempts to become a writer. When Norpois criticizes an essay which Marcel has shown him on grounds that it lacks a noble purpose and seems an example of art-for-art's-sake, Marcel attempts to take advantage of Norpois' practical advice, but "after a few laboured pages, weariness made the pen drop from my fingers; I cried with anger at the thought that I should never have any talent, that I was not 'gifted.' " [15]

Despairing of his ability to write, Marcel develops, in the years that follow, into a man of the world. He becomes a regular visitor to the fashionable salon of the Duchesse de Guermantes and the more bourgeois but culture-centered salon of Madame Verdurin. He falls in love, first with Gilberte Swann, later with Albertine. He travels when his health permits. He accepts the friendship of Robert de Saint-Loup. Yet during these years and in the midst of distraction Marcel retains his notion of an artistic vocation and collects mental notes for the book which he will someday write. Society, friendship, love, travel, the theater all prove inadequate pleasures, and it is note-worthy that he can enjoy them only when he can see them "in the perspective of imagination and art." [16]

Always there is the silent testimony of the artists he knows. From the writer Bergotte, the painter Elstir, and the composer Vinteuil, he gains a vague sense of the "hidden country" of the true artist. The conflict between art and life is brought out most dramatically in the account of Marcel's love affair with Albertine. In spite of his careful investigations and every effort of his rational intelligence, he never succeeds in really knowing Albertine. It is only when he is hurt by her, as when he is most jealous, that he seems to love her. When everything is going smoothly, his life with Albertine is unin-terrupted boredom, but even then her character seems apparitional. The conflict is symbolized by the intrusion of the passage on the death of Bergotte, whose beautiful life is juxtaposed against Alber-tine's trivial lies. In his suffering state, Marcel feels the passing of Bergotte not so much because of the loss of a friend as because his

14. I, 337.   16. II, 417.
15. I, 338.

death has provided him with an opportunity to catch Albertine telling a lie, for she swears that she has seen Bergotte on, it turns out, the day after his death.

The most striking contrast to the love affair, however, is provided by Vinteuil's septet. The famous "little phrase" from Vinteuil's sonata had earlier served as a symbol—the objective correlative or "spiritual equivalent"—of Swann's love for Odette and Marcel's love for Gilberte Swann. Now, from a study of the more significant and complete septet, Marcel comes to realize that it is only through art that the individual can be known.

> But is it not the fact then that from those elements, all the real residuum which we are obliged to keep to ourselves, which cannot be transmitted in talk, even by friend to friend, by master to disciple, by lover to mistress, that ineffable something which makes a difference in quality between what each of us has felt and what he is obliged to leave behind at the threshold of the phrases in which he can communicate with his fellows only by limiting himself to external points common to us all and of no interest, art, the art of a Vinteuil like that of an Elstir, makes the man himself apparent, rendering externally visible in the colours of the spectrum that intimate composition of those worlds which we call individual persons and which, without the aid of art, we should never know? [17]

And Marcel succeeds finally in linking the essence of Vinteuil's music, the quality which the "little phrase" shares with the complete septet, with the feeling which had been aroused in him by the steeples at Martinville. From this realization Marcel discovers the nature of art, though the means of attainment remain a mystery.

> I might be sure that this new tone of joy, this appeal to a super-terrestial joy, was a thing I would never forget. But should I be able, ever, to realise it? This question seemed to me all the more important, inasmuch as this phrase was what might have seemed most definitely to characterise—from the sharp contrast with all the rest of my life, with the visible world—those impressions which at remote intervals I recaptured in my life as starting-points, foundation-stones for the construction of a true life: the impression that I had felt at the sight of the steeples at Martinville, or of a line of trees near Balbec.[18]

Marcel's next lesson on the nature of the artistic experience is a negative one. Opening Figaro one morning, he is surprised to see an essay

17. II, 559.	18. II, 561.

which he had submitted months before printed as the lead article. Immediately he is overcome by visions of the many homes into which *Figaro* enters. He imagines the effect his article may have upon various readers, and takes comfort in the thought that certain passages that may not appeal to M. de Guermantes would perhaps strike a responsive chord in the vulgar Bloch. He is later disabused of this idea when he realizes that none of his friends has noticed the article, but even at the moment of highest gratification, upon rereading the essay, he is sceptical of its merit. The implication is that Marcel's essay is composed of a series of separate passages which fail to express the special consciousness of a real artist. This writing, like parliamentary reports, can be judged only in terms of its popularity, of its striking a responsive chord in the minds of its readers. "And as a crowd, even a select crowd, is not an artist, this final seal of approval which it sets upon the article must always retain a certain element of vulgarity." [19] But from his experience with the *Figaro* article Marcel learns that he need not concern himself with appealing to an audience. True art, produced in silence, is a personal experience and needs no justification.

Another occurrence tends both to increase and to lessen his regret at having no talent for literature. He picks up a volume of the unpublished journal of the Goncourt brothers. The passage he reads— one of Proust's most clever pastiches—deals with the early days of the Verdurin salon, and Marcel is surprised to discover here an intelligent M. Verdurin, a ridiculous Elstir, a charming Cottard. His first reaction is one of appreciation of that "magical power of literature" which makes him desire once again to see acquaintances who have bored him. But this, he reflects, is why he can never be a great writer himself: he is incapable of seeing things as they are. "Goncourt knew how to listen, as he knew how to observe; I did not." [20] It is only when another writer has brought their image before him that Marcel's imagination is aroused concerning individuals whom he has known. As for his own powers of observation:

> Like a geometrician who, stripping things of their perceptible qualities, sees only their linear substratum, what people said escaped me because what interested me was not what they wanted to say, but the way they said it in so far as it revealed their characters or their ludicrous traits; or, rather, there was one thing which had always been the object of my investigation because it gave me a very special pleasure, and that was the point that two human beings had in common. . . . It was of no use for me to go out to

19. II, 782.   20. II, 890.

dinner, I did not see the guests because, when I thought I was looking at them, I was looking through them as with an X-ray.[21]

But if literature, as evidenced by the Goncourt brothers, is simply the record of appearances and has no obligation to reveal spiritual truths, then Marcel's failure to write seems less tragic. At the same time, it is unfortunate that his passion for analogy prevented him from making the most of the particular reality of the scenes he has witnessed.

After several years of solitude and unhappiness, spent partly in a sanitarium, Marcel returns to Paris and decides to spend an evening with the Princesse de Guermantes. Any enjoyment which might be derived from such a visit now seems to him a "purely frivolous one," but he has no reason for refusing such dubious pleasures, "since I now had the proof that I was not good at anything, that I could no longer hope to find joy in literature, whether through my own fault, for lack of talent, or because literature itself was less pregnant with reality than I had thought." [22] But the revelation which he had sought in vain through his reason now appears to him as if by inspiration: "But sometimes it is just at the moment when all appears lost that a signal comes which may save us; after knocking at all the doors that lead nowhere, the only one through which we can enter, one which we might have sought in vain for a hundred years, we stumble against unwittingly, and it opens." [23] It is while Marcel is on his way to the Princesse de Guermantes that a series of involuntary memories show him the path to art. Once before, in the taste of the celebrated madeleine, he had been transported to the past. But the isolated experience was not enough to sustain the reaction. Now, the feel of curbstones, the clink of a spoon against a plate, the feel of a napkin, the sight of a copy of George Sand's *François le Champi*, restore to him past experiences embodied in the new.

He now realizes that his experience with the madeleine opened up the realm of essence. Earlier, he had discovered transcendent reality in the steeples at Martinville and the trees at Balbec, and he knew that in dreams or the sensation of first awakening from sleep, when he was still on the threshold between the conscious and the unconscious, he could escape temporarily from contemporaneous existence, the realm of matter to which everyone is chained by habit, to the timeless realm of essence. Yet, because the sensation experienced in awakening fades in an instant, a particular essence cannot

21. II, 888.   23. II, 991.
22. II, 991.

be captured in half sleep. To capture these fragments of transcendent reality is to find those "foundation-stones for the construction of a true life" which he has been long seeking.

These essences are complete in themselves, but are lost forever in a realm of nothingness until they are responded to by the individual who has experienced them: "When from a long-distant past nothing subsists, after the people are dead, after the things are broken and scattered, still, alone, more fragile, but with more vitality, more unsubstantial, more persistent, more faithful, the smell and taste of things remain poised a long time, like souls, ready to remind us, waiting and hoping for their moment, amid the ruins of all the rest; and bear unfaltering, in the tiny and almost impalpable drop of their essence, the vast structure of recollection." [24] These essences cannot be captured through a deliberate effort of memory, but come involuntarily to the person prepared to receive them.

Let a sound already heard or an odour caught in bygone years be sensed anew, simultaneously in the present and the past, real without being of the present moment, ideal but not abstract, and immediately the permanent essence of things, usually concealed, is set free and our true self, which had long seemed dead but was not dead in other ways, awakes, takes on fresh life as it receives the celestial nourishment brought to it. A single minute released from the chronological order of time has re-created in us the human being similarly released, in order that he may sense that minute. And one comprehends readily how such a one can be confident in his joy; even though the mere taste of a *madeleine* does not seem to contain logical justification for this joy, it is easy to understand that the word "death" should have no meaning for him; situated outside the scope of time, what could he fear from the future? [25]

Because of this revelation, Marcel now feels himself prepared to create a work of art.

And so I was decided to consecrate myself to this study of the essence of things, to establish its true nature, but how should I do this, by what means? . . .

The only way to get more joy out of them was to try to know them more completely at the spot where they were to be found, namely, within myself, and to clarify them to their lowest depths. . . .

For the truths that the intelligence grasps directly and openly

24. II, 991.   25. II, 996.

in the full-lighted world are somehow less profound, less indispensable than those which life has communicated to us without our knowledge through the form of impressions, material because they have come to us through our senses, but the inner meaning of which we can discern. In short, in this case as in the other, whether objective impressions such as I had received from the spires of Martinville or subjective memories like the unevenness of the two steps or the taste of the *madeleine,* I must try to interpret the sensations as the indications of corresponding laws and ideas; I must try to think, that is to say, bring out of the obscurity what I had felt, and convert it into a spiritual equivalent. Now this method, which seemed to me the only one, what was it other than to create a work of art? [26]

As long as these essences are captured only in involuntary memories, they remain personal and incommunicable. But it is in the artist's power to relate these personal essences to the essences of others, to connect the past to the present, the inanimate to the living, art to life.

> An hour is not merely an hour. It is a vase filled with perfumes, sounds, plans and climates. What we call reality is a certain relationship between these sensations and the memories which surround us at the same time . . . the only true relationship, which the writer must recapture so that he may link together in his phrase its two distinct elements. One may list in an interminable description the objects that figured in the place described, but truth will begin only when the writer takes two different objects, establishes their relationship . . . and encloses them in the necessary rings of a beautiful style, or even when, like life itself, comparing similar qualities in two sensations, he makes their essential nature stand out clearly by joining them in a metaphor, in order to remove them from the contingencies of time, and links them together with the indescribable bond of an alliance of words.[27]

Hence artistic representation of the realm of essence depends primarily on analogy and metaphor. In this sense, *A la Recherche du Temps perdu* is a giant metaphor, the little phrase of Vinteuil multiplied a thousand times, which conveys the true self of the artist in Proust.

There appear to be six important steps in Marcel's development as artist: (1) an awareness of the immobility of habit-chained existence and rational perception, (2) an increasing belief in the transcendent reality beneath the surface of things, (3) the conviction

26. II, 999–1001.   27. II, 1008–1009.

that only through art can the individual be known—hence, the theory of art as a reflection of consciousness, (4) the experience of involuntary memory, which captures the essences of hidden reality, (5) the compulsion to create the "spiritual equivalent" of these linked essences in the form of a work of art, and (6) the conception of art as a series of metaphors joining the essences of disparate experiences and reflecting the special universe of the artist's consciousness. Because all of these ideas appear in *Jean Santeuil*, we may assume that Proust, unlike Marcel, did not have to experience a sudden revelation such as that which shows Marcel the path to art at the conclusion of his story. However, by withholding the full theory and then presenting it as a climactic revelation, Proust succeeded in tying together the many parts of his novel; and just as this technique provided a means of unification, it revealed too that Marcel was not simply Proust, but a more ideal, more complete, more ordered self.

The series of discoveries Marcel made on his memorable journey to the Guermantes culminates in his decision to write the book which Proust has already written. Marcel has discovered the existence of his ideal self and learned how to give it artistic form, but the ideal self is still a mental concept as far as Marcel is concerned, for *he* has not yet created it. Therefore, to understand the nature of that self we must turn first to the proven artists who serve as surrogates for the post-conversion Marcel and then to the form of the work itself.

Stendhal called the novel "a mirror carried along a high road." [28] Proust retained the notion of the mirror, but felt that it reflected the traveler more than the road.

> To mount the skies it is not necessary to have the most powerful of motors, one must have a motor which, instead of continuing to run along the earth's surface, intersecting with a vertical line the horizontal which it began by following, is capable of converting its speed into ascending force. Similarly the men who produce works of genius are not those who live in the most delicate atmosphere, whose conversation is most brilliant or their culture broadest, but those who have had the power, ceasing in a moment to live only for themselves, to make use of their personality as of a mirror, in such a way that their life, however unimportant it may be socially, and even, in a sense, intellectually speaking, is reflected by it, genius consisting in the reflective power of the writer and not in the intrinsic quality of the scene reflected. [29]

28. *The Red and the Black,* trans.   Heritage Press, 1947), p. 321.
C. K. Scott Moncrieff (New York: 29. I, 422–423.

"Ceasing in a moment to live only for themselves"—this phrase provides a first clue to the ranking of the artists in *A la Recherche du Temps perdu*. As in the world of Henry James, the artists in Proust's fictional milieu are more numerous than in real society. In addition to Marcel and his three principal masters—Vinteuil, Elstir, and Bergotte—there are, to name but a few, Berma and Rachel the actresses, Morel the violinist, Legrandin the novelist, Bloch the playwright, Ski the sculptor, Madame de Villeparesis the memoir writer, an unnamed naturalist who wanders through a drawing room muttering "I observe," Charles Swann the amateur critic, and Baron de Charlus, who lacks a specific art but is "an artist to his finger-tips." With the exception of Berma, however, these lesser artists lack the ability to project beyond themselves. Legrandin, for example, uses his meager talent as a stepping stone to a position in polite society, and this novelist of the people, "too frank, too honest," he says, for snobs and esthetes like Marcel, emerges as Legrandin de Méséglise. The diabolic Morel, protegé of Baron de Charlus, would do anything for money though he "set above money his certificate as first-prize winner at the Conservatoire," cannot get beyond his "admirable virtuosity." Ski is an ex-prodigy who has developed more temperament than art. Swann and Charlus, however, illustrate the point more fully because they fail more emphatically. Swann's predominance in the novel is justified in that he serves as alter ego for Marcel and illustrates the course which the latter might have taken had he not experienced his revelation. Swann submerges himself in life and never finishes his book on Vermeer. The Baron de Charlus is based on the same prototype as Huysman's des Essentes and Wilde's Dorian Gray and, like them, is a victim of misplaced sensibility. Because of his sexual inversion, the baron cannot see himself objectively, and this brilliant man who could have become, if not a great artist, then a great impressario like Diaghilev, is doomed to perpetual self-defense and self-dramatization—"This willing Prometheus had had himself chained by force to the rock of pure Matter." [30]

The sufferings of a great artist are of a different kind from the self-imposed flagellations of a Charlus. Like Balzac, Proust believes in the value of suffering: "Works of art, like artesian wells, mount higher in proportion as the suffering has more deeply pierced the heart." [31] Suffering is the tool which penetrates the shield of habit ruling normal lives and allows the truth to be perceived. A certain Dr. du Boulbon appears in the novel long enough to say: "All the

30. II, 971.   31. II, 1022.

greatest things we know have come to us from neurotics. It is they and they only who have founded religions and created great works of art. Never will the world be conscious of how much it owes to them, nor above all of what they have suffered in order to bestow their gifts on it. We enjoy fine music, beautiful pictures, a thousand exquisite things, but we do not know what they cost those who wrought them in sleeplessness, tears, spasmodic laughter, rashes, asthma, epilepsy, a terror of death which is worse than any of these." [32] Until his daughter's Lesbianism plunges him into the deepest grief he has ever known, Vinteuil is simply a provincial music teacher. From his personal tragedy emerges his innate genius. As if Proust sought to symbolize the reliance of art upon suffering, the seducer of Vinteuil's daughter is the only person capable of deciphering the almost illegible scraps of music produced by her victim's father and organizing them into his greatest composition. But though suffering may help an artist, the budding man of genius should not deliberately seek pain and sorrow, as Charlus does; rather, it must come to him naturally, as it will inevitably so long as his talent demands of living more than life, chaotic and unruled, can offer. No doubt it was the very untidiness of Proust's life that impelled him to create a more ordered self in art.

Once the artist has been jolted into self-discovery, he is then justified in retreating to the Ivory Tower, as Proust did when he retired to his cork-lined study. There is Bergotte, for example: "Perhaps the more the great writer was developed in Bergotte at the expense of the little man with the beard, so much the more his own personal life was drowned in the flood of all the lives that he imagined, until he no longer felt himself obliged to perform certain practical duties, for which he had substituted the duty of imagining those other lives." [33] Hence, Marcel, even before his consecration to art, finds the need to escape from the distractions of society to the rejuvenating experience of solitude: "I had not been wrong, perhaps, after all, in sacrificing not only the vain pleasures of the world but the real pleasure of friendship to that of spending the whole day in this green garden. People who enjoy the capacity—it is true that such people are artists, and I had long been convinced that I should never be that—are also under an obligation to live for themselves." [34] Later, in describing the revelation, he is more emphatic: "For whatever moral reasons he may do it, the artist who gives up an hour of work for an hour's conversation with a friend knows that he is sacrificing a reality for something which is non-existent." [35] The most dangerous vices for

32. I, 933–934.   34. I, 679.
33. I, 426.   35. II, 998.

the artist are the greatest virtues of society—friendship, loyalty, patriotism, piety, and good fellowship—for the artist must deny anything that drives him away from his work. The vice of the artist is in giving way to distractions. "Real books must be the product, not of broad daylight and small talk but of darkness and silence." [36]

Perhaps one reason for the artist's basic isolation is to be found in the nature of talent itself. Talent, "an instinct religiously hearkened to," [37] is scarcely to be distinguished from individuality, the propensity of living one's life for oneself. Genius is to be distinguished from talent by the extent to which it is capable of taking this independent path and transforming it into a reflection of a unique world. Because every true work of art is stamped with the artist's individuality, there is no such thing as an imitative masterpiece. Except for the established materials with which it must work, art cannot be explained in terms of traditions, schools, or fashions. It is great art not because of what it shares, but because of what distinguishes it from all other art. "One feels unmistakably," Marcel notes, "when one sees side by side ten portraits of different people painted by Elstir, that they are all, first and foremost, Elstirs." [38] Thus, "A well-read man will at once begin to yawn with boredom when anyone speaks to him of a new 'good book,' because he imagines a sort of composite of all the good books that he has read and knows already, whereas a good book is something special, something incalculable, and is made up not of the sum of all previous masterpieces but of something which the most thorough assimilation of every one of them would not enable him to discover, since it exists not in their sum but beyond it." [39] The word "beyond" appears frequently in Proust's discourses on art. The "something beyond" external reality that is the great work of art is like a special universe, hidden and secret until the man of genius reveals it. The writer conveys his awareness through the medium of his special style.

> Style is for the writer, as for the painter, a question, not of technique but of vision. It is the revelation—impossible by direct and conscious means—of the qualitative differences in the way the world appears to us . . . Only by art can we get outside ourselves, know what another sees of his universe, which is not the same as ours and the different views of which would otherwise have remained as unknown to us as those there may be on the moon. Thanks to art, instead of seeing only one world, our own, we see it under multiple forms, and as many as there are original artists,

36. II, 1015.   38. I, 640.
37. II, 1012.   39. I, 498.

just so many worlds have we at our disposal, differing more widely from one another than those that roll through infinite space, and years after the glowing center from which they emanated has been extinguished, be it called Rembrandt or Vermeer, they continue to send us their own rays of light.[40]

Believing that no other aspect of art is more primary than individual vision, Proust can tell us much about that aura which I discussed in the Balzac chapter; and if the abundance of literary criticism in Proust's novel is justified, it is as an invitation to discover the unique, the individual characteristics of the work we are reading. In a footnote to the preface of his translation of Ruskin's *The Bible of Amiens*, Proust explains why he quotes so liberally from Ruskin's other books in order to explain the one. To read but a single book by an author, says Proust, is merely to make his acquaintance. One may notice certain peculiarities, but he is likely to attribute them as much to the subject as to the author. It is only after one reads numerous works by the same author that the reader is able to separate and distinguish the characteristic aspects of his artistic personality: "From comparing a number of different works, we are able to isolate those features, common to all of them, which, in their totality, compose the artist's moral physiognomy. . . . Fundamentally, some such attempt to help the reader to feel the impact of an artist's unique characteristics, to put before him those traits whose similarity with what he is reading at the moment may enable him to realise the essential part they play in the genius of a particular writer, should be the first part of every critic's task."[41]

If Proust came to this conclusion from his extended study of Ruskin, Marcel attains the same realization from his reflections on the music of Vinteuil. At first, the little phrase in Vinteuil's sonata, though it suggested a unique point of view, was isolated. It is only after Marcel has studied the more ambitious septet that he is able to link the little phrase with others in Vinteuil's music and to discover the characteristic genius of the Combray music master, "for with other and more profound gifts Vinteuil combined that which few composers, and indeed few painters have possessed, of using colours not merely so lasting but so personal that, just as time has been powerless to fade them, so the disciples who imitate him who discovered them, and even the masters who surpass him do not pale their originality."[42] His early works were merely exercises in

40. II, 1013.
41. *Marcel Proust: A Selection from His Miscellaneous Writings*, ed.
Gerard Hopkins (London: Allan Wingate, 1948), p. 24.
42. II, 556.

the style of other composers—like Proust's pastiches—and it was only when he tried to do something entirely new that his essential nature was revealed. From his study of Vinteuil Marcel concludes that "each artist seems thus to be the native of an unknown country, which he himself has forgotten, different from that from which will emerge, making for the earth, another great artist." [43]

When Marcel suggests to Albertine that it is in this "unknown quality of a unique world . . . that the most authentic proof of genius consists, even more than in the content of the work itself," she politely inquires, "Even in literature?" [44] This provides Marcel with an opportunity to illustrate what Proust meant by saying, in the Ruskin preface, that the first task of the critic is to identify the unique characteristics of an author. Distinguishing qualities of Thomas Hardy, for example, include his "stone-mason's geometry" and his structural parallelism. The novels of Stendhal are individualized by, among other things, " a certain sense of altitude combining with the life of the spirit: the lofty place in which Julien Sorel is imprisoned, the tower on the summit of which Fabrice is confined, the belfry in which the Abbé Blanès pores over his astrology and from which Fabrice has such a magnificent bird's-eye view." [45] Just as each of Vermeer's pictures is a fragment of the same world, so the women and the houses of murder in Dostoevsky's works are always the same woman and the same house, and his novels could all be called *The Story of a Crime*: "That novel and terrible beauty of a house, that novel beauty blended with a woman's face, that is the unique thing which Dostoevsky has given to the world, and the comparisons that literary critics may make, between him and Gogol, or between him and Paul de Kock, are of no interest, being external to this secret beauty." [46]

These, however, are detachable qualities, and it is the "something beyond" their sum total that makes the real artist. At this point, Proust's theory of the artist verges on the mystical. The second duty of the critic, Proust continues in the Ruskin preface, is to attempt to reveal that particular frame of mind from which all the special characteristics emanate.

In my view, however, the critic should go further still. He should try to reconstruct the peculiar life of the spirit which belongs to every writer who is obsessed by his own special view of reality, whose inspiration can be measured by the degree to which he has attained to the vision of that reality, whose talent can be

43. II, 558.   45. II, 644.
44. II, 643.   46. II, 645.

estimated by the extent to which he can re-create it in his work, whose morality can be interpreted as the instinct which, by compelling him to see life under the aspect of Eternity (no matter how peculiar to himself that life may seem, to us, to be), forces him to sacrifice to the urgency of visualising it, and the necessity of reproducing it, and, thereby, assuring a vision of it that shall be durable and lucid, every duty, and even existence itself, because existence for him has no justification save as being the sole possible medium through which he can make contact with reality, no value other than that which an essential instrument may have for a doctor engaged on an experiment.[47]

Something of this Marcel realized when, as a young boy, he read the works of Bergotte. Although he fancied that he was interested in the story alone, it was the image of Bergotte that enchanted him, and almost unconsciously he found himself entered into the special world of the great writer. He found in the peculiar phrases of the book "something ethereal and sublime":

> One of these passages of Bergotte, the third or fourth which I had detached from the rest, filled me with a joy to which the meagre joy I had tasted in the first passage bore no comparison, a joy which I felt myself to have experienced in some innermost chamber of my soul, deep, undivided, vast, from which all obstructions and partitions seemed to have been swept away. For what had happened was that, while I recognised in this passage the same taste for uncommon phrases, the same bursts of music, the same idealist philosophy which had been present in the earlier passages without my having taken them into account as the source of my pleasure, I now no longer had the impression of being confronted by a particular passage in one of Bergotte's works, which traced a purely bi-dimensional figure in outline upon the surface of my mind, but rather of the "ideal passage" of Bergotte, common to every one of his books, and to which all the earlier, similar passages, now becoming merged in it, had added a kind of density and volume, by which my own understanding seemed to be enlarged.[48]

Such is the art of Bergotte, but the "ideal passage" is not reproduced, perhaps because it is in the mind of Marcel even more than on the pages of Bergotte's book. The same is true of the music of Vinteuil and the paintings of Elstir. In describing them, Proust

47. *Marcel Proust: A Selection* . . . , 48. I, 71–72.
p. 109.

created new works of art, but the music and the paintings, until they can be heard and seen, remain apart. Perhaps it is just as well. What remains of Vinteuil's sonata, Bergotte's books, and Elstir's seascapes can be visualized in imagination. Berma "made her words, her lines, her whole speeches even, flow into lakes of sound vaster than themselves, at the margins of which it was a joy to see them obliged to stop, to break off." [49]

To see life always "under the aspect of Eternity" is the mission of the true artist, Proust insists, and if his novel is a search for lost time, it is also a search for what transcends chronological time. Proust's description of Bergotte's death illustrates his theory of the artist's immortality, the basis of his spiritualized conception of art. When the ailing writer reads an account of a recent art exhibition and finds the critic mentioning a little patch of yellow wall in Vermeer's *Street in Delft*, which, though he fancied that he knew the picture by heart, he cannot remember, he gets out of bed and makes his way to the gallery. He sees the yellow wall, feels that it is greater than all his books, and is overcome with giddiness. "In a celestial balance there appeared to him, upon one of its scales, his own life, while the other contained the little patch of wall so beautifully painted in yellow. He felt that he had rashly surrendered the former for the latter." [50] Despite the word "rashly," which brings out the pathos of his situation as a human being, this passage may be said to symbolize the sacrifice made by every great artist—the giving of life that little patches of yellow wall may live on. While Bergotte mutters to himself, "little patch of yellow wall, with a sloping roof, little patch of yellow wall," he slumps to the floor. Proust revised the following passage just before his own death.

He was dead. Permanently dead? Who shall say? Certainly our experiments in spiritualism prove no more than the dogmas of religion that the soul survives death. All that we can say is that everything is arranged in this life as though we entered it carrying the burden of obligations contracted in a former life; there is no reason inherent in the conditions of life on this earth that can make us consider ourselves obliged to do good, to be fastidious, to be polite even, nor make the talented artist consider himself obliged to begin over again a score of times a piece of work the admiration aroused by which will matter little to his body devoured by worms, like the patch of yellow wall painted with so much knowledge and skill by an artist who must for ever remain unknown and is barely identified under the name Vermeer. All

49. I, 750.   50. II, 509.

these obligations which have not their sanction in our present life seem to belong to a different world, founded upon kindness, scrupulosity, self-sacrifice, a world entirely different from this, which we leave in order to be born into this world, before perhaps returning to the other to live once again beneath the sway of those unknown laws which we have obeyed because we bore their precepts in our hearts, knowing not whose hand had traced them there—those laws to which every profound work of the intellect brings us nearer and which are invisible only—and still!— to fools. So that the idea that Bergotte was not wholly and permanently dead is by no means improbable.

They buried him, but all through the night of mourning, in the lighted windows, his books arranged three by three kept watch like angels with outspread wings and seemed, for him who was no more, the symbol of his resurrection.[51]

If Bergotte is "not wholly and permanently dead," it is because his books, the reflection of his unique world, will live after "the common thick-set peering person" is entirely forgotten. From this we may see why Proust stressed involuntary memory in his theory of art, for the linking of the past and the present in one transcendent essence is a means of escaping the restrictions of time. The mere taste of a madeleine is not enough to explain the sense of joy experienced by Marcel; rather, as he says in a passage already quoted, the joy is brought about because death, continually present in all temporal life, is momentarily forgotten: "It is easy to understand that the word 'death' should have no meaning for him; situated outside the scope of time, what could he fear from the future?"

It is by creating things anew in the way that only he can see them that the artist attains personal immortality through his art. When Marcel visits Elstir's studio and looks at the painter's most recent works, he decides that "the charm of each of them lay in a sort of metamorphosis of the things represented in it, analogous to what in poetry we call metaphor, and that, if God the Father had created things by naming them, it was by taking away their names or giving them other names that Elstir created them anew. The names which denote things correspond invariably to an intellectual notion, alien to our true impressions, and compelling us to eliminate from them everything that is not in keeping with itself." [52] Thus, for example, a characteristic metaphor in Elstir's seascapes is the suppression of the line of separation between the sea and the land, as in the picture of the harbor at Carquethuit, where he "prepared the mind

51. II, 509–510.   52. I, 628.

of the spectator by employing, for the little town, only marine terms, and urban terms for the sea." [53] Such devices, Marcel insists, are not arbitrary or ingenious; they are the products of a special "impression" of a scene. Elstir, who had, in reality, "an exceptionally cultivated mind," made every effort to "strip himself, when face to face with reality, of every intellectual concept." [54] He attempted to "wrest from what he had just felt what he already knew, his effort had often been to break up the aggregate of impressions which we call vision." [55] The paintings of the great artists are unique because they combine elements which logic seldom associates. Habit, the champion of logic, determines one's usual perception of things; the artist breaks through the shield of rational associations and sees the world anew: "artistic genius in its reactions is like those extremely high temperatures which have the power to disintegrate combinations of atoms which they proceed to combine afresh in a diametrically opposite order, following another type." [56]

"I believe that metaphor alone can give a species of eternity to style," Proust wrote in an essay on Flaubert. [57] Not only are Elstir's seascapes composed of analogies between disparate elements, but Proust describes them in verbal terms. Similarly, in attempting to depict the music of Vinteuil, Proust uses words more appropriate to the visual arts. For example:

> Whereas the sonata opened upon a dawn of lilied meadows, parting its slender whiteness to suspend itself over the frail and yet consistent mingling of a rustic bower of honeysuckle with white geraniums, it was upon continuous, level surfaces like those of the sea that, in the midst of a stormy morning, beneath an already lurid sky, there began in an eery silence, in an infinite void, this new masterpiece, and it was into a roseate dawn that, in order to construct itself progressively before me, this unknown universe was drawn from silence and from night. This so novel redness, so absent from the tender, rustic, pale sonata, tinged all the sky, as dawn does, with a mysterious hope. [58]

The realm of essence can be perceived only when the startling likenesses between objects are noted by the sensitive observer. And since the prime duty of the artist is to reveal the realm of essence, analogy is his appropriate medium. Almost every page of Proust's novel is studded with figures of speech which seem arbitrary but

53. I, 629.
54. I, 632.
55. I, 1018.
56. I, 647.

57. *Marcel Proust: A Selection* . . . , p. 224.
58. II, 554.

which Proust would insist are inevitable. It seemed to young Marcel that whenever Bergotte "spoke of something whose beauty had until then remained hidden from me . . . by some piece of imagery he would make their beauty explode and drench me with its essence." [59] What Marcel says of Bergotte applies also to Proust:

> Above all, he was a man who in his heart of hearts loved nothing really except certain images and (like a miniature set in the floor of a casket) the composing and painting of them in words. For a trifle that some one had sent him, if that trifle gave him the opportunity of introducing one or two of these images, he would be prodigal in the expression of his gratitude, while showing none whatever for an expensive present. And if he had to plead before a tribunal, he would inevitably have chosen his words not for the effect that they might have on the judge but with an eye to certain images which the judge would certainly never have perceived.[60]

Elstir's method of working—his effort to strip himself of intellectual concepts and, seeing the truth beneath appearance, to reveal its "spiritual equivalent" in visual metaphors, thus demonstrating the unity between apparently disparate elements—is a demonstration of two key ideas in Proust's theory of the artist: his belief that the artist must be passive before his vision and, a consequence of this, the theory that style is not so much a matter of technique as of the artist's particular way of seeing things. The question remains, how does this apply to a work of literature? Since Bergotte's methods of writing are not described in detail, the best answer is to be found in the novel written after Marcel achieves his theory of art. By looking at *A la Recherche du Temps perdu* in this light, it will be possible to show not only Proust's use of metaphor but also the way in which he unified in one work these "foundation-stones for the construction of a true life."

we have seen that the basic discovery made by Marcel is that art must reveal the reality behind the appearance. This reality is attained through the experience of involuntary memory. However, a novel, particularly one as long as this, cannot be made up entirely of momentary perceptions. The madeleine and its counterparts are stimuli, and the response is the product of involuntary memory, the rediscovery of the past. Once the veil of habit and reason is broken, memories of the past flood upon Marcel. His task, he decides, is to

59. I, 72.   60. I, 426.

reestablish "the significance of even the slightest signs by which I was surrounded (the Guermantes, Albertine, Gilberte, Saint-Loup, Balbec and so forth) long familiarity having destroyed their meaning for me." [61]

I felt it possible to shed light on this life which we live in darkness and to bring back to its former true character this life which we distort unceasingly—in short, extract the real essence of life in a book. Happy the man who could write such a book, I thought to myself; what a mighty task before him! To convey an idea of it, one would have to go to the noblest and most varied arts for comparisons; for this writer, who, moreover, would have to shew the most contradictory sides of each of his characters in order to give his volume the effect of a solid, would need to prepare it with minute care, constantly regrouping his forces as if for an attack, endure it like an exhausting task, accept it like a rule of conduct, build it like a church, follow it like a regimen, overcome it like an obstacle, win it like a friendship, feed it intensively like a child, create it like a world, without overlooking those mysteries whose explanation is probably to be found only in other worlds and the presentiment of which is the quality in life and art which moves us most deeply. [62]

"The effect of a solid" describes Proust's eagerness to show the oneness of disparate elements. Stylistically, the long sentences, the abundance of imagery, and the block-like paragraphs suggest a solid, as if any break in the typography would be artificial, a reluctant concession to publishers and readers. As for the matter of which the book is composed, the effect of a solid is maintained by the complete relevance of everything it contains. This does not mean that the novel could not be shortened, but the task would require an exceptional editor. Events which first appear insignificant prove to be turning points in the narrative, and the most trivial details eventually take on meaning.

"To shew the most contradictory sides of each of his characters in order to give his volume the effect of a solid"—this passage also reveals a peculiarity of Proust's theory of essences. Essences never come singly. Nothing exists without its opposite; the ego is meaningless without what is outside it. Nineteenth-century fiction proceeded on the assumption that character is more or less stationary, and the novelist was usually content to set down his characters, give them certain arbitrary qualities, place them in opposition to one an-

61. II, 1014.   62. II, 1112.

other, and describe their conflicts. The geometrical pattern in this fictional structure is the curved or straight line. Proust believed that such a method, failing to account for the contradictions and apparent lack of rule in the life about him, was actually unrealistic (even though it might call itself "realism") because it ignored "those mysteries whose explanation is probably to be found only in other worlds and the presentiment of which is the quality in life and art which moves us most deeply." The lines of realism must run parallel to each other until they cross, thus denying—a crossing is but a momentary joining—the alliances revealed by "those mysteries," which because they *are* mysteries cannot be fully understood. But until these mysteries, vaguely perceived in the experience of waking and proved by involuntary memory, can be understood fully, the artist must not commit himself. By showing the two, actually the countless, sides to every fact and situation, by setting in juxtaposition the tragic and the ludicrous, the good and the bad, the artist is able to show the connection between things which, taken singly, appear to be illusions.

This explains perhaps why Marcel is such a puzzling character, a bewildering mixture of the benevolent and the malicious. Is the Marcel who treats his grandmother kindly, tips waiters lavishly, and writes a passage like the one on the death of Bergotte the same Marcel who peeks over the transom at Charlus and Jupien, lies to Albertine, employs after her death a spy to investigate her character, and proves unjust to his friend Saint-Loup? To readers accustomed to the traditional hero, such a mingling of characteristics may seem incomprehensible. Proust would reply that people in life are as contradictory as Marcel and that any fictional character can be convincing only to the extent that he is many sided. Truth varies according to the point of view, and it is the "something beyond" the sum of all possible viewpoints that constitutes the spiritual reality. It would be impossible to reveal in any novel, however long, all these focal points. But it is the novelist's duty to suggest the total through a multiplicity of possibilities.

Thus in *A la Recherche du Temps perdu* nothing is significant only in itself, and its hundreds of pages are among the most economical in literature. The long Swann and Charlus episodes, for example, are complete narratives in themselves, but have the additional function of showing several alternate paths for the man of sensibility. Swann and Charlus must be kept in mind if one is to appreciate the course of Marcel's life. Vinteuil, Elstir, and Bergotte have been discussed here as if they were detachable from the novel in which they appear. Yet even these artists serve functional roles in the development of the narrative in addition to representing the goal to which Marcel aspires. Vinteuil's music becomes a symbol for the love theme, and it is because of him specifically that Marcel discovers the lesbianism of Albertine. He visits Elstir in the hope that the painter will introduce him to the "little band" of young girls at Balbec. Even the death of Bergotte, as we have seen, has narrative significance in that it permits Marcel to discover one of Albertine's lies. A small detail, such as the hawthornes or the number three (the steeples at Martinville, the trees at Balbec, Bergotte's books arranged three by three, and so on) is made to function again and again as a unifying link between past and present. "We have put something of ourselves everywhere," says Marcel, "everything is fertile, everything is dangerous, and we can make discoveries no less precious than Pascal's *Pensées* in an advertisement of soap." [63] What appears to be trivial at first glance gradually expands, collects new elements, and, like Tennyson's flower, emerges as a world in itself.

Essences and their literary representation as images depend upon the particular point of view of the perceiver: "The only way to get any joy out of them," Marcel says in a passage previously quoted, "was to try to know them more completely at the spot where they were to be found, namely, within myself." Therefore the necessary base of the novel, the stage on which the drama is being enacted, is the consciousness of Marcel. Essences exist permanently in a realm which has no relation to time or personality, but they cannot be captured and represented until they are recognized. Once they are captured, they serve as static points of reference in what is otherwise flux, providing the themes by which Marcel can construct the pattern of the novel with architectural precision. In doing so, he creates a better self as well.

Most of the ideas expressed by Proust have been found in some of the writers previously discussed, but it is Proust's distinction to have given them dramatic representation in what is probably the greatest single portrait of the artist in fiction. It deserves this ranking not merely because it is brilliantly unified and saturated with Proustian aura, but also because Proust found his own solution to the problem of the artist's relation to life. If we think of Balzac as primarily a creator of a world and James as an observer of the world around him, Proust may be considered an explorer of the unknown country within the artist. Like James, he demands detachment from a certain kind of life that a more transcendent life may be attained, and though there is less emphasis in James on the timeless essences

63. II, 763.

which link the disparate elements of consciousness, the two novelists share a similar conviction that art is a reflection of life at its most significant. But whereas James's artists seem to have a share in what he called the "fountain source of being," the primary consciousness of things, Proust's ideal artist acknowledges the role of the Sacred Fount but insists that it differs with each artist and thus may be represented only as seen from the Ivory Tower.

CHAPTER SEVEN

JAMES JOYCE:

The Return From Exile

JAMES Joyce's *A Portrait of the Artist as a Young Man* has been imitated so often since it appeared in 1915 that we are likely to think of it as the beginning of a literary movement rather than its climax. But if many a young writer or would-be artist has found a mirror in the *Portrait,* it is because Joyce succeeded in giving definitive treatment to an archetype that was firmly established long before the twentieth century. The first of the many sensitive young men who have followed Stephen Dedalus into exile was Joyce himself, who, like Proust, discovered that "he could become an artist by writing about the process of becoming an artist." [1] The *Portrait* sets down an esthetic of art and a program for the development of *the* artist which Joyce did his best to follow. However, no novelist becomes great merely by following a guidebook, even one that he has written himself, and though Joyce followed Stephen into exile, he found his own way back.

One reason why the *Portrait* still seems revolutionary to the young is that it argues for the necessary alienation of the artist from God, home, and country. "Alienation," an overworked word in modern criticism, is not synonymous with "detachment," for the former implies estrangement from something previously accepted, whereas detachment, as in James, may be an innate quality in temperament. Joyce's insistence that the artist must withdraw from life, using it in

1. Richard Ellmann, *James Joyce* (New York: Oxford University Press, 1959), p. 149.

his art but isolating himself from its interests, has been encountered frequently in the writers already discussed. But just as James and Proust, for instance, disagree with Joyce on the purpose of detachment—James making the artist aloof so that he may observe life more objectively; Proust, that he may penetrate into his own subjectivity—another distinction may be made between Joyce and these two writers. Detachment from life was easier for James and Proust than it was for Joyce. As a small boy James was already aware of his natural aloofness from the normal concerns of the world, and he was fortunate to have a family environment that encouraged freedom and independence. Proust's divided religious background helped him to escape spiritual dogmas, and he was a member of a social class capable of accepting eccentricity. Joyce, on the other hand, came into the world encumbered with religious and domestic obligations. Reared in strict Irish Catholicism, in a large middle-class family devoted to Irish nationalism, he had to shed imposed loyalties so that he might develop in his own way. For Joyce, alienation had to precede detachment.

Although the *Portrait* has been traditionally and, I think, correctly read as a novel which defends the need of the artist to withdraw from the normal commitments of life, this does not mean that Stephen rejects life itself. The artist dies to a certain kind of life that he may be reborn into another. Hence, just as Stephen, poised for exile after having denied the claims of country, religion, family, and friendship, calls out "Welcome, O life," [2] and conceives of his mission as being "to live, to err, to fall, to triumph, to recreate life out of life!," [3] so Joyce at the parallel period of his own life was both detaching himself from life and committing himself to living. "I want to live," he told his brother, "I should be supported at the expense of the state because I am capable of enjoying life." [4] But at about the same time he was writing, "My mind rejects the whole present social order and Christianity—home, the recognised virtues, classes of life, and religious doctrines." [5] This is not simply a matter of his rejecting the life about him for art; rather, the Joyce who wrote the story of Stephen was aware that it is possible to be both the detached, godlike artist and a participating human being. Joyce, an exemplar of the Ivory Tower, also acknowledged the Sacred Fount. Not only is his art based on his experience, but he was also one of the most domestic of writers—"very much a family man, a

2. *A Portrait of the Artist as a Young Man* (New York: Modern Library, 1928), p. 299. Passages from the *Portrait* are reprinted by permission of Viking Press.
3. *Portrait*, p. 200.
4. Ellmann, p. 137.
5. Ellmann, p. 175.

devoted husband, a good father, and a loyal son." [6] Ezra Pound was shocked when he first met Joyce. Expecting to see the "artist" of the *Portrait,* he met a scholarly appearing, domestic-minded man whose Paris flat was furnished in a conventional, middle-class way.[7] Apparently, then, Joyce, like many of the writers already discussed in these pages, had resolved the conflict between art and life by recognizing the divided nature of the artist. But before we can see how Joyce presented this solution in the symbolic substructure of his work, it is necessary to investigate one of the crucial issues of Joyce criticism—the relationship between Joyce and Stephen Dedalus.[8]

The case against Stephen Dedalus has been made most emphatically by Wyndham Lewis:

> He is the really wooden figure. He is "the poet" to an uncomfortable, a dismal, a ridiculous, even a pulverizing degree. His movements in the Martello-tower, his theatrical "bitterness," his cheerless, priggish stateliness, his gazings into the blue distance, his Irish Accent, his exquisite sensitiveness, his "pride" that is so crude as to be almost indecent, the incredible slowness with which he gets about from place to place, up the stairs, down the stairs, like a funereal stage-king; the time required for him to move his neck, how he raises his hand, passes it over his aching eyes, or his damp brow, even more wearily drops it, closes his dismal little shutters against his rollicking Irish-type of a friend (in his capacity of a type-poet), and remains sententiously secluded, shut up in his own personal Martello-tower—a Martello-tower within a Martello-tower—until he consents to issue out, tempted by the opportunity of making a "bitter"—a very "bitter" jest, to show up against the really idiotic background provided by Haines; all this has to be read to be believed.[9]

If charges like this were made only by frankly anti-Joycean critics like Wyndham Lewis, it would be unnecessary to reply to them. But

6. Lucie Noel, *James Joyce and Paul L. Léon: The Story of a Friendship* (New York: Gotham Book Mart, 1950), p. 12. See also Silvio Benco, "James Joyce in Trieste," *Bookman,* LXXII (December, 1930), 376; and Mary Colum, *Life and the Dream* (Garden City, New York: Doubleday, 1947), p. 397.

7. Herbert Gorman, *James Joyce* (New York: Rinehart, 1948), pp. 272–273.

8. See my "Joyce and Stephen Dedalus: The Problem of Autobiography," in Marvin Magalaner, ed., *A James Joyce Miscellany: Second Series* (Carbondale, Illinois: Southern Illinois University Press, 1959), pp. 67–77. Portions of the discussion that follows are from this more extended study.

9. *Time and Western Man* (New York: Harcourt, Brace and Co., 1928), p. 97.

such attacks on the character of Stephen, who, admittedly, is a hero difficult to like, have led some pro-Joycean critics to a misdirected defense of the author by dissociating him from his hero. His first novel, these critics suggest, is not so much a portrait as a parody of the artist as a young man. William York Tindall, for example, writes: "Those who find a sentimental attachment in *A Portrait of the Artist* have failed to notice the tone. To his friend Frank Budgen, Joyce once said, 'I haven't let this young man off very lightly, have I?' A careful reading makes it apparent that Joyce is aloof and generally ironic in his treatment of Stephen. But Joyce's attitude is never explicit. Stephen is allowed to expose himself. Joyce limits his assistance to arranging contrasts and juxtapositions and to using a style which, following the contours of the hero's passion, becomes that passion while parodying it." [10] Hugh Kenner finds it difficult to reconcile "an indigestibly Byronic hero" with respect for Joyce's artistic achievement:

> [Stephen] does not, as is frequently supposed, become an artist by rejecting church and country. Stephen does not become an artist at all. Country, church and mission are an inextricable unity, and in rejecting the two that seem to hamper him he rejects also the one on which he has set his heart. . . . Stephen becomes, not an artist, but an esthete: he has rejected the humility before being proper to artists [*sic*]. . . . It is high time, in short, to point out once and for all that Stephen's flight into adolescent "freedom" is not meant to be the "message" of the book. (Joyce observed to Frank Budgen that people often forgot the last four words of his title, A Portrait of the Artist AS A YOUNG MAN.) *Ulysses* securely places Stephen as an esthete, not an artist, as Wyndham Lewis saw; his mistake was to suppose that Joyce did not see it too.[11]

It is only in recent years, with the publication of Joyce's letters and critical writings, and other primary source materials, including the memoirs of his brother Stanislaus and Richard Ellmann's thorough and careful biography, that it has become possible to compare the fiction with the reality and to decide, with partial assurance at least, the extent to which Stephen is modelled upon the young Joyce. Because of this new evidence, views of Stephen such as those expressed by Tindall and Kenner no longer seem tenable, for the

10. *James Joyce: His Way of Interpreting the Modern World* (New York: Scribners, 1950), p. 17.
11. "The Portrait in Perspective," in Seon Givens, ed., *James Joyce: Two Decades of Criticism* (New York: Vanguard Press, 1948), pp. 150–153.

autobiographical basis of the *Portrait* must now be conceded. But if in many respects Stephen now seems to be even more of a self-portrait than had been assumed, we must concede also that in other ways he is quite different from Joyce. Because we find in the *Portrait* both sympathy for the artist-hero and a certain amount of ironic detachment, it is no longer possible to argue that Stephen is Joyce or he is not; rather, we must compromise by seeing that Stephen is both Joyce and not Joyce. There are several ways of compromising.

Stanislaus Joyce says that his brother drew "very largely upon his own life and his own experience. . . . But *A Portrait of the Artist* is not an autobiography; it is an artistic creation." [12] This explanation seems only to avoid the issue, for if we put "autobiography" on one side, "artistic creation" on the other, where do we put such works as the *Confessions* of Rousseau or *The Education of Henry Adams?* Just as an autobiography may be a work of art, a work of art may also be an autobiography. And because even an autobiography must alter and rearrange events to some extent, it is easy to see why many of the divergences between reality and fiction derive simply from Joyce's need to economize, to transform the multitude of chaotic impressions which made up Joyce's experience into a compact, unified novel. This process has been apparent since the publication of *Stephen Hero*, which allows us to isolate a midway stage between Joyce's experience and the finished work of art. The most important example of how Joyce altered reality, and why, is to be found in the almost entire omission from the *Portrait* of Stephen's brother Maurice, who has an important part in the earlier version. Playing down the role of Maurice helps to emphasize the proud independence of Stephen and to place greater stress on his quest for vocation. But now that the memoirs of Stanislaus Joyce, the real Maurice, have been published, we can see an additional reason. It turns out that Stanislaus was even more estranged from his family, his country, and church than was his brother. It was Stanislaus, not James, who refused to make his Easter duty. If Joyce had wanted only to strengthen the impression of Stephen's uniqueness and his staunch withstanding of opposition, he could have given him a brother who opposed his views, as Shaun opposes Shem in *Finnegans Wake*. Joyce, in the *Portrait* still generally faithful to his experience, though less so than in *Stephen Hero*, could not go that far. Rather than oppose Stephen with a strong spokesman or weaken his triumph by providing moral support within his family, Joyce combined key aspects of his brother's character with his own and gave Stephen the

12. *My Brother's Keeper: James Joyce's Early Years* (New York: Viking Press, 1958), p. 17.

strength of both young Joyces. In this way the need for artistic economy results in a distortion of reality in Stephen's favor.

The second alternative to deciding whether Joyce champions or repudiates Stephen is to fall back on the convenient critical doctrine of the irony of noncommittal. In his later works, certainly, Joyce is free of opinions and judgments, and it may well be that in the *Portrait*, too, he attempted to avoid either favoring Stephen or making him the object of ridicule. Whether deliberate or not, much of the author's seeming aloofness from his subject is the inevitable detachment of time. The Joyce writing is a different person from the Joyce depicted. If Stephen's life parallels Joyce's, the story ends in 1902. Joyce did not finish writing the novel until 1915. The mixture of irony and sympathy may be explained as the half-apologetic, half-proud attitude of an older man looking back on the foibles of his youth. This, I take it, is the sense of Joyce's frequently quoted remarks to Frank Budgen—his assertion that people too often forget the words "as a young man" in his title, and his statement, "I haven't let this young man off very lightly, have I?" In neither statement does Joyce disown the autobiographical relation nor imply an attack upon the character of Stephen. The words "as a young man" do not eradicate the word "artist." And Joyce immediately followed his first remark with two sentences that are never quoted by Stephen detractors: "Many writers have written about themselves. I wonder if any of them has been as candid as I have?" [13] All that Joyce probably meant by saying that he had not let Stephen off lightly was that he had tried to draw an uncompromisingly truthful portrait of his earlier self. The objectivity of the picture demonstrates Joyce's artistic ideal of the author's detachment from his subject, even when that subject is the author's self.

In striving for a balance between self-exaltation and self-disparagement, Joyce tended to strengthen the artistic nature of Stephen and weaken his human nature. Thus Stephen is given many artistic beliefs and convictions which Joyce himself did not attain until after 1902. For example, when Joyce gave his paper on "Drama and Life" in 1900 he replied to his critics at length and with considerable spirit. In *Stephen Hero*, after Stephen's reading of his paper and the attack upon it, he maintains a dignified silence in keeping with Joyce's later theory that the artist ought to be indifferent to his critics. As for the talk itself, the "Drama and Life" essay has an exhortatory, life-exalting message that makes it seem dated and juvenile beside the cool exposition in the *Portrait* when Stephen expounds

13. Frank Budgen, *James Joyce and*   Grayson, 1934), p. 52.
the Making of Ulysses (London:

on the three stages of art, from lyrical to epical to dramatic.[14] But though Joyce gave Stephen a more invulnerable esthetic than he himself possessed at the equivalent period of his life, he balanced this by making Stephen a more disagreeable person than Joyce appears to have been. According to Stanislaus, Joyce was fairly athletic, a good swimmer, and so goodnatured as a child that he earned the nickname "Sunny Jim." Stephen, of course, shuns the playing field, is frightened of the water, and is definitely not sunny of temperament. Joyce, it is clear, was a better rounded person than his fictional surrogate. It is the lack of roundness which makes many readers dislike Stephen. If Joyce had given him more of his own features— had, that is, been even more truthful—Stephen would not have seemed the poet to so dismal and pulverizing a degree as he struck Wyndham Lewis and the other Stephen haters.

The whole point, though, is that Stephen is *the poet* or, as Joyce's carefully worded title tells us, *the artist*. One of Joyce's first critics, Valery Larbaud, said that the *Portrait* should be read as "l'histoire de la jeunesse de l'artiste en général, c'est-à-dire de tout homme doué du tempérament artiste." [15] One way in which Joyce sought to detach himself from his hero was to depict not James Joyce, but the universal, representative, archetypal artist, the ideal which Joyce could achieve only partially in reality. Thus he had to omit certain features of his personality that seemed to him out of keeping with the conventional idea of the artist. In terms of the stereotype available to Joyce, a well-rounded, athletic poet would have seemed an anomaly, and everyone knows that poets are supposed to be gloomy rather than sunny. The Stephen haters may recognize that he is the stereotyped artist, but they err in assuming that he therefore cannot be a true artist. The cumulative weight of the stereotype, the frequency with which it appears in other portraits of the artist, may, on the contrary, actually convince us that whether we like the type or not, it may well characterize the essential, universal qualities of the artistic temperament. Byron, Baudelaire, Rimbaud, Baron Corvo, and many other artists of distinction had unbalanced and disagreeable personalities; and to dislike Stephen because of his lack of human roundness does not justify the opinion that he cannot therefore be an artist. Proust's Marcel is a sickly, effeminate, posturing creature whom few of us would care to know personally, but that he is also an artist is proved by the novel in which he appears.

14. See *The Critical Writings of James Joyce*, ed. Ellsworth Mason and Richard Ellmann (New York: Viking Press, 1959), pp. 38–46.

15. "James Joyce," *La Nouvelle Revue Française*, XVIII (April, 1922), 395.

Joyce is known to have been acquainted with many works in the artist-hero tradition. The *Kunstlerdrama* form was especially influential during his college years, and works like Ibsen's *When We Dead Awaken,* Hauptmann's *Michael Kramer,* and Sudermann's *Magda* (of which Joyce said to his family, "The subject of the play is genius breaking out in the home and against the home. You needn't have gone to see it. It's going to happen in your own house"),[16] all with the common theme of the artist versus society, helped to establish in Joyce's mind the conviction that the artist is inevitably in conflict with his environment. There was Giordano Bruno, proud and eccentric rebel, who helped Joyce form his scorn of the "rabblement" and may even have suggested the name "Daedalus." [17] There were Byron, Blake, and the other early Romantics; Pater and Wilde; the French writers Flaubert, Baudelaire, Rimbaud, Mallarmé, and Huysmans; the Irish poet James Clarence Mangan, on whom Joyce wrote two essays (in 1902 and 1907), which may be considered his first creative portrait of the artist-type; Goethe's *Wilhelm Meister,* which not only founded the tradition of the portrait-of-the-artist novel but established the convention of *Hamlet* criticism which Joyce, in *Ulysses,* was not the first writer to continue; the artist stories of Yeats; Butler's *The Way of All Flesh* and Meredith's *The Ordeal of Richard Feverel,* with their direct appeal for revolt against the fathers; the cool detachment of a Henry James, whose *Portrait of a Lady,* Stanislaus tells us, suggested the title of Joyce's novel.[18] From sources such as these Joyce could readily have learned the traditional features of the artist archetype—sensitivity, passivity, egotism, introversion, the faculty of absorption in a single activity, a sense of divine vocation, aloofness from society, and the ability as artist to stand detached even from self. Stephen has all of these traits.

It would seem therefore that in depicting Stephen, Joyce drew not only on his own character and experience, modified by the artistic need for selection and economy, but also on the artist-heroes of life and fiction. From these sources he developed the image of an archetypal artist, gave it the symbolic name of "Dedalus," and carefully removed any traits of his own character that conflicted with the stereotype. In developing his composite artist, Joyce, who had long been seeking a pose, provided for himself a personal model, a Mallarméan mask, which he seems to have put on once he knew what it looked like. Commenting on how Joyce "adjusted his life to art's

16. Stanislaus Joyce, *My Brother's Keeper,* p. 87.
17. See my "James Joyce and Giordano Bruno: A Possible Source for 'Dedalus,'" *James Joyce Review,* I (Dec. 15, 1957), 41–44.
18. *My Brother's Keeper,* p. 242.

exigencies," Richard Ellmann says, "The fact that he was turning his life to fiction at the same time that he was living it encouraged him to feel a certain detachment from what happened to him, for he knew he could reconsider and re-order it for the purpose of his book. At the same time, since he felt dependent for material upon actual events, he had an interest in bringing simmering pots to a strong boil, in making the events through which he lived take on as extreme a form as possible." [19]

Yet the most extreme and dramatic event in Joyce's life—his falling in love with Nora Barnacle in June 1904 and his eloping with her to the continent—is not depicted directly in Joyce's fiction. The *Portrait* ends with Stephen preparing to leave Ireland for Paris, as Joyce did late in 1902. "Bloomsday," June 16, 1904, finds Stephen back in Dublin, somewhat chastened, but on the eve of what in Joyce's life was the most crucial event of all. Now that we know that the date of *Ulysses* is the day Joyce fell in love,[20] we can say with certainty that Joyce deliberately dropped Stephen while he was still only *the artist*. But though Joyce's solution to the conflict between art and life was presumably one that he felt was too intimately personal to be depicted directly at the narrative level, he nonetheless both disguised his secret and revealed it in the symbolic substructure of the *Portrait* and *Ulysses*. These novels, we must remember, were written *a posteriori*, and Joyce knew, even if Stephen did not, how his hero was to return from exile without losing his artistic integrity.

In the *Portrait*, however, the emphasis properly falls on the route *to* exile. Theodore Spencer finds in *Stephen Hero* and the *Portrait* five themes subordinate to Stephen himself: his family; his friends, male and female; the life of Dublin; Catholicism; and art. The structure of the novel, which is identical with the development of Stephen, "may be described," says Spencer, "as a process which sloughs off the first four in order that the fifth may stand clear." [21] Granted the circumstances, Stephen has but one way to go. With a temperament which combines emotional sensitivity with intellectual rigidity, Stephen is the type who never enters into anything halfway. Proudly demanding more from life than it has to offer, he is a representative "totality-type" artist, subject to fanatic conversions and bitter revulsions. He is impelled to be an artist when all else fails, and only art is capable of retaining his enthusiasm. Until

19. *James Joyce*, p. 154.
20. *James Joyce*, p. 162.
21. "Introduction," *Stephen Hero: A Part of the First Draft of "A Por-* *trait of the Artist as a Young Man,"* ed. Theodore Spencer (Norfolk, Connecticut: New Directions, 1944), p. 13.

his consecration as artist, his development proceeds in a negative fashion as he discards one by one the loyalties which have been imposed upon him.

A Portrait of the Atrist is written in the indirect first person. Everything is seen through the eyes of Stephen, but he does not narrate his autobiography nor describe his perceptions. Joyce's method is similar to James's center of consciousness, and Stephen's character, like that of James's sensitive observers, can be determined only by noting his subjective reactions to the world about him. A typical passage is the following:

> The wide playgrounds were swarming with boys. All were shouting and the prefects urged them on with strong cries. The evening air was pale and chilly and after every charge and thud of the footballers the greasy leather orb flew like a heavy bird through the grey light. He kept on the fringe of his line, out of sight of his prefect, out of the reach of the rude feet, feigning to run now and then. He felt his body small and weak amid the throng of players and his eyes were weak and watery. Rody Kickham was not like that: he would be captain of the third line all the fellows said.[22]

It is difficult to separate the third person from the indirect first person. At first reading, the passage seems to progress evenly from the third person, "the wide playgrounds were swarming with boys," to the statement of emotion, "he felt," to complete immersion in Stephen's consciousness, "Rody Kickham was not like that." But is it to Stephen or Joyce that the football seems to fly "like a heavy bird through the grey light" and the player's feet seem "rude"? The mingling of auctorial description with character response allows Joyce to suggest precocious powers of observation and verbalization in his young hero. It is a method well adapted to the depiction of a child whose most characteristic feature is extreme sensitivity.

"He felt his body small and weak"—here is not only the traditional sensitive young boy unhappy and awkward among his athletic schoolmates, but also a boy capable of recognizing his uniqueness. Self-awareness must precede self-realization, and Stephen's ability to place himself in a setting, to realize his differences from the world in which he is merged (this feeling boy against the "swarming" playgrounds and the "throng"), encourages him eventually to define himself by learning the personal significance of his name.[23] In an effort

22. *Portrait*, p. 3.
23. Stephen's quest for a name is discussed by William R. Mueller in

The Prophetic Voice in Modern Fiction (New York: Association Press, 1959), pp. 27–55.

to identify himself, Stephen writes on the flyleaf of his geography his complete address, beginning with his name and ending with "the universe." Looking at his inscription, Stephen wonders, "What was the universe? Nothing. But was there anything round the universe to show where it stopped before the nothing place began? It could not be a wall but there could be a thin thin line there all round everything. It was very big to think everything and everywhere. Only God could do that." From God—"it made him feel his head very big"—he turns again to the textbook, looking at the "green round earth in the middle of the maroon clouds," and the association of colors makes him think of Parnell and Irish politics. "It pained him that he did not know what politics meant and that he did not know where the universe ended," Joyce says, then, once again, "He felt small and weak." [24] The method is not unlike that which Dickens used in fusing childhood impressions through the reminiscence of the mature David Copperfield.

Stephen's sensitivity includes not only the desire to understand things which most people take for granted, but also a continual awareness of sights, sounds, and smells. The emphasis on sensual images in the early pages of the *Portrait* is not without purpose. These images allow the reader to recognize in Stephen a basic conflict between feeling and knowing. The extravertive child asks a thousand questions because he wants to know how things work; the introspective child like Stephen wants to know things because he feels them. As the *Portrait* develops, these sensual images become less frequent as Stephen moves closer to the detachment which results from emotionless understanding.

Stephen's loneliness and self-awareness have been forced upon him at an earlier age than is usual among children. At Clongowes Wood College, away from home for the first time, he is painfully conscious of his inability to compete with his fellows on their own terms—terms of physical ability and worldly knowledge. This sense of displacement makes him yearn for the warm, protective atmosphere of the home he has left: "All the boys seemed to him very strange. They had all fathers and mothers and different clothes and voices. He longed to be at home and lay his head on his mother's lap. But he could not. . . . He thought that he was sick in his heart if you could be sick in that place." [25] So intense does his homesickness become that the mere approach of Christmas vacation brings on a state resembling physical illness. He is sent to the infirmary, where another boy asks him riddles he cannot answer be-

24. *Portrait*, pp. 12–13.   25. *Portrait*, pp. 8–9.

cause they are like the questions other boys ask—how-is-it? questions
—and where he thinks it "queer that they had not given him any
medicine." Going home for Christmas, everyone thinks, will be the
only medicine he needs.

The Christmas dinner scene must be placed in this context. Composed with meticulous skill, it reveals subtly a main theme in the
pre-revolt sections of the novel: the victimization of Stephen, his
betrayal by his elders. It is through this experience that Stephen discovers what Hermann Hesse has called "the first cleft in the sacred-
ness of parenthood . . . the first split in the pillar . . . which
everyone must overthrow, before he can attain to self-realization." [26]
The scene opens with the appropriate images of warmth and ex-
pectancy: the fire in the grate, the ivy-twined chandelier, the big
dishes covered with heavy metal covers, Mr. Dedalus parting his
coattails before the fire and pouring a drink for his friend Mr. Casey.
This is the first Christmas that Stephen has been allowed to stay
"downstairs," and he expects much from it. The theme of deception
is early suggested:

> Mr Casey leaned his head to one side and, smiling, tapped the
> gland of his neck with his fingers. And Stephen smiled too for
> he knew now that it was not true that Mr Casey had a purse
> of silver in his throat. He smiled to think how the silvery noise
> which Mr Casey used to make had deceived him. And when he
> had tried to open Mr Casey's hand to see if the purse of silver
> was hidden there he had seen that the fingers could not be
> straightened out: and Mr Casey had told him that he had got
> those three cramped fingers making a birthday present for Queen
> Victoria.[27]

Stephen has begun to question what his elders tell him and to perceive the difference between real truth and that which grownups
reserve for children. Mr. Dedalus and Mr. Casey laugh together over
a story of a bartender friend who has succeeded in watering some
champagne and thereby gained a dishonest profit.

> Mr Casey was still struggling through his fit of coughing and
> laughter. Stephen, seeing and hearing the hotel keeper through
> his father's face and voice, laughed.
> Mr Dedalus put up his eyeglass and, staring down at him, said
> quietly and kindly:
> —What are you laughing at, you little puppy, you? [28]

26. *Demian: The Story of a Youth*   27. *Portrait*, pp. 26–27.
  (New York: Holt, 1948), p. 20.   28. *Portrait*, p. 28.

Their admiration of the bartender's cunning and dishonesty is thus suddenly juxtaposed against the innocent presumption of the youngster, who is not supposed to know about such things. Stephen, who wants to know everything, can expect little help from his elders, who persist in protecting him through lies. At the dinner table Mrs. Riordan quotes from the Bible:

—Woe be to the man by whom the scandal cometh! . . . *It would be better for him that a millstone were tied about his neck and that he were cast into the depths of the sea rather than that he should scandalise one of these, my least little ones.* That is the language of the Bible.

—And very bad language if you ask me, said Mr Dedalus coolly.

—Simon! Simon! said Uncle Charles. The boy.

—Yes, yes, said Mr Dedalus. I meant about the . . . I was thinking about the bad language of that railway porter. Well now, that's all right. Here, Stephen, show me your plate, old chap. Eat away now. Here.[29]

This attempt by the father to cover up his lack of caution fails with the adults as with Stephen. After a few moments of silence, Mr. Dedalus explodes bitterly, "Well, my Christmas dinner has been spoiled anyhow." This is the end of the pretense, the cue for the others to renew their argument over Parnell and the Church. When Stephen's father calls a certain priest "tub of guts,"

—Really, Simon, you should not speak that way before Stephen. It's not right.

—O, he'll remember all this when he grows up, said Dante hotly —the language he heard against God and religion and priests in his own home.

—Let him remember too, cried Mr Casey to her from across the table, the language with which the priests and the priests' pawns broke Parnell's heart and hounded him into his grave. Let him remember that when he grows up.

—Sons of bitches! cried Mr Dedalus. When he was down they turned on him to betray him and rend him like rats in a sewer. Lowlived dogs! And they look it! By Christ, they look it![30]

Thus the argument continues, reaching finally the dramatic moment when Mr. Casey stands up to proclaim "No God for Ireland!" and Mrs. Riordan runs out of the room shouting "Devil out of hell! We

29. *Portrait*, p. 32.   30. *Portrait*, p. 34.

won! We crushed him to death! Fiend!" and Stephen, "raising his terrorstricken face, saw that his father's eyes were full of tears." [31]

With this betrayal, Stephen is thrown upon his own resources. The home for which he yearned no longer exists. He is "terrorstricken" because he has clearly seen, if not understood, the truth from which he has been protected. Adults have two worlds, each with its own "truth": on the one hand, the ideal, convenient-for-children world of Christmas, prayers, and God; on the other, the real world of dishonest bartenders, screaming curses, and politics. Mr. Dedalus can move easily from one to the other, while Mr. Casey is a more tragic figure because he has had to choose between them. As for Mrs. Riordan, the fanatic egotism of her final outburst reveals her failure to stay immersed in spirituality. Stephen is left without props, the victim of his elders' hypocrisy.

Against the unjust world of the adults and their alliance against sensitivity, Stephen begins to yearn for an ideal that will compensate for his aloneness. At first it takes a natural form in Eileen, a Protestant girl who is "forbidden" him:

> Eileen had long thin cool white hands too because she was a girl. They were like ivory; only soft. That was the meaning of *Tower of Ivory* but protestants could not understand it and made fun of it. One day he had stood beside her looking into the hotel grounds. A waiter was running up a trail of bunting on a flagstaff and a fox terrier was scampering to and fro on the sunny lawn. She had put her hand into his pocket where his hand was and he had felt how cool and thin and soft her hand was. She had said that pockets were funny things to have; and then all of a sudden she had broken away and had run laughing down the sloping curve of the path. Her fair hair had streamed out behind her like gold in the sun. *Tower of Ivory. House of Gold.* By thinking of things you could understand them.[32]

Whereas Stephen at this point in his childhood seems vaguely aware of the religious associations of "Tower of Ivory," he characteristically confuses it with sensuality. The artistic meaning of "Ivory Tower" is one he could not be expected to know at this time, but just as he comes eventually to know the sacramental meaning of "Daedalus," the religious and sensuous associations of "Tower of Ivory" will give way before the artistic.

The ideal next takes the form of Mercedes, the inspiration for which is not actuality, as in the case of Eileen, but a work of liter-

31. *Portrait,* p. 41.   32. *Portrait* p. 45.

ature. A lonely isolation causes Stephen, like so many artists-to-be, to retreat to the dream world of literature. During this period, the book which most fascinates him is *The Count of Monte Cristo* with its "figure of the dark avenger." He makes a model of the island cave, and "when he had broken up this scenery, weary of its tinsel, there would come to his mind the bright picture of Marseilles, of sunny trellises and of Mercedes."

> He returned to Mercedes and, as he brooded upon her image, a strange unrest crept into his blood. Sometimes a fever gathered within him and led him to rove alone in the evening along the quiet avenue. The peace of the gardens and the kindly light in the windows poured a tender influence into his restless heart. The noise of children at play annoyed him and their voices made him feel, even more keenly than he had felt at Clongowes, that he was different from others. He did not want to play. He wanted to meet in the real world the unsubstantial image which his soul so constantly beheld. He did not know where to seek it or how, but a premonition which led him on told him that this image would, without any overt act of his, encounter him. They would meet quietly as if they had known each other and had made their tryst, perhaps at one of the gates or in some more secret place. They would be alone, surrounded by darkness and silence: and in that moment of supreme tenderness he would be transfigured. He would fade into something impalpable under her eyes and then in a moment, he would be transfigured. Weakness and timidity and inexperience would fall from him in that magic moment.[33]

The idea that the image will appear to him without any "overt act of his" suggests Stephen's passive nature. Waiting patiently for whatever Mercedes will show him the way, he becomes accustomed to his distinction and begins to "taste the joy of his loneliness." He has already set aside the claims of family and country; as yet, however, he does not know whether "the great part which he felt awaited him the nature of which he only dimly apprehended"[34] is to come in the form of love, religion, or art.

"Before the savage desire within him to realise the enormities which he brooded on nothing was sacred."[35] Stephen is not the first artist to attempt self-discovery through sinning, but it is a precocious sexuality that in early adolescence drives him to prostitutes. Joyce's style is lushly romantic as he describes Stephen's sexual initiation, but the mingling of the coarse details—"Good night,

33. *Portrait*, pp. 70–71.   35. *Portrait*, p. 111.
34. *Portrait*, p. 68.

Willie dear," the huge doll in the armchair, the "tinkling hand," the perfume—with the heavy prose creates a repulsion which Joyce undoubtedly intended as preparation for Stephen's own remorse and guilt: "Only the morning pained him with its dim memory of dark orgiastic riot, its keen and humiliating sense of transgression." [36]

Granting Stephen's intense nature, his loneliness, and the remorse induced by his sexual experiments, his religious conversion is inevitable. The histrionic abilities of the priest who conducts the retreat, the vision of an omnipotent God and an eternal punishment, and his deep sense of divine mission produce in Stephen a conversion as fanatic as it is brief. Most readers find the sermon tedious, but its presence is justified in that it balances Stephen's exposition of his personal religion of art. The sermon is thoroughly conventional and derivative in content, and it uses the time-honored persuasive devices: rhetorical questions, a cataloging of horrors, extreme contrasts, and skillful use of the second person. All these devices are aimed to frighten young boys into piety, and with Stephen they succeed. The contrast which the priest draws between time and eternity is especially vivid to the imaginative boy. Even before the retreat, Stephen wanted to turn away from the temporal world of sordidness and sin; now he sees in the Church the path to an infinite universe and an eternal heaven.

So intense are Stephen's revulsion and conversion that he becomes physically ill and experiences a mystical vision of hell. Crying for help and frantic lest he die before he can confess, he leaves his room, and even now too proud to offer his confession at school, hurries along the sordid streets until he find an obscure church. There he makes a pained and difficult confession to a weary old priest, who can only advise: "As long as you commit that sin, my poor child, you will never be worth one farthing to God." [37] Nonetheless, as Stephen returns home, he feels that "the muddy streets were gay" and that "the world lay all before him." [38] After this, Stephen divides his day into devotional areas, carries his beads in his pocket that he may say his rosary as he walks the streets, obeys all the rituals of the Church, attempts to mortify his physical senses, and sees continually before him "the one omnipresent perfect reality." [39]

At one time it seemed to Stephen that "from the evil seed of lust all other deadly sins had sprung forth: pride in himself and contempt of others." [40] He is surprised after his conversion to discover that

36. *Portrait*, p. 111.
37. *Portrait*, p. 167.
38. *Portrait*, p. 168.

39. *Portrait*, p. 173.
40. *Portrait*, p. 120.

though "he had no temptations to sin morally," he is subject to scarcely suppressed outbursts of anger "at hearing his mother sneeze or at being disturbed in his devotions." [41] Actually, the pride precedes the lust, and it is pride which lies behind his conversion. When the director of the school suggests that he consider entering the priesthood, Stephen visualizes himself as the Reverend Stephen Dedalus, S. J. And when the director tells him, "No king or emperor on this earth has the power of the priest of God," Stephen hears "in this proud address an echo of his own proud musings. How often had he seen himself as a priest wielding calmly and humbly the awful power of which angels and saints stood in reverence! . . . He would know obscure things, hidden from others, from those who were conceived and born children of wrath. He would know the sins, the sinful longings and sinful thoughts and sinful acts, of others, hearing them murmured in his ears in the confessional under the shame of a darkened chapel by the lips of women and of girls." [42] But if it is pride which makes him yearn to know "obscure things," it is also pride which turns him away from the idea of the priesthood. A sudden recollection of the "raw reddish glow he had so often seen on wintry mornings on the shaven gills of the priests" makes him realize that "he would never swing the thurible before the tabernacle as priest. His destiny was to be elusive of social or religious orders. The wisdom of the priest's appeal did not touch him to the quick. He was destined to learn his own wisdom apart from others or to learn the wisdom of others himself wandering among the snares of the world." [43]

Just as reaction from sensual excesses led Stephen to religion, the excessive religiosity of his conversion leads directly to his consecration as artist. The conversion has been a temporary halt on his path to his vocation, but it has helped him in several ways: it has drawn him away from the other distractions of life, brought him knowledge of his capacity for asceticism, and increased his sense of divinely led vocation. It is no coincidence therefore that Stephen's long-awaited moment of self-discovery and consecration to art occurs almost immediately after his interview with the director. That evening, as he walks alone, he undergoes a series of mystic experiences which enable him to understand the significance of his name and, in the figure of the young girl standing in midstream, to meet at last in the real world that "unsubstantial image" which he has long sought: "Her image had passed into his soul for ever and no word had broken the holy silence of his ecstasy. Her eyes had called

41. *Portrait*, p. 175.   43. *Portrait*, p. 188.
42. *Portrait*, pp. 183–185.

him and his soul had leaped at the call. To live, to err, to fall, to trumph, to recreate life out of life!" [44]

After this moment of transformation Stephen sees in art the means by which he may be reconciled to his aloneness and his pride. His mission *is to recreate life out of life*—how much more godlike this seems than the mere powers of the priesthood. Knowing this, Stephen need not retreat from intercourse with his fellows since, even in participation, he can be detached. He can observe the life of the Dublin streets, forge an esthetic theory which justifies the artist's detachment, drink beer in pubs, and even ask the respectable Emma Cleary to sleep with him. Nothing, he thinks, will make him indignant or bitter because he bears always with him the idea that if he is to create art, he must use life with the dispassionateness of a god. Once he has accepted his mission, everything else pales into insignificance except to the extent that it is raw material for his craft. The physical exile from Ireland, family, and friends begins at the end of the novel when, after the deliberate breaking of the last worldly bond, his friendship with Cranly, Stephen realizes that to express himself in "unfettered freedom" he had best "go away." [45] He is not fleeing to an Ivory Tower, however, for he goes to encounter "the reality of experience." [46]

In spite of the emphasis on alienation in the *Portrait*, the ambivalence of Stephen's dedication to art *and* life anticipates Joyce's personal, post-Stephen solution to the conflict between the Ivory Tower and the Sacred Fount. The answer is revealed most effectively in *Ulysses,* as we may see by examining a group of related images which symbolize the artist's relationship to life—the images of moon and water, of drowning and rising from an earthy or watery grave, of birds and flight.[47]

The theme of the Sacred Fount, we have found, is best dramatized in terms of the artist's relationship to woman. Joyce too equates woman with the life principle. Stephen finds that estrangement from life is most difficult when it means alienation from his mother, and Joyce often personified the life principle in feminine guise, just as "life" appeared before him in its most tempting—and for the exile most dangerous—form when he met Nora Barnacle. The artist's relationship to life is dramatized in "A Painful Case" in terms of the relationship between Mr. Duffy and Mrs. Sinico; in "The Dead" in terms of Gabriel and Gretta Conroy; in the *Portrait* with, on the

44. *Portrait*, p. 200.
45. *Portrait*, pp. 289–290.
46. *Portrait*, p. 299.
47. Much of the discussion that fol- lows appears, in somewhat different form, in my "James Joyce: Barnacle Goose and Lapwing," *PMLA, LXXI* (June, 1956), pp. 302–320.

the one hand, Stephen and his mother, and on the other, Stephen
and the Girl-Muse of the *Portrait* and Molly Bloom of *Ulysses;* in
Exiles as Richard Rowan and his common-law wife Bertha; and in
Finnegans Wake as Shem the Penman and Anna Livia Plurabelle,
of whom Molly Bloom is the symbolic precursor.

In Joyce's iconography, Woman, Moon, Water, and Life are
closely associated: the Moon is the peculiar image of Woman, who
is also identified with Water, which is the stream of Life. These
images are sanctioned by literary and mythic tradition, and the
abundance of allusions, especially in *Ulysses,* proves that Joyce was
aware of the frequency with which they appear in earlier literature.
By using these symbols, he could stimulate a tradition-based response in his readers and thus, while remaining inexplicit, convey
the meaning which he intended. Images of moon and water are
especially well adapted to this purpose because their appeal depends
as much on the subconscious as on a knowledge of the literary
tradition. For example, Joyce introduces the thematic symbol of
water-woman-drowning at the beginning of *Ulysses* when Buck
Mulligan says, "Isn't the sea what Algy calls it: a grey sweet mother?
The snot-green sea." [48] Like most of Joyce's allusions, this one takes
on richer meaning if the reader can supply the original lines. In
"The Triumph of Time," Swinburne writes:

> I will go back to *the great sweet mother,*
>   Mother and lover of men, the sea. . . .

> O fair *green*-girdled mother of mine,
>   Sea, that art clothed with the sun and the rain,
> Thy sweet hard kisses are strong like wine,
>   Thy large embraces are keen like pain.
> Save me and hide me with all thy waves,
> Find me *one grave of thy thousand graves.*
> Those pure cold populous graves of thine
>   Wrought without hand in a world without stain.[49]

Although not all readers could be expected to identify the source
of Buck Mulligan's distorted allusion, it would be an unusual reader
who was not familiar with the sea-as-mother concept. Even such a
reader may feel the appropriateness of the association, if the discoveries and conjectures of certain scientists may be taken seriously.

48. *Ulysses* (New York: Modern Library, 1934), p. 7. Passages from
Ulysses are reprinted by permission
of Random House.

49. *Complete Works,* ed. Edmund
Gosse and Thomas James Wise
(London, 1925), I, 177. (My
italics.)

The first part of Rachel Carson's *The Sea Around Us* is entitled "Mother Sea." According to Miss Carson, the ocean is the source of organic life, and the powerful appeal of the sea may be attributed to man's interest in "a world long lost, but a world that, in the deepest part of his sub-conscious, he has never wholly forgotten." Each living creature not only carries in its veins a salty stream chemically similar to sea water and has a bone structure which is a heritage from the calcium-rich ocean of Cambrian times, but also "as life itself began in the sea, so each of us begins his individual life in a miniature ocean within his mother's womb, and in the stages of his embryonic development repeats the steps by which his race evolved, from gill-breathing inhabitants of a water world to creatures able to live on land." [50] The phylogenetic appeal of Mother Sea is substantiated by at least one psychiatrist. Sandor Ferenczi, in *Thalassa: A Theory of Genitality*, writes: "Individual observations of the symbolism of dreams and neuroses reveal a fundamental symbolic identification of the mother's body with the water of the sea and the sea itself on the one hand, and on the other with 'Mother Earth,' provider of nourishment." [51]

Robert Graves has attempted to show that much great poetry is an invocation, conscious or unconscious, to the many-named Moon-Earth-Sea Goddess of pre-Christian times.[52] Moon, sea, earth, and woman are traditionally related. The effect of the moon on the tides of the sea is a commonplace. Not so well known is the fact that the moon may once have been a part of earth: according to Miss Carson, the moon probably once rested in the cavity now formed by the Pacific Ocean and was torn off into space by a great tidal wave. A long passage in *Ulysses*, we shall see, points out similarities between the moon and woman, including the ancient theory of the influence of the phases of the moon on the twenty-eight day cycle of the female menses. In popular folklore the best time for romance is during a full moon, and we find in William Faulkner's fiction an instance of the folk belief that a woman may encourage pregnancy by lying naked before the awesome force of a full moon—a belief which has a natural explanation, according to one of his sceptical characters.[53] Water too is associated with love and fertility, and it is no accident that Niagara Falls remains the favorite resort of honeymooners. Seen against this literary-mythic-phylogenetic background, Molly Bloom, goddess of

50. (New York: Oxford University Press, 1951), pp. 12–13.

51. Translated by Henry Alden Bunker (Albany, New York: Psychoanalytic Quarterly, Inc., 1938), p. 47.

52. *The White Goddess: A Historical Grammar of Poetic Myth* (New York: Creative Age Press, 1948).

53. *The Hamlet* (New York: Modern Library Paperbacks, 1956), p. 312.

the moon and "liquid formless earth," is twin sister to the Girl-Muse standing in midstream in the *Portrait* and to Anna Livia Plurabelle, who is, symbolically, the River Liffey and, as A. L. P., Alph the Sacred River.

Closely related to Joyce's images of moon and sea are those of drowning and rising from a grave, which represent the possible fates of the woman-trapped artist, who may lose his independence as artist by submerging himself in life or transcend the commonplace by producing art which is universal and timeless. These images are, again, psychologically appropriate. If woman is the sea, she offers possibilities of death by drowning and birth or rebirth. According to Swinburne, the Sea-Mother is both "strong for death and fruitful of birth." [54] And Ferenczi writes: "It would indeed seem as though there were discoverable in the symptoms of the death struggle regressive trends which might fashion dying in the image of birth and so render it less agonizing . . . the fact that in dreams and myths we find the same symbols for both death and birth cannot be a mere coincidence." [55] The White Goddess, says Graves, is both "the Mother of All Living" and "the female spider or the queen-bee whose embrace is death." [56]

Such speculations may well seem extravagant. Whether they are valid or not is of no real concern here; they are useful only to the extent that they help to clarify the psychological background of certain images used pervasively in the work of Joyce and other writers. Joyce, whose familiarity with mythology and the pioneer theories of psychology is well known, found that the images of moon, sea, earth, drowning, and rising from a grave provided archetypal symbols with which to convey his own experience with the life principle incarnate in Nora Barnacle. That she stood behind these images and that Joyce's use of them was deliberate is proved by a note for *Exiles* which he wrote in 1913, just before he began *Ulysses*. The significance of this somewhat obscure reference to moon and water can best be appreciated if it is approached chronologically. I would begin by tracing Stephen's changing attitude toward life-woman, moon and water in the period which corresponds to the time in Joyce's life before he found a personal solution to the conflict between life and art. After explaining Joyce's solution, I can then show more convincingly how it fits into the symbolic substructure of his fiction.

"How can you own water really?" Leopold Bloom asks himself, "It's always flowing in a stream, never the same, which in the stream

54. *Complete Works*, I, 178.   56. *The White Goddess*, p. 10.
55. *Thalassa*, p. 95.

of life we trace. Because life is a stream." [57] Life in this broad sense includes both the present moment and the All-Life of the past, present, and future: Yeat's "mackerel-crowded seas" of the passing generations versus "that dolphin-torn, that gong-tormented sea" of Byzantium. The kind of life to which Stephen in the *Portrait* calls "Welcome, O life!" appears to be primarily the All-Life later personified by Anna Livia. But water also symbolizes the rejected life. What is associated with triumphant consecration in the *Portrait* is in *Ulysses* associated with fear and guilt because Stephen does not yet know what his creator knew: that there are not only two kinds of life but also two sides to the artist. If water is a symbol of *this* life, it is also a symbol of death; if it is a symbol of the timeless Happy Other World of mythology or the ageless Byzantium of art, it is also a symbol of regeneration. Corresponding to the two kinds of life are the two sides of the man-artist: the man has to participate in life; the artist is inevitably detached.

Jerome Hamilton Buckley, in his *The Victorian Temper,* has traced at some length the use of water-baptism as a thematic symbol in nineteenth-century British literature.[58] The Victorian hero is baptized when he humbles his ego by immersing in the life around him. The process is fittingly reversed in Joyce's *Portrait,* in which Stephen's baptism as artist takes the form of a refusal to enter the water. Always different from his fellows, Stephen becomes reconciled to his otherness when he stands aloof from his schoolmates swimming in the mouth of the Liffey and realizes that he need not regret his inability or his reluctance to participate in the activities around him, that as detached artisan-artist his mission is to create "a living thing, new and soaring and beautiful, impalpable, imperishable." [59] He can do this by emulating the first Daedalus and staying *above* the sea. As Stephen walks by the river, the swimmers call out to him.

Stephanos Dedalos! Bous Stephanoumenos! Bous Stephaneforos! Their banter was not new to him and now it flattered his mild proud sovereignty. Now, as never before, his strange name seemed to him a prophecy. So timeless seemed the grey warm air, so fluid and impersonal his own mood, that all ages were as one to him. A moment before the ghost of the ancient kingdom of the Danes had looked forth through the vesture of the haze-wrapped city. Now, at the name of the fabulous artificer, he seemed to hear the noise of dim waves and to see a winged form flying above

57. *Ulysses,* p. 151.   versity Press, 1951), pp. 97–108.
58. (Cambridge, Mass.: Harvard Uni-   59. *Portrait,* p. 197.

the waves and slowly climbing the air. What did it mean? Was it a quaint device opening a page of some medieval book of prophecies and symbols, a hawklike man flying sunward above the sea, a prophecy of the end he had been born to serve and had been following through the mists of childhood and boyhood, a symbol of the artist forging anew in his workshop a new soaring impalpable imperishable being? [60]

Although Stephen wades along a rivulet in the strand, he feels that "his soul was soaring in an air beyond the world and the body he knew was purified in a breath and delivered of incertitude and made radiant and commingled with the element of the spirit." [61] This sensation of birdlike flight is objectified—held in a momentary stasis—when he comes upon the girl standing in midstream. Although she is "touched with the wonder of mortal beauty," she appears "like one whom magic had changed into the likeness of a strange and beautiful sea-bird." [62] She suffers the worship of his gaze, then quietly directs it to the water. In Joyce's description of Stephen's moment of transcendent dedication, images of flight and immersion, the eternal and the mortal, art and life, are fused into a unity. Accepting the totality, Stephen finds his mission as the life-creating artist.

Clearly, there are two kinds of life involved in this scene of the *Portrait*. Stephen's mystical exaltation causes him to perceive a reflection of the timeless world ("all ages were as one to him") represented by the best art ("imperishable being"), but even while he affirms the physical life about him, which he recognizes as the material of his art, he knows that "he was alone. He was unheeded, happy, and near to the wild heart of life." [63] The call he hears is "not the dull gross voice of the world of duties and despair"; through art he can transcend "the house of squalor and subterfuge." [64] To make art, to recreate life from life, he must first see the world clearly and distinterestedly, he must stand beyond participation and carnal desire. It is upon this basis that Stephen formulates his theory of esthetics, insisting that all true art is static and divorced from kinetic desire and that the artist must be godlike, "invisible, refined out of existence, indifferent, paring his fingernails." [65] Stephen's theory of art, cunningly presented as an exercise in pseudo-Thomistic dialectic, is rooted psychologically in this moment of vision—the Girl-Muse as stasis in a "timeless" setting—when he dedicates himself to his voca-

60. *Portrait*, p. 196.
61. *Portrait*, p. 196.
62. *Portrait*, p. 199.

63. *Portait*, pp. 198–199.
64. *Portrait*, pp. 197–198.
65. *Portrait*, p. 252.

tion and realizes that "his soul had arisen from the grave of boyhood, spurning her graveclothes." [66]

When Stephen, after his brief stay in Paris, returns to Dublin, he is much less confident of his ability to fulfill his mission. The change is represented in *Ulysses* by his increased hydrophobia. He has come to recognize the dangers inherent in his position as a youthful and non-established artist: he is balanced precariously between the high-flying Daedalus and the drowned son Icarus, who, it must be remembered, were trying to fly to their homeland, having grown weary of exile. The sixteenth day of June 1904 finds him tortured by a double sense of guilt; he has failed to live up to his own ideal of vocation, and he has treated his mother heartlessly. He has refused to pray at her bedside as she lay dying—just as in the *Portrait* he refused to make his Easter duty—because he is still convinced that to discard everyday loyalties and duties is a prerequisite to his career as artist. As yet, however, he has failed to justify through the production of art his repudiation of temporal values. The water images in *Ulysses* reveal Stephen's double guilt. After Buck Mulligan calls the sea "a grey sweet mother,"

> Stephen stood up and went over to the parapet. Leaning on it he looked down on the water and on the mailboat clearing the harbour mouth of Kingstown.
> —Our mighty mother, Buck Mulligan said.
> He turned abruptly his great searching eyes from the sea to Stephen's face.
> —The aunt thinks you killed your mother, he said.[67]

On the pages which follow, the words "mother" and "water" or "sea" appear together often enough to suggest that Joyce wanted to keep the reader aware of the conjunction and to prepare him for the key passages in which Stephen's sense of guilt is linked to the drowning image. "Your mother" is not equivalent to "our mighty mother" any more than Simon Dedalus is the spiritual father that Stephen insists is his true father. But for the time being at least, "your mother" has taken precedence over "our mighty mother" because on June 16, 1904, Stephen's need to reaffirm his devotion to All-Life is less pressing than his need to escape the traps which, guilt-stricken, he sees in the life around him.

Stephen's soliloquy as he walks along the beach in the early part of *Ulysses* is in ironic contrast to his meditations in the consecration scene of the *Portrait*. During that earlier walk, the tide had been

66. *Portrait,* p. 197.   67. *Ulysses,* p. 7.

going out; Stephen's thoughts of the early Danes had brought him
a sense of the timeless; the girl holding up her skirts had symbolized
purity and a-carnal desire; he strode "far out over the sands, singing
wildly to the sea, crying to greet the advent of the life that had
cried to him." [68] Now the tide is coming in; the Danes, compared
with the "jerkined dwarves, my people," suggest the decay of the
present; there is now "a woman and a man. I see her skirties. Pinned
up I bet"; Stephen urinates in the water. Whereas the images had
been all of life, they now are predominantly of death. Stephen
thinks of

> the man that was drowned nine days ago off Maiden's rock. They
> are waiting for him now. The truth, spit it out. I would want to.
> I would try. I am not a strong swimmer. Water cold soft. . . . A
> drowning man. His human eyes scream to me out of horror of his
> death. I. . . . With him together down. . . . I could not save
> her. Waters: bitter death: lost.[69]

Stephen compulsively associates the drowned man with his dead
mother. An echo of this guilt association appears later, in the book-
stall episode, when Stephen recognizes the mute appeal of one of
his sisters:

> She is drowning. Agenbite. Save her. Agenbite. All against us.
> She will drown me with her, eyes and hair. Lank coils of seaweed
> hair around me, my heart, my soul. Salt green death.[70]

Although the sea is the "grey sweet mother," Stephen realizes that
to submit to it, to become immersed in life, means death for the artist. Although Stephen is remorseful that others must be sacrificed
to the demands of his vocation, it is his own death as artist that he
fears above all else.

The conclusion of the *Portrait* found Stephen aspiring to a form
of godhood: the true artist, he said, is godlike in his role as life-
creator and in his sublime indifference. At the beginning of *Ulysses*,
Buck Mulligan addresses Stephen as "Ah, poor dogsbody." [71] In the
Circe episode, the Voice of the Damned pronounces the word *God*
backward, "Dooooooooooog!," [72] thus partly explaining Mulligan's
address to Stephen. "Dogsbody" appears also during the soliloquy
scene in the form of a dead dog lying on the beach which Stephen
identifies as "Ah, poor dogsbody. Here lies poor dogsbody's body." [73]
The process from grave to godhood of the *Portrait* is now ironically

68. *Portrait*, p. 200.
69. *Ulysses*, pp. 46–47.
70. *Ulysses*, p. 240.

71. *Ulysses*, p. 7.
72. *Ulysses*, p. 584.
73. *Ulysses*, p. 47.

reversed: "God becomes man becomes fish becomes barnacle goose becomes featherbed mountain." [74] The godlike artist becomes human, submerges in the sea of life, enters the gullet of a bird of prey, becomes dead goose. The word-conscious Joyce's selection of barnacle goose out of all possible birds of prey is perhaps significant.[75]

Several literary allusions intensify the sea-as-death connotation of the water symbol. The earlier Telemachus sought a father persecuted by Poseidon, god of the sea. During the history lesson at Mr. Deasy's school, the mention of Pyrrhus leads Stephen to think of a pier as a "disappointed bridge," of drowning, and then of the drowned poet Lycidas.[76] As Stephen walks by the strand, "Lycidas" joins with *The Tempest*.

> Five fathoms out there. Full fathom five thy father lies. At once he said. Found drowned. High water at Dublin bar. Driving before it a loose drift of rubble, fanshoals of fishes, silly shells. A corpse rising salt-white from the undertow, bobbing landward, a pace a pace a porpoise. There he is. Hook it quick. Sunk though he be beneath the watery floor.[77]

Stephen's theory of Hamlet includes the idea that paternity may be a "mystical estate, an apostolic succession," as opposed to a "legal fiction." [78] This provides Stephen with a rationalization for his denial of his legal father, Simon Dedalus. As in the *Portrait,* Stephen thinks of the mythical Daedalus as his real old father.

> Fabulous artificer, the hawklike man. You flew. Whereto? Newhaven-Dieppe, steerage passenger. Paris and back. Lapwing. Icarus. *Pater, ait.* Seabedabbled, fallen, weltering.[79]

Stephen as Icarus calls for help to his father. The spiritual father sought by Stephen is one who will save him from drowning in the sea of death-guilt, the "grey sweet mother," which is the sea of life.

There are several candidates for the fatherhood. Stephen has already rejected Simon Dedalus. Buck Mulligan has saved men from drowning, but Stephen quarrels with the aggressive Malachi and refuses to return to the Martello tower. There is Leopold Bloom, whose quest for a spiritual son is juxtaposed against Stephen's search

74. *Ulysses,* p. 51.
75. There is, of course, an obvious connection between *barnacle goose* and Nora Barnacle. In addition, Joyce may have chosen the barnacle goose because of the old belief that it is hatched from a barnacle: hence, "becomes fish becomes barnacle goose." See Graves, *The White Goddess,* p. 68.
76. *Ulysses,* p. 26.
77. *Ulysses,* p. 50.
78. *Ulysses,* pp. 204–205.
79. *Ulysses,* p. 208.

for a spiritual father. But when Bloom and Stephen meet at the end of the day, there is little evidence that either has succeeded. Bloom is identified as "waterlover, drawer of water, watercarrier," [80] and one of the first things he offers his guest is a washbasin.

What reason did Stephen give for declining Bloom's offer?
That he was hydrophobe, hating partial contact by immersion or total by submersion in cold water (his last bath having taken place in the month of October of the preceding year), disliking the aqueous substance of glass and crystal, distrusting aquacities of thought and language. [81]

Stephen's rejection of the washbasin seems to be more significant, considered in light of the centrality of the water image throughout *Ulysses*, than is his acceptance of the Epps's cocoa, a "massproduct," which for William York Tindall is a symbol of communion and represents the ultimate success of the two quests. [82] As Bloom and Stephen take leave of each other on the porch, they hear church bells sounding the hour. Immediately the bells echo for Stephen the phrase *Liliata rutilantium* from the prayer he had refused to say at his mother's bedside; this phrase, which has recurred throughout the day, would seem to indicate that Stephen's *Agenbite of Inwit*, another compulsive association of guilt, remains as sharp as ever. Bloom's day ends in the single question, "Where?"

Despite the failure on the narrative plane of the two quests which give *Ulysses* its connecting thread of plot, many readers persist in finding in Molly Bloom's soliloquy an affirmation of life. The idea makes sense only if one keeps in mind the two kinds of life which appear in the consecration scene of the *Portrait*. In the sequel, Stephen is not defeated; he does not submit to "the world of duties and despair," but remains loyal to the timeless world of art-life created from real life. He has not yet, however, discovered the means by which such a life may be presented in art nor managed to detach himself, conscience-free, from "the house of squalor and subterfuge." In *Ulysses*, which illustrates Joyce's theory of art as stasis, there can be no significant change in the character portrayal. Whereas the *Portrait* covers some nineteen years, *Ulysses* covers only nineteen hours: it is more a portrait than is the earlier novel. Affirmation of life—not the life of Dublin on June 16, 1904, but that transcendent life which includes the life of Dublin, June 16, 1904—must be found on the symbolic rather than the narrative level; and even then, it is not affirmation in the customary life-is-

80. *Ulysses*, p. 655.
81. *Ulysses*, p. 657.

82. *James Joyce: His Way of Interpreting the Modern World*, p. 29.

good sense so much as it is a restatement and an acceptance of the fact that life *is*.

A link between Bloom's day and the interior monologue of his wife is provided by the meditations of Bloom as, after Stephen has left, he stands on the porch and gazes at the moon.

> What special affinities appeared to him to exist between the moon and woman?
>
> Her antiquity in preceding and surviving successive tellurian generations: her nocturnal predominance: her satellitic dependence: her luminary reflection: her constancy under all her phases, rising and setting by her appointed times, waxing and waning: the forced invariability of her aspect: her indeterminate response to inaffirmative interrogation: her potency over effluent and refluent waters: her power to enamour, to mortify, to invest with beauty, to render insane, to incite to and aid delinquency: the tranquil inscrutability of her visage: the terribility of her isolated dominant implacable resplendent propinquity: her omens of tempest and of calm: the stimulation of her light, her motion and her presence: the admonition of her craters, her arid seas, her silence: her splendour, when visible: her attraction, when invisible.[83]

The obvious and traditional asociation of the moon with the sea—"handmaid of the moon," [84] "loom of the moon" [85]—clarifies the symbolic function of Molly Bloom. If Bloom and Stephen are both exiled, it is from what Molly represents. Her stream of consciousness is, in a sense, the stream of life in which Bloom's day takes place, and what seemed previously to be parallel lines (Bloom the artist as bourgeois and Stephen the artist as would-be god: Joyce as both Bloom and Stephen) occasionally intersecting and never merging are now seen as lines moving concentrically within a circle. The day of *Ulysses* is exaggeratedly temporal; but in what is symbolized by Molly (B)loom-of-the-moon, Joyce reaffirms the kind of time-transcendent life to which Stephen has dedicated himself. Seen thus, *this* woman, Molly Bloom, is also Nora Barnacle and all women, the Moon-Muse, the Mother of All Living; and *Ulysses* is something of an invocation. If Stephen's mother represents the threat of drowning, the life that kills, Molly Bloom, both earth-held and spiritual, lusty and amoral, represents the life that transcends death, and those critics who hold that *Ulysses* ends on the eve of Stephen's rebirth are perhaps right after all.

83. *Ulysses*, p. 686.   85. *Ulysses*, p. 50.
84. *Ulysses*, p. 48.

But this interpretation must be drawn from the symbolism rather than the narrative. In the *Portrait*, water seemed to represent both the life of art ("to recreate life") and the life of Stephen's Dublin ("out of life"). In contrast to Stephen's schoolmates frolicking in the river, the girl standing in midstream is symbolically equivalent to the life-force represented by Molly Bloom and thus seems both an angel and an image of mortal beauty. However, Stephen does not meet Molly during the hours covered by *Ulysses*, and in the later novel the thought of water evokes for Stephen only the dread of losing his artistic identity, his individuality, by submersion in the physical life around him. Whether he is to drown in the watery grave of life or ascend through art is a problem never answered directly in *Ulysses*.

Joyce not only fulfilled Stephen's mission as artist, but also became what Stephen feared to become, a participant in life, a family man with responsibilties to others as well as to himself and his art. If Stephen did likewise, it was not until after June 16, 1904. According to Ellmann, Joyce met Nora Barnacle on June 10, 1904, and made an appointment with her "for the evening of June 16, when they went walking at Ringsend, and thereafter began to meet regularly. To set *Ulysses* on this date was Joyce's most eloquent if indirect tribute to Nora, a recognition of the determining effect upon his life of his attachment to her. On June 16 he entered into relation with the world around him and left behind him the loneliness he had felt since his mother's death. He would tell her later, 'You made me a man.' June 16 was the sacred day that divided Stephen Dedalus, the insurgent youth, from Leopold Bloom, the complaisant husband." [86]

Falling in love with Nora Barnacle did not immediately cause Joyce to repudiate his (and Stephen's) insistence that the artist must scorn all legal and religious ties. It was not until late 1927 that Joyce and Nora were married, and then only in a civil ceremony instigated by J. F. Byrne, the original of Cranly. Byrne tells how Nora mentioned to him the "one fly in the amber of my happiness," in the hope that he would broach the subject to Joyce. Byrne did, and Joyce "assented warmly." [87] The story is revealing. After twenty-three years of cohabitation with Joyce, Nora retained one of the cherished convictions of her middle-class Irish upbringing. Yet she was reluctant to mention to the father of her children her desire for a legal wedding. Joyce's response seems to have been one of surprise,

86. *James Joyce*, pp. 162–163.
87. *Silent Years: An Autobiography with Memoirs of James Joyce and*   *Our Ireland* (New York: Farrar, Straus and Young, 1953), pp. 149–150.

as if the idea had never occurred to him or as if he no longer had to prove his independence. Perhaps he would have acceded years earlier, though what Mary Colum says of the baptizing of his grandchildren without Joyce's knowledge argues otherwise.[88] If those who knew him intimately hesitated to suggest the desirability of the most conventional civil and religious ceremonies, we may assume that Joyce retained even after twenty years much of Stephen's alienation from state and church.

The union appears to have been more successful than some of Joyce's friends had expected. Those who knew the late Mrs. Joyce agree that her pleasant appearance and cheerful disposition, rather than any affinity of intellectual interests, must have captivated the young writer. "Her mind and her attitude towards life," says Herbert Gorman, "seem to have been essentially practical, in other words, a direct reverse of her husband's mind and attitude towards life. This was a lucky state of affairs for Joyce, perhaps the most impractical man in the world, because it gave a stabilizing influence to the household." Significantly, she "was assiduous in guarding her husband from the many hangers-on and victimizers of genius who sought for anything they could get out of the writer and she transformed his home into a place where he could work in peace." [89]

Hawthorne asked, "Why are poets so apt to choose their mates, not for any similarity of poetic endowment, but for qualities which might make the happiness of the rudest handicraftsman as well as that of the ideal craftsman of the spirit?" And he answered his own question, "Because, probably, at his highest elevation, the poet needs no human intercourse; but he finds it dreary to descend, and be a stranger." [90] The artist is an artist only when he is creating art, but he is a man too, and when he descends from his Ivory Tower he is likely to find that he wants such things as a drink, a dinner, conversation, a woman. If he does not find them at home, he is all too likely to dissipate his creative energy in a search for them. Joyce's union with Nora was a form of economy. It was a partial compact with life which, while taking care of his mortal needs and rescuing him from a restless quest for distraction in Bohemias and Nighttowns which plagued the Joyce of pre-1904 and the Stephen of *Ulysses,* yet left the creative personality free to produce art. Through a partial bondage Joyce achieved the environment in which, for the first time, "he could work in peace."

88. *Life and the Dream,* pp. 388–389.
89. *James Joyce,* p. 336.
90. *The Complete Works of Na-* *thaniel Hawthorne,* Riverside Edition (Boston: Houghton Mifflin, 1884), III, 171.

"A Painful Case," written within a year of the elopement, may be read as Joyce's justification of the change in his life.[91] Mr. Duffy, the translator, like Joyce, of Hauptmann's *Michael Kramer*, has clung jealously to his independence from spiritual and domestic ties. It is only when he reads of the death of the one woman who tried to break through his isolation that he realizes the full extent of his loneliness: "He felt his moral nature falling to pieces. . . . No one wanted him; he was outcast from life's feast. . . . He felt that he was alone." [92] Mr. Duffy, whose attempts to establish himself as a writer have been ineffectual, stands for the man that Joyce might have been, the Stephen who may be.

The alternate fate, the man Joyce did become, is Richard Rowan of *Exiles* and the Shakespeare of Stephen's Hamlet theory. Such a hypothesis may be drawn in part from the following passage in Joyce's notes for *Exiles*:

N. (B.)—*13 Nov. 1913.*

Moon: Shelley's grave in Rome. He is rising from it: blond she weeps for him. He has fought in vain for an ideal and died killed by the world. Yet he rises. Graveyard at Rahoon by the moonlight where Bodkin's grave is. He lies in the grave. She sees his tomb (family vault) and weeps. The name is homely. Shelley's is strange and wild. He is dark, unrisen, killed by love and life, young. The earth holds him.

Bodkin died. Kearns died. In the convent they called her the man-killer: (woman-killer was one of her names for me). I live in soul and body.

She is the earth, dark, formless mother, made beautiful by the moonlit night, darkly conscious of her instincts. Shelley whom she has held in her womb or grave rises: the part of Richard which neither love nor life can do away with; the part for which she loves him: the part she must try to kill, never be able to kill and rejoice at her impotence. Her tears are of worship. Magdalen seeing the rearisen Lord in the garden where he had been laid in the tomb. Rome is the strange world and strange life to which Richard brings her. Rahoon her people. She weeps over Rahoon too, over him whom her love has killed, the dark boy whom,

---

91. On the autobiographical relevance of "A Painful Case," see Marvin Magalaner, *Time of Apprenticeship: The Fiction of Young James Joyce* (New York: Abelard-Schuman, 1959), pp. 34–45. Stanislaus Joyce's claim that he is the original of Mr. Duffy (see *My Brother's Keeper*, p. 54) does not refute the autobiographical relevance, since Stanislaus, a would-be writer, may be considered in many respects his brother's "double."

92. *Dubliners* (New York: Modern Library, 1926), pp. 146–147.

as the earth, she embraces in death and in disintegration. He is her buried life, her past. Her attendant images are the trinkets and toys of girlhood (bracelet, cream sweets, palegreen lily of the valley, the convent garden). His symbols are music and the sea, liquid formless earth, in which are buried the drowned sea and body.[93]

Here in compact form are the images of moon and sea, drowning and resurrection. The *she*—the "N. (B.)" of the heading—is Nora Barnacle and Bertha of *Exiles*. She is the earth, which is equivalent to the sea ("liquid formless earth"), and the moon, which looks down on the earth held graves of Shelley and Bodkin. For Bodkin, her tears are of pity; for Shelley, of worship. The artist Shelley is here Joyce, and "I live in soul and body" is equivalent to "Yet he rises." The *he* of the passage, Bodkin, "dark, unrisen, killed by love and life," is Michael Furey of "The Dead," Icarus, and the drowned man off Maiden's rock in *Ulysses*. The moon-sea-earth *she* of the note becomes, in addition to Nora and Bertha, Gretta Conroy of "The Dead," the girl-muse of the *Portrait*, the "she" of the poem "She Weeps over Rahoon," the earth- and moon-like Molly Bloom, and Anna Livia.

The similarity of theme between "The Dead" and *Exiles* was apparent long before the publication of Joyce's note. The passage above, with its references to Rahoon (according to Padraic Colum, Michael Furey lies buried at Rahoon) [94] and the convent garden, makes the identification explicit. Gabriel Conroy, however, perceives no clear distinction between Michael Furey and himself; the snow "falling upon every part of the lonely churchyard on the hill where Michael Furey lay buried" is "falling faintly through the universe and faintly falling, like the descent of their last end, upon all the living and the dead." [95] The sense of loss and change and humility which Gabriel Conroy feels upon hearing his wife's story of a young man who loved her and whose love she may have returned is similar to Richard Rowan's uncertainty at the conclusion of *Exiles*, when he is "wounded" by the fact that he "can never know the truth" about the relationship between Bertha and Robert Hand.

Yet it is Richard's wound that sets him free. Robert Hand tells Bertha that her submission to him would free Richard "from every

93. *Exiles: A Play in Three Acts, Including Hitherto Unpublished Notes by the Author, Discovered after His Death; and an Introduction by Padraic Colum* (New York: Viking Press, 1951), pp. 117–118. Reprinted by permission of Viking Press.

94. "Introduction" to *Exiles*, pp. 9–10.

95. *Dubliners*, p. 288.

law . . . from every bond. All his life he has sought to deliver himself. Every chain but one he has broken and that one we are to
break." [96] At the end of the play, Richard tells Bertha, "To hold
you by no bonds, even of love, to be united with you in body and
soul in utter nakedness—for this I longed. And now I am tired for
a while, Bertha." [97] In one way, Richard has been defeated. He returned to Ireland hoping to justify his exile, but his failure to withstand the test of Bertha—his test as well as hers—and his guilt over
his mother's never having forgiven him his apostasy force him to
participate more fully in life. He will probably accept the professor-
ship at the university, his son Archie will continue to be "brought
up on Robert's principles," [98] and he will probably legitimize his
union with Bertha. Joyce wrote in his notes, "Exiles—also because
at the end either Robert or Richard must go into exile. . . . Robert
will go." [99] The point, however, is that Richard can stay in Ireland
because the artist in his personality is detached and he no longer requires bodily exile. What was to have been a pure and complete
union with Bertha becomes an expediency, and the play concludes
with Bertha's crying for the return of her "strange, wild lover," who
is equivalent to the Shelley-Joyce-Dedalus (his name is "strange and
wild") of the note: "Shelley whom she has held in her womb or
grave rises: the part of Richard which neither love nor life can
do away with; the part for which she loves him: the part she must
try to kill, never be able to kill and rejoice at her impotence."

The part of Richard which is made free is clarified by examina-
tion of the theory of Hamlet which Stephen advances in *Ulysses*.
Stephen's description of Shakespeare's marital difficulties arouses the
sympathies of his listeners, but Stephen insists, "The man of genius
makes no mistakes. His errors are volitional and are the portals of
discovery." [100] By marrying Ann Hathaway, a woman with whom
he could not live, Shakespeare forced himself into the exile necessary to the development of his genius: "Belief in himself has been
untimely killed. He was overborne in a cornfield (ryefield, I should
say) and he will never be a victor in his own eyes after nor play
victoriously the game of laugh and lie down." [101] A later indignity,
which may have been his cuckolding by one or all of his three
brothers in Stratford, impelled him to produce his greatest tragedy.
Shakespeare is the ghost in *Hamlet*. "He goes back, weary of the
creation he has piled up to hide him from himself, an old dog licking

96. *Exiles*, p. 87.
97. *Exiles*, p. 112.
98. *Exiles*, p. 117.
99. *Exiles*, p. 123.
100. *Ulysses*, p. 188.
101. *Ulysses*, p. 194.

an old sore. But, because loss is his gain, he passes on towards eternity in undiminished personality, untaught by the wisdom he has written or by the laws he has revealed. His beaver is up. He is a ghost, a shadow now, the wind by Elsinore's rocks or what you will, the sea's voice, a voice heard only in the heart of him who is the substance of his shadow, the son consubstantial with the father." [102] Stephen, like Shakespeare, is "untaught by . . . the laws he has revealed." He dreads life because he fears that he may not be a Shakespeare, that he may be a Bodkin instead of a Shelley. What Stephen has not yet learned on June 16, 1904, is that he need not fear participation in life. Just as on that earlier occasion, "his soul had arisen from the grave of boyhood, spurning her graveclothes," he may as artist be detached and exalted even in participation. Although at the moment he is fallen, in a sense dead ("Here lies poor dogsbody's body"), he may rise from the gave, like the Shelley and the Christ of Joyce's note to *Exiles*. Shakespeare, *an old dog*—the reverse of "the playwright who wrote the first folio of this world" [103] —attains strength through a volitional error and, a ghost, rises from the grave to become "the sea's voice." That is what Stephen had tried to do when, dedicating himself to art, he cried "wildly to the sea, crying to greet the advent of the life that had cried to him." It is what the Stephen-like Shem the Penman of *Finnegans Wake* accomplishes when he records the "all marryvoising mood-moulded cyclewheeling history" symbolized by Anna Livia.

In Stephen's theory of Shakespeare, then, the sea becomes a symbol of redemption: the artist Shakespeare (and, by projection, Shelley and Joyce and Stephen) becomes through art the sea's voice. If we look again at the literary allusions to drowning in *Ulysess*, we may see that they are ambivalent, containing not only connotations of death and extinction but also, when read in context, implications of redemption and transformation. The passage previously quoted on the "corpse rising saltwhite from the undertow" contains quotations from "Lycidas" and *The Tempest* which suggest permanent extinction by drowning. Lycidas, "sunk though he be beneath the wat'ry floor," is raised to heaven by "the dear might of Him that walked the waves." Ferdinand's father, who presumably lies "full fathom five," is not actually dead; and the lines of Ariel's song suggest transformation:

> Of his bones are coral made,
> Those are pearls that were his eyes.

102. *Ulysses*, p. 194.   103. *Ulysses*, p. 210.

Nothing of him that doth fade
But doth suffer a sea change
Into something rich and strange.   (I, ii. 397–402)

Interrupting Stephen's exposition of his Hamlet theory is a passage which critics cite as evidence that Stephen has come to realise that his mission has failed. This passage must be quoted once again to show that it is also subject to the redemption interpretation.

Fabulous artificer, the hawklike man. You flew. Whereto? New-haven-Dieppe, steerage passenger. Paris and back. Lapwing. Icarus. *Pater, ait.* Seabedabbled, fallen, weltering. Lapwing you are. Lapwing he.

"Seabedabbled" suggests that "day of dappled seaborne clouds" which marked Stephen's consecration as artist in the *Portrait.* Representing, ironically, the height of Stephen's aspiration, it is the antithesis of "fallen"; but "weltering" is to rise and fall tumultuously. As Harry Levin has pointed out, the *"pater, ait"* has Icarus calling to his father for help instead of Daedalus calling to his fallen son, as in Ovid's version of the myth.[104] We may note, however, that this change need not be interpreted as intentionally ironic. In the version which Joyce presumably knew best (C. Witt's *Myths of Hellas,* one of the books in Joyce's pre-*Portrait* library), "Icarus felt the strokes becoming more feeble and called to his father for help." [105] And why did Joyce choose, of all birds, the lapwing? According to *Funk and Wagnalls Standard Dictionary of Folklore, Mythology, and Legend,* the lapwing is best known for "its famous trick of screaming in distress to lure passersby in the opposite direction from its nest." Robert Graves says in *The White Goddess:* "The Greeks called the lapwing *polyplagktos,* luring on deceitfully, and had a proverbial phrase 'more beseechful than a lapwing,' which they used for artful beggars. . . . The lapwing's poetic meaning is 'Disguise the Secret' and it is her extraordinary discretion which gives her the claim to sanctity. According to the Koran she was the repository of King Solomon's secrets and the most intelligent of the flock of prophetic birds that attended him." [106] Thus, when Stephen identifies himself as a lapwing, he may mean that he is an artful deceiver feigning injury. The idea of transformation or shape-shifting may also be suggested by the lapwing: in one Greek myth, Graves

104. *James Joyce* (Norfolk, Conn.: New Directions, 1941), pp. 61–62.
105. Translated by Frances Younghusband (London, 1883), p. 53. See Thomas Connolly, *The Personal*
Library of James Joyce, University of Buffalo Studies, XXII (1955), item 310.
106. *The White Goddess,* p. 37.

tells us, Zeus took the form of the lapwing. At any rate, Stephen,
even in this moment of self-doubt, remains proud enough to identify
himself with the most intelligent of the sacred birds. The secret
disguised by lapwing Stephen is perhaps his theory of Hamlet,
which reveals Joyce's mature theory of the artist's relationship to
life. The circle is now completed: God becomes man becomes fish
becomes barnacle goose becomes featherbed mountain becomes lapwing becomes God.

If the above interpretation of a group of related images, autobiographical in source, is valid, we may conclude that Joyce modifies
Stephen's theories. Joyce grants to the artist the right, even the
need, to form at least a partial compact with life. But he also extends
and intensifies Stephen's alienation, for the partial compact releases
the artist from the man and provides him with the conditions under
which he can best work. Just as there is the life that ends with death
and the All-Life that transcends death and time, the River Liffey
and Alph the Sacred River, every true artist is both the mortal man
whose name is on his works and the godlike creator whose art world,
like Keat's Grecian Urn, is universal in time and place. The young
Stephen, denying this inevitable split, thought that he could be a
Shelley or a Shakespeare only by not being a Bodkin. Joyce realized
that Shelley and Shakespeare were Bodkins—men who loved and
lived and died—as well as artists whose art became "the sea's voice."
When Joyce learned this, he could write triumphantly, "In the
convent they called her the man-killer: . . . I live in soul and body."
Stephen may well be the drowned Icarus, but if he stands for Joyce,
then he too, like Daedalus, may as artist fly high above the sea of
life as he makes his way back from exile.

Conclusion

ANOTHER book could be written on the portrait-of-the-artist novel after Joyce, for publication of the story of Stephen Dedalus in the *Portrait* and *Ulysses* did not, of course, end the tradition of the artist as hero. In fact, a bibliography of artist-novels would probably show more entries for the past four decades than for the preceding century and a half. With Joyce, however, the archetype of the artist became firmly established, and later contributors to the genre have done little to alter that image. Additional chapters on such writers as Thomas Mann, André Gide, Thomas Wolfe, Samuel Beckett, and Lawrence Durrell would reveal variations on the pattern I have sought to illustrate, but my reading of their artist-novels has not convinced me that they have changed that pattern in any really significant way. They would only provide further examples of what I hope has already been established.

Indeed, some readers may well feel that I have too fully illustrated the artist and his situation, for it is apparent that the artist-hero, like the hero with a thousand faces, is always the same man and the conflicts he faces are essentially the same conflicts. In defense, I would say that it is that sameness which justifies a comparative study such as this. Considered as a group, portraits of the artist have a cumulative force that provides us with an inside-out view of art and artist. Works of art about art, they are exercises in criticism and esthetic theory as well as products of the creative imagination.

Therefore, we should expect to find in what they have in common certain implications relevant to problems in modern criticism.

THE split between man and artist which we have found to be a dominant theme in the artist-novel is similar to a division in modern literary theory and critical practice. The dispute between "old scholars" and "new critics" is essentially a conflict between those who place their emphasis on the man who makes the work and those who stress the work itself. Extremists on the one side often assume that to know the cause is to understand the effect and therefore that to know the man—his experiences, his intentions, the literary and social influences upon him, the milieu in which he lived —is to understand his work. At the other extreme, some critics argue that the artist can be found only in what he produces, which they would consider apart from all external factors. That both extremes have severe limitations is increasingly apparent, but there are welcome signs that some scholar-critics are seeking a meeting ground between author and creation. Just as the greatest writers resolve the conflict between their two selves, the best criticism of the future may be that which emphasizes neither the maker nor the work, but finds a link between them in that *persona* of the artist which functions like a Holy Ghost in linking the Creator with the created.

Joseph Conrad will serve as an example of the disparity between the critical and scholarly approaches to literature, and of one way in which the conflict may be resolved. Many critics have given us close readings of his stories, but their interpretations have so often contradicted one another that we have grown suspicious of the critic's ability to achieve true objectivity. Most critics see Conrad as "one of us," for all too often "nose to nose, the critic confronts the writer and, astonished, discovers himself." [1] But there are many "I's" among "us" and therefore many different Conrads. It is our growing awareness of this limitation of criticism that has led to renewed faith in biography. Of late we have heard little about "the biographical heresy," and books like Richard Ellmann's *James Joyce* and Mark Schorer's *Sinclair Lewis* are almost universally acclaimed. We are now told that the critic must rely on biography if only to the extent that it sets *the limits of rational interpretation* by laying down cautionary principles: This particular writer, being the kind of man he was, working as he did, living in the age in which he lived, could *not*, whatever he meant, have meant *that*." [2]

1. Marvin Mudrick, "Conrad and the Terms of Modern Criticism," *Hudson Review*, VI (Autumn, 1954), 421.

2. Patrick Cruttwell, "Makers and Persons," *Hudson Review*, XII (Winter, 1959–1960), 504–505.

True enough, but if we are now aware that there are dangers in ignoring the maker of the work, there are equally strong dangers in an uncritical acceptance of biography. The life of an author is as subject to individual interpretation as are his writings. The Conrad of Jean-Aubry is not quite the Conrad of Jocelyn Baines or Jerry Allen. Yet each of these biographers assumes that to know the man Conrad is to know the writer. They go further and equate the fiction with the experience. Thus, Jean-Aubry tells us solemnly that *Youth* narrates "the exact, authentic circumstances of the wreck of the *Palestine*" and that *Heart of Darkness* is "nothing but a detailed account of his [Conrad's] ill-fated Congo adventure." [3] Baines is not quite so literalistic, but his impatience with the critics of Conrad betrays his conviction that because the man Conrad—that is, *his* Conrad—was a simple fellow, the fiction must be simple too. "I do not believe," Baines tells us, "that Conrad intended 'The Secret Sharer' to be interpreted symbolically," [4] and any reader who sees something beneath the surface of a Conrad story is dismissed as "fantastic" or "alchemical." The premise shared by Conrad's biographers is that if we could know everything about Conrad's experience the mysteries in his writing would be solved. Miss Allen, in a recent essay, [5] describes the long search by scholars for the real river where Almayer lived. That river has been found at last—in Borneo—and in an overgrown cemetery on a nearby hill is the grave marker of a Charles Olmeyer. Unfortunately, we do not know enough about the life of the real "Almayer" to say with certainty that Conrad's first novel is a true story; but how does a scholar justify travelling halfway around the world in search of a river and a grave marker unless he equates source with result and assumes that to know the Pole, Captain Korzeniowski, is to know Conrad the writer?

Somewhere between these two extremes—the many Conrads of the interpreters and the several Conrads of the literal-minded biographers—there is another Conrad who is neither the man nor the writer but that creative spirit which joins the maker with the creation. Or, to put the matter differently, there was first the man, Korzeniowski, who was born in 1857 and died officially in 1924, though he virtually disappeared from life some time during the 1890's when Joseph Conrad, the British man of letters, was born. Just as we cannot determine the exact birthdate of Joseph Conrad, so is the date of his death uncertain, for he remains alive in the works he

3. Gerard Jean-Aubry, *The Sea Dreamer: A Definitive Biography of Joseph Conrad*, trans. Helen Sebba (Garden City, New York: Doubleday, 1957), p. 238.
4. Jocelyn Baines, *Joseph Conrad: A Critical Biography* (New York: McGraw-Hill, 1959), p. 358.
5. Jerry Allen, "Conrad's River," *Columbia University Forum*, V (Winter, 1962), 29–35.

wrote. We use the past tense in writing of Korzeniowski, the present tense in writing of Conrad; but the latter was also a citizen of public record. Joseph Conrad married, fathered sons, paid taxes, had literary friends, and conducted business with publishers. Sometimes, in fact, the man of letters was ready to receive personal as well as financial credit for the products of his pen, but a study of his correspondence and memoirs reveals that he did not pretend to understand fully what he had written and that he liked to insist that he was but an agent for still another Conrad, a creative force that operated through him, making use of the physical energy of the mortal Conrad but remaining apart from the man.

Consider Conrad's own account of how he began to write. In *A Personal Record* he tells us that one morning, while he was between voyages and residing in a London boardinghouse, he ordered the breakfast dishes removed from the table, called for paper and pen, and then, without clear intention, wrote the first lines of what was to become *Almayer's Folly*.

> It was not the outcome of a need—the famous need for self-expression which artists find in their search for motives. The necessity which impelled me was a hidden, obscure necessity, a completely masked and unaccountable phenomenon. Or perhaps some idle and frivolous magician . . . had cast a spell over me through his parlour window as I explored the maze of streets east and west in solitary leisurely walks without chart and compass. Till I began to write that novel I had written nothing but letters, and not very many of these. I never made a note of a fact, of an impression or of an anecdote in my life. The conception of a planned book was entirely outside my mental range when I sat down to write; the ambition of being an author had never turned up amongst those gracious imaginary existences one creates fondly for oneself at times in the stillness and immobility of a daydream.[6]

It makes a good story—this account of a man of thirty-eight suddenly cast under a mysterious spell that made him an author in spite of himself—but, unfortunately, it is not true. Baines has shown that Conrad began writing much earlier than he claimed and that he had literary pretensions from an early age. What interests me here is not whether the story holds up factually, but why Conrad bothered to invent it. Perhaps because, as his friend Ford Madox Ford would have said, even if the facts are false, the "impression" is true. For, after all, Conrad was not the first nor the last artist to suppose that

6. (New York: Harper, 1912), pp.
114–115.

he was the vehicle of a force greater than himself. If we had not encountered the same insistence in many of the writers discussed in this study, we could dismiss Conrad's account as a protective pose. But the archetype of the divided artist lends support to Conrad's claim.

That archetype implies that there are always two selves within the artist, that these selves are in conflict, and that the conflict may be found within the work produced. Therefore, to accept wholly Conrad's story of the magician's spell and to assume that everything he wrote was produced unconsciously would be to make as serious an error as to assume that everything in his fiction can be explained in terms of the experiences of Captain Korzeniowski or the values of the man of letters. Except for rare works created in a trance, art is the result of a collaboration, usually unfriendly, between the man and the artistic *persona*. The man may function as editor, as censor, sometimes even as critic; he may, in fact, be the sole author if the story produced is only the working out of a formula designed to attract a wide audience. But in serious, noncommercial fiction we find almost always a clash between the life affirming values of the man-self and the life denying values of the artist-self. "Ah, Davidson," cries Axel Heyst at the end of *Victory*, "woe to the man whose heart has not learned while young to hope, to love—and to put its trust in life!" Many critics have interpreted the novel in terms of that simple moral, but, as I tried to show in my third chapter, awareness of Conrad's *persona* forces us to recognize a strongly nihilistic strain in the novel, a contrary moral which affirms that life is expendable for the artist, who finds *his* victory in the destruction of life that it may be transformed into art. To counteract the conventional readings of *Victory* I have probably overemphasized the message of Conrad's buried self. A more complete interpretation of the novel would concede that both the patriotic man of letters and the detached artist are at work and that the resulting conflict is never fully resolved.

Victory is, I think, a good example of a work of fiction split between man values and art values, for it was produced under the special conditions of wartime (even Henry James visited army hospitals) and because we very soon forget the sketch pad that Axel Heyst brought with him to the islands. Axel Heyst is not a producing artist at all, and *Victory* is hardly a portrait-of-the-artist novel in the usual sense. In many of the works I have discussed we find all too readily the divided self of the artist and the conflict between the Ivory Tower and the Sacred Fount because these are books that tell how they came to be written. They are "reflexive," inside-out novels that analyze themselves.[7] We recognize the form easily in *A la Recherche du Temps perdu,* a *Counterfeiters,* or an *Alexandrian Quartet;* and we may acknowledge that when Lily Briscoe puts the finishing touch to her picture, Virginia Woolf achieves the artistic triumph of *To the Lighthouse.* But we may feel that these are special cases if we forget that all good novels are written by artists who embody the divided nature of the archetype. Perhaps, then, all serious fiction is partly reflexive. If so, a conflict between life-denial and life-affirmation may be basic to the nature of fiction. The test would seem to lie outside the artist-novel, but to prove the hypothesis would require another book. Here I can give only brief examples.

We are not likely to consider Hawthorne's *The Scarlet Letter* a portrait of the artist, but when it is placed in perspective against the works that preceded and followed it, we can find in it some of the reasons for Hawthorne's decline as an artist. He seems to have moved steadily from Ivory Tower to Sacred Fount and only seldom to have maintained a balance along the way. During the twelve "solitary years" when he lived in the attic of his mother's house and set himself to learning his craft, he obviously held himself aloof from the normal claims of life. Yet, looking up from his work to gaze in the mirror that faced his desk, he must have often thought about the nature of the "double" imaged there, for we find in some of his early stories a growing sense of guilt at setting himself apart from what he and his age called "the great chain of human sympathy." [8] His early ideal of the artist is given to us in "The Artist of the Beautiful." Owen Warland creates ideal beauty only after he has cast aside both love and social duty. So complete is his triumph that he remains sanguine even when the object he created is destroyed. Hawthorne tells us, "When the artist rose high enough to achieve the beautiful, the symbol by which he made it perceptible to mortal senses became of little value in his eyes while his spirit possessed itself in enjoyment of the reality." [9] He, at least, has attained the ideal; he is not required to communicate the symbol of it to less appreciative souls. If the vision of the multitude is too crude to recognize the truly beautiful, the artist may simply remain in the clouds. However, it is significant that Warland's art is impersonal: the "beautiful" he creates is a mechanical butterfly which actually flies. Richard Harter Fogle has noted that Owen Warland differs from Miles Coverdale

7. For a good discussion of the "reflexive" novel, see Albert Cook, *The Meaning of Fiction* (Detroit: Wayne State University Press, 1960), p. 25ff.

8. *Complete Works,* Riverside Edition (Boston: Houghton Mifflin, 1883), III, 171. See also Malcolm Cowley, "Hawthorne in the Looking Glass," *Sewanee Review,* LVI (October–December, 1948), 552.

9. *Complete Works,* II, 535–536.

in *The Blithedale Romance* or the painter of "The Prophetic Pictures" in that "in the peculiar nature of his art he runs no risk of violating the human heart, of losing the respect for the sanctity of the human spirit, as do those who imitate the human form or delve into human psychology." [10] However, because Hawthorne as novelist was committed to observation of his fellowmen and had to explore psychology, he came to feel that the artist's power to expose the human soul could lead him to the "unforgivable sin." In *The Scarlet Letter*, written after Hawthorne's marriage to Sophia Peabody, his sense of guilt emerges in the equation of art with sin. It may seem to stretch a point to say that Hester Prynne represents the type of the alienated artist, though she is obviously an outcast from the community and we are told specifically that "she possessed an art that sufficed, even in a land that afforded comparatively little scope for its exercise, to supply food for her thriving infant and herself. It was the art—then, as now, almost the only one within a woman's grasp—of needlework. She bore on her breast, in the curiously embroidered letter, a specimen of her delicate and imaginative skill." [11] The example of her art is also the emblem of her sin, and it is the mysterious sensitiveness in the letter embroidered on her bodice that gives her "sympathetic knowledge of the hidden sin in other hearts." [12] Whereas Chillingworth exults in his ability to probe the secrets of the human heart, Hester considers the power which the emblem of her art gives her the most terrible of her punishments. She is an outcast, but not a rebel from society. As sinning mortal, she accepts the moral code of her persecutors, and as artist refuses to set herself above society. Ultimately the emblem stands for not only Hester's particular adultery, but also sin in general, the bond which links all men since the Fall, and when its specific meaning is forgotten by the people of the community, the redeemed Hester is no longer an exile from society. *The Scarlet Letter*, however, is set comfortably in the past; it is introduced by one of the most elaborate and extended examples of the "lost-manuscript device" in all fiction; and what autobiographical significance it may contain is heavily disguised. In the two novels which immediately follow— *The House of the Seven Gables* and *Blithedale Romance*—Hawthorne deals more directly with his own experience and with people he has known, and he discovers in the process that he can no longer commit the sin of exposing the human heart.[13] Like Miles Cover-

10. *Hawthorne's Fiction: The Light and the Dark* (Norman: University of Oklahoma Press, 1952), p. 88.
11. *Complete Works*, V, 105.
12. *Complete Works*, V, 110.
13. See my "The Fall of the House of Pyncheon," *Nineteenth-Century Fiction*, XI (June, 1956), 1–17.

dale, he is overwhelmed by life and ceases to be a real artist.

Whereas Hawthorne shows how art may be defeated by life, Ernest Hemingway demonstrates the triumph of art over life. Because Hemingway lived adventurously and exalted the physical pleasures of life—hunting big game, fighting bulls, and making love—we are likely to think of him as perhaps the most conspicuous life affirmer among modern novelists. That such a man should have killed himself seems inappropriate, yet when we look back upon his career we find that a life-negating, suicidal impulse was there from the beginning, as Philip Young argued long before Hemingway's death,[14] and that this impulse was as strong as his tendency to affirm the value of life at its most sensual and physical level. When *For Whom the Bell Tolls* appeared in 1940, it was widely praised by critics as an eloquent appeal for social engagement; and there are still those who reduce the meaning of the novel to the "moral" suggested by its title. Forgetting that the bell tolls death in Donne's poem, many readers have assumed that the bell is a summons to action, an appeal for social cooperation. Hemingway's own efforts in support of the Loyalists in Spain would seem to verify such an interpretation. However, it was the man Hemingway, not the artist, who during the late thirties travelled to Spain, wrote *The Fifth Column,* and addressed the Marxist-dominated Writers' Congress. The man may well have been embarrassed when leftist critics attacked *For Whom the Bell Tolls* because it showed that there was as much cruelty and inhumanity among the Loyalists as among the Fascists or when Lionel Trilling said that here was a "novel which, undertaking to celebrate the community of men, actually glorifies the isolation of the individual ego." [15] But the artist in Hemingway was anything but democratic or liberal, and must have known that Trilling was right. Robert Jordan is the typical Hemingway hero—a strong man who separates his mission from his feelings, persists against impossible odds, and proves willing to martyr himself in a losing cause. Maria symbolizes the appeal of love and life, but Jordan can respond to her with only a part of himself, and it is clear that his mission, his work as a man, must come first. We tend to overlook the fact that his mission is not only to fight the Fascists, but also to write a book—"He would write a book when he got through with this. But only about the things he knew, truly, and about what he knew." [16] If Jordan is a surrogate for Hemingway both as man of action and as artist, then the man

14. *Ernest Hemingway* (New York: Rinehart, 1952).

15. "An American in Spain," in William Phillips and Philip Rahv, eds., *Partisan Reader* (New York: Dial

Press, 1946), pp. 639–644.

16. *For Whom the Bell Tolls* (New York: Charles Scribner's Sons, 1940), p. 248.

is sacrificed to the artist, for the only real victory in *For Whom the Bell Tolls* is that of the writer—just as the *Victory* of Conrad's novel is that of the artist. The man Jordan is last seen as, crippled, he waits for death, but the target in his gun sights is Lieutenant Berrendo, who was previously shown as a compassionate human being doing his duty much as Jordan. Hemingway's hero fulfills his destiny as martyr but not before he has destroyed life and sent Maria on her way. *For Whom the Bell Tolls* is a nihilistic, perhaps arrogant novel which affirms only the success of the artist. We should not be surprised when after Pilar has described the murder of the Fascists in her home village, Jordan reflects, "If that woman could only write. . . . I wish I could write well enough to write that story," [17] for this is the artist in Hemingway reminding us that he has just written that story.

Once we become aware of the life negating aspect of the artist's *persona*, we are no longer free to interpret fiction as if it were written by "one of us." There is, I think, a fundamental difference between the creative and the critical minds. The good critic, particularly if he is a teacher-critic, is less interested in expressing himself than in understanding someone else, and the acts of teaching and explaining a work of literature imply a certain degree of social responsibility. The archetypal artist, on the other hand, is an anarchist: he seeks not only to express his individuality, but also to free himself from the obligations which would entrap him. As Morse Peckham has demonstrated at length,[18] both society and religion strive to impose uniformity, whereas the mission of art is to break down all orientations. However, there is one commitment which the individual artist cannot deny—his duty to the artist-type he represents. And that type insists that art is justified to the extent that it improves upon life. "It is art that *makes* life," Henry James insisted to H. G. Wells. To assume, however, that the archetypal artist is merely nihilistic, continually shouting "no! in thunder" to the prevailing values of his time, as Leslie Fiedler has argued,[19] is to overlook the positive side to the artist's rebellion.

WE have seen that the usual situation of the artist-hero involves a conflict between those opposing ideals which I have characterized as the Ivory Tower and Sacred Fount traditions. The former insists that the true artist must hold himself aloof from life,

17. *For Whom the Bell Tolls*, p. 134.
18. *Beyond the Tragic Vision: The Quest for Identity in the Nineteenth Century* (New York: George Braziller, 1962).
19. *No! In Thunder: Essays on Myth and Literature* (Boston: Beacon Press, 1960), pp. 1–18.

while the latter finds the source of art in experience. The artist is pulled in both directions simultaneously because his needs as a human being are not those of his creative self. Almost always the two selves are at odds, and it is a rarely fortunate artist who achieves happiness and success both as a man and a creator. Yet the artist who moves too far in either direction and separates art from life is more likely to fail than the artist who attains a balance between his two selves. That balance may be achieved in different ways, as I have sought to show in my chapters on Balzac, James, Proust, and Joyce. These novelists are unique in certain respects, but that they may all be approached both as realists and as visionaries shows that they managed to resolve the conflict between the outside world and their internal vision. Their fiction supports Mark Schorer's observation that the finest novels exist at the crossroads of "social history" and "sensibility."

But if it were always easy to remain at that crossroads, there would be more major novelists; and knowing that the conflict may be resolved should not cause us to forget that it does exist. Failure to recognize the inevitable division of man from artist is, I think, the chief limitation of most discussions of the alienation of the modern artist. The man may or may not be exiled from the life about him. We may think of Balzac in his monastic cell or Proust in his cork-lined bedroom, but these images are countered with the knowledge that Balzac was also a man with a voracious appetite for all kinds of experience and that Proust was a Jockey Club aristocrat. Henry James is the epitome of a man innately detached in temperament, yet he had a wide circle of friends and he made his province the novel of manners. Joyce insisted that the artist must exile himself from God, home, and country, but we have seen that he was a domestic-minded man who lived a normal, bourgeois life. Nonetheless, though these four writers show that it is possible to move back and forth between the Tower and the Fount, they have a common insistence that the artist *as artist* must turn his back on life.

Nor should this surprise us. Just as editoralists in the popular journals from time to time urge our younger writers to take an affirmative view of American society, most discussions of the alienation of the modern artist proceed from the assumption that the artist may change his vision of life at will. The authors of such discussions usually attribute to the artist-as-exile the main evils of modern art— obscurity, dehumanization, failure to communicate, and so on—but we cannot blame the artist for his aloofness from society unless we assume that he voluntarily chooses detachment. One of the principal conclusions which may be drawn from a study of the alienated artists of fiction is that their detachment is rooted in a certain basic kind of temperament over which the person has very little control. The artist, unlike the man of action, is essentially passive; and just as no one can "elect" to become an artist and expect to achieve success unless he is blessed with innate talent, the artist of fiction discovers in himself a *persona* with an unchangeable nature. The man-self of the artist may hold standards and values quite different from those of his creative self, and though it is possible for the man-self to revise or suppress the products of his creative imagination, more often than not he does not even understand them. There is considerable justification for Lawrence's statement, "Never trust the author—trust the tale."

Another reason for the inevitable detachment of the artist may be found in the nature of the creative process. In a sense all creative work must be a solitary endeavor. Before an artist can begin to compose, he must abstract himself from the distractions around him. Often he attains the proper creative mood by performing a special ritual, such as Balzac's donning his monkish robe and drinking a particular blend of coffee. Some artists feel that they can create only at certain hours of the day or night, and was it Schiller who was said to have required the smell of a rotting apple in his desk drawer before he could begin to write? Even scholars may have their pencil sharpening rituals or find that they cannot write unless surrounded by a screen of tobacco smoke. Whatever form the ritual may take, its purpose is to set up barriers between the worker and whatever may interfere with his concentration.

The exact nature of the artist's concentration remains a mystery, though most modern authorities on the creative process agree that the artist's subconsciousness plays a more important role in imaginative creation than does the conscious, reasoning mind. Since Plato and Aristotle, writers have differed on the question of inspiration versus calculation. Against Blake's statement, "I have written his poem from immediate Dictation, twelve or sometimes twenty or thirty lines at a time without Premeditation & even against my will," may be set Poe's "Philosophy of Composition," in which he insisted that every element in "The Raven" was the product of a reasoned calculation such as one applies to solving a puzzle. Against Coleridge's account of the opium-inspired writing of "Kubla Khan" may be opposed his statement that each line of "Christabel" cost him "labor pains." As usual, the truth seems to lie somewhere between the two poles. In a passage that influenced Joyce, Shelley wrote: "Poetry is not like reasoning, a power to be exerted according to the determination of the will. A man cannot say: 'I will compose poetry.' The greatest poet cannot even say it; for the mind in creation is as a fading coal, which some invisible influence, like an inconstant wind, awakens to transitory brightness; this power arises from within, . . . and the conscious portions of our natures are unprophetic either of its approach or departure." [20] The only lyric which Stephen Dedalus is shown composing in the *Portrait* seems to emerge spontaneously, but it obviously derives from his erotic subconsciousness, reflecting his experiences and desires as a young man. Joyce would agree with Shelley that though a man cannot will poetry, the "invisible influence" which sets the poet in motion arises from within. They would agree too that the product of the creative mood may be subjected to revision requiring careful deliberation. "The idea, of course, simply comes," T. S. Eliot has said, "but upon arrival is subject to prolonged manipulation." [21]

Similarly, what begins with calculation may end with something like inspiration. For years the favored approach to Henry James was through the statements of intention in his *Notebooks,* and few writers have seemed more conscious of their craft than he. More recently, however, it has become the fashion to turn James's intended heroes into villains, and his intended villains into heroes, and to argue that James often put more turns on the screw than he realized. No other type of fiction would seem to require more careful planning than the mystery novel—it is no accident that the author of "The Philosophy of Composition" invented the detective story—but one highly successful writer of mysteries, Dorothy L. Sayers, has admitted that certain of her characters have refused to perform according to plan.[22] Anyone who has written anything at all, even a college theme or a long letter, knows that there may occur during the process of composition a moment when "some obstruction is momentarily whisked away," [23] when something seems to take over for the calculating mind of the author.

In earlier times this "something" was thought of as a divine afflatus descending upon the artist. More recent writers have thought of it as a demon casting a spell. But since the something arises from within the subconsciousness, it seems more reasonable to identify it as the *persona,* the second self, which we have found to be im-

20. *The Works in Verse and Prose,* ed. H. B. Forman (London, 1880), V, 137.
21. *Selected Essays, 1917–1932* (New York: Harcourt, Brace, 1932), p. 276.
22. *The Mind of the Maker* (New York: Harcourt, Brace, 1941), pp. 63–83.

23. T. S. Eliot, *The Use of Poetry and the Use of Criticism* (Cambridge: Harvard University Press, 1933), p. 138. On the creative process in fiction see the symposium on "Intention and Unconscious Creation in the Novel," *Daedalus,* XCII (Spring, 1963), 297–382.

plicit in the archetype of the artist. If the creative process requires in most instances a fusion of calculation with inspiration, we may say also that each work of art requires collaboration between the man and the creative self, but that both cannot be in control at the same time. When the man dominates, the work is largely the product of calculation; when the second self takes over, inspiration is ascendant.

The relationship of these two selves to each other and to the life-in-general which is their ultimate source may be illustrated through Joyce's *Finnegans Wake*. Anna Livia Plurabelle, a personification of both the river Liffey and Alph the Sacred River, symbolizes all that water-moon-woman meant to Joyce, and thus represents the life principle itself. Her two sons, Shaun the Postman and Shem the Penman, represent the two selves of Joyce. Shaun is the postman in that he is a kinetic, communicating personality, the conformist, a would-be author of best-sellers. Because he exploits life, he "points the deathbone and the quick are still." Shem is static and solipsistic, the non-conformist, the exile, and the true artist. Nonacquisitive and nonexploiting, he has but to lift his lifewand and the dumb speak. Anna Livia's personal manifesto, which some interpreters of the novel take to be *Finnegans Wake* itself, is dictated to Shem, but Shaun tries to pass it off as his own creation, though he is incapable of understanding it. Shaun, in fact, would destroy Shem if he could, but the true artist is protected by his time-transcendent mother, who serves as the muse of his writing. Shem, "self exiled in upon his ego," pens the eternal vision not merely by transcribing his mother's dictation, but by "reflecting from his own individual person life unlivable, transaccidentated through the slow fires of consciousness into a dividual chaos." [24] I think that this is precisely what Stephen Dedalus meant to accomplish when, at the conclusion of the *Portrait*, he wrote in his diary that he was going forth in exile "to forge in the smithy of my soul the uncreated conscience of my race."

"To make life out of life" was Stephen's mission. Joyce implies that Shem is incomplete without Shaun—as the one Clare Vawdrey in James's "The Private Life" or the one Octave in Proust's novel would be incomplete without the other. Shem may write the manifesto, but he needs his brother to communicate it to the world, for the second self must always find a mortal body through whom to act. Just as the most extreme champions of the Sacred Fount tradition could hardly deny that the artist must isolate himself from life at least long enough to record what has already happened to him,

24. (New York: Viking Press, 1939), pp. 185–186.

the most extreme of Ivory Tower artists could scarcely deny that he must use life as the raw material of his art.

However, as Meyer Abrams has shown, the modern artist sees himself as more a lamp than a mirror—to express himself is more important than to reflect the life around him. We have seen that every true artist must share certain characteristics of the archetype. Yet each individual artist insists that his own consciousness is unique. Around him spins a special, private universe—the world revealed from his special perspective—composed of a multitude of fleeting impressions: "air-blown grains" for James, "essences" for Proust, "epiphanies" for Joyce. These elements are in themselves empty and disparate; they take on meaning only when they are unified by the consciousness of the individual observer. The artist arrests these fleeting particles and transforms them into an art world complete in itself and independent of the real world. Therefore, we must accept the validity of each unique perspective and concede that any form of alienation short of suicide is not absolute: the artist-as-exile rejects one kind of life that another may be attained. He attempts to escape the restrictions of temporal life only because he would achieve transcendent life in the art which defeats time.

Paradoxically, however, the modern artist is likely to imitate a God in whom he does not believe. If what seems to be a disordered world was created by God, then he would seem to be detached from his creation. "The artist," Flaubert said, "must stand to his work as God to his creation, invisible and all powerful; he must be everywhere felt but nowhere seen." Joyce's artist-god is "invisible, indifferent, paring his fingernails." But instead of emulating in the structure of their works the disorder implied by their concept of a God who does not care, most modern novelists strive for order and harmony, thus revealing a yearning for a super-subjective harmony which they fail to find outside themselves and which, indeed, is foreign to their concept of life. In a world without a maker, why should order be considered better than disorder, unity better than variety, pattern better than formlessness? The subjective novelists with whom I have been dealing are likely to insist that art is better than life, but their concept of value is determined by what life was thought to be several centuries ago—ordered and harmonious. There is a sense of something lost, an awareness of dissociation which distinguishes the subjective novelists from the naturalists, who, with their alleged indifference to pattern and structure, their eagerness to present life as it is, achieve a truth-to-life which corresponds to the view of life which the authors of the "well-made novel" find outside their fiction. In earlier times a patterned work of fiction was considered realistic on the assumption that life itself is patterned; today pattern is considered arbitrary, unnatural, false to life. The subjective novelist resolves this seeming paradox by restricting "truth" to the particular angle from which it is perceived. The author conceals himself—becomes detached—by fusing impressions through the mind of an observer, who, if he is like Proust's Marcel, has the ability to see the relations between things and to tie them together in a way neglected by the creator of the world. Such novelists present not *the* world, but *a* world. But because the observers, surrogates for their authors, usually have the attributes of that God in whom their authors do not believe, the worlds thus created are well made.

To concede this paradox in much modern art is not necessarily to regret it. Our own religious and social views must ultimately determine our attitude toward the private universes of modern art, but for many men there may be a lesson in the example set by the artist. Just as every artist is a man, every man is to some extent an artist, a maker of things, and the alienation of the artist is not unlike that of many men in a world where the center does not hold and where even the crowd is a lonely one. To try to create something out of chaos, if only by cultivating our gardens, is to heed the lesson of the artist. But to offer such a moral is to move beyond the province of the literary historian.

Index

INDEX